Frank Wood's
Book-keeping and Accounts

Frank Wood's
Book-keeping and Accounts

Fourth Edition

Frank Wood BSc(Econ), FCA

and

Sheila Robinson BA(Hons), Cert Ed, MAAT

PITMAN
PUBLISHING

London · Hong Kong · Johannesburg · Melbourne · Singapore · Washington DC

PITMAN PUBLISHING
128 Long Acre, London WC2E 9AN
Tel: +44 (0)171 447 2000
Fax: +44 (0)171 240 5771

A Division of Pearson Professional Limited

Fourth edition first published in Great Britain in 1997

© Pearson Professional Limited 1997

The right of Frank Wood and Sheila Robinson to be identified
as authors of this work has been asserted by them in accordance
with the Copyright, Designs and Patents Act 1988.

ISBN 0 273 62695 7

British Library Cataloguing in Publication Data
A CIP catalogue record for this book can be obtained from the British Library.

10 9 8 7 6 5 4 3 2 1

Typeset by Land & Unwin (Data Sciences) Limited
Printed and bound in Great Britain by Clays Ltd, St Ives plc

The Publishers' policy is to use paper manufactured from sustainable forests.

Contents

Preface to the fourth edition

This book was written specifically to cover a number of examination syllabuses. It covers the work to be carried out for the following courses:

Royal Society of Arts (RSA) Examinations Board, Book-keeping Stage 1
London Chamber of Commerce and Industry (LCCI), Book-keeping First Level
Pitman Qualifications, Book-keeping and Accounts Level 1
Edexcel Foundation (BTEC), Book-keeping requirements
International Association of Book-keeping (IAB), Foundation Level

It may also be used by students undertaking courses based on the Accounting Standards at NVQ Level 2. Such courses include the Association of Accounting Technicians (AAT) Foundation Level and the Association of Chartered Certified Accountants (ACCA) Technician course, Foundation Level. The chapter on Wages and Salaries, while meeting the requirements of the RSA, IAB and BTEC syllabuses, does not fully meet the requirements of the NVQ Level 2 unit, Recording Payroll Transactions, and the student is referred to the specific text for this unit by the same author, *NVQ Level 2 Accounting, Unit 3 Recording Payroll Transactions*, published by Pitman Publishing.

This fourth edition of *Frank Wood's Book-keeping and Accounts* has been reorganised to bring a comprehensive and structured approach to book-keeping, enabling the student to develop knowledge in a logical sequence. In the main, the examples and questions on final accounts use the vertical method of presentation. The chapters on VAT and Wages and Salaries have been revised and incorporate current rates relevant to VAT and Income Tax.

An extensive range of questions is provided at the end of each chapter, with a range of multi-choice questions at the end of the book. It is strongly recommended that students work through these to develop their under-standing and competence. Answers to most of the questions are clearly presented at the back of the book. Answers to those with the suffix 'X', e.g. 21.4X, are provided in a separate *Teacher's Manual* and this is available free to teaching staff who recommend this book.

We are grateful to the examining bodies who have allowed us to reproduce questions from their examination papers.

We acknowledge with thanks the contributions of Adrian Veale, FMAAT, to certain aspects of this edition.

We welcome any suggestions as to how the book might be improved; these should be sent to the publishers who will pass them on to us.

Frank Wood
Sheila Robinson

Matrix of subjects covered and examining bodies

Chapters	Subjects covered	AAT Foundation NVQ 2	AACA Technician NVQ 2	BTEC GNVQ	IAB Foundation	LCCI	Pitman Levels 1 & 2	RSA Stage 1
1–7	Double entry to Trial Balance	✓	✓	✓	✓	✓	✓	✓
8–10 & 27–30	Final accounts	✗	✗	✗	✗	✓	✓	✓
11	Accounting concepts & conventions	✓	✓	✗	✓	✓	✓	✓
12	Division of the Ledgers	✓	✓	✗	✓	✓	✓	✓
13	Petty cash	✓	✓	✓	✓	✓	✓	✓
14	Banking system	✓	✓	✓	✓	✓	✓	✓
15–16	Recording cash transactions	✓	✓	✓	✓	✓	✓	✓
17	Bank reconciliation	✓	✓	✓	✓	✓	✓	✓
18	Capital & revenue expenditure	✓	✓	✓	✓	✓	✓	✓
19–22 & 24–25	Recording credit transactions	✓	✓	✓	✓	✓	✓	✓
23	Value added tax	✓	✓	✓	✓	✓	✓	✓
25	Control Accounts	✓	✓	✗	✗	✓	✓	✓
26	The Journal	✓	✓	✗	✓	✓	✓	✓
31	Trial Balance – errors	✓	✓	✗	✗	✓	✓	✓
32	Suspense Accounts and errors	✓	✓	✗	✗	✓	✓	✓
33	Single entry/incomplete records	✗	✗	✗	✗	✗	✗	✓
34	Income & Expenditure Accounts	✗	✗	✗	✗	✓	✗	✓
35	Valuation of stock	✗	✗	✓	✓	✓	✓	✓
36	Wages and salaries	✓	✓	✓	✓	✗	✗	✓
37	Manufacturing Accounts	✗	✗	✗	✗	✗	✗	✗
38	Accounting ratios	✗	✗	✗	✗	✓	✗	✗

Key:
✓ = included in syllabus
✗ = not in syllabus

Note: As Syllabuses do change from time to time, check that the above details still apply to your examination.

PART 1

Introduction to double entry accounting

Introduction to accounting

1.1 What is accounting?

People and businesses

Accounting is something that affects people in their personal lives just as much as it affects very large businesses. We all use accounting ideas when we plan what we are going to do with our money. We have to plan how much of it we will spend and how much we will save. We may write down a plan, known as a **budget**, or we may simply keep it in our minds.

Recording accounting data

However, when people normally talk about accounting it means the type used by businesses and other organisations. They cannot keep all the details in their minds so they have to write it all down.

They will not only record cash received and paid out. They will also record goods bought and sold, items bought to use rather than to sell, and so on. This part of accounting is usually called the *recording of data*.

Classifying and summarising

When the data is being recorded this has to be sorted out so as to be most useful to the business. This is known as *classifying* and *summarising* data.

Following such classifications and summaries, it will be possible to work out how much profit or loss has been made by the business during a period of time. It will also be possible to show what resources are owned by the business, and what is owed by it, on the closing date of the period.

Communicating information

From the data, those who are skilled in accounting should be able to tell whether or not the business is performing well financially. They should be able to work out what are the strengths and weaknesses of the business.

Finally, they should be able to tell or *communicate* their results to the owners of the business, or to others allowed to receive this information.

Accounting is, therefore, concerned with:

- Recording data.
- Classifying and summarising data.
- Communicating what has been learned from the data.

1.2 What is book-keeping?

The part of accounting that is concerned with recording data is often known as book-keeping. Until about one hundred years ago all accounting data was recorded in books, hence the term book-keeping.

Nowadays, although books may be used, quite obviously a lot of accounting data is recorded by using computers.

1.3 Users of accounting information

The possible users can be:

- Owner(s) of the business. They want to be able to see whether or not the business is profitable. In addition they want to know what the financial resources of the business are.
- A prospective buyer. When the owner wants to sell his business the buyer will want to see such information.
- The bank. If the owner wants to borrow money for use in the business then the bank will need such information.
- Tax inspectors. They need it to be able to calculate the taxes payable.
- A prospective partner. If the owner wants to share ownership with someone else, then the would-be partner will want it.

There could also be other users. It is obvious that without recorded accounting data a business would have many difficulties.

New terms

Book-keeping (p 4): The recording of accounting data
Budget (p 3): A plan shown expressed in money

4

2 The accounting equation and the balance sheet

2.1 The accounting equation

The whole of accounting is based upon a very simple idea. This is called the *accounting equation*, which sounds complicated, but in fact it is easy to understand.

It can be explained by saying that if a firm is to set up, and start trading, then it needs resources. Let us assume that in the first place it is the owner of the business who has supplied all of the resources. This can be shown as:

> **Resources in the business = Resources supplied by the owner**

In accounting, terms are used to describe things. The amount of the resources supplied by the owner is called **capital**. The actual resources that are then in the business are called **assets**. This means that the accounting equation above, when the owner has supplied all of the resources, can be shown as:

> **Assets = Capital**

Usually, however, someone other than the owner has supplied some of the assets. **Liabilities** is the name given to the amount owing to this person for these assets. This equation has now changed to:

> **Assets = Capital + Liabilities**

It can be seen that the two sides of the equation will have the same totals. This is because we are dealing with the same thing from two different points of view. It is:

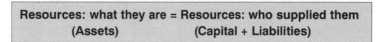

> **Resources: what they are = Resources: who supplied them**
> **(Assets)   (Capital + Liabilities)**

It is a fact that the totals of each side will always equal one another, and that this will always be true no matter how many transactions there may be. The actual assets, capital and liabilities may change, but the total of the assets will always equal the total of capital + liabilities.

Assets consist of property of all kinds, such as buildings, machinery, stocks of goods and motor vehicles. Also benefits such as debts owed by customers and the amount of money in the bank account are included.

Liabilities consist of money owing for goods supplied to the firm and for expenses. Also loans made to the firm are included.

Capital is often called the owner's **equity** or net worth.

2.2 The balance sheet – horizontal presentation

The accounting equation is shown in a statement called the **balance sheet**. It is not the first book-keeping record to be made, but it is a good place to start to consider accounting.

The introduction of capital

On 1 May 1997 B Blake started in business and put £5,000 into a bank account for the business. The balance sheet would appear:

B Blake
Balance Sheet as at 1 May 1997

Assets	£		£
Cash at bank	5,000	Capital	5,000
	5,000		5,000

The purchase of an asset by cheque

On 3 May 1997 Blake buys fixtures for £3,000. The effect of this transaction is that the cash at the bank is reduced and a new asset, fixtures, appears.

B Blake
Balance Sheet as at 3 May 1997

Assets	£		£
Fixtures	3,000	Capital	5,000
Cash at bank	2,000		
	5,000		5,000

The purchase of an asset and the incurring of a liability

On 6 May 1997 Blake buys some goods for £500 from D Smith, and agrees to pay for them some time within the next two weeks. There is now a new asset, **stock** of goods, and there is also a new liability because Blake owes money to D Smith for the goods.

A person to whom money is owed for goods is known in accounting language as a **creditor**.

B Blake
Balance Sheet as at 6 May 1997

Assets	£	Capital and Liabilities	£
Fixtures	3,000	Capital	5,000
Stock of goods	500	Creditor	500
Cash at bank	2,000		
	5,500		5,500

Sale of an asset on credit

On 10 May 1997 goods which had cost £100 were sold to J Brown for the same amount, the money to be paid later. This means a reduction in the stock of goods and there will now be a new asset. A person who owes money to the firm is known in accounting language as a **debtor**. The balance sheet now appears as:

B Blake
Balance Sheet as at 10 May 1997

Assets	£	Capital and Liabilities	£
Fixtures	3,000	Capital	5,000
Stock of goods	400	Creditor	500
Debtor	100		
Cash at bank	2,000		
	5,500		5,500

Sale of an asset for immediate payment

On 13 May 1997 goods which had cost £50 were sold to D Daley for the same amount, Daley paying for them immediately by cheque. Here one asset, stock of goods, is reduced, while another asset, bank, is increased. The balance sheet now appears:

B Blake
Balance Sheet as at 13 May 1997

Assets	£	Capital and Liabilities	£
Fixtures	3,000	Capital	5,000
Stock of goods	350	Creditor	500
Debtor	100		
Cash at bank	2,050		
	5,500		5,500

The payment of a liability

On 15 May 1997 Blake pays a cheque for £200 to D Smith in part payment of the amount owing. The asset of bank is therefore reduced, and the liability of the creditor is also reduced. The balance sheet now appears:

B Blake
Balance Sheet as at 15 May 1997

Assets	£	Capital and Liabilities	£
Fixtures	3,000	Capital	5,000
Stock of goods	350	Creditor	300
Debtor	100		
Cash at bank	1,850		
	5,300		5,300

Collection of an asset

On 31 May 1997 J Brown, who owes Blake £100, makes a part payment of £75 by cheque. The effect is to reduce one asset, debtor, and to increase another asset, bank. This results in a balance sheet as follows:

B Blake
Balance Sheet as at 31 May 1997

Assets	£	Capital and Liabilities	£
Fixtures	3,000	Capital	5,000
Stock of goods	350	Creditor	300
Debtor	25		
Cash at bank	1,925		
	5,300		5,300

It can be seen that every transaction has affected two items. Sometimes it has changed two assets by reducing one and increasing the other. Other times things have changed differently. A summary of the effect of transactions upon assets, liabilities and capital is shown in Exhibit 1.1.

Exhibit 1.1

Example of transaction	Effect			
1 Buy goods on credit	⬆	Increase asset (Stock of goods)	⬆	Increase liability (Creditors)
2 Buy goods by cheque	⬆	Increase asset (Stock of goods)	⬇	Decrease asset (Bank)
3 Pay creditor by cheque	⬇	Decrease asset (Bank)	⬇	Decrease liability (Creditors)
4 Owner pays more capital into the bank	⬆	Increase asset (Bank)	⬆	Increase capital
5 Owner takes money out of the business bank account for his own use	⬇	Decrease asset (Bank)	⬇	Decrease capital
6 Owner pays creditor from private money outside the firm	⬇	Decrease liability (Creditors)	⬆	Increase capital

Each transaction has, therefore, maintained the same total for assets as that of capital + liabilities. This can be shown:

Number of transactions as above	Assets	Capital and Liabilities	Effect on balance sheet totals
1	+	+	Each side added to equally
2	+ −		A *plus* and *minus* both on the assets side *cancelling out* each other
3	−	−	Each side has equal deductions
4	+	+	Each side has equal additions
5	−	−	Each side has equal deductions
6		− +	A *plus* and *minus* both on the liabilities side *cancelling out* each other

2.3 The balance sheet – vertical presentation

You will notice that in the previous section the balance sheet has been shown using the horizontal method of presentation. However, nowadays almost everyone uses the vertical method of presentation.

The format for the presentation of final accounts, which includes the trading and profit and loss account and the balance sheet, is governed by the Companies Acts of 1985 and 1989. At this initial stage of the study of accounting, limited company accounts are not examinable, but it is considered an advantage to understand and be able to prepare final accounts, including balance sheets, using the vertical method of presentation.

2.4 B Blake's balance sheet as at 31 May 1997 – vertical presentation

The balance sheet of B Blake using the vertical method of presentation would appear as follows:

B Blake
Balance Sheet as at 31 May 1997

	£	£	£
Fixed assets			
Fixtures			3,000
Current assets			
Stock	350		
Debtors	25		
Cash at bank	1,925	2,300	
Less: Current liabilities			
Creditors	300	300	
Net current assets			2,000
			5,000
Financed by:			
Capital			5,000

You will have noticed the use of the terms 'fixed assets', 'current assets' and 'current liabilities'. Chapter 9 contains a full and proper examination of these terms. At this point we will simply say that:

- Fixed assets: are assets to be kept as such for a few years at least, e.g. buildings, machinery, fixtures, motor vehicles.
- Current assets: are assets which change from day to day, e.g. the value of stock in hand goes up and down as it is bought and sold. Similarly, the amount of money owing to us by debtors will change quickly, as we sell more to them on credit and they pay their debts. The amount of money in the bank will also change as we receive and pay out money.
- Current liabilities: are those liabilities which have to be paid within the near future, e.g. creditors for goods bought.

Note: Generally, the figures used for exhibits and for exercises have been kept down to relatively small amounts. This has been done deliberately to make the work of the user of this book that much easier. Constantly handling large figures does not add anything to the study of the principles of accounting, instead it simply wastes a lot of the student's time, and they will probably make many more errors if larger figures are used.

It could lead to the accusation of not being 'realistic' with the figures given, but we believe that it is far more important to make learning easier for the student.

New terms

Assets (p 5): Resources owned by the business.

Balance sheet (p 6): A statement showing the assets, capital and liabilities of a business.

Capital (p 5): The total of resources supplied to a business by its owner.

Creditor (p 6): A person to whom money is owed for goods or services.

Debtor (p 7): A person who owes money to the business for goods or services supplied.

Equity (p 6): Another name for the capital of the owner.

Liabilities (p 5): Total of money owed for assets supplied to the business.

Stock (p 6): Unsold goods.

Exercises

Note: *Questions with the letter X shown after the question number do **not** have answers shown at the back of the book. Answers to the other questions are shown on page 428 onwards.*

2.1 You are to complete the gaps in the following table:

	Assets	Liabilities	Capital
	£	£	£
(a)	?	5,750	20,000
(b)	?	10,520	62,300
(c)	38,400	3,420	?
(d)	55,300	6,700	?
(e)	92,500	?	80,000
(f)	152,320	?	121,700

2.2X You are to complete the gaps in the following table:

	Assets	Liabilities	Capital
	£	£	£
(a)	75,428	12,300	?
(b)	?	4,562	63,400
(c)	122,500	?	110,900
(d)	88,700	16,212	?
(e)	?	29,200	42,500
(f)	99,100	?	85,100

2.3 From the following list show which are assets and which are liabilities:

(a) Office machinery
(b) Loan from C Shirley
(c) Fixtures and fittings
(d) Motor vehicles
(e) We owe for goods
(f) Bank balance

2.4X Which of the following are assets and which are liabilities?

(*a*)   Motor vehicles
(*b*)   Premises
(*c*)   Creditors for goods
(*d*)   Stock of goods
(*e*)   Debtors
(*f*)   Owing to bank
(*g*)   Cash in hand
(*h*)   Loan from D Jones
(*i*)   Machinery

2.5 State which of the following are shown under the wrong headings for J White's business:

Assets	*Liabilities*
Loan from C Smith	Stock of goods
Cash in hand	Debtors
Machinery	Money owing to bank
Creditors	
Premises	
Motor vehicles	

2.6X Which of the following are shown under the wrong headings:

Assets	*Liabilities*
Cash at bank	Loan from J Graham
Fixtures	Machinery
Creditors	Motor vehicles
Building	
Stock of goods	
Debtors	
Capital	

2.7 A Smart sets up a new business. Before he actually sells anything he has bought Motor vehicles £2,000, Premises £5,000, Stock of goods £1,000. He did not pay in full for his stock of goods and still owes £400 in respect of them. He had borrowed £3,000 from D Bevan. After the events just described, and before trading starts, he has £100 cash in hand and £700 cash at bank. You are required to calculate the amount of his capital.

2.8X T Charles starts a business. Before he actually starts to sell anything he has bought Fixtures £2,000, Motor vehicle £5,000 and a stock of goods £3,500. Although he has paid in full for the fixtures and the motor vehicle, he still owes £1,400 for some of the goods. J Preston had lent him £3,000. Charles, after the above, has £2,800 in the business bank account and £100 cash in hand. You are required to calculate his capital.

2.9 Draw up T Lymer's balance sheet, using the vertical presentation method, from the following information as at 31 December 1997.

	£
Capital	34,823
Delivery van	12,000
Debtors	10,892
Office furniture	8,640
Stock of goods	4,220
Cash at bank	11,722
Creditors	12,651

2.10X Draw up A Pennington's balance sheet as at 31 March 1998 from the following information:

	£
Premises	50,000
Plant and machinery	26,500
Debtors	28,790
Creditors	32,320
Bank overdraft	3,625
Stock	21,000
Cash in hand	35
Capital	90,380

2.11 Look at this list:

(a) We pay a creditor £70 in cash.
(b) Bought fixtures £200 paying by cheque.
(c) Bought goods on credit £275.
(d) The proprietor introduces another £500 cash into the firm.
(e) J Walker lends the firm £200 in cash.
(f) A debtor pays us £50 by cheque.
(g) We return goods costing £60 to a supplier whose bill we had not paid.
(h) Bought additional shop premises paying £5,000 by cheque.

For each item shown, you are to state how it changes assets, capital or liabilities. For example the answer to (a) will be:

(a) – Assets £70
– Liabilities £70

2.12X Show how each item on the following list changes assets, capital and liabilities.

(a) Bought a motor van on credit £500.
(b) Repaid by cash a loan owed to P Smith £1,000.
(c) Bought goods for £150 paying by cheque.
(d) The owner puts a further £5,000 cash into the business.
(e) A debtor returns to us £80 goods. We agree to make an allowance for them.
(f) Bought goods on credit £220.
(g) The owner takes out £100 cash for his personal use.
(h) We pay a creditor £190 by cheque.

2.13 C Sangster has the following items in his balance sheet as on 30 April 1998: Capital £18,900; Loan from T Sharples £2,000; Creditors £1,600; Fixtures £3,500; Motor vehicle £4,200; Stock of Goods £4,950; Debtors £3,280; Cash at bank £6,450; Cash in hand £120.

During the first week of May 1998 Sangster:
(*a*) Bought extra stock of goods £770 on credit.
(*b*) One of the debtors paid us £280 in cash.
(*c*) Bought extra fixtures by cheque £1,000.

You are to draw up a balance sheet as on 7 May 1998 after the above transactions have been completed.

2.14X H Charles has the following balance sheet as at 31 March 1999:

Balance Sheet as at 31 March 1999

Assets	£	*Capital and Liabilities*	£
Buildings	6,000	Capital	14,400
Motor vehicle	4,000	Loan from W Young	2,000
Stock of goods	2,000	Creditors	1,600
Debtors	2,800		
Cash at bank	3,200		
	18,000		18,000

The following transactions occur:

2 April Paid a cheque of £500 to a creditor.
8 April A debtor paid H Charles £300 by cheque.
10 April W Young is repaid £1,000 by cheque.

Write up a balance sheet on 10 April 1999 after the transactions have been completed.

3 The double entry system: assets, liabilities and capital

3.1 The double entry system

We have seen that every transaction affects two items. If we want to show the effect of every transaction when we are doing our book-keeping, we will have to show the effect of a transaction on each of the two items. For each transaction this means that a book-keeping entry will have to be made to show an increase or decrease of that item, and another entry to show the increase or decrease of the other item. From this you will probably be able to see that the term **double entry system** of book-keeping is a good one, as each entry is made twice.

In Chapter 2 we drew up a new balance sheet after each transaction. You could do this easily if you had only a few transactions per day, but if there were hundreds of transactions each day it would become impossible for you to draw up hundreds of different balance sheets. You simply would not have enough time.

The double entry system has an **account** (meaning details of transactions relating to a particular item) for every asset, every liability and for capital. Thus there will be a shop premises account (for transactions in shop premises), a motor vans account (for transactions in motor vans), and so on for every asset, liability and for capital.

3.2 The accounts for double entry

An account shows us the 'history of' a particular asset, liability, capital or indeed any business transaction. Each account is usually shown on a separate page which is divided into two halves. The left-hand side of each page is known as the **debit** side and is abbreviated **Dr**, the right-hand side is known as the **credit** side and is abbreviated **Cr**.

The words debit and credit in book-keeping terms do not mean the same as in normal language and should be viewed differently from the start to avoid confusion. Students new to studying double entry may find is useful to use 'IN' and 'OUT' initially, in addition to debit and credit.

The name of each account is usually written across the centre and each account has a reference number, which is essential both in manual and computerised systems. An example of an account is shown below:

Name of Account – Reference No

Date	Details 'IN'	£	Date	Details 'OUT'	£
	Debit side			Credit side	

Dr ... *Cr*

You will notice that the account looks rather like a letter 'T' and indeed accounts are often referred to as 'T Accounts'.

As mentioned above, the words 'debit' and 'credit' in book-keeping terms have different meanings to those in normal language. In book-keeping terms the word 'debit' refers to something from which the business benefits (IN), e.g. an asset such as land, buildings and machinery, or an expense item which the business needs in order to operate, such as electricity, rent and stationery. The expense item may seem wrong as a benefit, but in fact serves to explain the concept of double entry book-keeping in the following example:

Paid cash £200 for rent of premises.

The double entry for this transaction would be as follows:

1   Cash goes 'OUT' – a credit entry in the Cash Account.
2   Rent goes 'IN' – a debit entry in the Rent Account. Rent is a benefit to the business, because it benefits from the use of the premises.

A 'credit' refers to a liability such as a debt owed, or capital, which is money owed by the business to the owner or owners of the business and income, such as that received from sales. Again, the latter item, sales, seems wrong, but if we follow through the double entry concept it is easy to understand, i.e.:

Sold goods for cash £100.

This would be entered as follows:

1   Cash goes 'IN' – a debit entry in the Cash Account.
2   Goods go 'OUT' – a credit entry in the Sales Account.

Rules for double entry

Double entry is relatively easy to learn and understand if the following rules are learnt and understood:

1   Double entry means that every transaction affects two things and should, therefore, be entered twice:

Once on the *Debit* side
and
Once on the *Credit* side

2   The order in which the items are entered does not matter. Although students may find it easier to deal with any cash or bank transaction first using the 'IN' and 'OUT' principle.

3   A **Debit entry** is always an asset or an expense.
A **Credit entry** is a liability, capital or income.

4   To increase or decrease assets, liabilities or capital, as seen in Chapter 2, the double entry rules are:

Accounts	To record	Entry in the account
Assets	an increase a decrease	Debit Credit
Liabilities	an increase a decrease	Credit Debit
Capital	an increase a decrease	Credit Debit

Let us now look at the accounting equation:

	Assets	= Liabilities	and Capital
To increase each item	Debit	Credit	Credit
To decrease each item	Credit	Debit	Debit

The double entry rules for liabilities and capital are the same, but they are the opposite of those for assets. This is because assets are on the opposite side of the equation and, therefore, follow opposite rules. Looking at the accounts the rules will appear as:

Any asset account		*Any liability account*		*Capital account*	
Increases	*Decreases*	*Decreases*	*Increases*	*Decreases*	*Increases*
+	–	–	+	–	+

We have not enough space in this book to put each account on a separate page, so we will have to list the accounts under each other. In a real firm at least one full page would be taken for each account.

3.3 Worked examples

The entry of a few transactions can now be attempted:

1 The proprietor starts the firm with £1,000 in cash on 1 August 1997.

Effect	Action
1 Increases the *asset* of cash 2 Increases the capital	Debit the cash account – Cash goes 'IN' Credit the capital account – Cash comes 'OUT' of the owners' money

These are entered:

Cash Account

Dr				Cr
1997 Aug 1		£ 1,000		

Capital Account

Dr				Cr
		1997 Aug 1		£ 1,000

The date of the transaction has already been entered. Now there remains the description which is to be entered alongside the amount. The double entry to the item in the cash account is completed by an entry in the capital account, therefore the word 'Capital' will appear in the cash account. Similarly, the double entry to the item in the capital account is completed by an entry in the cash account, therefore the word 'Cash' will appear in the capital account.

The finally completed accounts are therefore:

Cash Account

Dr				Cr
1997 Aug 1 Capital		£ 1,000		

Capital Account

Dr				Cr
		1997 Aug 1 Cash		£ 1,000

This method of entering transactions therefore fulfils the requirements of the double entry rules as shown on page 17. Now let us look at the entry of some more transactions.

2   A motor van is bought for £275 cash on 2 August 1997.

Effect	Action
1 Decreases the *asset* of cash 2 Increases the *asset* of motor van	Credit the cash account – Cash goes 'OUT' Debit the motor van account – Motor van comes 'IN'

Cash Account

Dr		Cr
	1997	£
	Aug 2 Motor van	275

Motor Van Account

Dr		Cr
1997	£	
Aug 2 Cash	275	

3   Fixtures bought on credit from Shop Fitters for £115 on 3 August 1997.

Effect	Action
1 Increases the *asset* of Fixtures	Debit the Fixtures account – Fixtures go 'IN'
2 Increases the *liability* to Shop Fitters	Credit the Shop Fitters' account – Fixtures come 'OUT' of the supplier's account

Fixtures Account

Dr		Cr
1997	£	
Aug 3 Shop Fitters	115	

Shop Fitters' Account

Dr		Cr
	1997	£
	Aug 3 Fixtures	115

4   Paid the amount owing in cash to Shop Fitters on 17 August 1997.

Effect	Action
1 Decreases the *asset* of cash	Credit the cash account – Cash goes 'OUT'
2 Decreases the *liability* to Shop Fitters	Debit the Shop Fitters' account – Cash goes 'IN' to the Supplier's account

Cash Account

Dr			Cr
		1997	£
		Aug 17 Shop Fitters	115

Shop Fitters' Account

Dr			Cr
1997	£		
Aug 17 Cash	115		

5 Transactions to date.

Taking the transactions numbered **1** to **4** above, the records will now appear:

Cash Account

Dr				Cr
1997	£	1997		£
Aug 1 Capital	1,000	Aug 2 Motor Van		275
		Aug 17 Shop Fitters		115

Capital Account

Dr			Cr
		1997	£
		Aug 1 Cash	1,000

Motor Van Account

Dr		Cr
1997	£	
Aug 2 Cash	275	

Shop Fitter's Account

Dr			Cr
1997	£	1997	£
Aug 17 Cash	115	Aug 3 Fixtures	115

Fixtures Account

Dr		Cr
1997	£	
Aug 3 Shop Fitters	115	

Before you read further you are required to work through questions 3.1 and 3.2.

3.4 A further worked example

Now you have actually made some entries in accounts you are to go carefully through the following example. Make certain you can understand every entry.

Transactions		Effect	Action	IN/OUT
1998 May 1	Started an engineering business putting £1000 into a business bank account.	Increases *asset* of bank.	Debit bank account.	IN
		Increases *capital* of owner.	Credit capital account.	OUT
May 3	Bought works machinery on credit from Unique Machines £275.	Increases *asset* of machinery.	Debit machinery account.	IN
		Increases *liability* to Unique Machines.	Credit Unique Machines account.	OUT
May 4	Withdrew £200 cash from the bank and placed it in the cash box.	Decreases *asset* of bank.	Credit bank account.	OUT
		Increases *asset* of cash.	Debit cash account.	IN
May 7	Bought a motor van paying in cash £180.	Decreases *asset* of cash.	Credit cash account.	OUT
		Increases *asset* of motor van	Debit motor van account.	IN
May 10	Sold some of the machinery for £15 on credit to B Barnes.	Decreases *asset* of machinery.	Credit machinery account.	OUT
		Increases *asset* of money owing from B Barnes.	Debit B Barnes account.	IN
May 21	Returned some of the machinery, value £27 to Unique Machines.	Decreases *asset* of machinery.	Credit machinery account.	OUT
		Decreases *liability* to Unique Machines.	Debit Unique Machines.	IN
May 28	B Barnes pays the firm the amount owing, £15, by cheque.	Increases *asset* of bank.	Debit bank account.	IN
		Decreases *asset* of money owing by B Barnes.	Credit B Barnes account.	OUT
May 30	Bought another motor van paying by cheque £420	Decreases *asset* of bank.	Credit bank account.	OUT
		Increases *asset* of motor vans.	Debit motor van account.	IN
May 31	Paid the amount of £248 to Unique Machines by cheque.	Decreases *asset* of bank.	Credit bank account.	OUT
		Decreases *liability* to Unique Machines.	Debit Unique Machines.	IN

In account form this is shown as:

Bank Account

Dr				Cr
1998			£	
May 1	Capital	1,000		
May 28	B Barnes	15		

1998		£
May 4	Cash	200
May 30	Motor van	420
May 30	Unique Machines	248

Cash Account

Dr		£	Cr		£
1998			1998		
May 4	Bank	200	May 7	Motor van	180

Capital Account

Dr	Cr		£
	1998		
	May 1	Bank	1,000

Machinery Account

Dr		£	Cr		£
1998			1998		
May 3	Unique Machines	275	May 10	B Barnes	15
			May 21	Unique Machines	27

Motor Van Account

Dr		£	Cr
1998			
May 7	Cash	180	
May 30	Bank	420	

Unique Machines Account

Dr		£	Cr		£
1998			1998		
May 21	Machinery	27	May 3	Machinery	275
May 31	Bank	248			

B Barnes Account

Dr		£	Cr		£
1998			1998		
May 10	Machinery	15	May 28	Bank	15

3.5 Abbreviation of 'Limited'

In this book when we come across transactions with limited companies the letters 'Ltd' are used as the abbreviation for 'Limited Company'. So we will know that if we see the name of a firm as T Lee Ltd, then that firm will be a limited company. In our books the transactions with T Lee Ltd will be entered the same as for any other customer or supplier.

New terms

Account (p 15): The place in a ledger where all the transactions relating to a particular asset, liability or capital, expenses for revenue item are recorded. Accounts are part of the double entry book-keeping system. They are sometimes referred to as 'T accounts' or ledger accounts.

Credit (p 15): The right-hand side of the accounts in double entry.

Debit (p 15): The left-hand side of the accounts in double entry.

Double entry book-keeping (p 15): A system where each transaction is entered twice, once on the debit side and once on the credit side.

Exercises

3.1 Complete the following table showing which accounts are to be credited and which to be debited:

	Account to be debited	Account to be credited
(a) Bought motor van for cash		
(b) Bought office machinery on credit from J Grant & Son		
(c) Introduced capital in cash		
(d) A debtor, J Beach, pays us by cheque		
(e) Paid a creditor, A Barrett, in cash.		

3.2 The following table is also to be completed, showing the accounts to be debited and credited:

	Account to be debited	Account to be credited
(a) Bought machinery on credit from A Jackson & Son		
(b) Returned machinery to A Jackson & Son		
(c) A debtor, J Brown, pays us in cash		
(d) J Smith lends us money, giving it to us by cheque		
(e) Sold office machinery for cash		

3.3X Complete the following table:

	Account to be debited	Account to be credited
(a) Bought office machinery on credit from D Isaacs Ltd		
(b) The proprietor paid a creditor, C Jones, from his private monies outside the firm		
(c) A debtor, N Fox, paid us in cash		
(d) Repaid part of loan from P Exeter by cheque		
(e) Returned some of office machinery to D Isaacs Ltd		
(f) A debtor, N Lyn, pays us by cheque		
(g) Bought motor van by cash.		

3.4X Complete the following table showing which accounts are to be debited and which to be credited:

	Account to be debited	Account to be credited
(a) Bought motor lorry for cash		
(b) Paid creditor, T Lake, by cheque		
(c) Repaid P Logan's loan by cash		
(d) Sold motor lorry for cash		
(e) Bought office machinery on credit from Ultra Ltd		
(f) A debtor, A Hill, pays us by cash		
(g) A debtor, J Cross, pays us by cheque		
(h) Proprietor puts a further amount into the business by cheque		
(i) A loan of £200 in cash is received from L Lowe		
(j) Paid a creditor, D Lord, by cash.		

3.5 Write up the asset and liability accounts in the records of D Coy to record these transactions:

1999
May   1   Started business with £1,000 cash
May   3   Bought a motor lorry on credit from Speed & Sons for £698
May   14   Bought office machinery by cash for £60
May   31   Paid Speed & Sons the amount owing to them, £698, in cash.

3.6 Write up the asset and liability and capital accounts to record the following transactions in the records of G Powell.

1998
July   1   Started business with £2,500 in the bank
July   2   Bought office furniture by cheque £150
July   3   Bought machinery £750 on credit from Planers Ltd
July   5   Bought a motor van paying by cheque £600

July 8 Sold some of the office furniture – not suitable for the firm – for £60 on credit to J Walker & Sons
July 15 Paid the amount owing to Planers Ltd £750 by cheque
July 23 Received the amount due from J Walker £60 in cash
July 31 Bought more machinery by cheque £280.

3.7X You are required to open the asset, liability and capital accounts, and record the following transactions for June 1998 in the records of C Williams.

1998
June 1 Started business with £2,000 in cash
June 2 Paid £1,800 of the opening cash into a bank account for the business
June 5 Bought office furniture on credit from Betta-Built Ltd for £120
June 8 Bought a motor van paying by cheque £950
June 12 Bought works machinery from Evans & Sons on credit £560
June 18 Returned faulty office furniture costing £62 to Betta-Built Ltd
June 25 Sold some of the works machinery for £75 cash
June 26 Paid amount owing to Betta-Built Ltd £58 by cheque
June 28 Took £100 out of the bank and put it in the cash till
June 30 J Smith lent us £500 – giving us the money by cheque.

3.8 Write up the asset, capital and liability accounts in the books of C Walsh to record the following transactions:

1997
June 1 Started business with £5,000 in the bank
June 2 Bought motor van paying by cheque £1,200
June 5 Bought office fixtures £400 on credit from Young Ltd
June 8 Bought motor van on credit from Super Motors £800
June 12 Took £100 out of the bank and put it into the cash till
June 15 Bought office fixtures paying by cash £60
June 19 Paid Super Motors a cheque for £800
June 21 A loan of £1,000 cash is received from J Jarvis
June 25 Paid £800 of the cash in hand into the bank account
June 30 Bought more office fixtures paying by cheque £300.

3.9X Write up the various accounts needed in the books of S Russell to record the following transactions:

1998
April 1 Opened business with £10,000 in the bank
April 3 Bought office equipment £700 on credit from J Saunders Ltd
April 6 Bought motor van paying by cheque £3,000
April 8 Borrowed £1,000 from H Thompson – he gave us the money by cheque
April 11 Russell put further capital into the firm in the form of cash £500
April 12 Paid £350 of the cash in hand into the bank account
April 15 Returned some of the office equipment costing £200 – it was faulty – to J Saunders Ltd
April 17 Bought more office equipment, paying by cash £50
April 19 Sold the motor van, as it had proved unsuitable, to R Jones for £3,000. R Jones will settle for this by three payments later this month
April 21 Received a loan in cash from J Hawkins £400
April 22 R Jones paid us a cheque for £1,000
April 23 Bought a suitable motor van £3,600 on credit from Phillips Garages Ltd
April 26 R Jones paid us a cheque for £1,800
April 28 Paid £2,000 by cheque to Phillips Garages Ltd
April 30 R Jones paid us cash £200.

4 The double entry system: The treatment of stock

4.1 Stock movements

The stock of goods in a business is constantly changing because some of it is bought, some of it is sold, some is returned to the suppliers and some is returned by the firm's customers.

To keep a check on the movement of stock, an account is opened for each type of dealing in goods. Thus we will have the following accounts:

Account	Reason
Purchases Account	For the purchase of goods
Sales Account	For the sale of goods
Returns Inwards Account	For goods returned to the firm by its customers
Returns Outwards Account	For goods returned by the firm to its suppliers

As stock is an asset, and these four accounts are all connected with this asset, the double entry rules are those used for assets.

We shall now look at some entries in the following sections.

4.2 Purchase of stock on credit

On 1 August 1998 goods costing £165 are bought on credit from D Henry.

First, the twofold effect of the transaction must be considered so that the book-keeping entries can be worked out.

1 The asset of stock is increased. An increase in an asset needs a debit entry in an account. Here the account is a stock account showing the particular movement of stock, in this case it is the 'purchases' movement so that the account must be the purchases account.

2 An increase in a liability. This is the liability of the firm to D Henry because the goods bought have not yet been paid for. An increase in a liability needs a credit entry, so that to enter this part of the transaction a credit entry is made in D Henry's account.

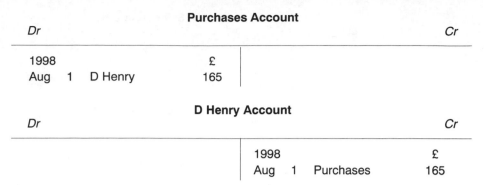

Purchases Account

Dr				Cr
1998			£	
Aug	1	D Henry	165	

D Henry Account

Dr				Cr
	1998			£
	Aug	1	Purchases	165

4.3 Purchases of stock for cash

On 2 August 1998 goods costing £22 are bought, cash being paid for them immediately.

1   The asset of stock is increased, so that a debit entry will be needed. The movement of stock is that of a purchase, so that it is the purchases account which needs debiting.
2   The asset of cash is decreased. To reduce an asset a credit entry is called for, and the asset is that of cash so that the cash account needs crediting.

Cash Account

Dr				Cr
	1998			£
	Aug	2	Purchases	22

Purchases Account

Dr				Cr
1998			£	
Aug	2	Cash	22	

4.4 Sales of stock on credit

On 3 August 1998 sold goods on credit for £250 to K Leach.

1   The asset of stock is decreased. For this a credit entry to reduce an asset is needed. The movement of stock is that of 'Sales' so the account credited is the sales account.
2   An asset account is increased. This is the account showing that K Leach is a debtor for the goods. The increase in the asset of debtors requires a debit and the debtor is K Leach, so that the account concerned is that of K Leach.

Sales Account

Dr		Cr
	1998	£
	Aug 3 K Leach	250

K Leach Account

Dr		Cr
1998	£	
Aug 3 Sales	250	

4.5 Sales of stock for cash

On 4 August 1998 goods are sold for £55, the cash being received at once upon sale.

1   The asset of cash is increased. A debit in the cash account is needed to show this.
2   The asset of stock is reduced. The reduction of an asset requires a credit and the movement of stock is represented by 'Sales'. So the entry needed is a credit in the sales account.

Sales Account

Dr		Cr
	1998	£
	Aug 4 Cash	55

Cash Account

Dr		Cr
1998	£	
Aug 4 Sales	55	

4.6 Returns inwards

These represent goods sold which have now been returned. Just as the original sale was entered in a double entry fashion, so also is the return of those goods.

On 5 August 1998 goods which had previously been sold to F Lowe for £29 are now returned by him.

1   The asset of stock is increased by the goods returned. So a debit representing an increase of an asset is needed, and this time the movement of stock is that of 'Returns Inwards'. The entry required therefore is a debit in the returns inwards account.
2   A decrease in an asset. The debt of F Lowe to the firm is now reduced, and to record this a credit is needed in F Lowe's account.

Returns Inwards Account

Dr·				Cr
1998			£	
Aug	5	F Lowe	29	

F Lowe Account

Dr				Cr
		1998		£
		Aug 5 Returns inwards		29

An alternative name for a returns inwards account is a sales returns account.

4.7 Returns outwards

These represent goods which were purchased, and are now being returned to the supplier. As the original purchase was entered in a double entry fashion, so also is the return to the supplier of those goods.

On 6 August 1998 goods previously bought for £96 are returned by the firm to K Howe.

1 The asset of stock is decreased by the goods sent out. So a credit representing a reduction in an asset is needed, and the movement of stock is that of 'Returns Outwards' so that the entry will be a credit in the returns outwards account.
2 The liability of the firm to K Howe is decreased by the value of the goods returned to him. The decrease in a liability needs a debit, this time in K Howe's account.

Returns Outwards Account

Dr				Cr
		1998		£
		Aug 6 K Howe		96

K Howe Account

Dr				Cr
1998			£	
Aug	6	Returns outwards	96	

An alternative name for a returns outwards account is a purchases returns account.

4.8 A worked example

Enter the following transactions in suitable double entry accounts:

1998
May   1   Bought goods on credit £68 from D Small
May   2   Bought goods on credit £77 from A Lyon & Son
May   5   Sold goods on credit to D Hughes for £60
May   6   Sold goods on credit to M Spencer for £45
May 10   Returned goods £15 to D Small
May 12   Goods bought for cash £100
May 19   M Spencer returned £16 goods to us
May 21   Goods sold for cash £150
May 22   Paid cash to D Small £53
May 30   D Hughes paid the amount owing by him £60 in cash
May 31   Bought goods on credit £64 from A Lyon & Son.

The double entry accounts can now be shown as:

Purchases Account

Dr				Cr
1998		£		
May 1	D Small	68		
May 2	A Lyon & Son	77		
May 12	Cash	100		
May 31	A Lyon & Son	64		

Sales Account

Dr				Cr
		1998		£
		May 5 D Hughes		60
		May 6 M Spencer		45
		May 21 Cash		150

Returns Outwards Account

Dr				Cr
		1998		£
		May 10 D Small		15

Returns Inwards Account

Dr				Cr
1998		£		
May 19	M Spencer	16		

D Small Account

Dr			Cr		
1998		£	1998		£
May 10	Returns outwards	15	May 1	Purchases	68
May 22	Cash	53			

A Lyon & Son Account

Dr				Cr
		1998		£
		May 2	Purchases	77
		May 31	Purchases	64

D Hughes Account

Dr			£	1998		Cr	£
1998							
May 5	Sales		60	May 30	Cash		60

M Spencer Account

Dr			£	1998		Cr	£
1998							
May 6	Sales		45	May 19	Returns inwards		16

Cash Account

Dr			£	1998		Cr	£
1998							
May 21	Sales		150	May 12	Purchases		100
May 30	D Hughes		60	May 22	D Small		53

4.9 Special meaning of 'sales' and 'purchases'

It must be emphasised that 'Sales' and 'Purchases' have a special meaning in accounting language.

'Purchases' in accounting means *the purchase of those goods which the firm buys with the prime intention of selling.* Sometimes the goods may be altered, added to, or used in the manufacture of something else, but it is the element of *resale* that is important. To a firm that deals in typewriters for instance, typewriters are purchases. If something else is bought, such as a motor van, such an item cannot be called purchases, even though in ordinary language it may be said that a motor van has been purchased. The prime intention of *buying* the motor van is for use by the company and not for resale.

Similarly, 'Sales' means the *sale of those goods in which the firm normally deals and which were bought with the prime intention of resale.* The word 'Sales' must never be given to the disposal of other items.

If we did not keep to these meanings, it would result in the different kinds of stock accounts containing something other than goods sold or for resale.

4.10 Comparison of cash and credit transactions for purchases and sales

The difference between the records needed for cash and credit transactions can now be seen.

The complete set of entries for purchases of goods where they are paid for immediately by cash would be:

1 Credit the cash account.
2 Debit the purchases account.

On the other hand the complete set of entries for the purchase of goods on credit can be broken down into two stages. First, the purchase of the goods and second, the payment for them.

The first part is:

1 Debit the purchases account.
2 Credit the supplier's account.

The second part is:

1 Credit the cash account.
2 Debit the supplier's account.

The difference can now be seen; with the cash purchase no record is kept of the supplier's account. This is because cash passes immediately and therefore there is no need to keep a check of indebtedness (money owing) to a supplier. On the other hand, in the credit purchase the records should show to whom money is owed until payment is made.

A study of cash sales and credit sales will reveal a similar difference.

Cash Sales	Credit Sales

Complete entry:
  Debit cash account
  Credit sales account
	First part:
	  Debit customer's account
	  Credit sales account
	Second part:
	  Debit cash account
	  Credit customer's account

New terms

Purchases (p 31): Goods bought by the business for the purpose of selling them again.
Returns inwards (p 28): Goods returned to the business by its customers.
Returns outwards (p 29): Goods returned by the business to its suppliers.
Sales (p 31): Goods sold by the business.

Exercises

4.1   Complete the following table showing which accounts are to be credited and which are to be debited:

	Account to be debited	Account to be credited
(a) Goods bought, cash being paid immediately		
(b) Goods bought on credit from E Flynn		
(c) Goods sold on credit to C Grant		
(d) A motor van sold for cash		
(e) Goods sold for cash.		

4.2X   Similarly, complete this next table:

	Account to be debited	Account to be credited
(a) Goods returned to H Flynn		
(b) Goods bought on credit from P Franklin		
(c) Goods sold on credit to S Mullings		
(d) M Patterson returns goods to us		
(e) Goods bought being paid for by cheque immediately.		

4.3   Complete the following table showing which accounts are to be credited and which are to be debited:

	Account to be debited	Account to be credited
(a) Goods bought on credit from J Reid		
(b) Goods sold on credit to B Perkins		
(c) Motor vans bought on credit from H Thomas		
(d) Goods sold, a cheque being received immediately		
(e) Goods sold for cash		
(f) Goods we returned to H Hardy		
(g) Machinery sold for cash		
(h) Goods returned to us by J Nelson		
(i) Goods bought on credit from D Simpson		
(j) Goods returned to H Forbes		

4.4X   Complete the following table:

	Account to be debited	Account to be credited
(a) Goods bought on credit from T Morgan		
(b) Goods returned to us by J Thomas		
(c) Machinery returned to L Jones Ltd		
(d) Goods bought for cash		
(e) Motor van bought on credit from D Davies Ltd		
(f) Goods returned by us to I Prince		
(g) D Picton paid us his account by cheque		
(h) Goods bought by cheque		
(i) We paid creditor, B Henry, by cheque		
(j) Goods sold on credit to J Mullings.		

4.5   You are to write up the following in the books:

1998
July   1   Started business with £500 cash
July   3   Bought goods for cash £85
July   7   Bought goods on credit £116 from E Morgan
July   10   Sold goods for cash £42
July   14   Returned goods to E Morgan £28
July   18   Bought goods on credit £98 from A Moses
July   21   Returned goods to A Moses £19
July   24   Sold goods to A Knight £55 on credit
July   25   Paid E Morgan's account by cash £88
July   31   A Knight paid us his account in cash £55.

4.6   You are to enter the following in the accounts needed:

1998
Aug   1   Started business with £1,000 cash
Aug   2   Paid £900 of the opening cash into the bank
Aug   4   Bought goods on credit £78 from S Holmes
Aug   5   Bought a motor van by cheque £500
Aug   7   Bought goods for cash £55
Aug   10   Sold goods on credit £98 to D Moore
Aug   12   Returned goods to S Holmes £18
Aug   19   Sold goods for cash £28
Aug   22   Bought fixtures on credit from Kingston Equipment Co £150
Aug   24   D Watson lent us £100 paying us the money by cheque
Aug   29   We paid S Holmes his account by cheque £60
Aug   31   We paid Kingston Equipment Co by cheque £150.

4.7 Enter up the following transactions in the records of E Sangster:

1999

July	1	Started business with £10,000 in the bank
July	2	T Cooper lent us £400 in cash
July	3	Bought goods on credit from F Jones £840 and S Charles £3,600
July	4	Sold goods for cash £200
July	6	Took £250 of the cash and paid it into the bank
July	8	Sold goods on credit to C Moody £180
July	10	Sold goods on credit to J Newman £220
July	11	Bought goods on credit from F Jones £370
July	12	C Moody returned goods to us £40
July	14	Sold goods on credit to H Morgan £190 and J Peat £320
July	15	We returned goods to F Jones £140
July	17	Bought motor van on credit from Manchester Motors £2,600
July	18	Bought office furniture on credit from Faster Supplies Ltd £600
July	19	We returned goods to S Charles £110
July	20	Bought goods for cash £220
July	24	Goods sold for cash £70
July	25	Paid money owing to F Jones by cheque £1,070
July	26	Goods returned to us by H Morgan £30
July	27	Returned some of office furniture costing £160 to Faster Supplies Ltd
July	28	E Sangster put a further £500 into the business in the form of cash
July	29	Paid Manchester Motors £2,600 by cheque
July	31	Bought office furniture for cash £100.

4.8X Enter up the following transactions in the records:

1999

May	1	Started business with £2,000 in the bank
May	2	Bought goods on credit from C Shaw £900
May	3	Bought goods on credit from F Hughes £250
May	5	Sold goods for cash £180
May	6	We returned goods to C Shaw £40
May	8	Bought goods on credit from F Hughes £190
May	10	Sold goods on credit to G Wood £390
May	12	Sold goods for cash £210
May	18	Took £300 of the cash and paid it into the bank
May	21	Bought machinery by cheque £550
May	22	Sold goods on credit to L Moore £220
May	23	G Wood returned goods to us £140
May	25	L Moore returned goods to us £10
May	28	We returned goods to F Hughes £30
May	29	We paid Shaw by cheque £860
May	31	Bought machinery on credit from D Lee £270.

4.9X You are to enter the following in the accounts needed:

1999

June	1	Started business with £1,000 cash
June	2	Paid £800 of the opening cash into a bank account for the firm
June	3	Bought goods on credit from H Grant £330
June	4	Bought goods on credit from D Clark £140
June	8	Sold goods on credit to B Miller £90
June	8	Bought office furniture on credit from Barrett's Ltd £400
June	10	Sold goods for cash £120
June	13	Bought goods for credit from H Grant £200
June	14	Bought goods for cash £60
June	15	Sold goods on credit to H Sharples £180
June	16	We returned goods £50 to H Grant
June	17	We returned some of the office furniture £30 to Barrett's Ltd
June	18	Sold goods on credit to B Miller £400
June	21	Paid H Grant's account by cheque £480
June	23	B Miller paid us the amount owing in cash £490
June	24	Sharples returned to us £50 goods
June	25	Goods sold for cash £150
June	28	Bought goods for cash £370
June	30	Bought motor van on credit from J Kelly £600.

5 The double entry system: expenses and revenue

5.1 The calculation of capital

On 1 January the assets and liabilities of a firm are:

Assets: Fixtures £10,000, Stock £7,000,
               Cash at the bank £3,000.
Liabilities: Creditors £2,000.

The capital is found by the formula

> **Assets – Liabilities = Capital**

In this case capital works out at £10,000 + £7,000 + £3,000 – £2,000 = £18,000.

During January the whole of the £7,000 stock is sold for £11,000 cash. On 31 January the assets and liabilities have become:

Assets: Fixtures £10,000, Stock nil, Cash at the bank £14,000.
Liabilities: Creditors £2,000.

The capital can be calculated:

$$\text{Assets } £10,000 + £14,000 - \text{liabilities } £2,000 = £22,000$$

It can be seen that capital has increased from £18,000 to £22,000 = £4,000 increase because the £7,000 stock was sold for £11,000, a profit of £4,000. Profit, therefore, increases capital.

> **Old Capital + Profit = New Capital**
> **£18,000 + £4,000 = £22,000**

On the other hand a loss would reduce the capital so that it would become:

> **Old Capital – Loss = New Capital**

5.2 Profit or loss and sales

Profit will be made when goods are sold at more than cost price, while the opposite will mean a **loss**.

5.3 Profit or loss and expenses

While the firm is selling its goods there will be other **expenses** on top of the cost of the goods being sold. Every firm has other expenses such as rent, salaries, wages, telephone expenses, motor expenses and so on. Every extra £1 of expenses will mean £1 less profit.

It would be possible simply to have one account with the title 'Expenses Account'. However, rather than just know that the total expenses were £50,000 it would be more useful if we knew exactly how much of that figure was for rent, how much for motor expenses and so on. An expense account is, therefore, opened for each type of expense.

5.4 Debit or credit

We have to decide whether expense accounts are to be debited or credited with the costs involved. Assets involve expenditure by the firm and are shown as debit entries. Expenses also involve expenditure by the firm and therefore should also be debit entries.

An alternative explanation may also be used for expenses. Every expense results in a decrease in an asset or an increase in a liability, and because of the accounting equation this means that the capital is reduced by each expense. The decrease of capital needs a debit entry and therefore expense accounts contain debit entries for expenses.

5.5 Effect of transactions

A few illustrations will demonstrate the double entry required.

1   The rent of £20 is paid in cash.
   Here the twofold effect is:
   (*a*) The asset of cash is decreased – money goes 'OUT'. This means crediting the cash account to show the decrease of the asset.
   (*b*) The total of the expenses of rent is increased – the benefit goes 'IN'. As expense entries are shown as debits, and the expense is rent, so the action required is the debiting of the rent account.

   Summary: Credit the cash account with £20 – 'OUT'.
                    Debit the rent account with £20 – 'IN'.

2   Motor expenses are paid with a cheque for £55.
   The twofold effect is:
   (*a*) The asset of money in the bank is decreased – money goes 'OUT'. This means crediting the bank account to show the decrease of the asset.
   (*b*) The total of the motor expenses paid is increased – a benefit is received 'IN'. To increase an expenses account needs a debit, so the action required is to debit the motor expenses account.

Summary: Credit the bank account with £55 – 'OUT'.
Debit the motor expenses account with £55 – 'IN'.

3   £60 cash is paid for telephone expenses.
   (a) The asset of cash is decreased – money goes 'OUT'. This needs a credit in the cash account to decrease the asset.
   (b) The total of telephone expenses is increased – a benefit received goes 'IN'. Expenses are shown by a debit entry, therefore to increase the expense account in question the action required is to debit the telephone expenses account.

Summary: Credit the cash account with £60 – 'OUT'.
Debit telephone expenses account with £60 – 'IN'.

It is now possible to study the effects of some more transactions showing the results in the form of a table:

		Increase	**Action**	**Decrease**	**Action**
1997 June	1 Paid for postage stamps by cash £5	Expense of postages	Debit postages account	Asset of cash	Credit cash account
	2 Paid for advertising by cheque £29	Expense of advertising	Debit advertising account	Asset of bank	Credit bank account
	3 Paid wages by cash £90	Expense of wages	Debit wages account	Asset of cash	Credit cash account
	4 Paid insurance by cheque £42	Expense of insurance	Debit insurance account	Asset of bank	Credit bank account

The above four examples can now be shown in account form:

Cash Account

Dr			Cr
	1997		£
	June 1	Postages	5
	June 3	Wages	90

Bank Account

Dr			Cr
	1997		£
	June 2	Advertising	29
	June 4	Insurance	42

Advertising Account

Dr				Cr
1997			£	
June	2	Bank	29	

Insurance Account

Dr				Cr
1997			£	
June	4	Bank	42	

Postages Account

Dr				Cr
1997			£	
June	1	Cash	5	

Wages Account

Dr				Cr
1997			£	
June	3	Cash	90	

Sometimes the owner will want to take cash out of the business for his private use. These are known as **drawings**. Any money taken out as drawings will reduce capital.

The capital account is a very important account. To help to stop it getting full of small details, each item of drawings is not entered in the capital account. Instead a drawings account is opened, and the debits are entered there.

The following example illustrates the entries for drawings.

5.6 A worked example

25 August 1997. Proprietor takes £50 cash out of the business for his own use.

Effect	Action
1 Capital is decreased by £50	Debit the drawings account £50
2 Cash is decreased by £50	Credit the cash account £50

Cash Account

Dr				Cr
	1997			£
	Aug	25	Drawings	50

Drawings Account

Dr   Cr

1997		£	
Aug 25	Cash	50	

Sometimes goods are also taken for private use. These are also known as drawings. Entries for such transactions will be described later in the book.

New terms

> **Drawings** (p 40): Cash or goods taken out of a business by the owner for his private use.
>
> **Expenses** (p 38): Costs of operating the business.
>
> **Profit**: (p 37): When goods are sold for more than they cost, the result is a *profit*; if they are sold for less than they cost, then a *loss* would be incurred.

Exercises

5.1 Complete the following table, showing the accounts to be debited and those to be credited:

	Account to be debited	Account to be credited
(a) Paid rates by cheque		
(b) Paid wages by cash		
(c) Rent received by cheque		
(d) Received by cheque refund of insurance previously paid		
(e) Paid general expenses by cash.		

5.2 Complete the following table:

	Account to be debited	Account to be credited
(a) Paid rent by cash		
(b) Paid for goods by cash		
(c) Received by cheque a refund of rates already paid		
(d) Paid general expenses by cheque		
(e) Received commissions in cash		
(f) Goods returned by us to T Jones		
(g) Goods sold for cash		
(h) Bought office fixtures by cheque		
(i) Paid wages in cash		
(j) Took cash out of business for private use.		

5.3X Complete the following table, showing the accounts to be debited and those to be credited:

	Account to be debited	Account to be credited
(a) Paid insurance by cheque		
(b) Paid motor expenses by cash		
(c) Rent received in cash		
(d) Paid rates by cheque		
(e) Received refund of rates by cheque		
(f) Paid for stationery expenses by cash		
(g) Paid wages by cash		
(h) Sold surplus stationery receiving proceeds by cheque		
(i) Received sales commission by cheque		
(j) Bought motor van by cheque.		

5.4X The following table should be completed:

	Account to be debited	Account to be credited
(a) Sold surplus stationery, receiving proceeds in cash		
(b) Paid salaries by cheque		
(c) Rent received for premises sublet, by cheque		
(d) Goods returned to us by Royal Products		
(e) Commission received by us previously in error, we now refund this by cheque		
(f) Bought machinery by cheque		
(g) Paid lighting expenses in cash		
(h) Insurance rebate received by cheque		
(i) Buildings bought by cheque		
(j) Building repairs paid in cash.		

5.5 Enter the following transactions in the necessary accounts in double entry:

1998
Jan 1 Started business with £200 in the bank
Jan 2 U Surer lent us £1,000 giving us the money by cheque
Jan 3 Bought goods on credit £296 from T Parkin
Jan 5 Bought motor van by cheque £250
Jan 6 Cash sales £105
Jan 7 Paid motor expenses in cash £15
Jan 8 Paid wages in cash £18
Jan 10 Bought goods on credit from C Moore £85
Jan 12 Paid insurance by cheque £22
Jan 25 Received commission in cash £15
Jan 31 Paid electricity bill by cheque £17.

5.6 You are to enter the following transactions, completing double entry in the books for the month of May 1997.

1997
May 1 Started business with £2,000 in the bank
May 2 Purchased goods £175 on credit from M Mills
May 3 Bought fixtures and fittings £150 paying by cheque
May 5 Sold goods for cash £275
May 6 Bought goods on credit £114 from S Waites
May 10 Paid rent by cash £15
May 12 Bought stationery £27, paying by cash
May 18 Goods returned to M Mills £23
May 21 Let off part of the premises receiving rent by cheque £5
May 23 Sold goods on credit to U Henry for £77
May 24 Bought a motor van paying by cheque £300
May 30 Paid the month's wages by cash £117
May 31 The proprietor took cash for himself £44.

5.7 Write up the following transactions in the books of L Thompson:

1998
March 1 Started business with cash £1,500
March 2 Bought goods on credit from A Hanson £296
March 3 Paid rent by cash £28
March 4 Paid £1,000 of the cash of the firm into a bank account
March 5 Sold goods on credit to E Linton £54
March 7 Bought stationery £15 paying by cheque
March 11 Cash sales £49
March 14 Goods returned by us to A Hanson £17
March 17 Sold goods on credit to S Morgan £29
March 20 Paid for repairs to the building by cash £18
March 22 E Linton returned goods to us £14
March 27 Paid A Hanson by cheque £279
March 28 Cash purchases £125
March 29 Bought a motor van paying by cheque £395
March 30 Paid motor expenses in cash £15
March 31 Bought fixtures £120 on credit from A Webster.

5.8X Enter the following transactions in double entry:

July 1 Started business with £8,000 in the bank
July 2 Bought stationery by cheque £30
July 3 Bought goods on credit from I Walsh £900
July 4 Sold goods for cash £180
July 5 Paid insurance by cash £40
July 7 Bought machinery on credit from H Morgan £500
July 8 Paid for machinery expenses by cheque £50
July 10 Sold goods on credit to D Small £320
July 11 Returned goods to I Walsh £70
July 14 Paid wages by cash £70
July 17 Paid rent by cheque £100
July 20 Received cheque £200 from D Small
July 21 Paid H Morgan by cheque £500
July 23 Bought stationery on credit from Express Ltd £80
July 25 Sold goods on credit to N Thomas £230
July 28 Received rent £20 in cash for part of premises sublet
July 31 Paid Express Ltd by cheque £80.

5.9X You are to enter the following transactions, completing double entry in the records of J Collins for the month of June 1999:

June   1   Started business with £10,000 in the bank and £300 cash

June   1   Bought goods on credit from: J Carby £400; F McIntyre £1,188; C Morrison £1,344

June   2   Bought shop fittings by cheque £240

June   3   Bought shop fittings on credit from M Johnson Ltd £575

June   5   Paid insurance by cash £88

June   6   Bought motor van paying by cheque £3,200

June   7   Sold goods for cash £140

June   7   Sold goods on credit to: W Graham & Co £450; F Phillips Ltd £246; D R Edwards £80

June   8   Bought office stationery £180 on credit from D Ball & Co

June   9   Paid rent by cheque £75

June 10   Paid rates by cheque £250

June 11   We returned goods to F McIntyre £168

June 12   Paid D Ball & Co £180 by cheque

June 13   Sold goods on credit to K P Prince & Co £220; F Phillips Ltd £154; Kay & Edwards Ltd £270

June 14   Goods returned to us by W Graham & Co £40

June 15   Paid wages by cash £120

June 16   Loan from D Clayton by cheque £500

June 17   W Graham & Co paid us the amount owing by cheque £410

June 18   Some of the stationery was bought unwisely. We sell it for cash £15

June 20   We had overpaid insurance. A refund of £8 received by cheque

June 21   Paid motor expenses by cash £55

June 23   Paid wages by cash £120

June 25   Cheques received from K P Prince & Co £220; F Phillips Ltd £100 (as part payment)

June 26   Some of the shop fillings were unsuitable and were returned to M Johnson Ltd £25

June 28   Paid F McIntyre £1,188, rent £75, both by cheque

June 30   J Collins took drawings by cheque £200.

6 The double entry system: closing balances

6.1 Accounts for debtors

Where debtors have paid their accounts

What you have been reading so far is the recording of transactions in the books by means of debit and credit entries. At the end of each period we will have to look at each account to see what is shown by the entries.

Probably the most obvious reason for this is to find out how much our customers owe us for goods we have sold to them. In most firms this is done at the end of each month. Let us look at the account of one of our customers, K Tandy, for transactions in August 1998.

K Tandy Account

Dr				Cr			
1998			£	1998			£
Aug	1	Sales	144	Aug	22	Bank	144
Aug	19	Sales	300	Aug	28	Bank	300

This shows that during the month we sold a total of £444 goods to Tandy, and have been paid a total of £444 by him. At the close of business at the end of August he therefore owes us nothing. His account can be closed off on 31 August 1998 by inserting the totals on each side, as follows:

K Tandy Account

Dr				Cr			
1998			£	1998			£
Aug	1	Sales	144	Aug	22	Bank	144
Aug	19	Sales	300	Aug	28	Bank	300
			444				444

Notice that totals in accounting are shown with a single line above them, and a double line underneath. Totals on accounts at the end of a period are always shown on a level with one another, as shown in the following completed account for C Lee.

C Lee Account

Dr			£	Cr			£
1998				1998			
Aug	11	Sales	177	Aug	30	Bank	480
Aug	19	Sales	203				
Aug	22	Sales	100				
			480				480

In this account, C Lee also owed us nothing at the end of August 1998, as he had paid us for all sales to him.

If an account contains only one entry on each side and they are equal, totals are unnecessary. For example:

K Wood Account

Dr			£	Cr			£
1998				1998			
Aug	6	Sales	214	Aug	12	Bank	214

Where debtors still owe for goods

On the other hand, some of our customers will still owe us something at the end of the month. In these cases the totals of each side would not equal one another. Let us look at the account of D Knight for August 1998.

D Knight Account

Dr			£	Cr			£
1998				1998			
Aug	1	Sales	158	Aug	28	Bank	158
Aug	15	Sales	206				
Aug	30	Sales	118				

If you add the figures you will see that the debit side adds up to £482 and the credit side adds up to £158. You should be able to see what the difference of £324 (i.e. £482 – £158) represents. It consists of sales of £206 and £118 not paid for and therefore owing to us on 31 August 1998.

In double entry we only enter figures as totals if the totals on both sides of the account agree. We do, however, want to close off the account for August, but showing that Knight owes us £324. If he owes £324 at close of business on 31 August 1998 then he will still owe us that same figure when the business opens on 1 September 1998.

We show this by **balancing the account**. This is done in five stages:

1   Add up both sides to find out their totals. Do not write anything in the account at this stage.
2   Deduct the smaller total from the larger total to find the balance.

3　Now enter the balance on the side with the smallest total. This now means the totals will be equal.

4　Enter totals on a level with each other.

5　Now enter the balance on the line below the totals. The balance below the totals should be on the opposite side to the balance shown above the totals.

Against the balance above the totals, complete the date column by showing the last day of that period. Below the totals show the first day of the next period against the balance. The balance above the totals is described as balance *carried down*. The balance below the total is described as balance *brought down*.

Knight's account when 'balanced off' will appear as follows:

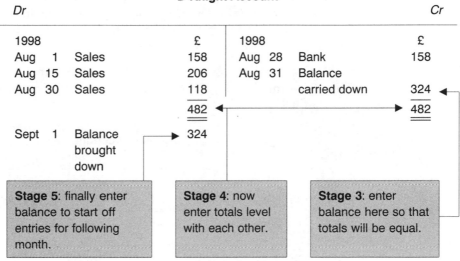

D Knight Account

Dr			£				Cr
1998				1998			
Aug	1	Sales	158	Aug	28	Bank	158
Aug	15	Sales	206	Aug	31	Balance	
Aug	30	Sales	118			carried down	324
			482				482
Sept	1	Balance brought down	324				

Stage 5: finally enter balance to start off entries for following month.

Stage 4: now enter totals level with each other.

Stage 3: enter balance here so that totals will be equal.

We can now look at another account prior to balancing:

H Henry Account

Dr			£				Cr
1998				1998			
Aug	5	Sales	300	Aug	24	Returns inwards	50
Aug	28	Sales	540	Aug	29	Bank	250

We will abbreviate 'carried down' to 'c/d' and 'brought down' to 'b/d' from now on.

H Henry Account

Dr						Cr
1998			£	1998		£
Aug	5	Sales	300	Aug 24	Returns inwards	50
Aug	28	Sales	540	Aug 29	Bank	250
				Aug 31	Balance c/d	540
			840			840
Sept	1	Balance b/d	540			

Notes:

- The date given to balance c/d is the last day of the period which is finishing and balance b/d is given the opening date of the next period.
- As the total of the debit side originally exceeded the total of the credit side, the balance is said to be a debit balance. This being a personal account (for a person), the person concerned is said to be a debtor – the accounting term for anyone who owes money to the firm. The use of the term debtor for a person whose account has a debit balance can again thus be seen.

If accounts contain only one entry it is unnecessary to enter the total. A double line ruled under the entry will mean that the entry is its own total. For example:

B Walters Account

Dr						Cr
1998			£	1998		£
Aug	18	Sales	51	Aug 31	Balance c/d	51
Sept	1	Balance b/d	51			

6.2 Account for creditors

Exactly the same principles will apply when the balances are carried down to the credit side. We can look at two accounts of our suppliers which are to be balanced off.

E Williams Account

Dr						Cr
1998			£	1998		£
Aug	21	Bank	100	Aug 2	Purchases	248
				Aug 18	Purchases	116

K Patterson Account

Dr							Cr
1998			£	1998			£
Aug 14	Returns outwards		20	Aug 8	Purchases		620
Aug 28	Bank		600	Aug 15	Purchases		200

We now add up the totals and find the balance, i.e. stages 1 and 2.
When balanced these will appear as:

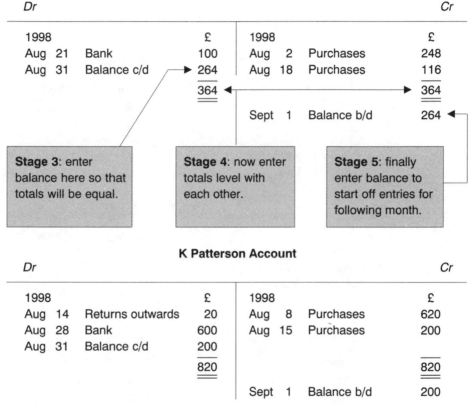

E Williams Account

Dr			£	1998			Cr £
1998							
Aug 21	Bank		100	Aug 2	Purchases		248
Aug 31	Balance c/d		264	Aug 18	Purchases		116
			364				364
				Sept 1	Balance b/d		264

Stage 3: enter balance here so that totals will be equal.

Stage 4: now enter totals level with each other.

Stage 5: finally enter balance to start off entries for following month.

K Patterson Account

Dr			£	1998			Cr £
1998							
Aug 14	Returns outwards		20	Aug 8	Purchases		620
Aug 28	Bank		600	Aug 15	Purchases		200
Aug 31	Balance c/d		200				
			820				820
				Sept 1	Balance b/d		200

Before you read further attempt exercises 6.1, 6.2 and 6.3 on pages 51–52.

6.3 Computers and accounts

Through the main part of this book the type of account used shows the left-hand side of the account as the debit side, and the right-hand side as the credit side. However, when most computers are used the style of the ledger account is different. It appears as three columns of figures, there being one column for debit entries, another column for credit entries, and the last column for the balance. If you have a current account at a bank your bank statements will normally be shown using this method.

The accounts used in this chapter will now be redrafted to show the ledger accounts drawn up in this way.

K Tandy Account

1998		Debit	Credit	Balance (and whether debit or credit)
		£	£	£
Aug 1	Sales	144		144 Dr
Aug 19	Sales	300		444 Dr
Aug 22	Bank		144	300 Dr
Aug 28	Bank		300	0

C Lee Account

1998		Debit	Credit	Balance
		£	£	£
Aug 11	Sales	177		177 Dr
Aug 19	Sales	203		380 Dr
Aug 22	Sales	100		480 Dr
Aug 30	Bank		480	0

K Wood Account

1998		Debit	Credit	Balance
		£	£	£
Aug 6	Sales	214		214 Dr
Aug 12	Bank		214	0

D Knight Account

1998		Debit	Credit	Balance
		£	£	£
Aug 1	Sales	158		158 Dr
Aug 15	Sales	206		364 Dr
Aug 28	Cash		158	206 Dr
Aug 31	Sales	118		324 Dr

H Henry Account

1998		Debit	Credit	Balance
		£	£	£
Aug 5	Sales	300		300 Dr
Aug 24	Returns		50	250 Dr
Aug 28	Sales	540		790 Dr
Aug 29	Bank		250	540 Dr

B Walters Account

1998		Debit £	Credit £	Balance £
Aug 18	Sales	51		51 Dr

E Williams Account

1998		Debit £	Credit £	Balance £
Aug 2	Purchases		248	248 Cr
Aug 18	Purchases		116	364 Cr
Aug 21	Bank	100		264 Cr

K Patterson Account

1998		Debit £	Credit £	Balance £
Aug 8	Purchases		620	620 Cr
Aug 14	Returns	20		600 Cr
Aug 15	Purchases		200	800 Cr
Aug 28	Bank	600		200 Cr

It will be noticed that the balance is calculated again after every entry. This can be done quite simply when using a computer because it is the machine which calculates the new balance.

However, when manual methods are being used it is often too much work to have to calculate a new balance after each entry. It also means that the greater the number of calculations the greater the possibility of errors. For these reasons it is usual for students to use two-sided accounts. However, it is important to note that there is no difference in principle, the final balances are the same using either method.

New term

Balancing the account (p 46): Finding and entering the difference between the two sides of an account.

Exercises

6.1 Enter the following items in the necessary debtors and creditors accounts only, do *not* write up other accounts. Then balance down each personal account at the end of the month. (Keep your answer – it will be used as a basis for question 6.3.)

1998
May 1 Sales on credit to H Harvey £690, N Morgan £153, J Lindo £420
May 4 Sales on credit to L Masters £418, H Harvey £66

May 10 Returns inwards from H Harvey £40, J Lindo £20
May 18 N Morgan paid us by cheque £153
May 20 J Lindo paid us £400 by cheque
May 24 H Harvey paid us £300 by cash
May 31 Sales on credit to L Masters £203.

6.2 Enter the following in the personal accounts only. Do *not* write up the other accounts. Then balance down each personal account at the end of the month. (Keep your answer – it will be used as the basis of question 6.4X.)

1998
June 1 Purchases on credit from J Young £458, L Williams £120, G Norman £708
June 3 Purchases on credit from L Williams £77, T Harris £880
June 10 We returned goods to G Norman £22, J Young £55
June 15 Purchases on credit from J Young £80
June 19 We paid T Harris by cheque £880
June 28 We paid J Young by cash £250
June 30 We returned goods to L Williams £17.

6.3 Redraft each of the accounts given in your answer to 6.1 in three column ledger style accounts.

6.4X Redraft each of the accounts given in your answer to 6.2 in three column ledger style accounts.

6.5 Enter the following in the personal accounts only, do *not* write up the other accounts. Balance down each personal account at the end of the month. After completing this, state which of the balances represent debtors and those which are creditors.

1999
Sept 1 Sales on credit to D Williams £458, J Moore £235, G Grant £98
Sept 2 Purchases on credit A White £77, H Samuels £231, P Owen £65
Sept 8 Sales on credit to J Moore £444, F Franklin £249
Sept 10 Purchases on credit from H Samuels £12, O Oliver £222
Sept 12 Returns inwards from G Grant £9, J Moore £26
Sept 17 We returned goods to H Samuels £24, O Oliver £12
Sept 20 We paid A White by cheque £77
Sept 24 D Williams paid us by cheque £300
Sept 26 We paid O Oliver by cash £210
Sept 28 D Williams paid us by cash £100
Sept 30 F Franklin pays us by cheque £249.

6.6X Enter the following in the necessary personal accounts. Do *not* write up the other accounts. Balance each personal account at the end of the month. (Keep your answer – it will be used as the basis of question 6.8X.)

1999
Aug 1 Sales on credit to L Sterling £445, L Lindo £480, R Spencer £221
Aug 4 Goods returned to us by L Sterling £15, R Spencer £33
Aug 8 Sales on credit to L Lindo £66, R Spencer £129, L Banks £465
Aug 9 We received a cheque for £430 from L Sterling
Aug 12 Sales on credit to R Spencer £235, L Banks £777
Aug 19 Goods returned to us by L Banks £21, R Spencer £25
Aug 22 We received cheques as follows: R Spencer £300, L Lindo £414
Aug 31 Sales on credit to L Lindo £887, L Banks £442.

6.7X Enter the following, personal accounts only. Bring down balances at end of the month. After completing this state which of the balances represent debtors and those which are creditors.

1999
May 1 Credit sale B Flynn £241, R Kelly £29, J Long £887, T Fryer £124
May 2 Credit purchases from S Wood £148, T DuQuesnay £27, R Johnson £77, G Henriques £108
May 8 Credit sales to R Kelly £74, J Long £132
May 9 Credit purchases from T DuQuesnay £142, G Henriques £44
May 10 Goods returned to us by J Long £17, T Fryer £44
May 12 Cash paid to us by T Fryer £80
May 15 We returned goods to S Wood £8, G Henriques £18
May 19 We received cheques from J Long £500, B Flynn £241
May 21 We sold goods on credit to B Flynn £44, R Kelly £280
May 28 We paid by cheque the following: S Wood £140; G Henriques £50; R Johnson £60
May 31 We returned goods to G Henriques £4.

6.8X Redraft each of the accounts given in your answer to 6.6X in three column style accounts.

7 The trial balance

7.1 Total debit entries = total credit entries

You have already seen that the method of book-keeping in use is that of the double entry method. This means:

- For each debit entry there is a credit entry
- For each credit entry there is a debit entry

All the items recorded in all the accounts on the debit side should equal in *total* all the items recorded on the credit side of the books. We need to check that for each debit entry there is also a credit entry. To see if the two totals are equal, usually known as seeing if the two sides of the books 'balance', a **trial balance** may be drawn up at the end of a period.

A form of trial balance could be drawn up by listing all the accounts and adding together all the debit entries, at the same time adding together all the credit entries. Using the worked exercise on pages 29–31 such a trial balance would appear as below. Note that it could not be drawn up until after all the entries had been made. It will therefore be dated as on 31 May 1998.

Trial Balance as on 31 May 1998	Dr £	Cr £
Purchases	309	
Sales		255
Returns outwards		15
Returns inwards	16	
D Small	68	68
A Lyon & Son		141
D Hughes	60	60
M Spencer	45	16
Cash	210	153
	708	708

7.2 Total debit balances = total credit balances

Section 7.1 is not the normal method of drawing up a trial balance, but it is the easiest to understand at first. Usually, a trial balance is a list of balances only, arranged according to whether they are debit balances or credit balances. If the trial balance on page 54 had been drawn up using the normal balances method it would appear as below.

Trial Balance as on 31 May 1998		
	Dr	Cr
	£	£
Purchases	309	
Sales		255
Returns outwards		15
Returns inwards	16	
A Lyon & Son		141
M Spencer	29	
Cash	57	
	411	411

Here the two sides also 'balance'. The sums of £68 in D Small's account, £60 in D Hughes' account, £16 in M Spencer's account and £153 in the cash account have, however, been cancelled out from each side of these accounts by taking only the *balances* instead of *totals*. As equal amounts have been cancelled from each side, £297 in all, the new totals should still equal one another, as in fact they do at £411.

This form of trial balance is the easiest to extract when there are more than a few transactions during the period. Also the balances are either used later when the profits are being calculated, or else appear in a balance sheet. Trial balances, therefore, are not just done to find errors.

7.3 A worked example

The following accounts, for K Potter, have been entered up for May 2001 and balanced off.

K Potter's Books
Bank Account

Dr							Cr
2001			£	2001			£
May	1	Capital	9,000	May	21	Machinery	550
May	30	T Monk	300	May	29	T Wood	860
				May	31	Balance c/d	7,890
			9,300				9,300
June	1	Balance b/d	7,890				

Cash Account

Dr   *Cr*

2001			£	2001			£
May	5	Sales	180	May	30	K Young	170
May	12	Sales	210	May	31	Balance c/d	220
			390				390
June	1	Balance b/d	220				

T Wood Account

Dr   *Cr*

2001			£	2001			£
May	6	Returns outwards	40	May	2	Purchases	900
May	29	Bank	860				
			900				900

K Young Account

Dr   *Cr*

2001			£	2001			£
May	28	Returns outwards	80	May	3	Purchases	250
May	30	Cash	170	May	18	Purchases	190
May	31	Balance c/d	190				
			440				440
				June	1	Balance b/d	190

T Monk Account

Dr   *Cr*

2001			£	2001			£
May	10	Sales	590	May	23	Returns inwards	140
				May	30	Bank	300
				May	31	Balance c/d	150
			590				590
June	1	Balance b/d	150				

C Howe Account

Dr   *Cr*

2001			£	2001			£
May	22	Sales	220	May	25	Returns inwards	10
				May	31	Balance c/d	210
			220				220
June	1	Balance b/d	210				

AB Ltd Account

Dr				Cr
		2001		£
		May 31	Machinery	2,700

Capital Account

Dr				Cr
		2001		£
		May 1	Bank	9,000

Purchases Account

Dr					Cr
2001			£	2001	£
May 2	T Wood		900	May 31 Balance c/d	1,340
May 3	K Young		250		
May 18	K Young		190		
			1,340		1,340
June 1	Balance b/d		1,340		

Sales Account

Dr				Cr
2001		£	2001	£
May 31 Balance c/d		1,200	May 5 Cash	180
			May 10 T Monk	590
			May 12 Cash	210
			May 22 C Howe	220
		1,200		1,200
			June 1 Balance b/d	1,200

Returns Inwards Account

Dr				Cr
2001		£	2001	£
May 23 T Monk		140	May 31 Balance c/d	150
May 25 C Howe		10		
		150		150
June 1 Balance b/d		150		

Returns Outwards Account

Dr				Cr
2001		£	2001	£
May 31 Balance c/d		120	May 6 T Wood	40
			May 28 K Young	80
		120		120
			June 1 Balance b/d	120

Machinery Account

Dr			£	Cr			£
2001				2001			
May	21	Bank	550	May	31	Balance c/d	3,250
May	31	AB Ltd	2,700				
			3,250				3,250
June	1	Balance b/d	3,250				

The trial balance would appear as follows:

K Potter Trial Balance as on 31 May 2001		
	Dr	Cr
	£	£
Bank	7,890	
Cash	220	
K Young		190
T Monk	150	
C Howe	210	
AB Ltd		2,700
Capital		9,000
Purchases	1,340	
Sales		1,200
Returns inwards	150	
Returns outwards		120
Machinery	3,250	
	13,210	13,210

7.4 Trial balances and errors

It may at first sight appear that the balancing of a trial balance proves that the books are correct. This, however, is quite wrong. It means that certain types of error have not been made, but there are several types of error that will not affect the balancing of a trial balance, such as omitting a transaction altogether. Examples of the errors which would be revealed, provided there are no compensating errors which cancel them out, are errors in additions, using one figure for the debit entry and another figure for the credit entry, entering only one aspect of a transaction, and so on. We shall consider these in greater detail in later chapters.

7.5 Skeleton trial balance

Some examining bodies provide a list of balances from which a trial balance must be drawn up, whilst other questions involve correction of a trial balance. It is essential to understand the basic principles of double entry to carry out this task, i.e. a debit balance is always an asset, expense or loss and a credit balance is capital, a liability or income.

A skeleton trial balance is shown is shown on page 60 which will act as a guide, enabling you to answer such questions. Some of the items will be found in later chapters.

7.6 Multiple-choice self-test questions

A growing practice of examining boards is to set multiple-choice questions in Accounting.

Multiple-choice questions certainly give an examiner the opportunity to cover large parts of the syllabus briefly but in detail. Students who omit to study areas of the syllabus will be caught out by an examiner's use of multiple-choice questions. No longer will it be possible to say that it is highly probable a certain topic will not be tested – the examiner can easily cover it with a multiple-choice question.

We have deliberately set blocks of multiple-choice questions at given places in this textbook, rather than a few at the end of each chapter. Such questions are relatively easy to answer a few minutes after reading the chapter. By asking the questions later your powers of recall and understanding are far better tested. It also gives you practice at answering a few questions in one block, as in an examination.

Each multiple-choice question has a 'stem', this is a part which poses the problem, a 'key' which is the one correct answer, and a number of 'distractors', i.e. incorrect answers. The key plus the distractors are known as the 'options'.

If you do not know the answer you should guess. You may be right by chance, or you may remember something subconsciously. In any event, unless the examiner warns otherwise, he will expect you to guess if you don't know the answer.

You should now attempt Set No 1, which contains 20 multiple-choice questions, on page 412.

Skeleton trial balance
Trial balance as at 31 May 1999

	Dr	Cr

*All **debit** balances will include:*

Assets
- Stock (1 June 1999)
- Cash
- Bank
- Machinery
- Motor vans
- Fittings
- Debtors
- Premises
- Goodwill, patents and trade marks
- Investments

Expenses and losses
- Purchases
- Carriage in and out
- Wages and salaries
- Advertising
- Rent and rates
- Stationery
- Discounts allowed
- Bad Debts written off
- Depreciation
- Light and heat

Others
- Drawings
- Stock taken for own use

*All **credit** balances will include:*

Capital and liabilities
- Capital
- Creditors
- Loans *from* others

Income, profits and gains
- Sales
- Commissions received
- Rents received
- Discounts received
- Bad debts recovered

Others
- Balance of Provision for Depreciation Account
- Provision for bad debts

Notes: Closing stock appears as a note.

New term

Trial balance (p 54): A list of all the balances in the books at a particular point in time. The balances are shown in debit and credit columns. These columns should balance provided no errors have occurred. (*See* Chapter 31: Trial balance: correction of errors not affecting trial balance agreement; and correction of errors affecting trial balance agreement.)

Exercises

7.1 You are to enter up the necessary amounts for the month of May from the following details, and then balance off the accounts and extract a trial balance as at 31 May 1998:

1998
May	1	Started firm with capital in cash of £250
May	2	Bought goods on credit from the following persons: D Ellis £54; C Mendez £87; K Gibson £25; D Booth £76; L Lowe £64
May	4	Sold goods on credit to: C Bailey £43; B Hughes £62; H Spencer £176
May	6	Paid rent by cash £12
May	9	Bailey paid us his account by cheque £43
May	10	H Spencer paid us £150 by cheque
May	12	We paid the following by cheque: K Gibson £25; D Ellis £54
May	15	Paid carriage by cash £23
May	18	Bought goods on credit from C Mendez £43; D Booth £110
May	21	Sold goods on credit to B Hughes £67
May	31	Paid rent by cheque £18.

7.2 Enter up the books from the following details for the month of March, and extract a trial balance as at 31 March 1998.

1998
March	1	Started business with £800 in the bank
March	2	Bought goods on credit from the following persons: K Henriques £76; M Hyatt £27; T Braham £56
March	5	Cash sales £87
March	6	Paid wages in cash £14
March	7	Sold goods on credit to: H Elliott £35; L Lane £42; J Carlton £72
March	9	Bought goods for cash £46
March	10	Bought goods on credit from: M Hyatt £57; T Braham £98
March	12	Paid wages in cash £14
March	13	Sold goods on credit to: L Lane £32; J Carlton £23
March	15	Bought shop fixtures on credit from Betta Ltd £50
March	17	Paid M Hyatt by cheque £84
March	18	We returned goods to T Braham £20
March	21	Paid Betta Ltd a cheque for £50
March	24	J Carlton paid us his account by cheque £95
March	27	We returned goods to K Henriques £24
March	30	J King lent us £60 by cash
March	31	Bought a motor van paying by cheque £400

7.3 The following transactions are to be entered up in the books for June, and accounts balanced off and a trial balance extracted as at 30 June 1998:

1998

June	1	Started business with £600 in the bank and £50 cash in hand
June	2	Bought £500 goods on credit from C Jones
June	3	Credit sales: H Henry £66; N Neita £25; P Potter £43
June	4	Goods bought for cash £23
June	5	Bought motor van paying by cheque £256
June	7	Paid motor expenses by cheque £12
June	9	Credit sales: B Barnes £24; K Lyn £26; M Moore £65
June	11	Goods bought on credit: C Jones £240, N Moss £62; O Hughes £46
June	13	Goods returned by us to C Jones £25
June	15	Paid motor expenses by cash £5
June	19	Goods returned to us by N Neita £11
June	20	Cash taken for own use (drawings) £10
June	21	We paid the following by cheque: N Moss £62; O Hughes £46
June	23	H Henry paid us in cash £66
June	25	P Potter paid us by cheque £43
June	26	Cash sales £34
June	27	Cash taken for own use £24
June	28	Goods returned by us to C Jones £42
June	29	Paid for postage stamps by cash £4
June	30	Credit sales: N Neita £43; M Edgar £67; K Lyn £45.

7.4X Record the following transactions of D Chatsworth for the month of May 1999, balance off all the accounts, and then extract a trial balance as on 31 May 1999:

1999

May	1	D Chatsworth started business with £8,000 cash
May	2	Put £7,500 of the cash into a bank account
May	2	Bought goods on credit from: Burton Brothers £180; Lyew & Co £560; P McDonald £380; K Black Ltd £410
May	3	Bought office fixtures by cheque £185
May	4	Bought goods for cash £190
May	5	Cash sales £110
May	6	Goods sold on credit: J Gayle & Son £190; P Gentles £340; T Sutherland £110; T Brown Ltd £300
May	7	Paid rent by cheque £100
May	8	Paid wages by cash £70
May	10	Bought goods on credit from: Lyew & Co £340; C Rose £160
May	11	Goods returned to us by J Gayle & Son £60
May	13	Goods sold on credit to: N Mattis £44; J Gayle & Son £300
May	14	Bought office fixtures on credit from Tru-kits Ltd £178
May	15	Bought office stationery for cash £90
May	16	Paid cheques to the following: Tru-kits Ltd £178; Burton Brothers £180
May	17	Paid wages by cash £90
May	18	D Chatsworth takes £100 drawings in cash
May	20	We returned goods to P McDonald £60; K Black Ltd £44
May	22	Bought office stationery £220 on credit from EP & Co
May	24	Received cheques from N Mattis £44; T Brown Ltd £180
May	26	Cash sales £140
May	29	D Chatsworth took cash drawings £150
May	31	Paid sundry expenses by cash £5.

7.5X Record the following details for the month of November 1999 and extract a trial balance as at 30 November:

Nov 1 Started with £5,000 in the bank
Nov 3 Bought goods on credit from: T Henriques £160; J Smith £230; W Rogers £400; P Boone £310
Nov 5 Cash sales £240
Nov 6 Paid rent by cheque £20
Nov 7 Paid rates by cheque £190
Nov 11 Sold goods on credit to: L Matthews £48; K Allen £32; R Hall £1,170
Nov 17 Paid wages by cash £40
Nov 18 We returned goods to: T Henriques £14; P Boone £20
Nov 19 Bought goods on credit from: P Boone £80; W Rogers £270; D Diaz £130
Nov 20 Goods were returned to us by K Allen £2; L Matthews £4
Nov 21 Bought motor van on credit from UZ Motors £500
Nov 23 We paid the following by cheque: T Henriques £146; J Smith £230; W Rogers £300
Nov 25 Bought another motor van, paying by cheque immediately £700
Nov 26 Received a loan of £400 cash from A Williams
Nov 28 Received cheques from: L Matthews £44; K Allen £30
Nov 30 Proprietor brings a further £300 into the business, by a payment into the business bank account.

7.6X Record the following for the month of January, balance off all the accounts, and then extract a trial balance as at 31 January 1998:

1998
Jan 1 Started business with £3,500 cash
Jan 2 Put £2,800 of the cash into a bank account
Jan 3 Bought goods for cash £150
Jan 4 Bought goods on credit from: L Coke £360; M Burton £490; T Hill £110; C Small £340
Jan 5 Bought stationery on credit from: Swift Ltd £170
Jan 6 Sold goods on credit to: S Walters £90; T Binns £150; C Howard £190; P Peart £160
Jan 8 Paid rent by cheque £55
Jan 10 Bought fixtures on credit from Matalon Ltd £480
Jan 11 Paid salaries in cash £120
Jan 14 Returned goods to M Burton £40; T Hill £60
Jan 15 Bought motor van by cheque £700
Jan 16 Received loan from J Henry by cheque £600
Jan 18 Goods returned to us by: S Walters £20; C Howard £40
Jan 21 Cash sales £90
Jan 24 Sold goods on credit to: T Binns £100; P Peart £340; J Smart £115
Jan 26 We paid the following by cheque: M Burton £450; T Hill £50
Jan 29 Received cheques from: J Smart £115; T Binns £250
Jan 30 Received a further loan from J Henry by cash £200
Jan 30 Received £500 cash from P Peart.

7.7 Correct and balance the following trial balance.

Trial balance of P Brown as at 31 May 1999		
	Dr £	Cr £
Capital		20,000
Drawings	7,000	
General expenses		500
Sales	38,500	
Purchases		29,000
Debtors		6,800
Creditors	9,000	
Bank balance (Dr)	15,100	
Cash		200
Plant and equipment		5,000
Heating and lighting		1,500
Rent	2,400	

7.8 Reconstruct the trial balance after making the necessary corrections.

Trial Balance of S Higton as at 30 June 1998		
	Dr £	Cr £
Capital	19,956	
Sales		119,439
Stationery	1,200	
General expenses	2,745	
Motor expenses		4,476
Cash at bank	1,950	
Stock 1 July 1997	7,668	
Wages and salaries		9,492
Rent and rates	10,500	
Office equipment	6,000	
Purchases	81,753	
Heating and lighting		2,208
Rent received	2,139	
Debtors	10,353	
Drawings		4,200
Creditors		10,230
Motor vehicle	7,500	
Interest received	1,725	
Insurance		3,444
	153,489	153,489

7.9 From the following list of balances prepare a trial balance as at 31 December 1999 for Ms Anita Hall:

	£
Plant and machinery	21,450
Motor vehicles	26,000
Premises	80,000
Wages	42,840
Purchases	119,856
Sales	179,744
Rent received	3,360
Telephone, printing and stationery	3,600
Creditors	27,200
Debtors	30,440
Bank overdraft	2,216
Capital	131,250
Drawings	10,680
General expenses	3,584
Lighting and heating	2,960
Motor expenses	2,360

PART 2

The final accounts of a business

8 An introduction to trading accounts and profit and loss accounts

8.1 Purpose of trading and profit and loss account

People run businesses to try to make a profit. If they are not successful they may make a loss. To calculate how much profit or loss has been made over a period of time a **trading and profit and loss account** is prepared.

Normally, all businesses prepare trading and profit and loss accounts at least once a year. They could be prepared for a shorter period if required.

The main purpose of a trading and profit and loss account is for the owners to see how profitably the business is being run. It is also used for other purposes, for instance it will be used as a basis for calculating the owners' income tax liability under Self Assessment.

8.2 Format for the trading and profit and loss account

One of the most important uses of the trading and profit and loss account is the comparison of the results achieved in this period with those of previous periods.

The trading and profit and loss account is in fact two separate accounts in one:

1 The **trading account**

This shows the sales for the period, less the cost of buying or manufacturing the sales i.e. 'The cost of goods sold'. The end result shows us the **gross profit**:

Trading account	
	£
Sales	X
Less Cost of goods sold	(X)
Gross profit	X

2 The **profit and loss account**

This starts with the gross profit figure brought down from the trading account, from which are deducted all other expenses, overheads, and finance costs, not directly attributable to sales, and therefore not included in the trading account. The end result shows the **net profit**:

Profit and loss account

	£
Gross profit	X
Less Expenses	(X)
Net profit	$\overline{\underline{\underline{X}}}$

Normally, these two accounts are combined to form one account called 'The trading and profit and loss account'.

8.3 Information needed

Before drawing up a trading and profit and loss account you will need the trial balance. This contains nearly all the information needed. (Later on in this book you will see that certain adjustments have to be made, but we will ignore these at this stage.)

Set out in Exhibit 8.1 is the trial balance for K Wade, made up to the end of his first year in business. We will use this information to prepare his trading and profit and loss account for the year ended 31 December 1997. For now we will assume K Wade has no closing stock at 31 December 1997.

Exhibit 8.1

K Wade Trial Balance as on 31 December 1997		
	Dr £	*Cr* £
Sales		9,650
Purchases	7,150	
General expenses	550	
Fixtures and fittings	1,840	
Debtors	1,460	
Creditors		1,180
Capital		2,800
Drawings	1,750	
Bank	820	
Cash	60	
	13,630	13,630

8.4 Preparation of a trading and profit and loss account

To calculate gross profit

Remember that:

Sales – Cost of Goods Sold = Gross Profit

To do this in double entry, the following steps should be carried out.

1 Transfer the credit balance of the sales account to the credit of the trading account portion of the trading and profit and loss account.

Debit: Sales account
Credit: Trading account

2 Transfer the debit balance of the purchases account to the debit of the trading account.

Debit: Trading account
Credit: Purchases

Remember, in this case there is no stock of unsold goods. This means that Purchases = Cost of Goods Sold.

3 If sales are greater than the cost of goods sold the difference is gross profit. (If not, the answer would be a gross loss.) We will carry this gross profit figure from the trading account part down to the profit and loss part. The double entry for gross profit is:

Debit: Trading account
Credit: Profit and loss account

Now we can see this done for Exhibit 8.1:

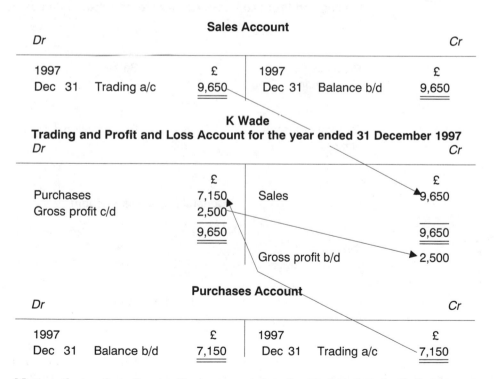

Sales Account

Dr						Cr
1997			£	1997		£
Dec 31	Trading a/c		9,650	Dec 31	Balance b/d	9,650

K Wade
Trading and Profit and Loss Account for the year ended 31 December 1997

Dr			Cr
	£		£
Purchases	7,150	Sales	9,650
Gross profit c/d	2,500		
	9,650		9,650
		Gross profit b/d	2,500

Purchases Account

Dr						Cr
1997			£	1997		£
Dec 31	Balance b/d		7,150	Dec 31	Trading a/c	7,150

Notice that, after the trading account has been completed, there are no balances remaining in the sales and purchases accounts. They are now *closed*.

To calculate net profit and record it

Remember that:

> **Gross Profit − Expenses = Net Profit**

Remember also (from Chapter 5) that:

> **Old Capital + Net Profit = New Capital**

Double entry needed to carry out these calculations:

1   Transfer the debit balances on expenses accounts to the debit of the profit and loss account.

Debit: Profit and loss account
Credit: Expenses accounts

2   Transfer the net profit, when found, to the capital account to show the increase in capital.

Debit: Profit and loss account
Credit: Capital account

K Wade
Trading and Profit and Loss Account for the Year ended 31 December 1997
Dr   Cr

	£		£
Purchases	7,150	Sales	9,650
Gross profit c/d	2,500		
	9,650		9,650
General expenses	550	Gross profit b/d	2,500
Net profit	1,950		
	2,500		2,500

General Expenses Account
Dr   Cr

1997		£	1997		£
Dec 31	Balance b/d	550	Dec 31	Profit and loss a/c	550

Capital Account
Dr   Cr

			1997		£
			Dec 31	Balance b/d	2,800
			Dec 31	Net profit	1,950
					4,750

Note: See 8.5 for completion of this account.

8.5 Completion of capital account

You have seen that we credit the capital account with the amount of net profit. We have, therefore, recorded the increase in capital.

In the trial balance, Exhibit 8.1, we can see that there are drawings of £1,750. Drawings means withdrawals of capital.

After entering the net profit in the capital account we can now complete the account. To do this we transfer the drawings to the capital account.

Debit: Capital account
Credit: Drawings account

The completed capital and drawings accounts are as follows:

Drawings Account

Dr					Cr
1997		£	1997		£
Dec 31	Balance b/d	1,750	Dec 31	Capital	1,750

Capital Account

Dr					Cr
1997		£	1997		£
Dec 31	Drawings	1,750	Dec 31	Balance b/d	2,800
Dec 31	Balance c/d	3,000	Dec 31	Net profit	1,950
		4,750			4,750
			1998		
			Jan 1	Balance b/d	3,000

8.6 Stock of unsold goods at end of period

Usually some of the goods bought (purchases) have not been sold by the end of the accounting period. We have already seen that gross profit is calculated as follows:

> **Sales – Cost of Goods Sold = Gross Profit**

However, purchases only equals cost of goods sold if there is no stock at the end of a period. We can calculate cost of goods sold as follows:

What we bought in this period:	Purchases
Less Goods bought but not sold in this period:	Closing Stock
	= Cost of Goods Sold

Let us look at the drawing-up of a trading and profit and loss account for B Swift. His trial balance is shown as Exhibit 8.2 and was drawn up after his first year of trading:

Exhibit 8.2

B Swift Trial Balance on 31 December 1997		
	Dr £	Cr £
Sales		3,850
Purchases	2,900	
Rent	240	
Lighting	150	
General expenses	60	
Fixtures and fittings	500	
Debtors	680	
Creditors		910
Bank	1,510	
Cash	20	
Drawings	700	
Capital		2,000
	6,760	6,760

Note: On 31 December 1997, at the close of trading, B Swift had goods costing £300 which were unsold.

1   The cost of goods sold figure will be:

	£
Purchases	2,900
Less Closing stock	(300)
Cost of goods sold	2,600

2   The gross profit will be:

	£
Sales	3,850
Less Cost of goods sold	(2,600)
Gross profit	1,250

3   The net profit will be:

	£	£
Gross profit		1,250
Less Expenses		
Rent	240	
Lighting	150	
General expenses	60	
		(450)
Net profit		800

We will now see this shown in double entry:

Sales Account

Dr						Cr
1997			£	1997		£
Dec 31	Trading a/c		3,850	Dec 31	Balance b/d	3,850

Purchases Account

Dr						Cr
1997			£	1997		£
Dec 31	Balance b/d		2,900	Dec 31	Trading a/c	2,900

Rent Account

Dr						Cr
1997			£	1997		£
Dec 31	Balance b/d		240	Dec 31	Profit and loss a/c	240

Lighting Account

Dr						Cr
1997			£	1997		£
Dec 31	Balance b/d		150	Dec 31	Profit and loss a/c	150

General Expenses Account

Dr						Cr
1997			£	1997		£
Dec 31	Balance b/d		60	Dec 31	Profit and loss a/c	60

Stock Account

Dr					Cr
1997			£		
Dec 31	Trading a/c		300 ◄		

B Swift
Trading and Profit and Loss Account for the year ended 31 December 1997

1997	£	1997	£
Purchases	2,900	Sales	3,850
Gross profit c/d	1,250	Closing stock	300 ◄
	4,150		4,150
Rent	240	Gross profit b/d	1,250
Lighting	150		
General expenses	60		
Net profit	800		
	1,250		1,250

To record the stock we have entered the following:

Debit: Stock account
Credit: Trading account

This means that there is now a balance on the stock account. We had to record it there because at 31 December 1997 we had an asset, £300 of stock, but there was no record of that fact in our books. We have now brought our records up-to-date by showing the stock in our accounts. Without the stock accounts at 31 December 1997 our records would have been incomplete.

The trading and profit and loss account shown above is written in the *horizontal format*, so as to demonstrate how the double entry system works.

However, the trading and profit and loss account is more often shown in the *vertical format*, and it is this format we will use in the future in this book. You may wish to carry on preparing the horizontal format trading and profit and loss account before drawing up the vertical format, until you are sure you understand how to double enter directly into the vertical format.

Exhibit 8.3 shows the trading and profit and loss account of B Swift, in the vertical format

Exhibit 8.3

B Swift
Trading and Profit and Loss Account for the year ended 31 December 1997

	£	£
Sales		3,850
Less Cost of goods sold		
Purchases	2,900	
less Closing stock	(300)	
		2,600
Gross profit		1,250
Less Overheads		
Rent	240	
Lighting	150	
General expenses	60	
		(450)
Net profit		800

8.7 The capital account

The capital account can now be completed.

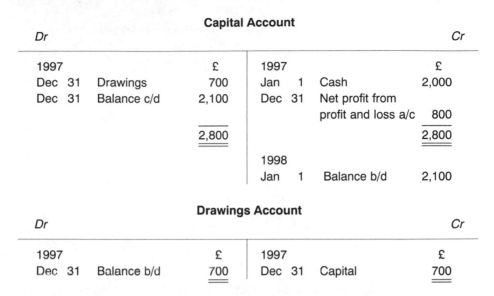

Capital Account

Dr			£	Cr			£
1997				1997			
Dec	31	Drawings	700	Jan	1	Cash	2,000
Dec	31	Balance c/d	2,100	Dec	31	Net profit from	
						profit and loss a/c	800
			2,800				2,800
				1998			
				Jan	1	Balance b/d	2,100

Drawings Account

Dr			£	Cr			£
1997				1997			
Dec	31	Balance b/d	700	Dec	31	Capital	700

8.8 The balances still in our books

Taking Exhibit 8.2, but including the adjustment for closing stock of £300, we can now see which balances still exist. We can do this by drawing up a trial balance as it would appear once the trading and profit and loss account was completed. We will show it as Exhibit 8.4.

Accounts closed

Sales
Purchases   } transferred to trading account

Rent
Lighting   } transferred to profit and loss account
General expenses

Drawings   } transferred to capital account

Accounts not closed

Exhibit 8.4

B Swift
Trial Balance as on 31 December 1997
(after Trading and Profit and Loss Accounts completed)

	Dr £	Cr £
Fixtures and fittings	500	
Debtors	680	
Creditors		910
Stock	300	
Bank	1,510	
Cash	20	
Capital		2,100
	3,010	3,010

The one account which was not in the original trial balance was stock account. It was not brought into our books until the trading account was prepared. These balances will be used by us when we look at the balance sheets.

New terms

Gross profit (p 69): Found by deducting cost of goods sold from sales.
Net profit (p 70): Gross profit less expenses.
Profit and loss account (p 69): Account in which net profit is calculated.
Trading account (p 69): Account in which gross profit is calculated.
Trading and profit and loss account (p 69): Combined account in which both gross and net profits are calculated.

Exercises

Note: All answers should show the vertical layout of the trading and profit and loss accounts.

8.1 From the following trial balance of B Webb, who has been in business for one year, extract a trading and profit and loss account for the year ended 31 December 1997. A balance sheet is not required.

Trial Balance as at 31 December 1997		
	Dr £	Cr £
Sales		18,462
Purchases	14,629	
Salaries	2,150	
Motor expenses	520	
Rent and rates	670	
Insurance	111	
General expenses	105	
Premises	1,500	
Motor vehicles	1,200	
Debtors	1,950	
Creditors		1,538
Cash at bank	1,654	
Cash in hand	40	
Drawings	895	
Capital		5,424
	25,424	25,424

Stock at 31 December 1997 was £2,548.

(Keep your answer – it will be used later in exercise 9.1.)

8.2 From the following trial balance of C Worth, who has been trading for one year, you are required to draw up a trading and profit and loss account for the year ended 30 June 1998. A balance sheet is not required.

Trial Balance as at 30 June 1998		
	Dr £	Cr £
Sales		28,794
Purchases	23,803	
Rent and rates	854	
Lighting expenses	422	
Salaries and wages	3,164	
Insurance	105	
Shop buildings	50,000	
Shop fixtures	1,000	
Debtors	3,166	
Trade expenses	506	
Creditors		1,206
Cash at bank	3,847	
Drawings	2,400	
Motor vans	5,500	
Motor running expenses	1,133	
Capital		65,900
	95,900	95,900

Stock at 30 June 1998 was £4,166.

(Keep your answer – it will be used later in exercise 9.2.)

8.3 Mrs P Stewart commenced trading as a card and gift shop with a capital of £6,855 on 1 April 1997. At the end of her first year's trading on 31 March 1998 she was able to identify from her accounting records that she had received £24,765 sales in the year. These sales had cost her £13,545 to purchase, and she had £2,345 cards and gifts at cost, in stock on 31 March 1998. In the year she had also spent £2,100 on staff wages, and drawn personal cash of £5,500. Other overhead costs incurred were:

	£
Rent and rates	1,580
Electricity	565
Motor expenses	845
Insurance	345
General expenses	245

On 31 March 1998 Mrs P Stewart had cash in hand of £135, a bank balance of £2,675, and owed £3,285 to creditors. Mrs Stewart's business owned a car which had a value of £5,875 at 31 March 1998. She had also bought shelving and fixtures and fittings in the year to the value of £1,495.

You are required to draw up the trading and profit and loss account for the first year's trading.

(*Exam hint*: Before you attempt to draw up the trading and profit and loss account, it would be a good idea to extract the trial balance at 31 March 1998 from the information given.)
Note: The closing stock figure should be shown as a note at the foot of the trial balance.

(Keep your answer – it will be used later in exercise 9.3.)

8.4X From the following trial balance of F Chaplin, draw up a trading and profit and loss account for the year ended 31 December 1998. A balance sheet is not required. He has been in business for one year only.

Trial Balance as at 31 December 1998	Dr £	Cr £
General expenses	210	
Rent and rates	400	
Motor expenses	735	
Salaries	3,560	
Insurance	392	
Purchases	18,385	
Sales		26,815
Motor vehicle	2,800	
Creditors		5,160
Debtors	4,090	
Premises	20,000	
Cash at bank	1,375	
Cash in hand	25	
Capital		24,347
Drawings	4,350	
	56,322	56,322

Stock at 31 December 1998 was £4,960.
(Keep your answer – it will be used later in exercise 9.5X.)

8.5X Miss R Burgess has just completed her first year of trading for the year ended 30 April 1998, as a manufacturer of model railway accessories. Her initial capital was £9,025.

At 30 April 1998, she was owed £5,600 by customers, and owed £4,825 to suppliers. She calculated she had stock on hand, at cost, at the year end of £7,670, and her bank account was overdrawn by £2,560. The petty cash float held £25 at 30 April 1998.

From her records, she calculated her income and expenditure for the year ended 30 April 1998 were:

	£
Sales	56,540
Purchases	34,315
Rent of factory	6,000
Drawings	10,000
Motor expenses	1,735
Insurance	345
General expenses	780
Salaries	7,550

Miss R Burgess had plant and equipment to the value of £3,750 and a van worth £2,850 at 30 April 1998.

You are required to draw up the trading and profit and loss account for the first year's trading.

(Keep your answer – it will be used later in exercise 9.6X.)

9 The balance sheet

9.1 Contents of the balance sheet

You saw in Chapter 2 that a balance sheet contains details of assets, capital and liabilities. These details have to be found in our records and then written out as a balance sheet.

It is easy to find these details. They consist of all the balances remaining in our records once the trading and profit and loss account for the period has been completed. All balances remaining have to be assets, capital or liabilities. All the other balances should have been closed off when the trading and profit and loss account was completed.

9.2 Drawing up a balance sheet

Let us now look at Exhibit 9.1, the trial balance of B Swift (from Exhibit 8.4) as on 31 December 1997 *after* the trading and profit and loss account had been prepared.

Exhibit 9.1

B Swift Trial Balance as on 31 December 1997 (after Trading and Profit and Loss Accounts completed)	Dr £	Cr £
Fixtures and fittings	500	
Debtors	680	
Creditors		910
Stock	300	
Bank	1,510	
Cash	20	
Capital		2,100
	3,010	3,010

We can now draw up a balance sheet as at 31 December 1997, Exhibit 9.2.

Exhibit 9.2

B Swift
Balance Sheet as at 31 December 1997

	£	£	£
Fixed assets			
Fixtures and fittings			500
Current assets			
Stock	300		
Debtors	680		
Cash at bank	1,510		
Cash in hand	20		
		2,510	
Current liabilities			
Creditors		910	
Net current assets			1,600
Long-term liabilities			
Long-term loan			–
Net assets			2,100
Financed by:			
Capital account			
Cash introduced			2,000
Add Net profit for the year			800
			2,800
Less Drawings			(700)
			2,100

This layout is discussed further in Section 9.4.

9.3 No double entry in balance sheets

It may seem very strange to you to learn that balance sheets are *not* part of the double entry system.

When we draw up accounts such as the cash account, rent account, sales account, trading and profit and loss account and so on, we are writing up part of the double entry system. We make entries on the debit side and the credit side of these accounts.

However, we do not enter or transfer any figures when drawing up a balance sheet. The balance sheet is a list of balances extracted from all the individual accounts which remain open at the balance sheet date, *after* the trading and profit and loss account has been drawn up for the period ending on the balance sheet date.

These balances then form the opening balances for the new accounting period.

If you see the word 'account' you will know that it is part of the double entry system, and will include debit and credit entries. If the word 'account' cannot be used it is not part of double entry. For instance:

Trial balance: A list of balances to see if the records are correct.

Balance sheet: A list of balances arranged according to whether they are assets, capital or liabilities.

9.4 Balance sheet layout

You would not expect to go into a department store and see goods for sale all mixed up and not laid out properly. You would expect that the goods would be displayed so that you could easily find them. Similarly in balance sheets we do not want all the items shown in any order. We want them displayed so that useful information can easily be seen.

For users of the accounts like bank managers, accountants and investors conformity of layout is needed in order to make a comparison of balance sheets easier. The standard layout is shown in Exhibit 9.2, and examined in more detail below.

Assets

The first section is Assets: Assets are shown under two headings, **Fixed Assets** and **Current Assets**.

Assets are called fixed assets when they:

1   are of long life;
2   are to be used in the business; and
3   were not bought only for the purposes of resale.

Examples: buildings, machinery, motor vehicles, fixtures and fittings.

Fixed assets are listed starting with those with the longest life expectancy down to those with the shortest life expectancy. For instance:

Fixed Assets
1 Land and buildings
2 Fixtures and fittings
3 Machinery
4 Motor vehicles

Current assets are cash in hand, cash at bank, items held for resale at a profit or items that have a short life.

These are listed starting with the asset furthest away from being turned into cash, finishing with cash itself. For instance:

Current Assets
1 Stock
2 Debtors
3 Cash at bank
4 Cash in hand

Liabilities

Liabilities are categorised under two headings:

1 **Current liabilities**. Current liabilities are liabilities due for repayment in the short term. Examples of current liabilities are bank overdraft, trade creditors and sundry creditors.

   Current liabilities are deducted from current assets, as shown in Exhibit 9.2, to give either net current assets or net current liabilities (also known as Working Capital).

2 **Long-term liabilities**. Long-term liabilities are liabilities not due for repayment in the short term. Examples of long-term liabilities are loans and mortgages.

   Long-term liabilities are deducted after the net current assets/liabilities figure in the balance sheet, also shown in Exhibit 9.2.

Capital account

This is the proprietor's or partner's account with the business. It will start with the balance brought forward from the previous accounts period, to which is added any personal cash introduced into the business and the net profit made by the business in this accounting period. Deducted from the capital account will be amounts drawn from the business and any loss made by the business. The final balance on the capital account should equal the net assets or net liabilities figure – and hence the balance sheet *balances*.

Exhibit 9.3

Capital Account

		£	£
Balance b/d			X
Add	Cash introduced		X
	Net profit for the period		X
Less	Drawings	X	
	Net loss for the period	X	
			X
			X

It is important to note that the balance sheet shows the position of the business at one point in time: the balance sheet date. It is like taking a snapshot of the business at one moment in time. The trading and profit and loss account shows the profit/loss of that business for a period of time (normally a year).

New terms

Current assets (p 84): Assets consisting of cash, goods for resale, or items having a short life.
Current liabilities (p 85): Liabilities to be paid for in the near future.
Fixed assets (p 84): Assets bought which have a long life and are to be used in the business.
Long-term liabilities (p 85): Liabilities not having to be paid for in the near future.

Exercises

9.1 Complete exercise 8.1 by drawing up a balance sheet as at 31 December 1997.

9.2 Complete exercise 8.2 by drawing up a balance sheet as at 30 June 1998.

9.3 Complete exercise 8.3 by drawing up a balance sheet as at 31 March 1998.

9.4 Miss V Holland had been trading for a number of years as a cheese retailer, making up accounts each year to 30 June. As at 30 June 1998 she was able to extract the following information from her accounting records, and has asked you as her accountant to draw up the balance sheet at that date:
   (a) She owed amounts to businesses that had supplied her with cheese, totalling £4,565
   (b) She was owed £2,375 by a customer who bought goods on credit
   (c) She had cash in hand of £150
   (d) Her bank account was overdrawn by £1,785
   (e) She had stock of cheese unsold totalling £1,465
   (f) She had a van which was used for deliveries which was valued at £3,400 on 30 June 1998
   (g) She had equipment valued at £2,885 at the year end
   (h) She had introduced £2,000 of her own money in the year, when she was nearing her overdraft limit
   (i) The business made a net profit of £2,525 in the year to 30 June 1998
   (j) Miss V Holland drew £50 each week, for the whole year, and had no other drawings from the business
   (k) The business had a loan from V Holland's mother for £2,000. This was not due to be repaid until the year 2004.

9.5X Complete exercise 8.4X by drawing up a balance sheet as at 31 December 1998.

9.6X Complete exercise 8.5X by drawing up a balance sheet as at 30 April 1998.

10 Further considerations regarding final accounts

10.1 Vertical format of trading and profit and loss account

In Chapter 8 we introduced the vertical format of the trading and profit and loss account. From now on you should get used to the vertical format, as this is the format we will use from this point on, and you will also come across it in your exams. Exhibit 10.1 shows the standard vertical format.

Exhibit 10.1

C Raines
Trading and Profit and Loss Account for the year ended 31 December 1999

	£	£
Sales		6,000
Less Cost of goods sold		
Opening stock	–	
Purchases	4,000	
Carriage inwards	350	
	4,350	
Less Closing stock	650	
		3,700
Gross Profit		2,300
Less Expenses		
Carriage outwards	280	
Other expenses	220	
		500
Net profit		1,800

Three new concepts shown in Exhibit 10.1 now need further consideration:

1 **Carriage inwards**
2 **Carriage outwards**
3 Opening stock

10.2 Carriage inwards

Carriage (the cost of transport of goods) into a firm is called carriage inwards.

When you buy goods the cost of carriage inwards may either be included as part of the price, or else the firm may have to pay separately for it. Suppose you were buying exactly the same goods. One supplier might sell them to you for £100, and he would deliver the goods and not send you a bill for carriage. Another supplier might sell the goods to you for £95, but you would have to pay £5 to a haulage firm for carriage inwards, i.e. a total cost of £100.

To keep the cost of buying goods shown on the same basis, carriage inwards is always added to the purchases in the trading account.

10.3 Carriage outwards

Carriage from a firm out to its customers is called carriage outwards.

This is always treated as an expense to be transferred to the debit of the profit and loss account.

Exhibit 10.2 shows extracts from the trial balance from which the trading and profit and loss account for the year ended 31 December 1999 in Exhibit 10.1 has been drawn up.

Exhibit 10.2

C Raines Trial Balance as at 31 December 1999 (extracts)		
	Dr £	Cr £
Sales		6,000
Purchases	4,000	
Carriage inwards	350	
Carriage outwards	280	
Other expenses	220	

The closing stock on 31 December 1999 was £650.

10.4 The second year of a business

Following on from Exhibit 9.2 in the last chapter, B Swift carries on his business for another year. He then extracts a trial balance as on 31 December 1998, shown as Exhibit 10.3.

Exhibit 10.3

B Swift Trial Balance as at 31 December 1998		
	Dr £	Cr £
Sales		6,700
Purchases	4,260	
Lighting	190	
Rent	240	
Wages: store assistant	520	
General expenses	70	
Carriage outwards	110	
Shop premises	2,000	
Fixtures and fittings	750	
Debtors	1,200	
Creditors		900
Bank	120	
Cash	40	
Loan from J Marsh		1,000
Drawings	900	
Capital		2,100
Stock (at 1 January 1998)	300	
	10,700	10,700

Closing stock at 31 December 1998 was £550.

Adjustments needed for stock

Previously we have done the accounts for new businesses only. They started without stock and therefore had closing stock only.

When we prepare the trading and profit and loss account for the second year we can now see the difference. Looking at Exhibits 9.1 (on p 82) and 10.3 for B Swift we can see the stock figures needed for the trading accounts:

Trading Account for period ⟶	Year to 31 December 1997	Year to 31 December 1998
Opening stock 1.1.1997	None	
Closing stock 31.12.1997	£300	
Opening stock 1.1.1998		£300
Closing stock 31.12.1998		£550

This means that calculations for the first year of trading, to 31 December 1997, had only one stock figure included in them. This was the closing stock. For the second year of trading, to 31 December 1998, both opening and closing stock figures will be in the calculations.

The stock shown in the trial balance, Exhibit 10.3, is that brought forward from the previous year on 31 December 1997; it is, therefore, the opening stock of 1998. The closing stock at 31 December 1998 can only be found by stocktaking. Assume it amounts at cost to be £550.

Let us first of all calculate the cost of goods sold for 1998.

	£
Stock of goods at start of year	300
Add Purchases	4,260
Total goods available for sale	4,560
Less What remains at the end of the year:	
i.e. stock of goods at end of year	550
Therefore cost of goods that have been sold =	4,010

The sales were £6,700, so Sales £6,700 Less Cost of Goods Sold £4,010 = Gross Profit £2,690.

Now the trading and profit and loss accounts can be drawn up using double entry, *see* exhibit 10.4. For purposes of illustration the stock account will be shown.

Exhibit 10.4

Stock Account

Dr				Cr
1997		£	1998	£
Dec 31 Balance b/d		300	Dec 31 Trading a/c	300
1998				
Dec 31 Trading a/c		550		

B Swift
Trading and Profit and Loss Account for the year ended 31 December 1998

	£		£
Opening stock	300	Sales	6,700
Purchases	4,260	Closing stock	550
Gross profit c/d	2,690		
	7,250		7,250
Wages	520	Gross profit b/d	2,690
Carriage outwards	110		
Lighting expenses	190		
Rent	240		
General expenses	70		
Net profit	1,560		
	2,690		2,690

The stock which at 31 December 1998 is £550, and has not been previously shown in the accounts, has been entered using double entry:

Debit: Stock account £550
Credit: Trading account £550

Display of cost of goods sold in the trading account

Accountants like to see a figure for **cost of goods sold** actually shown in the trading account. This is because they use it for various calculations to be described later in your course.

Exhibit 10.4 shows a trading account where the normal double entry is shown. However, although the stock account would stay exactly as in Exhibit 10.4, accountants would prefer to show the trading account part as in Exhibit 10.5. The figure of gross profit stays the same. The only difference is in display.

Exhibit 10.5

B Swift
Trading and Profit and Loss Account for the Year Ended 31 December 1998

	£	£
Sales		6,700
Less Cost of sales		
Opening stock	300	
Add purchases	4,260	
	4,560	
Less Closing stock	550	
Gross profit		4,010
		2,690
Less Expenses		
Wages	520	
Carriage outwards	110	
Lighting expenses	190	
Rent	240	
General expenses	70	
Net profit		1,130
		1,560

The balances remaining in the books, including the new balance on the stock account, are now drawn up in the form of a balance sheet (*see* Exhibit 10.6).

Exhibit 10.6

B Swift
Balance Sheet as at 31 December 1998

	£	£	£
Fixed assets			
Shop premises			2,000
Fixtures and fittings			750
			2,750
Current assets			
Stock	550		
Debtors	1,200		
Cash at bank	120		
Cash in hand	40		
		1,910	
Current liabilities			
Creditors		900	
Net current assets			1,010
			3,760
Long-term liabilities			
Loan from J Marsh			1,000
Net assets			2,760
Financed by			
Capital account			
Balance at 1 January 1998			2,100
Add Net profit for the year			1,210
			3,310
Less Drawings			550
			2,760

10.5 Final accounts

The term **final accounts** is used to describe the final figures of a period of account, and comprise the trading and profit and loss account (*see* Exhibit 10.5), the balance sheet (*see* Exhibit 10.6), and any notes written to attach to, and explain figures in the accounts.

10.6 Other expenses in the trading account

Sometimes the goods you buy to sell have to have something done to them before they can be sold. An example of this is a trader who sells clocks packed in boxes. To do this he:

1 Buys clocks from one supplier.
2 Buys boxes from a different supplier.
3 Pays wages to a person to pack the clocks into the boxes.

Expenses **1**, **2** and **3** will be transferred to the trading account when calculating gross profit.

Note that the wages of a person selling the clocks will *not* be transferred to the trading account. Instead these wages will be transferred to profit and loss account.

10.7 The accountant as a communicator

Quite often the impression is given that all that the accountant does is to produce figures, arranged in various ways. Naturally, such forms of computation do take up a great deal of the accountant's time, but what then takes up the rest of his time is exactly how he communicates these figures to other people.

The figures he has produced could be given to several people all of whom are very knowledgeable about accounting. He could, in such an instance, present the figures in a normal accounting way, knowing full well that the recipients of the information will understand it.

On the other hand, the accounting figures may well be needed by people who have little or no knowledge at all of accounting. In such a case a normal accounting statement would be no use to them at all, they would not understand it. In this case he might set out the figures in a completely different way to try make it easy for them to grasp. For instance, instead of preparing a normal trading and profit and loss account he might show the information in a more descriptive report as follows:

		£
In the year ended 31 December 1998 you sold goods for		50,000
Now how much had those goods cost you to buy?		
At the start of the year you had stock costing	6,000	
+ You bought some more goods in the year costing	28,000	
So altogether you had goods available to sell of	34,000	
− At the end of the year you had stock of goods unsold of	3,000	
So the goods you had sold in the year had cost you	31,000	
Let us deduct this from what you had sold the goods for		31,000
This means that you had made a profit on buying and selling goods, before any other expenses had been paid, amounting to (We call this sort of profit the Gross Profit)		19,000
But you suffered other expenses such as wages, rent, lighting and so on, and during the year the amount of these expenses, not including anything taken for yourself, amounted to		9,000
So for this year your sales value exceeded all the costs involved in running the business by (We call this sort of profit Net Profit)		10,000

If an accountant cannot arrange the figures to make them meaningful to the recipient then he is failing in his task. His job is not just to produce figures for himself to look at, his job is to communicate these results to other people.

Very often the accountant will have to talk to people to explain the figures, or send a letter or write a report concerning them. He will also have to find out exactly what sort of accounting information is required. This means that if accounting examinations consist simply of computational type questions then they will not test the ability of the candidate to communicate in any other way than by writing down accounting figures. In recent years more attention has been paid by examining boards to these other aspects of an accountant's work.

Note: Treatment of returns inwards, returns outwards, discounts allowed and discounts received in final accounts will be dealt with in Chapter 30. 'Accruals, prepayments and other adjustments' will be dealt with after we have covered the double entry of these items in Part 3 of the book: 'Books of original entry'.

New terms

Carriage inwards (p 87): Cost of transport of goods into a business.
Carriage outwards (p 88): Cost of transport of goods to the customers of a business.
Cost of goods sold (p 90): Cost of goods sold to customers during an accounting period.
Final accounts (p 92): At the end of the accounting period or year a business usually prepares its final accounts, which includes the trading and profit and loss account and balance sheet.

Exercises

10.1 From the following details draw up in vertical format, the trading account for the year ended 31 December 1997.

	£
Carriage inwards	670
Sales	38,742
Purchases	26,409
Stocks of goods: 1 January 1997	6,924
31 December 1997	7,489

10.2 From the following trial balance of R Graham draw up, in vertical format, a trading and profit and loss account for the year ended 30 September 1998, and a balance sheet as at that date.

	Dr	Cr
	£	£
Stock 1 October 1997	2,368	
Carriage outwards	200	
Carriage inwards	310	
Purchases	11,874	
Sales		18,600
Salaries and wages	3,862	
Rent and rates	304	
Insurance	78	
Motor expenses	664	
Office expenses	216	
Lighting and heating expenses	166	
General expenses	314	
Premises	5,000	
Motor vehicles	1,800	
Fixtures and fittings	350	
Debtors	3,896	
Creditors		1,731
Cash at bank	482	
Drawings	1,083	
Capital		12,636
	32,967	32,967

Stock at 30 September 1998 was £2,946.

10.3X The following details for the year ended 31 March 1998 are available. Draw up the trading account for that year, in vertical format.

	£
Stocks: 31 March 1997	16,492
31 March 1998	18,504
Purchases	36,905
Carriage inwards	1,122
Sales	54,600

10.4X The following trial balance was extracted from the books of B Jackson on 30 April 1998. From it, and the notes, prepare his trading and profit and loss account for the year ended 30 April 1998, and a balance sheet as at that date, in vertical format.

	Dr	Cr
	£	£
Sales		18,600
Purchases	11,556	
Stock 1 May 1997	3,776	
Carriage outwards	326	
Carriage inwards	234	
Salaries and wages	2,447	
Motor expenses	664	
Rent	456	
Rates	120	
Sundry expenses	1,202	
Motor vehicles	2,400	
Fixtures and fittings	600	
Debtors	4,577	
Creditors		3,045
Cash at bank	3,876	
Cash in hand	120	
Drawings	2,135	
Capital		12,844
	34,489	34,489

Stock at 30 April 1998 was £4,998.

10.5X G Bowyer manufactures sportswear, and for the year ended 31 October 1998, his sales were £76,540. He also paid carriage outwards of £4,275 to transport the sportswear to customers.

The materials purchased in the year amounted to £33,325, with an additional amount paid for carriage inwards of £2,715. G Bowyer had stock of £8,255 on 1 November 1997, and £7,985 on 31 October 1998.

He was owed £6,285 by customers, and owed £4,825 to suppliers on 31 October 1998. His bank balance was overdrawn by £3,335, and he had equipment valued at £11,125 and a van valued at £2,225 on that date.

His overheads for the year ended 31 October 1998 were:

	£
Rent and rates	6,000
Motor expenses	3,110
Salaries	7,450
Telephone	495
Insurance	500
General expenses	750

He drew £3,675 in the year to 31 October 1998 and had a balance brought forward on his capital account on 1 November 1997 of £5,485.

You are required to draw up in the vertical format, the trading and profit and loss account for the year ended 31 October 1998, and a balance sheet for G Bowyer at that date.

11 Accounting concepts and conventions

11.1 Introduction

So far we have been concerned with recording transactions in the books. While we have been making such records we have been following certain *rules*. These rules are known as concepts and conventions.

An owner of a business may not be the only person to see the final accounts. He may have to show them to his bank manager if he wants to borrow money, or to a potential buyer, if he is looking at selling his business. Under Self Assessment, accounts are used as a basis for completing the annual self assessment tax return, and may be required by the Inland Revenue if they enquire into the business's affairs.

11.2 One set of final accounts for all purposes

If it had always been the custom to draft different kinds of final accounts for different purposes, so that one type was given to a banker, another type to someone wishing to buy the business, etc., then Accounting would be different than it is today. However, copies of the same set of final accounts are given to all the different people.

This means that the banker, the prospective buyer of the business, the owner and the other people all see the same trading and profit and loss account and balance sheet. Interests of each party are different and different kinds of information are needed from that wanted by the others. For instance, the bank manager would really like to know how much the assets would sell for if the firm ceased trading. He could then see what the possibility would be of the bank obtaining repayment of its loan. Other people would also like to see the information in the way that is most useful to them. Yet normally only one sort of final accounts is available for these different people.

This means that trading and profit and loss accounts and balance sheets have to be used for different needs, and to be of any use, the different parties have to agree to the way in which they are drawn up.

Assume that you are in a class of students and that you have the problem of valuing your assets, which consist of ten text books. The first value you decide is that of how much you could sell them for. Your own guess is £30, but the other members of the class may give figures from £15 to £50.

Suppose that you now decide to put a value on their use to you. You may well think that the use of these books will enable you to pass your examinations and so you will get a good job. Another person may have the opposite idea concerning the use of the books to him. The use value placed on the books by others in the class will be quite different.

Finally you decide to value them by reference to cost. You take out of your pocket the bills for the books, which show that you paid a total of £60 for the books. If the rest of the class do not think that you have altered the bills, then they also can all agree that the value expressed as cost is £60. As this is the only value that you can all agree to, then each of you decides to use the idea of showing the value of his asset of books at the cost price.

11.3 Objectivity and subjectivity

The use of a method which all can agree to, instead of everyone using their own different method, is said to be **objective**. To use cost for the value of an asset is, therefore, a way to be objective.

When you are **subjective**, this means that you want to use your own method, even though no one else may agree to it.

Objectivity, using methods that all people can agree to, is what financial accounting ensures. The rules which state how the transactions are recorded are usually known as concepts.

11.4 Basic concepts

The cost concept

The need for this has already been described. It means that assets are normally shown at cost price, and that this is the basis for valuation of the asset.

The money measurement concept

Accounting is concerned only with those facts covered by **1** and **2** which follow:

1   it can be measured in money, and
2   most people will agree to the money value of the transaction.

This means that accounting can never tell you everything about a business. For example, accounting does not show the following:

1   whether the firm has good or bad managers,
2   that there are serious problems with the work-force,
3   that a rival product is about to take away a lot of our best customers,
4   that the government is about to pass a law which will cost us a lot of extra expense in future.

The reason that **1** to **4** or similar items are not recorded is that it would be impossible to work out a money value for them which most people would agree to.

Some people think that accounting tells you everything you want to know. The above shows that this is not true.

Going concern concept

Normally we assume that a business will continue for a long time. Only if the business was going to be sold would we show how much the assets would sell for. This is because we use the cost concept. If businesses were not assumed to be **going concerns**, the cost concept could not be used. Should firms be treated as to be sold immediately, then the saleable value of assets would be used instead of cost.

The business entity concept

The items recorded in a firm's books are limited to the transactions which affect the firm as a **business entity**. Suppose that a proprietor of a firm, from his personal monies outside the firm, buys a diamond necklace for his wife. As the money spent was not out of the firm's bank account or cash box, then this item will not be entered in the firm's books.

The only time that the personal resources of the proprietor affect the firm's accounting records is when he brings new capital into the firm, or takes drawings out of the firm.

The realisation concept

Normally, profit is said to be earned at the time when:

1 goods or services are passed to the customer, and
2 he then incurs liability for them.

This concept of profit is known as the **realisation concept**. Notice that it is *not*

1 when the order is received, or
2 when the customer pays for the goods.

The dual aspect concept

This states that there are two aspects of Accounting, one represented by the assets of the business and the other by the claims against them. The concept states that these two aspects are always equal to each other. In other words:

$$\text{Assets} = \text{Capital} + \text{Liabilities}$$

Double entry is the name given to the method of recording the transactions for the **dual aspect concept**.

The accrual concept

The **accrual concept** says that net profit is the difference between revenues and expenses, i.e.

> **Revenues – Expenses = Net Profit**

Determining the expenses used up to obtain the revenues is referred to as *matching* expenses against revenues.

Many people who have not studied Accounting do not understand this concept. They think that receipts of a period, less payments of the period, equal net profit.

You know that expenses consist of the assets used up in a period. You also know that cash paid in a period and expenses of a period are usually different figures.

You, however, know that we have to make adjustments for items such as expenses owing, payments in advance, depreciation and provisions for bad debts etc. Only then can we calculate net profit.

11.5 The assumption of the stability of monetary measures

As we have seen, accounting uses the cost concept, which states that the asset is normally shown at its cost price. This means that accounting statements can be misleading because assets will be bought at different times at the prices then ruling, and the figures will be totalled up to show the value of the assets in cost terms.

For instance, suppose that you bought a building 20 years ago for £20,000. You now decide to buy an identical additional building, but the price has risen to £40,000. You buy it, and the buildings account now shows buildings at a figure of £60,000. One building is in the currency of 20 years ago, while the other is at today's currency value. The figure of a total of £60,000 is historically correct, but cannot be used for much else.

When we look at final accounts we must understand such problems. There are ways of adjusting accounts to make the figures more useful, but these are not in your syllabus. You will have to study them if you take accounting examinations at an advanced level.

11.6 The conventions of accounting

The concepts of Accounting have become accepted in the business world. The concepts, however, could be looked at in many ways if nothing had been done to bring about standard methods.

Accounting therefore has tried to make certain that similar items are dealt with in similar ways. As a result we have the conventions of Accounting.

The main conventions may be said to be: **1 materiality**, **2 prudence**, **3 consistency**.

Materiality

This convention is to try to stop you wasting time and effort doing completely unnecessary work. Accounting does not serve a useful purpose if the effort of recording a transaction in a certain way is not worthwhile. As an example, if a box of paperclips was bought it would be used over a period of time, and this cost is used up every time someone uses a paperclip. It is possible to record this as an expense every time it happens, but obviously the price of a box of paperclips is so little that it is not worth recording it in this way.

The box of paperclips is not a material item, and, therefore, would be charged as an expense in the period it was bought even though it could last for more than one accounting period. You should not waste your time in the unnecessary recording of trivial items. Similarly, the purchase of a cheap metal ashtray would also be charged as an expense in the period it was bought because it is not a material item, even though it may last 20 years. It would not be worth calculating depreciation on it. Depreciation is dealt with in Chapters 27 and 28.

A motor lorry would be deemed to be a material item. We then calculate depreciation to charge each period, with the cost consumed in each period of its use.

You can see that small amounts are not material, while larger amounts are material. The question is, at what figure does an item become material? There is no fixed rule for this.

Firms make all sorts of rules to say what is material and what is not. There is no law that says what these should be. What is material and what is not depends upon judgement. A firm may decide that all items under £100 should be treated as expenses in the period in which they were bought, even though they may be in use in the firm for the following ten years. Another firm, especially a large one, may put the limit at £1,000. Different limits may be set for different types of items.

The size and type of firm will affect the decisions as to what is material, and what is not.

Prudence

Very often accountants have to use their judgement to decide which figure they will take for an item. Suppose a debt has been owing for quite a long time, and no one knows whether it will be paid. Should the accountant be an optimist in thinking that it will be paid, or be more pessimistic?

It is the accountant's duty to see that people get the proper facts about a business. They should make certain that assets are not valued too highly. Similarly, liabilities should not be shown at values too low. Otherwise, people might inadvisedly lend money to a firm, which they would not do if they had the proper facts.

The accountant should always be on the side of caution, and this is known as prudence. The prudence convention means that normally accountants will take the figure which will understate rather than overstate the profit. Thus they should choose the figure which will cause the capital of the firm to be shown at a lower amount rather than at a higher one. They will also normally make sure that all losses are recorded in the books, but profits should not be anticipated by recording them before they are realised. This concept used to be known as the 'conservatism' concept, although is now more commonly called the prudence concept.

Consistency

Even if we do everything already listed under concepts and conventions, there will still be quite a few different ways in which items could be recorded.

Each firm should try to choose the methods which give the most reliable picture of the business.

This cannot be done if one method is used in one year and another method in the next year and so on. Constantly changing the methods would lead to misleading profits being calculated from the accounting records. Therefore the convention of consistency is used. This convention says that when a firm has fixed a method for the accounting treatment of an item, it will enter all similar items in exactly the same way in following years.

However, it does not mean that the firm has to follow the method until the firm closes down. A firm can change the method used, but such a change is not taken without a lot of consideration. When such a change occurs and the profits calculated in that year are affected by a material amount, then either in the profit and loss account itself or in one of the reports with it, the effect of the change should be stated.

11.7 Accounting terminology

Unfortunately many of the terms used in the description of Accounting theory mean quite different things to different people. Things described as concepts and conventions in this book may well be called principles by someone else. They might be called concepts without any attempt to distinguish between concepts and conventions. Provided that the reader realises this, there is no problem.

Probably the most recent attempt to change a term is the use of the word *prudence* instead of **conservatism**. As most accounting books now use the word prudence, this is the one used in this book. Both of these words can be taken to mean the same.

Quantifiability means the ability to make a proper measure of the transaction. This must take place if the transaction is to be measured in money.

New terms

Accrual concept (p 100): Where net profit is the difference between revenues and expenses.

Business entity concept (p 99): Concerning only transactions which affect the firm, and ignoring the owner's private transactions.

Consistency (p 102): To keep to the same method, except in special cases.

Dual aspect concept (p 99): Dealing with both aspects of a transaction.

Going concern concept (p 99): Where a business is assumed to continue for a long time.

Materiality (p 101): To record something in a special way only if the amount is not a small one.

Objectivity (p 98): Using a method that everyone can agree to.

Prudence or **conservatism** (p 101): To ensure that profit is not shown as being too high, or assets shown at too high a value.

Realisation concept (p 99): The point at which profit is treated as being earned.

Subjectivity (p 98): Using a method which other people may not agree to.

Exercises

11.1 Which accounting concept is used in each of the following accounting treatments? Explain.

(a) The cost of a tape dispenser has been charged to an expense account, although in fact it could still be in use in ten years' time.

(b) A sole proprietor has sold his private house, but has not recorded anything about it in the business records.

(c) A debt has been written off as a bad debt even though there is still a chance that the debtor eventually may be able to pay it.

(d) A machine has been bought for an exceedingly low figure, and has been entered in the asset account at that figure even though it is worth more.

(e) An expert says that the value of the management team to the company is worth well over a million pounds, yet nothing is entered for it in the books.

(f) A motor van broke down in December 1997, but the repairs bill for it was not paid until 1998 yet it has been treated as a 1997 expense.

(g) A customer saw a carpet in 1997 and said he might well buy it. He phoned in 1998 to ask us to deliver the carpet. The item was not treated as a sale in 1997 but was treated instead as 1998 sales.

(h) The final day of the financial year saw the passing of a law which would render trading in our sort of goods illegal, and the business will have to close. The accountant says that our stock figure cannot be shown at cost in the balance sheet.

(i) We have been told that we cannot show our asset of motor cars at cost one year and at cost plus the next year when the manufacturer increases prices of all cars, which also includes our unsold stock.

(j) We have shown all items of machinery costing less than £100 as machinery operating expenses.

11.2X When preparing the final accounts of your company, name the accounting concepts you should follow to deal with each of the following:

(a) Electricity consumed during the accounting period is still unpaid at the year end.

(b) The owner of the company has invested his private assets in the company.

(c) A debtor who owes the company a large amount has been declared bankrupt. The outstanding amount due to the company is now considered to be irrecoverable.

(d) The company has suffered substantial losses in the past few years. It is extremely uncertain whether the company can continue to operate next year.

PART 3

Books of original entry

12 Division of the ledgers: books of original entry

12.1 Introduction

While a business is very small, all the double entry accounts can be kept in one book, which we would call the ledger. In a larger business it would be impossible to use one book, as the large number of pages needed for the numerous transactions would mean that the book would be too big to handle. Also, if there were several book-keepers, they could not all do their work properly if there was only one ledger.

The answer to this problem is to use different books, in which we put similar types of transactions together.

12.2 Books of original entry

These are books in which we record transactions first of all. We have a separate book for each different kind of transaction. The nature of the transaction affects which book it is entered into. Sales will be entered in one book, purchases in another book, cash in another book, and so on. We enter the transactions in these books as follows:

Date	Customer/Supplier detail	Invoice no	Folio no	Total (£)

The layouts for each of the types of **Books of original entry** are described in the appropriate chapters that follow.

12.3 Types of books of original entry

These are:

- **Sales Day Book** – for credit sales (Chapter 19).
- **Purchases Day Book** – for credit purchases (Chapter 20).
- **Returns Inwards Day Book** – for returns inwards (Chapter 21).

- **Returns Outwards Day Book** – for returns outwards (Chapter 21).
- **Cash Book** – for receipts and payments of cash (Chapters 15 and 16).
- **General Journal** – for other items (Chapter 26).

12.4 The ledgers

The books of original entry list the transactions, but do not show the effects of the transaction on the accounts.

We must therefore enter the transactions in the appropriate ledger. A separate ledger will be kept for different types of transactions, as listed in 12.5.

12.5 Types of ledgers

The different types of ledgers are:

- **Sales Ledger.** This is the record of customers' personal accounts.
- **Purchases Ledger.** This is the record of suppliers' personal accounts.
- **General Ledger.** This contains the remaining double entry accounts such as expenses, fixed assets, capital etc.

12.6 Diagram of books used

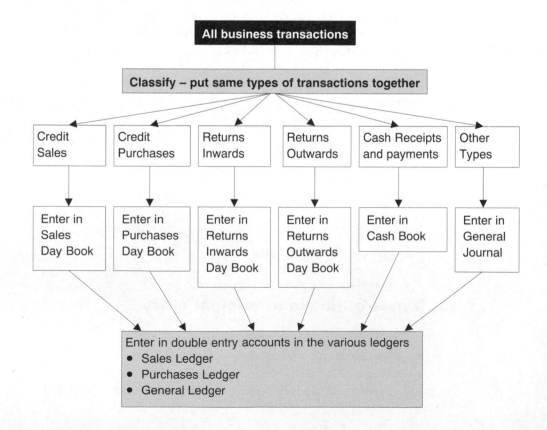

12.7 Types of accounts

Some people describe all accounts as **personal** accounts or as **impersonal** accounts.

- **Personal Accounts** – These are for debtors and creditors.
- **Impersonal Accounts** – These are all other accounts, divided between real accounts and nominal accounts.
- **Real Accounts** – Accounts in which property is recorded. Examples are buildings, machinery, fixtures and stock.
- **Nominal Accounts** – Accounts in which expenses, income and capital are recorded.

The following diagram may enable you to understand it better:

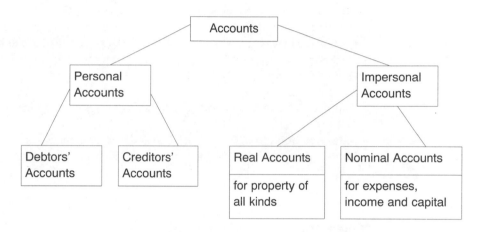

12.8 Nominal and private ledgers

The ledger in which the impersonal accounts are kept is known as the **nominal** (or general) **ledger**. Very often, to ensure privacy for the proprietor(s), the capital and drawing accounts and similar accounts are kept in a **private ledger**. By doing this office staff cannot see details of items which the proprietors want to keep a secret.

12.9 The use of computers in accounting

So far it has been assumed that all book-keeping procedures are carried out using manual systems, but nowadays many businesses use computer systems especially when dealing with large numbers of transactions. Computers are used for recording information in the same ways as manual systems, therefore, throughout the book the accounting terms of 'book' or 'journal' will be referred to for their use in either system.

New terms

Books of original entry (p 107): Books where the first entry of a transaction is made.

Cash book (p 108): Book of original entry for cash and bank receipts and payments.

General journal (p 108): Book of original entry for all items other than those for cash or goods.

General ledger (p 108): All accounts other than those for customers and suppliers.

Impersonal accounts (p 109): All accounts other than debtors' and creditors' accounts.

Nominal accounts (p 109): Accounts in which expenses, revenue and capital are recorded.

Nominal ledger (p 109): Ledger for impersonal accounts (also called General Ledger).

Personal accounts (p 109): Accounts for both creditors and debtors.

Private ledger (p 109): Ledger for capital and drawings accounts.

Purchases day book (p 107): Book of original entry for credit purchases.

Purchases ledger (p 108): A ledger for suppliers' personal accounts.

Real accounts (p 109): Accounts in which property of all kinds is recorded.

Returns inwards day book (p 107): Book of original entry for goods returned by customers.

Returns outwards day book (p 108): Book of original entry for goods returned to suppliers.

Sales day book (p 107): Book of original entry for credit sales.

Sales ledger (p 108): A ledger for customers' personal accounts.

Exercises

12.1   The following balances were taken from the ledger of Roger Craig at 31 December 1998:

		£
(1)	Customer account balances	2,620
(2)	Drawings	4,210
(3)	Sales	36,340
(4)	Wages and salaries	8,310
(5)	Supplier account balances	1,730
(6)	Fixed assets at net book value	14,500
(7)	Cash in hand	15
(8)	Capital (at 1 January 1998)	17,365
(9)	Cost of goods sold (Trading Account)	18,185
(10)	Rates	1,720
(11)	Insurances	680
(12)	Stock	1,836
(13)	Electricity	1,010
(14)	General expenses	550
(15)	Bank	1,799

Required

(*a*)   Calculate Roger Craig's **net** profit for the year.

(*b*)   Prepare a balance sheet as at 31 December 1998. (LCCI)

12.2 For each of the following types of transactions, state the book of original entry, and the ledger and type of account, in which you would enter the transaction:

(i)   Sales invoice
(ii)   Bank receipt
(iii)   Purchase invoice
(iv)   Bank payment
(v)   Sales credit note
(vi)   Returns inwards
(vii)   Purchases credit note
(viii) Closing stock

13 The analytical petty cash book and the imprest system

13.1 Division of the cash book

With the growth of the firm it has been seen that it becomes necessary to have several books instead of just one ledger.

These ideas can be extended to the cash book. It is obvious that in almost any firm there will be many small cash payments to be made. It would be an advantage if the records of these payments could be kept separate from the main cash book. Where a separate book is kept it is known as a **petty cash book**.

The advantages of such an action can be summarised:

- The task of handling and recording the small cash payments could be given by the cashier to a junior member of staff. He would then be known as the petty cashier. The cashier, who is a higher paid member of staff, would be saved from routine work. This would then be done by the petty cashier who is a junior and lower paid member of staff.
- If small cash payments were entered into the main cash book, these items would then need posting one by one to the ledgers. If travelling expenses were paid to staff on a daily basis this could mean over 250 postings to the staff travelling expenses account during the year, i.e. 5 days per week x 50 working weeks per year. However, if a special form of a petty cash book is kept, it would only be the monthly totals for each period that need posting to the general ledger. If this was done, only 12 entries would be needed in the staff travelling expenses account instead of over 250.

When the petty cashier makes a payment to someone, then that person will have to fill in a voucher showing exactly what the payment was for. He may have to attach bills – e.g. bills for petrol – to the petty cash voucher. An example of a Petty Cash Voucher is shown in Exhibit 13.1 He would sign the voucher to certify that his expenses had been paid to him by the petty cashier.

13.2 The imprest system

The **imprest system** is where the cashier gives the petty cashier enough cash to meet his needs for the following period. At the end of the period the cashier finds out the amounts spent by the petty cashier, and gives him an amount equal to that spent. The petty cash in hand should then be equal to the *original* amount with which the period was started. Exhibit 13.2 shows an example of this method.

Exhibit 13.1

This is an example of a petty cash voucher.

```
                                    No _____

    Petty Cash Voucher

                            Date _____
  _____
                                   Amount
      For what required          £        p
                               _____
                              |      |      |
                              |      |      |
                              |      |      |
  _____|_____|_____|

      Signature _____

      Passed by _____
```

Exhibit 13.2

		£
Period 1	The cashier gives the petty cashier	100
	The petty cashier pays out in the period	78
	Petty cash now in hand	22
	The cashier now gives the petty cashier the amount spent	78
	Petty cash in hand at the end of period 1	100
Period 2	The petty cashier pays out in the period	84
	Petty cash now in hand	16
	The cashier now gives the petty cashier the amount spent	84
	Petty cash in hand end of period 2	100

It may be necessary to increase the fixed sum, often called the cash 'float', to be held at the start of each period. In the above case if we had wanted to increase the 'float' at the end of the second period to £120, then the cashier would have given the petty cashier an extra £20, i.e. £84 + 20 = 104.

13.3 Illustration of an analytical petty cash book

An analytical petty cash book is often used. One of these is shown as Exhibit 13.3.

The receipts column is the debit side of the petty cash book. On giving £50 to the petty cashier on 1 September the credit entry is made in the cash book while the debit entry is made in the petty cash book. A similar entry is made on 30 September for the £44 paid by the chief cashier to the petty cashier. This amount covers all expenses paid by the petty cashier.

On the credit side:

1 Enter the date and details of each payment. Put the amount in the total column.
2 For **1** also put the amount in the column for the type of expense.
3 At the end of each period, add up the totals column.
4 Now add up each of the expense columns. The total of **3** should equal the total of all the expense columns. In Exhibit 13.3 this is £44.

To complete double entry for petty cash expenses paid:

1 Total of each expense column is debited to the expense account in the general ledger.
2 Enter folio number of each general ledger page under each of the expense columns in the petty cash book.
3 The last column in the petty cash book is a ledger column. In this column items paid out of petty cash which need posting to a ledger other than the general ledger are shown.

This would happen if a purchases ledger account was settled out of petty cash, or if a refund was made out of the petty cash to a customer who had overpaid his account.

The double entry for all the items in Exhibit 13.3 appears as Exhibit 13.4.

1998			£
Sept	1	The cashier gives £50 as float to the petty cashier	
		Payments out of petty cash during September:	
Sept	2	Petrol	6
Sept	3	J Green – travelling expenses	3
Sept	3	Postages	2
Sept	4	D Davies – travelling expenses	2
Sept	7	Cleaning expenses	1
Sept	9	Petrol	1
Sept	12	K Jones – travelling expenses	3
Sept	14	Petrol	3
Sept	15	L Black – travelling expenses	5
Sept	16	Cleaning expenses	1
Sept	18	Petrol	2
Sept	20	Postages	2
Sept	22	Cleaning expenses	1
Sept	24	G Wood – travelling expenses	7
Sept	27	Settlement of C Brown's account in the Purchases Ledger	3
Sept	29	Postages	2
Sept	30	The cashier reimburses the petty cashier the amount spent in the month.	

Exhibit 13.3

Page 31

Petty Cash Book

Receipts	Folio	Date		Details	Voucher No	Total	Motor expenses	Staff travelling expenses	Postages	Cleaning	Ledger folio	Ledger accounts
£		1998				£	£	£	£	£		£
50	CB 19	Sept	1	Cash								
		"	2	Petrol	1	6	6					
		"	3	J Green	2	3		3				
		"	3	Postages	3	2			2			
		"	4	D Davies	4	2		2				
		"	7	Cleaning	5	1				1		
		"	9	Petrol	6	1	1					
		"	12	K Jones	7	3		3				
		"	14	Petrol	8	3	3					
		"	15	L Black	9	5		5				
		"	16	Cleaning	10	1				1		
		"	18	Petrol	11	2	2					
		"	20	Postages	12	2			2			
		"	22	Cleaning	13	1				1		
		"	24	G Wood	14	7		7				
		"	27	C Brown	15	3					PL 18	3
		"	29	Postages	16	2			2			
						44	12	20	6	3		3
							GL 17	GL 29	GL 44	GL 64		
		Sept	30	Balance	c/d	6						
50						50						
6		Oct	1	Balance	b/d							
44	CB 22	"	1	Cash								

Exhibit 13.4

Cash Book
Page 19

Dr		Cr
	1998	£
	Sept 1 Petty cash PCB 31	50
	Sept 30 Petty cash PCB 31	44

General Ledger
Motor Expenses Account
Page 17

Dr		Cr
1998	£	
Sept 30 Petty cash PCB 31	12	

Staff Travelling Expenses Account   *Page 29*

Dr						Cr
1998			£			
Sept 30	Petty cash	PCB 31	20			

Postages Account   *Page 44*

Dr						Cr
1998			£			
Sept 30	Petty cash	PCB 31	6			

Cleaning Account   *Page 64*

Dr						Cr
1998			£			
Sept 30	Petty cash	PCB 31	3			

Purchases Ledger
C Brown Account   *Page 18*

Dr							Cr
1998			£	1998			£
Sept 30	Petty cash	PCB 31	3	Sept 1	Balance b/d		3

13.4 Bank cash book

In a firm with both a cash book and a petty cash book, the cash book is often known as a bank cash book. This means that *all* cash payments are entered in the petty cash book, and the bank cash book will contain *only* bank columns and discount columns. In this type of firm any cash sales will be paid direct into the bank.

In such a cash book, as in fact could happen in an ordinary cash book, an extra column could be added. In this would be shown the details of the cheques banked, just the total of the banking being shown in the total column.

Exhibit 13.5 shows the receipts side of the Bank Cash Book. The totals of the banking made on the three days were £192, £381 and £1,218. The details column shows what the bankings are made up of.

Exhibit 13.5

Dr	Bank Cash Book (Receipts side)		
Date	Details	Items	Total banked
1998		£	£
May 14	G Archer	95	
May 14	P Watts	57	
May 14	C King	40	192
May 20	K Dooley	114	
May 20	Cash Sales	55	
May 20	R Jones	60	
May 20	P Mackie	152	381
May 31	J Young	19	
May 31	T Broome	950	
May 31	Cash Sales	116	
May 31	H Tiller	133	1,218

New terms

Imprest system (p 112): A system used for controlling expenditure of small cash items which are recorded in the petty cash book. A cash 'float' of a fixed amount is provided initially to the person responsible for operating the petty cash system. Any cash paid out during a particular period, i.e. a week, is reimbursed to the petty cashier so restoring the 'float' to its original sum.

Petty cash book (p 113): A cash book used for making small (petty) payments. Payments are usually analysed and the totals of each column later posted to the various accounts in the general ledger. The source document used for entry into the petty cash book is a petty cash voucher.

Petty cash voucher (p 113): The form used by anyone requesting payment for a small item of expenditure incurred on behalf of the business. The form gives details of the expense and should be signed and duly authorised.

Exercises

13.1 Thomas Jones, a sole trader, keeps his petty cash on the imprest system and the imprest amount is £50. The petty cash transactions for the month of February 1998 were as follows:

1998
Feb 1 Petty cash in hand £4.67
" 1 Petty cash restored to imprest amount
" 3 Paid wages £8.76
" 7 Purchased postage stamps £2.94
" 10 Paid wages £9.11
" 14 Purchased envelopes £2.28
" 17 Paid wages £8.84
" 20 Paid cash to J Smith, a creditor, £4.16
" 21 Purchased stationery £2.75
" 24 Paid wages £8.48.

Required

Draw up Jones' petty cash book for the month of February 1998. The analysis columns should be as follows:

(a) Wages
(b) Stationery
(c) Postage
(d) Ledger

On 1 March 1998 show the restoration of the petty cash to the imprest amount. (LCCI)

13.2X O Zone, a sole trader, uses an analysed petty cash book with columns for travelling, postage and stationery, motor expenses, cleaning, ledger accounts.

The petty cash system is based on an imprest of £100 which Zone replenishes on the Monday following the period of expenditure. O Zone supplies the following information for the month of August.

			£
Aug	1	Petrol	4.00
"	3	Postage stamps	1.50
"	4	One ream of typing paper	3.00
"	6	H Wise – settlement of account	15.00
"	7	Office cleaning materials	2.00
"	8	Taxis	4.00
"	10	Refund of clerk's bus fares	2.00
"	14	Car polish	3.00
"	16	Petrol and oil	7.00
"	18	Registered mail	2.00
"	20	Office carpet shampoo	1.00
"	21	Petrol	7.00
"	25	Petrol	7.00
"	27	J Brown – settlement of account	25.00
"	28	W Smith – settlement of account	6.00
"	29	Carbon paper (one packet)	4.00

Required

(a) Enter the above transactions into a suitably ruled Petty Cash Book.
(b) Replenish the imprest on Monday, 3 September. (RSA)

13.3 You work for S Dickinson (Estate Agents) as receptionist, although some of your duties include administration tasks and dealing with the firm's petty cash, which is operated using the imprest system. A 'float' of £120 is used by the firm for petty cash and this is given to you on 1 March.

Required

(a) From the following petty cash vouchers (Fig. 13.1) you are required to enter them in the petty cash book, using analysis columns as you think appropriate. Balance off at the end of the month and obtain cash to restore the imprest from Ms Dickinson.
(b) Post the petty cash expense columns to the accounts in the general ledger and enter the cash obtained to restore the imprest in the cash book.
(c) What are the advantages to using the imprest system? Draft a short memo outlining these to Ms Dickinson.
(NVQ Level 2)

Fig 13.1

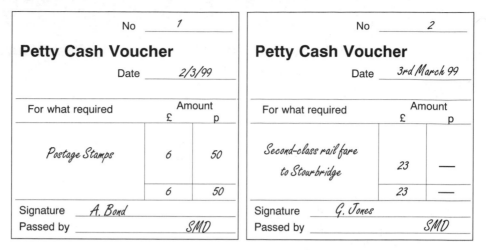

	No	1
Petty Cash Voucher		
	Date	2/3/99

For what required	Amount £	p
Postage Stamps	6	50
	6	50

Signature   A. Bond
Passed by   SMD

	No	2
Petty Cash Voucher		
	Date	3rd March 99

For what required	Amount £	p
Second-class rail fare to Stourbridge	23	—
	23	—

Signature   G. Jones
Passed by   SMD

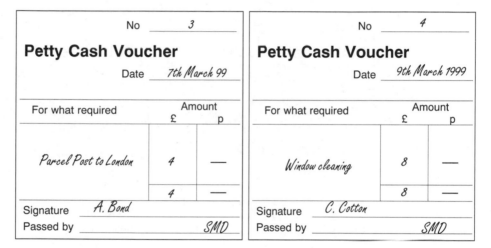

	No	3
Petty Cash Voucher		
	Date	7th March 99

For what required	Amount £	p
Parcel Post to London	4	—
	4	—

Signature   A. Bond
Passed by   SMD

	No	4
Petty Cash Voucher		
	Date	9th March 1999

For what required	Amount £	p
Window cleaning	8	—
	8	—

Signature   C. Cotton
Passed by   SMD

	No	5
Petty Cash Voucher		
	Date	12th March 1999

For what required	Amount £	p
Envelopes	2	64
VAT		46
	3	10

Signature   A. Bond
Passed by   SMD

	No	6
Petty Cash Voucher		
	Date	14th March 1999

For what required	Amount £	p
Tea etc, (Hospitality)	6	40
	6	40

Signature   A. Bond
Passed by   SMD

Fig 13.1 (*continued*)

No	7

Petty Cash Voucher

Date _16th March 1999_

For what required	Amount £	p
Petrol (including VAT)	10	—
	10	—

Signature _G Jones_

Passed by _SMD_

No	8

Petty Cash Voucher

Date _19th March 1999_

For what required	Amount £	p
3 1/4" Computer Discs	11	06
VAT @ 17.5%	1	94
	13	—

Signature _S. Dickinson_

Passed by _SMD_

No	9

Petty Cash Voucher

Date _20/3/99_

For what required	Amount £	p
Dusters & Polish	1	47
17.5% VAT		26
	1	73

Signature _J Pratt_

Passed by _SMD_

No	10

Petty Cash Voucher

Date _23 March 1999_

For what required	Amount £	p
Postage Stamps	2	40
	2	40

Signature _A. Bond_

Passed by _SMD_

No	11

Petty Cash Voucher

Date _27th March 1999_

For what required	Amount £	p
Payment of creditors:- J. Cheetham (A.c No C44)	7	30
	7	30

Signature _S. Dickinson_

Passed by _SMD_

No	12

Petty Cash Voucher

Date _31st March 1999_

For what required	Amount £	p
Magazines, Newspapers etc. (for reception)	6	40
	6	40

Signature _A. Bond_

Passed by _SMD_

13.4X You are employed as junior accountant's assistant of Morridge Products Ltd and one of your main tasks is that of petty cashier. The company uses an analytical petty cash book with columns for travelling expenses, postages, stationery, cleaning, sundry expenses and VAT and they operate the imprest system.

Required:

(a) On 1 January 1999 the company's accountant, Mr Brammer, restores the petty cash float to £100 and gives you the following petty cash vouchers (Fig. 13.2). You are required to enter them in the petty cash book, balance off the book at the end of January and obtain reimbursement from Mr Brammer to restore the imprest.

(b) Mr Brammer is anxious for you to become involved with all the financial aspects of the business and would like you to complete the book-keeping entries by posting the totals of the 'petty cash analysis columns' to the relevant accounts in the general ledger.

(c) Unfortunately you have to go in hospital for a few days and will probably be absent from work for a couple of weeks. Mr Brammer asks you to write out a set of instructions in note form on the operation of the petty cash book as Jenny Cadwaller, his secretary, will be taking over in your absence. Ensure the instructions are clear, concise and easy to follow.

(NVQ Level 2)

Fig 13.2

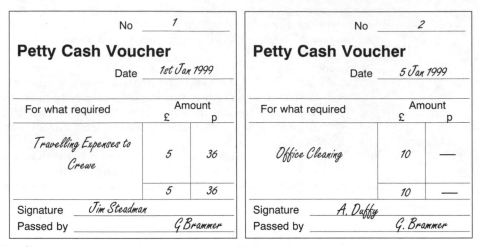

No	1

Petty Cash Voucher

Date _1st Jan 1999_

For what required	Amount £	p
Travelling Expenses to Crewe	5	36
	5	36

Signature _Jim Steadman_

Passed by _G Brammer_

No	2

Petty Cash Voucher

Date _5 Jan 1999_

For what required	Amount £	p
Office Cleaning	10	—
	10	—

Signature _A. Duffy_

Passed by _G. Brammer_

No	3

Petty Cash Voucher

Date _9 Jan 1999_

For what required	Amount £	p
Parcel to Northampton	1	98
	1	98

Signature _Tom Finikin_

Passed by _G Brammer_

No	4

Petty Cash Voucher

Date _10 Jan 1999_

For what required	Amount £	p
Milk & Coffee for Office	6	50
	6	50

Signature _J. Cadwaller_

Passed by _G. Brammer_

No	5

Petty Cash Voucher

Date _12 Jan 1999_

For what required	Amount £	p
Air-mail Stationery	7	15
VAT	1	25
	8	40

Signature _J. Cadwaller_

Passed by _G. Brammer_

No	6

Petty Cash Voucher

Date _15 Jan 1999_

For what required	Amount £	p
Light Bulbs & 3 plugs.	3	64
VAT		64
	4	28

Signature _Tom Finikin_

Passed by _G Brammer_

Fig 13.2 (*continued*)

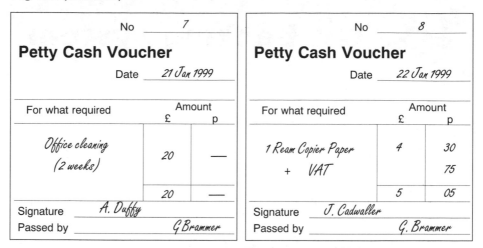

No	7

Petty Cash Voucher

Date 21 Jan 1999

For what required	Amount £	p
Office cleaning (2 weeks)	20	—
	20	—

Signature *A. Duffy*

Passed by *G Brammer*

No	8

Petty Cash Voucher

Date 22 Jan 1999

For what required	Amount £	p
1 Ream Copier Paper	4	30
+ VAT		75
	5	05

Signature *J. Cadwaller*

Passed by *G. Brammer*

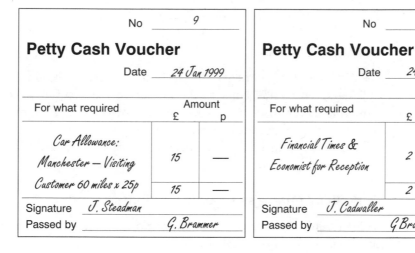

No	9

Petty Cash Voucher

Date 24 Jan 1999

For what required	Amount £	p
Car Allowance: Manchester — Visiting Customer 60 miles x 25p	15	—
	15	—

Signature *J. Steadman*

Passed by *G. Brammer*

No	10

Petty Cash Voucher

Date 24 Jan 1999

For what required	Amount £	p
Financial Times & Economist for Reception	2	10
	2	10

Signature *J. Cadwaller*

Passed by *G Brammer*

No	11

Petty Cash Voucher

Date 30 Jan 1999

For what required	Amount £	p
Milk	1	50
	1	50

Signature *G. Brammer*

Passed by *G. Brammer*

No	12

Petty Cash Voucher

Date 31 Jan 1999

For what required	Amount £	p
First Class Stamps	4	80
	4	80

Signature *J. Cadwaller*

Passed by *G. Brammer*

14 The banking system

14.1 Introduction

We will be looking at payments into and out of bank accounts in Chapters 15 and 16. You therefore need to know some details about bank accounts.

14.2 Types of account

There are two main types of bank account:

Current accounts

Used for regular payments into and out of a bank account. A **cheque book** will be given by the bank to the holder of the account, who will use it to make payments to people to whom they owe money. Payment may also be made by standing order or direct debit.

So that they can pay money into their current account, the holder will be given a paying-in book.

Deposit or business reserve accounts

Such a bank account is for holding money that is not needed for making payments in the foreseeable future.

Interest is given by the bank on money kept in such accounts. Current accounts do not usually earn interest.

14.3 Cheques

When the bank has agreed to let you open a current account it will ask you for a specimen signature. This allows them to prove that your cheques are in fact signed by you, and have not been forged. You will then be issued with a cheque book.

You can then use the cheques to make payments out of the account. Normally you must make sure that you have more money in the account then the amount paid out. If you wish to pay out more money than you have banked, you will need to discuss the reasons for this with your bank and if they agree they will give their permission for you to 'overdraw' your account. This is known as a **bank overdraft**.

The person writing the cheque and using it for payment is known as the **drawer**. The person to whom the cheque is paid is known as the **payee**.

We can now look at Exhibit 14.1, which is a blank cheque before it is filled in.

Exhibit 14.1

On the face of the cheque are various sets of numbers. These are:

914234   Every cheque printed for the Cheshire Bank will be given a different number, so that individual items can be traced.

09-07-99   Each branch of each bank in the United Kingdom has a different number given to it. Thus this branch has a 'code' number 09-07-99.

058899   Each account with the bank is given a different number. This particular number is kept only for the account of J Woodstock at the Stockport branch.

When we fill in the cheque we copy the details on the counterfoil which we then detach and keep for our records.

We can now look at the completion of a cheque. Let us assume that we are paying seventy-two pounds and eighty-five pence to K Marsh on 22 May 1998. Exhibit 14.2 shows the completed cheque.

Exhibit 14.2

In Exhibit 14.2:

The drawer is: J Woodstock
The payee is: K Marsh

The two parallel lines across the face of the cheque are drawn as a safeguard. If we had not done this the cheque would have been an 'uncrossed cheque'. If someone had stolen a signed uncrossed cheque he could have gone to the Stockport branch of the Cheshire Bank and obtained cash in exchange for the cheque. When the cheque is crossed it means it *must* be paid into a bank account, Post Office Giro bank or Savings Bank. Virtually all cheques today are pre-printed crossed, as 'Account payee'.

14.4 Cheque crossing

Cheques can be further safeguarded by using specific crossing, i.e. writing a form of instruction within the crossing on the cheques as shown in Exhibit 14.3.

Exhibit 14.3

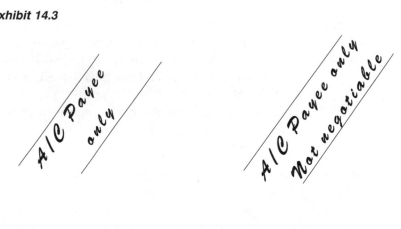

These are specific instructions to the banks about the use of the cheque. The use of 'A/c Payee only' means the cheques should be paid only into the account of the payee named. If cheques are lost or stolen the drawer must advise his bank immediately and confirm by letter. These cheques will be 'stopped', i.e. payment will not be made on these cheques, provided you act swiftly. The safest crossing is that of 'A/c Payee only, Not negotiable'. If the cheque is lost or stolen it will be of no use to the thief or finder. This is because it is impossible for this cheque to be paid into any bank account other than that of the named payee.

14.5 Paying-in slips

When we want to pay money into our current accounts, either cash or cheques or both, we use a **paying-in slip**. One of these is shown as Exhibit 14.4.

J Woodstock has banked the following items:

Four	£5 notes
Three	£1 coins
One	50p coin
Other silver	30p
Bronze coins	12p

Cheques received from:		Code numbers:
E Kane & Son	£184.15	02-58-76
J Gale	£65.44	05-77-85

Exhibit 14.4

Face of paying-in slip

Date *22 May* 19*98* Cashier's stamp and initials	Date *22 May* 19*98* Cashier's stamp and initials	**bank giro credit** Destination Branch Code number *09 - 07 - 99* Bank *Cheshire Bank* Branch *Stockport* Account Name (Block letters) & A/c. No		pounds	pence
		£5 notes and over		20	
		£1 coins		3	
		50p coins			50
		Other silver			30
		Bronze coin			12
A/c *J WOODSTOCK*			Total cash	23	92
Cash 23 - 92			Cheques, POs etc. (see over)	249	59
Cheques 249 - 59 POs etc			£	273	51
£ 273 - 51	Paid in by *J Woodstock*	Details for advice to recipient			

J. WOODSTOCK 058899

Counterfoil
retained by
Woodstock

Paying-in slip and cash and cheques handed in to bank

Reverse side of paying-in slip

Details of Cheques, POs etc

for cheques please specify Drawer's name and	Bank Code Number as shown in top right corner				
E. KANE & SON	02-58-76	184	15	184	15
J. GALE	05-77-85	65	44	65	44
In view of the risk of loss in course of clearing, customers are advised to keep an independent record of the drawers of cheques.	Total carried over £	249	59	249	59

Reverse of
counterfoil

14.6 Bank giro credits/credit transfer

Another way of paying creditors, wages and salaries etc. is by **bank giro credits**, also known as credit transfer. Here the business prepares payments in the usual way but in addition prepares a list and bank giro credit slips detailing each person's or organisation's name, account number, bank code number, bank name and branch title and lastly the amount of the payment. The list and slips are then sent to the bank with one cheque to cover all the payments and the payments are automatically credited to the various bank accounts via the banking system.

One distinct advantage is that only one cheque has to be made out and signed. The disadvantage is the preparation of the bank giro credit list and slips. However, this method is very outdated and very few organisations use this method of payment.

14.7 Payment by BACS

Many businesses are changing over from payment via bank giro credit to payment by **Banker's Automated Clearing Services**, known as BACS. BACS is a company owned by the Bank of England, the high street banks and some building societies, which offers a computerised payment transfer system that organisations may use to pay not only wages and salaries but also creditors, dividends, grants, pensions etc.

If an employer decides to use this method for paying creditors, wages and/or salaries, then they need to send to BACS a disk cassette or magnetic tape giving the following details of each employee organisation:

- Person's or organisation's name
- Bank name and branch title
- Bank sort code number
- Person's or organisation's bank account number.

The above information is sent prior to the payment and held permanently on computer file by BACS Processing Computer Centre at Edgware in London.

As the payment is prepared periodically on the business's own computer, a magnetic tape or disk containing details of the payment is prepared at the same time and the data is then sent by courier or telephone link to BACS which automatically processes the data, crediting each person's or organisation's bank or building society account and debiting the business's account. Processing the transfers is a three-day cycle; the information is received on the first day, processed on the second day and then sent for checking by the employers prior to the transfers being made on the third day.

Sometimes a business may not have the computer facilities to enable payment to be made in this way. In these circumstances they may wish to use the services of a computer bureau or bank, who, on receipt of a list of payments, will process the data to BACS via magnetic tape or disk.

14.8 Standing orders and direct debits

A person may make a regular payment from their bank account, or receive a regular amount into their account, by standing order or direct debit.

1   **Standing order**. The payer will instruct their bank to pay a fixed amount on a regular payment date to the payee. The payer can stipulate a time limit, or cancel the arrangement at any time.

  The payee will receive the money direct into their bank account, without the need for a paying-in slip to be completed.

2   **Direct debit**. The payer completes and signs a mandate form, instructing the payee's bank to take funds from the payer's bank account. The mandate may be for a fixed amount of money, or a variable amount.

  The payer can only cancel the arrangements by instructing the payee to ask their bank to stop withdrawing the funds.

  The payee will receive the money direct into their bank account.

  The variable direct debit is becoming a more common method of payment by businesses.

14.9 Cheque clearings

We will now look at how cheques paid from one person's bank account pass into another person's bank account.

Let us look at the progress of the cheque in Exhibit 14.2. We will assume that the post office is being very efficient and delivering all letters the following day after being posted.

1998

May 22   Woodstock, in Stockport, sends the cheque to K Marsh, who lives in Leeds. Woodstock enters the payment in his cash book.

May 23   Cheque received by Marsh. He banks it the same day in his bank account at Barclays Bank in Leeds. Marsh shows the cheque in his cash book as being received and banked on 23 May.

May 24   Barclays in London receive the cheque. They exchange it with the head office of the Cheshire Bank in London.
The Cheshire Bank send the cheque to their Stockport branch.

May 25   The Stockport branch of the Cheshire Bank examine the cheque. If there is nothing wrong with it, the cheque can now be debited by the bank to J Woodstock's account.

In Chapter 17 we will be examining bank reconciliation statements. What we have looked at –

1998

May 22   This is the day on which Woodstock has made the entry in his cash book.

May 25   This is the day when the bank makes an entry in Woodstock's account in respect of the cheque.

– will become an important part of your understanding such statements.

New terms

Bank giro credits (p 128): Method used by businesses to pay creditors, wages and/or salaries. A bank giro credit list and slips containing information about each person or organisation to be paid and the amount payable are sent to the bank, together with one cheque to cover all the payments. The bank then automatically transfers the funds from the business's account to the account of each of the respective people or organisations.

Bank overdraft (p 124): When we have paid more out of our bank account than we have paid into it.

Bankers' Automated Clearing Service (BACS) (p 128): Computerised payment transfer system which is a very popular way of paying creditors, wages and salaries.

Cheque book (p 124): Book containing forms (cheques) used to pay money out of a current account.

Current account (p 124): Bank account used for regular payments in and out of the bank.

Deposit or Business reserve account (p 124): Bank account for money to be kept in for a long time. Interest is given on money deposited.

Direct debit (p 129): Payment made out of payer's bank, direct to payee's bank, on *payee's* instructions.

Drawer (p 125): The person making out a cheque and using it for payment.

Payee (p 125): The person to whom a cheque is paid.

Paying-in slip (p 126): Form used for paying money into a bank account.

Standing order (p 129): Payment made out of payer's bank, direct to payee's bank, on *payer's* instructions.

Exercises

14.1 Explain the difference between a current account and a deposit account. Which account would be most suitable for making regular savings?

14.2 Describe the difference when making out a cheque between the drawer and payee.

14.3X Organisations today pay many of their creditors and staff salaries using BACS. Explain fully how the system operates and its main advantage.

14.4 Morridge Products Ltd receives a cheque which has a special crossing.

(*a*) Explain briefly what is meant by a special crossing.
(*b*) Explain briefly the effect of a special crossing.

14.5 Many payments are made by either standing order or direct debit. Explain these methods of payment and state the advantage of using each method.

15 Two-column cash books

15.1 Introduction

The cash book consists of the cash account and the bank account put together in one book. Initially we showed these two accounts on different pages of the ledger. Now it is easier to put the two sets of account columns together. This means that we can record all money received and paid out on a particular date on the same page.

In the cash book the debit column for cash is put next to the debit column for bank. The credit column for cash is put next to the credit column for bank.

15.2 Drawing up a cash book

We can now look at a cash account and a bank account in Exhibit 15.1 as they would appear if they had been kept separately. Then in Exhibit 15.2 they are shown as if the transactions had instead been kept in a cash book.

The bank column contains details of the payments made by cheque and of the money received and paid into the bank account. The bank will have a copy of the account in its own books.

The bank will send a copy of the account in its books to the firm, this copy usually being known as the **bank statement**. When the firm receives the bank statement, it will check it against the bank column in its own cash book to ensure that there are no errors.

Exhibit 15.1

Cash Account

Dr							*Cr*
1998			£	1998			£
Aug	2	T Moore	33	Aug	8	Rent	20
Aug	5	K Charles	25	Aug	12	C Potts	19
Aug	15	F Hughes	37	Aug	28	Wages	25
Aug	30	H Howe	18	Aug	31	Balance c/d	49
			113				113
Sept	1	Balance b/d	49				

Bank Account

Dr				Cr	
1998		£	1998		£
Aug 1	Capital	1,000	Aug 7	Rates	105
Aug 3	W P Ltd	244	Aug 12	F Small Ltd	95
Aug 16	K Noone	408	Aug 26	K French	268
Aug 30	H Sanders	20	Aug 31	Balance c/d	1,204
		1,672			1,672
Sept 1	Balance b/d	1,204			

Exhibit 15.2

Cash Book

Dr		Cash	Bank			Cr Cash	Bank
		£	£			£	£
1998				1998			
Aug 1	Capital		1,000	Aug 7	Rates		105
" 2	T Moore	33		" 8	Rent	20	
" 3	W P Ltd		244	" 12	C Potts	19	
" 5	K Charles	25		" 12	F Small Ltd		95
" 15	F Hughes	37		" 26	K French		268
" 16	K Noone		408	" 28	Wages	25	
" 30	H Sanders		20	" 31	Balance c/d	49	1,204
" 30	H Howe	18					
		113	1,672			113	1,672
Sept 1	Balances b/d	49	1,204				

15.3 Cash paid into the bank

In Exhibit 15.2 the payments into the bank have been cheques received by the firm which have been banked immediately. We must now consider cash being paid into the bank.

1   Let us look at the position when a customer pays his account in cash, and later a part of this cash is paid into the bank. The receipt of the cash is debited to the cash column on the date received, the credit entry being in the customer's personal account. The cash banked has the following effect needing action as shown:

Effect	Action
1 Asset of cash is decreased	Credit the asset account, i.e. the cash account which is represented by the cash column in the cash book.
2 Asset of bank is increased	Debit the asset account, i.e. the bank account which is represented by the bank column in the cash book.

A cash receipt of £100 from M Davies on 1 August 1998, later followed by the banking on 3 August of £80 of this amount would appear in the cash book as follows:

Cash Book						
Dr						Cr
	Cash	Bank			Cash	Bank
1998	£	£	1998		£	£
Aug 1 M Davies	100		Aug 3 Bank		80	
Aug 3 Cash		80				

The details column shows entries against each item stating the name of the account in which the completion of double entry has taken place. Against the cash payment of £80 appears the word 'bank', meaning that the debit £80 is to be found in the bank column, and the opposite applies.

2 Where the whole of the cash received is banked immediately the receipt can be treated in exactly the same manner as a cheque received, i.e. it can be entered directly in the bank column.

3 If the firm requires cash it may withdraw cash from the bank. This is done by making out a cheque to pay itself a certain amount in cash. The bank will give cash in exchange for the cheque.

The twofold effect and the action required may be shown:

Effect	Action
1 Asset of bank is decreased.	Credit the asset account, i.e. the bank column in the cash book.
2 Asset of cash is increased.	Debit the asset account, i.e. the cash column in the cash book.

A withdrawal of £75 cash on 1 June 1998 from the bank would appear in the cash book thus:

Cash Book						
Dr						Cr
	Cash	Bank			Cash	Bank
1998	£	£	1998		£	£
June 1 Bank	75		June 1 Cash			75

Both the debit and credit entries for this item are in the same book. When this happens it is known as a **contra** item.

15.4 The use of folio columns

As you have already seen, the details column in an account contains the name of the other account in which double entry has been completed. Anyone looking through the books would therefore be able to find where the other half of the double entry had been entered.

However, when many books are being used, just to mention the name of the other account would not be enough information to find the other account quickly. More information is needed, and this is given by using **folio columns**.

In each account and in each book being used, a folio column is added, always shown on the left of the money columns. In this column the name of the other book, in abbreviated form, and the number of the page in the other book where double entry is completed is stated against each and every entry in the books.

An entry of receipt of cash from C Kelly whose account was on page 45 of the sales ledger, and the cash recorded on page 37 of the cash book, would use the folio column thus:

In the cash book. In the folio column would appear SL 45.
In the sales ledger. In the folio column would appear CB 37.

By this method full cross reference would be given. Each of the contra items, being shown on the same page of the cash book, would use the letter 'C' in the folio column.

15.5 Advantages of folio columns

These are:

- As described in 15.4 it speeds up reference to the other book where double entry for the item is completed.
- The folio column is filled in when double entry has been completed. If it has not been filled in, double entry will not have been made.

Looking through the folio columns to ensure they have all been filled in will help us to detect such errors.

15.6 Example of a cash book with folio columns

The following transactions are written up in the form of a cash book. The folio columns are filled in as though double entry had been completed to other accounts.

1998		£
Sept	1	Proprietor puts capital into a bank account for the business	940
Sept	2	Received cheque from M Boon	115
Sept	4	Cash sales	102
Sept	6	Paid rent by cash	35
Sept	7	Banked £50 of the cash held by the firm	50
Sept	15	Cash sales paid direct into the bank	40
Sept	23	Paid cheque to S Wills	277
Sept	29	Withdrew cash from bank for business use	120
Sept	30	Paid wages in cash	118

Cash Book

Dr									Cr
		Folio	Cash	Bank			Folio	Cash	Bank
1998			£	£	1998			£	£
Sept 1	Capital	GL1		940	Sept 6	Rent	GL65	35	
" 2	M Boon	SL98		115	" 7	Bank	C	50	
" 4	Sales	GL87	102		" 23	S Wills	PL23		277
" 7	Cash	C		50	" 29	Cash	C		120
" 15	Sales	GL87		40	" 30	Wages	GL39	118	
" 29	Bank	C	120		" 30	Balances	c/d	19	748
			222	1,145				222	1,145
Oct 1	Balances	b/d	19	748					

The abbreviations used in the folio column are as follows:

GL = General Ledger: SL = Sales Ledger: C = Contra: PL = Purchases Ledger.

15.7 Receipts

When a cash sale is made it is not necessary for a receipt to be given. This is a form stating how much cash has been received and the date of payment. This is because the goods are handed over immediately and there is, therefore, no need to keep a check on the identity of the payer. However, quite a lot of businesses, for example Marks & Spencer, do give receipts in such cases even though it is not legally necessary. However, payment by cash for payments in respect of goods sold on credit would need the evidence of a receipt.

A receipt might be as follows:

Date .15 May. 1999.

Received from ...A Reader.........................

the sum of .....Fifty pounds 40p.................

in respect of ....Settlement of account.........

Signed ....J Hall....................

on behalf of Johnson and Longden Ltd

When payment is made by cheque a receipt is not necessary, as the paid cheque will act as evidence of payment. Similarly, payments by standing order and direct debit will mean that receipts are not needed.

New terms

Bank statement (p 131): Copy of our current account given to us by our bank.
Contra (p 132): A contra is where both the debit and credit entries are shown in the cash book.
Folio columns (p 134): Columns used for entering reference numbers.

Exercises

15.1 Write up a two-column cash book from the following details, and balance off as at the end of the month:

1997
May 1 Started business with capital in cash £100
May 2 Paid rent by cash £10
May 3 F Lake lent us £500, paying by cheque
May 4 We paid B McKenzie by cheque £65
May 5 Cash sales £98
May 7 N Miller paid us by cheque £62
May 9 We paid B Burton in cash £22
May 11 Cash sales paid direct into the bank £53
May 15 G Moores paid us in cash £65
May 16 We took £50 out of the cash till and paid it into the bank account
May 19 We repaid F Lake £100 by cheque
May 22 Cash sales paid direct into the bank £66
May 26 Paid motor expenses by cheque £12
May 30 Withdrew £100 cash from the bank for business use
May 31 Paid wages in cash £97.

15.2 Write up a two-column cash book from the following details, and balance off as at the end of the month:

1998
Mar 1 Balances brought down from last month:
Cash in hand £56; Cash in bank £2,356
Mar 2 Paid rates by cheque £156
Mar 3 Paid for postage stamps in cash £5
Mar 5 Cash sales £74
Mar 7 Cash paid into bank £60
May 8 We paid T Lee by cheque £75; we paid C Brooks in cash £2
Mar 12 J Moores pays us £150, £50 being in cash and £100 by cheque
Mar 17 Cash drawings by proprietor £20
Mar 20 P Jones pays us by cheque £79
Mar 22 Withdrew £200 from the bank for business use
Mar 24 Bought a new motor van for £195 cash
Mar 28 Paid rent by cheque £40
Mar 31 Cash sales paid direct into the bank £105.

15.3X A two-column cash book is to be written up from the following, carrying the balances down to the following month:

1998
Jan 1 Started business with £4,000 in the bank
Jan 2 Paid for fixtures by cheque £660
Jan 4 Cash sales £225: Paid rent by cash £140
Jan 6 T Thomas paid us by cheque £188
Jan 8 Cash sales paid direct into the bank £308
Jan 10 J King paid us in cash £300
Jan 12 Paid wages in cash £275
Jan 14 J Walters lent us £500 paying by cheque
Jan 15 Withdrew £200 from the bank for business use
Jan 20 Bought stationery paying by cash £60
Jan 22 We paid J French by cheque £166
Jan 28 Cash drawings £100
Jan 30 J Scott paid us by cheque £277
Jan 31 Cash sales £66.

15.4X Write up a two-column cash book from the following:

1998
Nov 1 Balance brought forward from last month: Cash £105; Bank £2,164
Nov 2 Cash sales £605
Nov 3 Took £500 out of the cash till and paid it into the bank
Nov 4 J Matthews paid us by cheque £217
Nov 5 We paid for postage stamps in cash £60
Nov 6 Bought office equipment by cheque £189
Nov 7 We paid J Lucas by cheque £50
Nov 9 Received rates refund by cheque £72
Nov 11 Withdrew £250 from the bank for business use
Nov 12 Paid wages in cash £239
Nov 14 Paid motor expenses by cheque £57
Nov 16 L Levy lent us £200 in cash
Nov 20 R Norman paid us by cheque £112
Nov 28 We paid general expenses in cash £22
Nov 30 Paid insurance by cheque £74.

15.5 You work for Stott & Co, a medium-sized clothes manufacturer, whose offices and works are situated in Derby. As book-keeper to the firm one of your main duties is to enter up the cash book on a regular basis.

Required

From the information given below enter up the transactions for May 1998, balance off at the end of the month and bring the balances down.

			£
May	1	Balances b/d	
		Cash in hand	14.72
		Bank (overdrawn)	820.54
May	2	Bought stationery by cash	10.00
May	3	Banked cheques received from:	
		P Wrench	432.36
		R Whitworth	634.34
		J Summers	341.00
May	6	South West Rail Ltd, cheque for travel expenses of company secretary to London	37.50
May	9	Paid the following accounts by cheque,	
		Fabulous Fabrics Ltd	450.80
		Mellors Manufacturing Co	348.32
May	12	Received from cash sale	76.00
May	14	Paid employees PAYE and NI to the Inland Revenue, by cheque	221.30
May	17	Received cheque from Trentam Traders	32.81
May	20	Foreign currency drawn from bank for director's visit to Italy	250.00
		Bank charges re currency	3.20
May	24	Received cash from sale of goods	350.00
May	26	Cash to bank	300.00
May	27	Salaries by cheque	5,720.00
May	31	Received cheques from the following:	
		J Summers	1,231.00
		Bradnop Manufacturing Co	725.00
		Taylors	2,330.50

(NVQ Level 2)

15.6 As a trainee accounts clerk at Jepsons & Co, one of your tasks is to enter up the firm's cash book at the end of each month.

Required

From the details listed below enter up the cash book for February, balance off at the end of the month and bring the balances down.

1998			£
Feb	1	Balances brought down from January	
		Cash in hand	76.32
		Cash at bank	2,376.50
Feb	2	Paid electricity bill by cheque	156.00
Feb	4	Paid motor expenses by cash	15.00
Feb	6	Received cheques from the following debtors:	
		D Hill	300.00
		A Jackson	275.00
		H Wardle	93.20
Feb	7	Paid for stationery by cash	3.70
Feb	10	Sold goods for cash	57.10
Feb	12	Paid for purchases from Palmer & Sons by cheque	723.50
Feb	14	Received loan by cheque from D Whitman	500.00
Feb	16	Paid Wright Brothers for repairs to office machinery by cheque	86.20
Feb	17	The proprietor, Stan Jepson, took cash for his own use.	50.00
		He asks you to pay his personal telephone bill by cheque to the post office	140.60
Feb	22	J Smith paid his account by cheque	217.00
Feb	23	Petrol bill paid by cash	21.00
Feb	26	Received cheque for sale of goods	53.00
Feb	27	Bought new photocopier from Bronsons of Manchester and paid by cheque	899.00
Feb	28	Paid monthly salaries by cheque	2,400.00

16 Three-column and analytical cash books and cash discounts

16.1 Cash discounts

It is better if customers pay their accounts quickly. A firm may accept a smaller sum in full settlement if payment is made within a certain period of time. The amount of the reduction of the sum to be paid is known as a *cash discount*. The term 'cash discount' thus refers to the allowance given for quick payment. It is still called cash discount, even if the account is paid by cheque.

The rate of cash discount is usually stated as a percentage. Full details of the percentage allowed, and the period within which payment is to be made, are quoted on all sales documents by the selling company. A typical period during which discount may be allowed is one month from the date of the original transaction.

16.2 Discounts allowed and discounts received

A firm may have two types of cash discounts in its books. These are:

1 **Discounts allowed**. Cash discounts allowed by a firm to its customers when they pay their accounts quickly.
2 **Discounts received.** Received by a firm from its suppliers when it pays their accounts quickly.

We can now see the effect of discounts by looking at two examples.

Example 1
W Clarke owed us £100. He pays on 2 September 1998 by cash within the time limit laid down, and the firm allows him 5 per cent cash discount. So he will pay £100 – £5 = £95 in full settlement of his account.

Effect	Action
1 Of cash: Cash is increased by £95. Asset of debtors is decreased by £95.	Debit cash account, i.e. enter £95 in debit column of cash book. Credit W Clarke £95.
2 Of discounts: Asset of debtors is decreased by £5. (After the cash was paid the balance of £5 still appeared. As the account has been paid this asset must now be cancelled.) Expenses of discounts allowed increased by £5.	Credit W Clarke £5. Debit discounts allowed account £5.

Example 2

The firm owed S Small £400. It pays him on 3 September 1998 by cheque within the time limit laid down by him and he allows 2½ per cent cash discount. Thus the firm will pay £400 – £10 = £390 in full settlement of the account.

Effect	Action
1 Of cheque: Asset of bank is reduced by £390. Liability of creditors is reduced by £390.	Credit bank, i.e. enter in credit bank column, £390. Debit S Small's account £390.
2 Of discounts: Liability of creditors is reduced by £10. (After the cheque was paid the balance of £10 remained. As the account has been paid the liability must now be cancelled.) Revenue of discounts received increased by £10.	Debit S Small's account £10. Credit discounts received account £10.

The accounts in the firm's books would appear:

Cash Book *(page 32)*

Dr						Cr
		Cash	Bank		Cash	Bank
1998		£	£	1998	£	£
Sept 2 W Clarke SL12		95		Sept 3 S Small PL75		390

Discounts Received Account (General Ledger *page 18*)

Dr			Cr
	1998		£
	Sept 2 S Small PL75		10

Discounts Allowed Account (General Ledger *page 17*)

Dr					Cr
1998				£	
Sept	2	W Clarke	SL12	5	

W Clarke Account (Sales Ledger *page 12*)

Dr							Cr
1998			£	1998			£
Sept 1	Balance b/d		100	Sept 2	Cash	CB32	95
				Sept 2	Discount	GL17	5
			100				100

S Small Account (Purchases Ledger *page 75*)

Dr							Cr
1998			£	1998			£
Sept 3	Bank	CB32	390	Sept 1	Balance b/d		400
Sept 3	Discounts	GL18	10				
			400				400

It is the accounting custom to enter the word 'Discount' in the personal accounts, not stating whether it is a discount received or a discount allowed.

16.3 Discount columns in cash book

The discounts allowed account and the discounts received account are in the general ledger along with all the other revenue and expense accounts. It has already been stated that every effort should be made to avoid too much reference to the general ledger.

In the case of discounts this is done by adding an extra column on each side of the cash book in which the amounts of discounts are entered. Discounts received are entered in the discounts column on the credit side of the cash book, and discounts allowed in the discounts column on the debit side of the cash book.

The cash book, if completed for the two examples so far dealt with, would appear:

Cash Book

Dr			Discount	Cash	Bank			Discount	Cash	Bank	Cr
			£	£	£			£	£	£	
1998			5	95		1998		10		390	
Sept 2	W Clarke	SL12				Sept 3	S Small PL75				

There is no alteration to the method of showing discounts in the personal accounts.

To make entries in the discounts accounts

Total of discounts
column on receipts } Enter on debit side of
side of cash book   discounts allowed account

Total of discounts
column on payments } Enter on credit side of
side of cash book   discounts received account

16.3 A worked example

1998			£
May	1	Balances brought down from April:	
		Cash Balance	29
		Bank Balance	654
		Debtors accounts:	
		B King	120
		N Campbell	280
		D Shand	40
		Creditors accounts:	
		U Barrow	60
		A Allen	440
		R Long	100
May	2	B King pays us by cheque, having deducted 2½ per cent cash discount £3	117
May	8	We pay R Long his account by cheque, deducting 5 per cent cash discount £5	95
May	11	We withdrew £100 cash from the bank for business use	100
May	16	N Campbell pays us his account by cheque, deducting 2½ per cent discount £7	273
May	25	We paid wages in cash	92
May	28	D Shand pays us in cash after having deducted 2½ per cent cash discount	38
May	29	We pay U Barrow by cheque less 5 per cent cash discount £3	57
May	30	We pay A Allen by cheque less 2½ per cent cash discount £11	429

Cash Book									page 64
Dr									Cr
	Folio	Discount	Cash	Bank		Folio	Discount	Cash	Bank
1998		£	£	£	1998		£	£	£
May 1					May 8				
Balances	b/d		29	654	R Long	PL58	5		95
May 2					May 11				
B King	SL13	3		117	Cash	C			100
May 11					May 25				
Bank	C		100		Wages	GL77		92	
May 16					May 29				
N Campbell	SL84	7		273	U Barrow	PL15	3		57
May 28					May 30				
D Shand	SL91	2	38		A Allen	PL98	11		429
					May 31				
					Balances	c/d		75	363
		12	167	1,044			19	167	1,044
Jun 1									
Balances	b/d		75	363					

Sales Ledger
B King Account
Page 13

Dr							Cr
1998			£	1998			£
May 1	Balance b/d		120	May 2	Bank	CB 64	117
				May 2	Discount	CB 64	3
			120				120

N Campbell Account
Page 84

Dr							Cr
1998			£	1998			£
May 1	Balance b/d		280	May 16	Bank	CB 64	273
				May 16	Discount	CB 64	7
			280				280

D Shand Account
Page 91

Dr							Cr
1998			£	1998			£
May 1	Balance b/d		40	May 28	Cash	CB 64	38
				May 28	Discount	CB 64	2
			40				40

Purchases Ledger

U Barrow Account *Page 15*

Dr								Cr

1998				£	1998			£
May	29	Bank	CB 64	57	May	1	Balance b/d	60
May	29	Discount	CB 64	3				
				60				60

R Long Account *Page 58*

Dr								Cr

1998				£	1998			£
May	8	Bank	CB 64	95	May	1	Balance b/d	100
May	8	Discount	CB 64	5				
				100				100

A Allen Account *Page 98*

Dr								Cr

1998				£	1998			£
May	30	Bank	CB 64	429	May	1	Balance b/d	440
May	30	Discount	CB 64	11				
				440				440

General Ledger

Wages Account *Page 77*

Dr					Cr

1998				£
May	25	Cash	CB 64	92

Discounts Received Account *Page 88*

Dr					Cr

	1998			£
	May 31	Total for the month	CB 64	19

Discounts Allowed Account

Dr					Cr

1998				£
May 31	Total for the month	CB 64	12	

Is the above method of entering discounts correct?
You can easily check. See the following:

Discounts in Ledger Accounts	Debits		Credits	
		£		
Discounts received	U Barrow	3	Discounts	
	R Long	5	Received	
	A Allen	11	Account	£19
		19		
				£
Discounts allowed	Discounts		B King	3
	Allowed		N Campbell	7
	Account	£12	D Shand	2
				12

You can see that proper double entry has been carried out. Equal amounts, in total, have been entered on each side of the accounts.

16.5   Bank overdrafts

A firm may borrow money from a bank by means of a bank overdraft. This means that the firm is allowed to pay more out of the bank account, by paying out cheques, than the total amount which is placed in the account.

Up to this point the bank balances have all been money at the bank, so they have all been assets, i.e. debit balances. When the account is overdrawn the firm owes money to the bank, so the account is a liability and the balance becomes a credit one.

Taking the cash book last shown, suppose that the amount payable to A Allen was £1,429 instead of £429. Thus the amount in the bank account, £1,044, is exceeded by the amount withdrawn. The cash book would appear as follows:

Dr				Cash Book					Cr
		Discount	Cash	Bank			Discount	Cash	Bank
1998		£	£	£	1998		£	£	£
May 1	Balances b/d		29	654	May 8	R Long	5		95
" 2	B King	3		117	" 11	Cash			100
" 11	Bank		100		" 25	Wages		92	
" 16	N Campbell	7		273	" 29	U Barrow	3		57
" 28	D Shand	2	38		" 30	A Allen	11		1,429
" 31	Balance c/d			637	" 31	Balance c/d		75	
		12	167	1,681			19	167	1,681
Jun 1	Balance b/d		75		Jun 1	Balance b/d			637

On a balance sheet a bank overdraft will be shown as an item included under the heading current liabilities.

16.6   Analytical cash book

Many businesses use an analytical cash book in a similar way to the analytical petty cash book. This has several advantages.

One advantage is that it enables the business to have the use of a VAT (Value Added Tax) column to record payments/receipt of VAT. At the end of the month the VAT columns are added up and the totals transferred to the VAT account in the general ledger. This VAT column is especially useful if the business buys and sells goods and/or services for immediate payment. The topic of value added tax will be dealt with more fully in Chapter 23.

Another advantage is that it allows for analysis of, say sales or purchases. In the example (Exhibit 16.1) Whiteheads Electrical Co sells television sets, radios, videos, as well as washing machines, dryers, fridges, etc. To monitor the sales and profit margins of the various lines, the owner of Whiteheads uses four analysis columns:

Electrical goods
'White' goods (e.g. washing machines, which are usually white)
Sundry sales
VAT

Payments from the cash book are analysed in a similar way.

Some businesses have a separate sales ledger and purchase ledger which are self-balancing by the use of control accounts. Analysis columns are used in an analytical cash book to record monies received from debtors or paid to creditors. At the end of the month the columns are added up and the totals posted to the respective sales and purchased ledger control accounts.

There is no set format for the number and names of the columns used; it is up to the organisation to adapt the cash book to meet its own requirements.

Exhibit 16.1   A worked example

Whiteheads Electrical Co is an independent electrical shop which sells television sets, radios and videos, as well as washing machines, dryers, fridges, etc. In order to monitor sales and profit margins, Mr Whitehead operates a columnar cash book, as follows.

Receipts
These are split between four main headings, namely:

Electrical goods
'White' goods
Sundry sales
a VAT column

Payments

The payments side of the cash book has headings as follows:

VAT
Electrical purchases
White goods purchases
Wages and salaries
General overheads

During October 1999 the following transactions took place:

1999

| Oct | 1 | Balance of cash in hand | £64.92 |
| | | Balance at bank | £416.17 |

2   Bought radios from Shaws (Wholesalers) Ltd,
£187.36 plus VAT of £32.78 paid by cheque.

4   Sold goods as follows:
– Washing machine £360.00 plus VAT of £63
to K Walters who paid by cheque
– Video to S Worrall who paid by cheque £330.00
plus VAT of £57.75

Both cheques were paid into the bank.

– Sundry cash sales, plugs, etc., £27.50 including
VAT of £4.10

7   Paid electricity account £76.30 by cheque.

7   Paid wages £245. Drew cash from bank for this purpose.

10   Sold goods as follows:

Mrs J White – Colour TV	£550	(including VAT £81.92)
Dr V Ford – Fridge	£180	(including VAT £26.81)
Mr J Summers – Dryer	£225.50	(including VAT £33.59)

Cheques were received in respect of the above and duly banked.

12   Cash sales: radio, £80.00 (including VAT £11.91).

14   Purchased the following goods from Allan's Electrical Ltd,
and paid by cheque. This totalled £2,056.25.

| Fridges | £450.00 plus VAT |
| Televisions | £1,300.00 plus VAT |

14   Paid wages £245.00. Drew cash from bank.

18   Cash sale, one fridge £163.50 (including VAT).

20   Paid cash for petrol £20.00 (including VAT).

23   Paid wages £252.00. Drew cash from bank.

24   Sold TV and video to J Pratt £964.67
(including VAT £143.67). He paid by cheque.

26   Bought electrical clocks and radios from B McDonald and Son
for £327.50 (including VAT). Paid by cheque.

30   Sundry cash sales paid direct into the bank £367.00 (including VAT).

31   Paid rent £200.00 in cash.

Cash Book (debit side only)

Dr   CB 1

Date	Details	Folio	VAT	Electrical sales	White goods sales	Sundry sales	Cash	Bank
1999			£	£	£	£	£	£
Oct 1	Balance b/d						64.92	416.17
4	K Walters		63.00		360.00			423.00
"	S Worrall		57.75	330.00				387.75
	Cash sales		4.10			23.40	27.50	
10	Mrs J White		81.92	468.08				550.00
"	Dr V Ford		26.81		153.19			180.00
"	Mr J Summers		33.59		191.91			225.50
12	Cash sales		11.91	68.09			80.00	
18	"		24.35	139.15			163.50	
24	J Pratt		143.67	821.00				964.67
30	Cash sales		54.66			312.34		367.00
			501.76	1,687.17	844.25	335.74	335.92	3,514.09
Nov 1	Balance b/d						115.92	91.90
			GL1	GL2	GL3	GL4		

Cash Book (credit side only)

Cr   CB 1

Date	Details	Folio	VAT	Electrical purchases	White goods purchases	Wages and salaries	General overheads	Cash	Bank
1999			£	£	£	£	£	£	£
Oct 2	Shaws (Wholesalers) Ltd		32.78	187.36					220.14
7	Electricity						76.30		76.30
7	Wages					245.00			245.00
14	Allan's Electrical Ltd		306.25	1,300.00	450.00				2,056.25
"	Wages					245.00			245.00
20	Petrol		2.98				17.02	20.00	
23	Wages					252.00			252.00
26	B McDonald & Son		48.78	278.72					327.50
31	Rent						200.00	200.00	
31	Balance c/d							115.92	91.90
			390.79	1,766.08	450.00	742.00	293.32	335.92	3,514.09
			GL1						

Note: Full coverage of the treatment of discounts allowed and discounts received in final accounts is shown in Chapter 30: 'Accruals, prepayments and other adjustments'.

New terms

Discounts allowed (p 140): A reduction given to customers who pay their accounts within the time allowed.

Discounts received (p 140): A reduction given to us by a supplier when we pay their account before the time allowed has elapsed.

Exercises

16.1   Enter up a three column cash book from the details following. Balance off at the end of the month, and show the relevant discount accounts as they would appear in the general ledger.

1998

May   1   Started business with £6,000 in the bank
May   1   Bought fixtures paying by cheque £950
May   2   Bought goods paying by cheque £1,240
May   3   Cash sales £407
May   4   Paid rent in cash £200
May   5   N Morgan paid us his account of £220 by a cheque for £210, we allowed him £10 discount
May   7   Paid S Thompson & Co £80 owing to them by means of a cheque £76, they allowed us £4 discount
May   9   We received a cheque for £380 from S Cooper, discount having been allowed £20
May   12 Paid rates by cheque £410
May   14 L Curtis pays us a cheque for £115
May   16 Paid M Monroe his account of £120 by cash £114, having deducted £6 cash discount
May   20 P Exeter pays us a cheque for £78, having deducted £2 cash discount
May   31 Cash sales paid direct into the bank £88.

16.2   A three column cash book is to be written up from the following details, balanced off and the relevant discount accounts in the general ledger shown.

1998

Mar   1   Balances brought forward: Cash £230; Bank £4,756
Mar   2   The following paid their accounts by cheque, in each case deducting 5 per cent cash discounts. Accounts: R Burton £140; E Taylor £220; R Harris £300
Mar   4   Paid rent by cheque £120
Mar   6   J Cotton lent us £1,000 paying by cheque
Mar   8   We paid the following accounts by cheque, in each case deducting a 2½ per cent cash discount: N Black £360; P Towers £480; C Rowse £800
Mar   10 Paid motor expenses in cash £44
Mar   12 H Hankins pays his account of £77 by cheque £74, deducting £3 cash discount
Mar   15 Paid wages in cash £160
Mar   18 The following paid their accounts by cheque, in each case deducting 5 per cent cash discount. Accounts: C Winston £260; R Wilson & Son £340; H Winter £460
Mar   21 Cash withdrawn from the bank £350 for business use
Mar   24 Cash drawings £120
Mar   25 Paid T Briers his account of £140, by cash £133, having deducted £7 cash discount
Mar   29 Bought fixtures paying by cheque £650
Mar   31 Received commission by cheque £88.

16.3 From the following details write up a three-column cash book, balance off at the end of the month, and show the relevant discount accounts as they would appear in the general ledger.

1999

Mar 1 Balances brought forward:
Cash in hand £211
Cash at bank £3,984

Mar 2 We paid each of the following accounts by cheque, in each case we deducted a 5 per cent discount: T Adams £80; C Bibby £260; D Clarke £440

Mar 4 C Potts pays us a cheque for £98

Mar 6 Cash sales paid direct into the bank £49

Mar 7 Paid insurance by cash £65

Mar 9 The following persons pay us their accounts by cheque, in each case they deducted a discount of 2½ per cent: R Smiley £160; J Turner £640; R Pimlott £520

Mar 12 Paid motor expenses by cash £100

Mar 18 Cash sales £98

Mar 21 Paid salaries by cheque £120

Mar 23 Paid rent by cash £60

Mar 28 Received a cheque for £500 being a loan from R Godfrey

Mar 31 Paid for stationery by cheque £27.

16.4X Enter the following in a three-column cash book. Balance off the cash book at the end of the month and show the discount accounts in the general ledger.

1998

June 1 Balances brought forward: Cash £97; Bank £2,186

June 2 The following paid us by cheque, in each case deducting a 5 per cent cash discount: R Harris £1,000; C White £280; P Peers £180; O Hardy £600

June 3 Cash sales paid direct into the bank £134

June 5 Paid rent by cash £88

June 6 We paid the following accounts by cheque, in each case deducting 2½ per cent cash discount: J Charlton £400; H Sobers £640; D Shallcross £200

June 8 Withdrew cash from the bank for business use £250

June 10 Cash sales £206

June 12 D Deeds paid us their account of £89 by cheque less £2 cash discount

June 14 Paid wages by cash £250

June 16 We paid the following accounts by cheque: L Lucas £117 less cash discount £6; D Fisher £206 less cash discount £8

June 20 Bought fixtures by cheque £8,000

June 24 Bought motor lorry paying by cheque £7,166

June 29 Received £169 cheque from D Steel

June 30 Cash sales £116

June 30 Bought stationery paying by cash £60.

16.5X You are to write up a three-column cash book for M Pinero from the details which follow. Then balance off at the end of the month and show the discount accounts in the general ledger.

1999

May 1 Balances brought forward:
    Cash in hand £58
    Bank overdraft £1,470

May 2 M Pinero pays further capital into the bank £1,000

May 3 Bought office fixtures by cheque £780

May 4 Cash sales £220

May 5 Banked cash £200

May 6 We paid the following by cheque, in each case deducting 2½ per cent cash discount: B Barnes £80; T Horton £240; T Jacklin £400

May 8 Cash sales £500

May 12 Paid motor expenses in cash £77

May 15 Cash withdrawn from the bank £400

May 16 Cash drawings £120

May 18 The following firms paid us their accounts by cheque, in each case deducting a 5 per cent discount: L Graham £80; B Crenshaw £140; H Green £220

May 20 Salaries paid in cash £210

May 22 T Weiskopf paid us his account in cash £204

May 26 Paid insurance by cheque £150

May 28 We banked all the cash in our possession except for £20 in the cash till

May 31 Bought motor van, paying by cheque £4,920.

16.6

(a) List *three* ways in which a trader can pay debts other than by cash or cheque.
(b) On 1 July 1998 the debit balances in the cash book of E Rich were:

Cash   £419
Bank £3,685

His transactions for the month of July were:

2 July   Received cheque from A Wood £296

6 July   Paid wages in cash £102

9 July   Paid C Hill £211 by cheque in full settlement of his account of £224

12 July   Received £146 cash for sale of damaged stock
    Paid T Jarvis £1,023 by cheque in full settlement of his account of £1,051

13 July   Paid wages in cash £104

17 July   Received cheque for £500 from Atlas & Company

19 July   Paid £21 in cash for postage stamps

20 July   Paid wages in cash £102

23 July   Withdrew £200 from bank for office cash

25 July   Paid W Moore £429 by cheque

26 July   Paid wages in cash £105

28 July   Received £317 cash from T Phillips in full settlement of his account of £325, paid into bank the same day

31 July   Paid £260 cash into bank

Required
Prepare the three-column cash book for the month of July 1998 and balance it at 31 July, bringing the balances down at 1 August.
(LCCI)

17 Bank reconciliation statements

17.1 The need for bank reconciliation statements

At the end of each period we will balance off our cash book. At the same time we should ask our bank for a copy of our bank statement. When we look at the closing balance in our cash book, and then compare with the balance on that date on the bank statement, we will usually find that the two balances are different.

We should then draw up a **bank reconciliation statement**, and the methods for doing this are shown in this chapter. This will either show:

1 that the reasons for the difference in balances are valid ones, showing that it has not been as a result of errors made by us or the bank, or
2 that there is not a good reason for the difference between the balances.

In the case of **2** we will have to find out exactly what the errors are. They can then be corrected.

17.2 An example of a bank reconciliation statement

Let us assume that we have just written up our cash book. We call at the bank on 30 June 1997 and get from the bank manager a copy of our bank statement. On our return we tick off in our cash book and on the bank statement the items that are similar. A copy of our cash book (bank columns only) and of our bank statement are now shown as Exhibit 17.1.

Exhibit 17.1

Dr				£	Cr				£
			Cash Book (bank columns only)						
1997					1997				
June	1	Balance b/f	✓	80	June	27	I Gordon	✓	35
June	28	D Jones	✓	100	June	29	B Tyrell		40
					June	30	Balance c/d		105
				180					180
July	1	Balance b/d		105					

Bank Statement

1997			Dr £	Cr £	Balance £
June 26	Balance b/f	✓			80 Cr
June 28	Banking	✓		100	180 Cr
June 30	I Gordon	✓	35		145 Cr

By comparing the cash book and the bank statement, it can be seen that the only item that was not in both of these was the cheque payment to B Tyrell £40 in the cash book.

The reason this was in the cash book, but not on the bank statement, is simply one of timing. The cheque had been posted to B Tyrell on 29 June, but there had not been time for it to be banked by Tyrell and passed through the banking system. Such a cheque is called an **unpresented cheque** because it has not yet been presented at the drawer's bank.

To prove that, although they are different figures the balances are not different because of errors, a bank reconciliation statement is drawn up. This is as follows:

Bank Reconciliation Statement as at 30 June 1997

	£
Balance in hand as per cash book	105
Add unpresented cheque: Tyrell	40
Balance in hand as per bank statement	145

It would have been possible for the bank reconciliation statement to have started with the bank statement balance:

Bank Reconciliation Statement as at 30 June 1997

	£
Balance in hand as per bank statement	145
Less unpresented cheque: Tyrell	40
Balance in hand as per cash book	105

You should notice that the bank account is shown as a debit balance in the firm's cash book because to the firm it is an asset. In the bank's books the bank account is shown as a credit balance because this is a liability of the bank to the firm.

17.3 Some reasons for differences in balances

We can now look at a more complicated example in Exhibit 17.2. Similar items in both cash book and bank statement are shown ticked.

Exhibit 17.2

Cash Book

Dr				£	Cr				£
1997					1997				
Dec	27	Total b/f		2,000	Dec	27	Total b/f		1,600
Dec	29	J Potter	✓	60	Dec	28	J Jacobs	✓	105
Dec	31	M Johnson (B)		220	Dec	30	M Chatwood (A)		15
					Dec	31	Balance c/d		560
				2,280					2,280
1998									
Jan	1	Balance b/d		560					

Bank Statement

				Dr	Cr	Balance
				£	£	£
1997						
Dec	27	Balance b/f				400 CR
Dec	29	Cheque	✓		60	460 CR
Dec	30	J Jacobs	✓	105		355 CR
Dec	30	Credit transfers: L Shaw (C)			70	425 CR
Dec	30	Bank charges (D)		20		405 CR

The balance brought forward in the bank statement £400 is the same figure as that in the cash book, i.e. totals b/f £2,000 – £1,600 = £400. However, items (A) and (B) are in the cash book only, and (C) and (D) are on the bank statement only. We can now examine these in detail:

(A) This is a cheque recently sent by us to Mr Chatwood. It has not yet passed through the banking system and been presented to our bank, and is therefore an 'unpresented cheque'.

(B) This is a cheque banked by us on our visit to the bank when we collected the copy of our bank statement. As we handed this banking over the counter at the same time as the bank clerk gave us our bank statement, naturally it has not yet been entered on the statement.

(C) A customer, L Shaw, has paid his account by instructing his bank to pay us direct through the banking system, instead of paying by cheque. Such a transaction is usually called a **credit transfer**.

(D) The bank has charged us for the services given in keeping a bank account for us. It did not send us a bill: it simply takes the money from our account by debiting it and reducing the amount of our balance.

We can show these differences in the form of a table. This is followed by bank reconciliation statements drawn up both ways. This is for illustration only; we do not have to draw up a table or prepare two bank reconciliation statements. All we need in practice is one bank reconciliation statement, drawn up whichever way we prefer.

Items not in both sets of books	Effect on Cash Book balance	Effect on Bank Statement	Adjustment required to one balance to reconcile it with the other	
			To Cash Book balance	To Bank Statement balance
1. Payment M Chatwood £15	reduced by £15	none – not yet entered	add £15	deduct £15
2. Banking M Johnson £220	increased by £220	none – not yet entered	deduct £220	add £220
3. Bank Commission £20	none – not yet entered	reduced by £20	deduct £20	add £20
4. Credit Transfers £70	none – not yet entered	increased by £70	add £70	deduct £70

Bank Reconciliation Statement as on 31 December 1997

	£	£
Balance in hand as per cash book		560
Add Unpresented cheque – M Chatwood	15	
Credit transfers	70	
		85
		645
Less Bank commission	20	
Bank lodgement not yet entered on bank statement	220	
		240
Balance in hand as per bank statement		405

Bank Reconciliation Statement as on 31 December 1997

	£	£
Balance in hand as per bank statement		405
Add Bank commission	20	
Bank lodgement not yet entered on bank statement	220	
		240
		645
Less Unpresented cheque – M Chatwood	15	
Traders credit transfers	70	
		85
Balance in hand as per bank statement		560

17.4 Writing up the cash book before attempting a reconciliation

The easiest way to do a reconciliation is to complete the cash book first. All items on the bank statement will then be in the cash book. This means that the only differences will be items in the cash book but not on the bank statement. In an examination it is possible that the examiner will ask you not to do it this way.

If, in Exhibit 17.2 the cash book had been written up before the bank reconciliation statement had been drawn up, then the cash book and reconciliation statement would have appeared as follows in Exhibit 17.3.

Exhibit 17.3

Cash Book

Dr   Cr

1997			£	1997			£
Dec	27	Total b/fwd	2,000	Dec	27	Total b/fwd	1,600
Dec	29	J Potter	60	Dec	28	J Jacobs	105
Dec	31	M Johnson	220	Dec	30	M Chatwood	15
Dec	31	Credit transfers		Dec	31	Bank commission	20
		L Shaw	70	Dec	31	Balance c/d	610
			2,350				2,350
1998							
Jan	1	Balance b/d	610				

Bank Reconciliation Statement as on 31 December 1996

	£
Balance in hand as per cash book	610
Add Unpresented cheque – M Chatwood	15
	625
Less Bank lodgement not yet entered on bank statement	220
Balance in hand as per bank statement	405

17.5 Bank overdrafts

When there is a bank overdraft the adjustments needed for reconciliation work are opposite to those needed for a balance.

Exhibit 17.4 is of a cash book, and a bank statement, showing an overdraft. Only the cheque for G Cumberbatch (A) £106 and the cheque paid to J Kelly (B) £63 need adjusting. Work through the reconciliation statement and then see the note after it.

Exhibit 17.4

Cash Book (Bank Columns only)

Dr   Cr

1999			£	1999			£
Dec	5	I Howe	308	Dec	1	Balance b/f	709
Dec	24	L Mason	120	Dec	9	P Davies	140
Dec	29	K King	124	Dec	27	J Kelly (B)	63
Dec	31	G Cumberbatch (A)	106	Dec	29	United Trust	77
Dec	31	Balance c/f	380	Dec	31	Bank charges	49
			1,038				1,038
				2000			
				Jan	1	Balance b/f	380

Bank Statement

1999			Dr £	Cr £	Balance £
Dec	1	Balance b/f			709 O/D
Dec	5	Cheque		308	401 O/D
Dec	14	P Davies	140		541 O/D
Dec	24	Cheque		120	421 O/D
Dec	29	K King: Credit transfer		124	297 O/D
Dec	29	United Trust: Standing order	77		374 O/D
Dec	31	Bank charges	49		423 O/D

Note: On a bank statement an overdraft is often shown with the letters O/D following the amount or else shown as a debit balance, indicated by the letters DR after the amount.

Bank Reconciliation Statement as on 31 December 1999

	£
Overdraft as per cash book	380
Add Bank lodgements not on bank statement	106
	486
Less Unpresented cheque	63
Overdraft per bank statement	423

Note: now compare the reconciliation statements in Exhibit 17.3 and 17.4. This shows:

	Exhibit 17.3 Balances	Exhibit 17.4 Overdrafts
Balance/Overdraft per cash book	XXXX	XXXX
Adjustments		
Unpresented cheque	PLUS	LESS
Banking not entered	LESS	PLUS
Balance/Overdraft per bank statement	XXXX	XXXX

Adjustments are, therefore, made in the opposite way when there is an overdraft.

17.6 Dishonoured cheques

When a cheque is received from a customer and paid into the bank, it is recorded on the debit side of the cash book. It is also shown on the bank statement as a banking by the bank. However, at a later date it may be found that the customer's bank will not honour it. They will not let it go through the customer's account. It is called a **dishonoured cheque**.

There are several possible reasons for this. Let us suppose that K King gave us a cheque for £5,000 on 20 May 1998. We bank it, but a few days later our bank returns the cheque to us. Typical reasons are:

1   King had put £5,000 in figures on the cheque, but had written it in words as five thousand five hundred pounds. You will have to give the cheque back to King for amendment.

2   Normally cheques are considered *stale* six months after the date on the cheque, in other words the banks will not pay cheques over six months old. If King had put the year 1997 on the cheque instead of 1998, then the cheque would be returned to us by our bank.

3   King simply did not have sufficient funds in his bank account. Suppose he had previously only got a £2,000 balance and yet he has given us a cheque for £5,000. His bank has not allowed him to have an overdraft.

   In such a case the cheque would be dishonoured. The bank would write on the cheque *refer to drawer*, and we would have to get in touch with King to see what he was going to do about it.

In all of these cases the bank would show the original banking as being cancelled, by showing the cheque paid out of our bank account. As soon as this happens they will notify us. We will then also show the cheque being cancelled by a credit in the cash book. We will then debit that amount to this account.

When King originally paid his account our records would appear as:

K King Account

Dr			£				Cr £
1998				1998			
May	1	Balance b/d	5,000	May 20	Bank		5,000

Bank Account Account

Dr			£		Cr
1998					
May 20	K King		5,000		

After our recording the dishonour, the records will appear as:

K King Account

Dr			£				Cr £
1998				1998			
May	1	Balance b/d	5,000	May 20	Bank		5,000
May	25	Bank: cheque dishonoured	5,000				

Bank Account Account

Dr						Cr
1998			£	1998		£
May 20	K King		5,000	May 25	K King: cheque	
					dishonoured	5,000

In other words King is once again shown as owing us £5,000.

17.7 Some other reasons for differences in balances

1 **Standing orders**. A firm can instruct its bank to pay regular amounts of money at stated dates to persons or firms. For instance you may ask your bank to pay £200 a month to a building society to repay a mortgage.

2 **Direct debits**. These are payments which have to be made, such as rates, insurance premiums and similar items. Instead of asking the bank to pay the money, as with standing orders, permission is given to the creditor to obtain the money direct out of their bank account. This is particularly useful if the amounts payable may vary from time to time, as it is the creditor who changes the payments, not you. With standing orders, if the amount is ever to be changed then you have to inform the bank. With direct debits it is the creditor who arranges that, not you.

As far as bank reconciliation statements are concerned, both of the above types of payments may have passed through the bank account but have not been entered in the cash book.

17.8 Reconciliation of our ledger accounts with suppliers' statements

Because of differences in timing, the balance on a supplier's statement on a certain date can differ from the balance on that supplier's account in our purchases ledger. This is similar to the fact that a bank statement balance may differ from the cash book balance. In a similar fashion a reconciliation statement may also be necessary. This can now be shown.

Our Purchases Ledger
C Young Ltd Account

Dr							Cr
1999			£	1999			£
Jan 10	Bank		1,550	Jan 1	Balance b/d		1,550
Jan 29	Returns	(1)	116	Jan 6	Purchases		885
Jan 31	Balance c/d		1,679	Jan 18	Purchases		910
			3,345				3,345
				Feb 1	Balance b/d		1,679

Supplier's statement

C Young Ltd
Market Place, Leeds

STATEMENT

Account Name: A Hall Ltd
Account Number: H93

Date: 31 January 1999

			Debit	Credit	Balance
1999			£	£	£
Jan	1	Balance			1,550 Dr
Jan	4	Invoice No 3250	885		2,435 Dr
Jan	13	Payment received		1,550	885 Dr
Jan	18	Invoice No 3731	910		1,795 Dr
Jan	31	Invoice No 3894	425		2,220 Dr

Comparing our purchases ledger account with the supplier's statement, two differences can be seen.

1   We sent returns £116 to C Young Ltd, but they had not received them and recorded them in their books by the end of January.
2   Our supplier has sent goods to A Hall Ltd (our company), but we had not received them and entered the £425 in our books by the end of January.

A reconciliation statement can be drawn up by us, A Hall Ltd, as on 31 January 1999.

Reconciliation of Supplier's Statement
C Young Ltd as on 31 January 1999

		£	£
Balance per our purchases ledger			1,679
Add Purchases not received by us	(2)	425	
Returns not received by supplier	(1)	116	
			541
Balance per supplier's statement			2,220

New terms

Bank reconciliation statement (p 154): A calculation comparing the cash book balance with the bank statement balance.
Credit transfer (p 156): An amount paid by someone direct into our bank account.
Dishonoured cheque (p 159): A cheque which is found to be worth nothing.
Unpresented cheque (p 155): A cheque which has been sent but has not yet gone through the bank account of the receiver of it.

Exercises

17.1 From the following draw up a bank reconciliation statement from details as on 31 December 1997.

	£
Cash at bank as per bank column of the cash book	678
Unpresented cheques	256
Cheques received and paid into the bank, but not yet entered on the bank statement	115
Credit transfers entered as banked on the bank statement but not entered in the cash book	56
Cash at bank as per bank statement	875

17.2X On 30 September 1997 George Snow's statement of account from his bank showed a credit balance in his favour of £1,024.66. On comparing the statement with his cash book he found the following entries in the cash book did not appear on the statement:

Cheques paid in 30 Sept	£342.51
Cheques drawn on 30 Sept	£297.82

The following entries on the statement did not appear in his cash book:

Bank charges to 30 Sept 1997	£15.48
Payment direct to the bank by one of his debtors	£230.17

Prepare a bank reconciliation statement to show the bank balance in his cash book on 30 September 1997.
(Pitman Qualifications)

17.3 At the close of business on 31 March 1999, William Robinson's bank balance according to his cash book was £787. This does not agree with the balance at the bank as shown by the bank statement, and the following items account for the entire difference:

(a) Frank Gibson, one of Robinson's debtors, had paid the sum of £73 direct into Robinson's banking account. This had not been entered in the cash book although it was recorded in the bank statement on 29 March 1999.

(b) A bankers standing order for a trade subscription of £25 was paid by the bank during March but the transaction has not yet been shown in the cash book.

(c) The following cheques – drawn by Robinson during March 1999 and entered in the cash book – had not been presented for payment at his bank by the close of business on 31 March 1999: £34, £41 and £52.

(d) The sum of £112 was paid into his banking account by Robinson on 31 March 1999 but this item did not appear on his bank statement until after that date.

Required
Prepare the bank reconciliation statement as at 31 March 1999, commencing with the cash book balance of £787 and ending with the bank statement balance.
(LCCI)

17.4X Cunningham & Co is an old-established firm of accountants in Huddersfield. You have been employed as book-keeper to the company to assist the senior partner, Mr Cunningham, with the accounting records and day-to-day routine duties.

The company's policies when dealing with both payments and receipts is extremely strict. All cash and cheques received are to be banked immediately. Any payments over £10 must be made by cheque. Small cash payments are all paid by the petty cash system.

One of your tasks is to enter the company's cash book and reconcile this with the bank statement. This task must be carried out on a weekly basis.

Required

(a) Having obtained the company's cheque book and paying-in book (Figs 17.1 and 17.2), enter up the cash book (bank column only) for the period commencing 3 November 1999. Unfortunately, on that date the company was overdrawn by £2,356.00.

(b) Balance up the cash book at the end of the week and bring the balance down.

(c) From the bank statement (Fig 17.3) you are required to prepare:
   (i) The corrected cash book balance as at 10 November 1999;
   (ii) A bank reconciliation statement as at 10 November 1999.

(NVQ Level 2)

Fig. 17.1   Details of cheque book stubs – Cunningham & Co

Date _3 Nov 1999_ Payee _Post Office_ _Stamps_ **Amount £ _146.50_** 001763	Date _3 Nov 1999_ Payee _The Law_ _Society_ **Amount £ _121.80_** 001764	Date _4 Nov 1999_ Payee _Bayleys_ _Office Supplies_ **Amount £ _94.10_** 001765
Date _5 Nov 1999_ Payee _Lower Bents_ _Garage_ _(Petrol A/c – Sept)_ **Amount £_450.15_** 001766	Date _6 Nov 1999_ Payee _Wages_ **Amount £ _489.20_** 001767	Date _10 Nov 1999_ Payee _Petty Cashier_ _(Restoring_ _Imprest)_ **Amount £ _46.00_** 001768

Fig 17.2 Details from paying-in book – Cunningham & Co

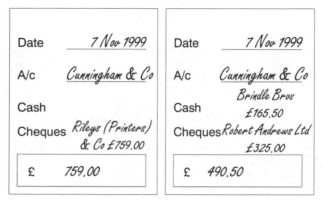

Date	3 Nov 1999
A/c	Cunningham & Co
Cash	
Cheques	Mrs Stoddard £540.00
£	540.00

Date	5 Nov 1999
A/c	Cunningham & Co
Cash	Bent Garage £221.00 P Ralphs £ 53.00
Cheques	Gardeners £1500.00
£	1774.00

Date	6 Nov 1999
A/c	Cunningham & Co
Cash	Mr Prince £130.50
Cheques	Stephens & Smith £523.10
£	653.60

Date	7 Nov 1999
A/c	Cunningham & Co
Cash	
Cheques	Rileys (Printers) & Co £759.00
£	759.00

Date	7 Nov 1999
A/c	Cunningham & Co
Cash	Brindle Bros £165.50
Cheques	Robert Andrews Ltd £325.00
£	490.50

Fig 17.3 Bank Statement – Cunningham & Co

TUDOR BANK	CONFIDENTIAL

High Street Huddersfield	**Account:** Cunningham & Co Chestergate Huddersfield
Account No: 0012770123	Sheet No: 67 Date: 8 November 1999

1999			Dr	Cr	Balance
Nov 3	Balance b/f				2,356.00 O/D
4	Cheque	001763	146.50		2,502.50 O/D
3	Deposit			540.00	1,962.50 O/D
5	Deposit			1,774.00	188.50 O/D
6	S/O Noble Insurance		62.00		250.50 O/D
6	Cheque	001767	489.20		739.70 O/D
6	Deposit			653.60	86.10 O/D
7	Deposit			759.00	672.90
7	Bank charges		22.45		650.45
7	Cheque	001765	94.10		556.35

17.5X William Kay's cash book on 28 February 1997 showed a balance at the bank of £456.48. On attempting a reconciliation with his bank statement the following matters were discovered:

(a) A payment from B Green to W Kay of £40 by direct bank transfer had not been recorded in the cash book.

(b) Cheques drawn but not presented to the bank were: A Roe £21.62; C Mills £36.55.

(c) A paying-in slip dated 27 February 1997 totalling £372.31 was not credited by the bank until 1 March 1997.

(d) A standing order for £21.58 payable on 20 February 1997 for fire insurance had been paid by the bank but not entered in the cash book.

(e) Bank charges £15 had not been entered in the cash book.

    (i) Open the cash book and make such additional entries as you consider necessary;

    (ii) Prepare a statement reconciling your *revised* cash book balance with the balance shown by the bank statement.

(RSA)

17.6 Mitchell's cash book showed a balance of £2,245 as at 31 December and his bank statement showed a balance of £2,195. A comparison of the two records showed the following outstanding items:

> non-presented cheques £250;
>
> payments made by the bank out of his account under a standing order but not yet recorded in the cash book £40;
>
> credit transfer from customer paid directly to bank account but not yet entered in cash book £175;
>
> bank charges not in cash book £40;
>
> takings deposited in night-safe on 31 December £300, but not recorded on bank statement.

Reconcile the two balances.
(Pitman Qualifications)

17.7 Finnikin Trading Co is situated on the outskirts of Uttoxeter and is a busy general supplier to the local traders and farming community.

As office trainee, one of your duties is to keep an eye on the firm's bank balance, as the owner, Joe Finnikin, never likes it to go into an overdraft situation.

You are given the following details of the firm's cash book (Fig 17.4) for July and a copy of their most recent bank statement (Fig 17.5).

Required

(a) You are to prepare:

    (i) The corrected cash book balance as at 31 July;

    (ii) A bank reconciliation statement as at 31 July.

(b) Explain briefly to Janice, one of the shop assistants, the difference between a standing order and a direct debit. Unfortunately Janice has only just opened her first bank account and is unfamiliar with some of the bank's terms.

(c) The firm's storekeeper asks you, in strict confidence, what position the firm is in financially. In particular he is interested to learn of the present bank position. What would be your reaction to this request?

(NVQ Level 2)

Fig 17.4

Finnikin Trading Co
Cash Book (Bank column only)

Dr   Cr

Date	Details	Folio	Bank	Date	Details	Folio	Bank
1999				1999			
Jul 1	Balance b/d		2,310.20	Jul 1	D Oultram Supplies	00236	54.00
3	F. Oakden		332.70	3	Electricity	00237	236.33
4	H. Mellor & Sons		110.00	4	Swindels & Co	00238	219.18
7	J. Mayer (Mfr) Co		249.00	6	Wages	00239	321.40
10	Geoff Burgess		180.20	9	A. & A. Parker	00240	7.42
17	Sales		522.66	10	Green Lane Garage	00241	450.25
20	G Biscoe Ltd		52.30	12	Drawings	00242	125.00
21	Johnson's		42.60	17	Wages	00243	336.10
23	Bentley & Bradley		152.00	21	Hudson Supplies Co	00244	1,427.30
27	Sales		629.30	24	Mace Stationers	00245	51.90
30	Alcock's		34.10	25	Wages	00246	316.50
				31	Balance c/d		1,069.68
			4,615.06				4,615.06
Aug 1	Balance b/d		1,069.68				

Fig 17.5

		Oak Bank			
		Market Square, Uttoxeter			

STATEMENT OF ACCOUNT

Account Name: Finnikin Trading Co
                        Nunn Lane
                        Uttoxeter

Account No: 00639972   Sheet No: 41

Date	Code	Reference	Debit	Credit	Balance
1999					
July 1		Brought forward			2,310.20
3	DEP			332.70	2,642.90
6	CHQ	0239	321.40		
		0237	236.33		
7	DD	United Insurance	35.00		2,050.17
	DEP			359.00	2,409.17
9	SO	Uttoxeter CC	76.00		
	CHQ	0240	7.42		
17	CHQ	0243	336.10		1,989.65
17	DEP			702.86	2,692.51
18	BC	Charges	24.40		2,668.11
23	DEP			246.90	2,915.01
	CHQ	0238	219.18		
25	CHQ	0246	316.50		2,379.33
	BGC	Wheeldons		217.00	
28	DEP			629.30	3,225.63

Note	BC	= Bank Charges	BGC	= Bank Giro Credit
	CHQ	= Cheque	DD	= Direct Debit
	DEP	= Deposit	SO	= Standing Order

17.8X   On 31 October 1999 the cash book of N Orange showed a balance at the bank of £570. An examination of his records located the following errors:

1   Orange paid to R Jones £175 by cheque on 15 October. This cheque was entered in the cash book as £195.

2   Bank charges not recorded in the cash book amounted to £25.

3   A cheque dated 19 October, value £150, payable to T Jack was not paid by the bank until 5 November.

4   Orange on 23 October received from W Green a cheque, value £125. This cheque was dishonoured on 29 October. No entry for the dishonour has been made in the cash book.

5   On 31 October a cheque, value £200, received from F Brown was banked; however, the bank statement was not credited until 1 November.

You are required to:

(a) Make the necessary entries in the cash book in order to show the revised cash book balance at 31 October 1999.

(b) Prepare a statement reconciling the corrected cash book balance with the bank statement at 31 October 1999.

(c) State the balance at bank at 31 October 1999 as shown by the bank statements.

(RSA)

17.9X From the following cash book and bank statement draw up a statement reconciling the two balances.

Cash Book (Bank columns only)

			£				£
April	1	Balance b/f	600.00	April	8	Rates	110.00
April	6	Cash paid in	75.20	April	15	Wages	40.00
April	12	Cheque from A	64.80	April	15	Electricity	60.42
April	18	Cheque from B	72.40	April	15	Paid X	72.15
April	28	Cash paid in	85.00	April	26	Rent	30.00
April	30	Cheque from C	54.62	April	26	Wages	40.00
				April	27	Paid Y	64.10
				April	30	Paid Z	24.10
				April	30	Balance c/f	511.25
			952.02				952.02
May	1	Balance b/f	511.25				

Bank statement

			Dr	Cr	Balance
April	1	Balance			600.00
April	6	Cash		75.20	675.20
April	12	A		64.80	740.00
April	12	Rates	110.00		630.00
April	15	Wages	40.00		590.00
April	18	B		72.40	662.40
April	19	Electricity	60.42		601.98
April	20	X	72.15		529.83
April	26	Wages	40.00		489.83
April	28	Cash		85.00	574.83

(Pitman Qualifications)

18 Capital and revenue expenditures

18.1 Expenditure

The term 'expenditure' refers to a payment (or promise to make a payment) for benefits received, either assets or services. Expenditure can be either capital expenditure or revenue expenditure.

18.2 Capital expenditure

Capital expenditure is made when a firm spends money to either:

1 Buy fixed assets, or
2 Add to the value of an existing fixed asset.

Included in such amounts should be those spent:

1 Acquiring fixed assets.
2 Bringing them into the firm.
3 Legal costs of buying buildings.
4 Carriage inwards on machinery bought.
5 Any other cost needed to get the fixed asset ready for use.

18.3 Revenue expenditure

Expenditure which does not increase the value of fixed assets, but is for running the business on a day-to-day basis, is known as **revenue expenditure**.

The difference can be seen clearly with the total cost of using a motor van for a firm. To buy a new motor van is capital expenditure. The motor van will be in use for several years and is, therefore, a fixed asset.

To pay for petrol to use in the motor van for the next few days is revenue expenditure. This is because the expenditure is used up in a few days and does not add to the value of fixed assets.

18.4 Difference between capital and revenue expenditure

The difference between capital and revenue expenditure can be seen in the following table (Exhibit 18.1). Revenue expenditure is a day-to-day running expense of the business and as such is chargeable to the trading and profit and loss account, whereas capital expenditure results in an increase in the fixed assets which are shown in the balance sheet.

Capital expenditure: further analysis

Capital expenditure not only consists of the cost of purchasing the fixed asset, but also includes other costs necessary to get the fixed asset operational. Some of the possible additional costs are now given:

1 Delivery cost
2 Installation costs
3 Inspection and testing the fixed asset before use
4 Legal costs in purchasing property and land
5 Architects' fees for building plans and for supervising construction of buildings
6 Demolition costs to remove something before new building can begin.

Exhibit 18.1 **Difference between capital and revenue expenditure**

Capital	Revenue
Premises purchased	Rent of premises
Legal charges for conveyancing	Legal charges for debt collection
New machinery	Repairs to machinery
Installations of machinery	Electricity costs of using machinery
Additions to assets	Maintenance of assets
Motor vehicles	Current Road Fund Tax
Delivery charges on new assets	Carriage on purchases and sales
Extension costs of new offices	Redecorating existing offices
Cost of adding air-conditioning to room	Interest on loan to purchase air-conditioning

18.5 Joint expenditure

Sometimes one item of expenditure will need dividing between capital and revenue expenditure.

A builder was engaged to tackle some work on your premises, the total bill being for £3,000. If one-third of this was for repair work and two-thirds for improvements, £1,000 should be charged in the profit and loss account as revenue expenditure, and £2,000 identified as capital expenditure and, therefore, added to the value of premises and shown as such in the balance sheet.

18.6 Incorrect treatment of expenditure

If one of the following occurs:

1 Capital expenditure is incorrectly treated as revenue expenditure, or
2 Revenue expenditure is incorrectly treated as capital expenditure,

then both the balance sheet figures and trading and profit and loss account figures will be incorrect.

This means that the net profit figure will also be incorrect. If the expenditure affects items in the trading account, then the gross profit figure will also be incorrect, e.g. if a motor vehicle was posted to motor expenses account instead of motor vehicle account, then:

Net profit would be understated
and
Balance sheet values would not include the value of the asset.

18.7 Treatment of loan interest

If money is borrowed to finance the purchase of a fixed asset then interest will have to be paid on the loan. The loan interest, however, is *not* a cost of acquiring the asset, but is simply a cost of financing it. This means that loan interest is revenue expenditure and *not* capital expenditure.

18.8 Capital and revenue receipts

When an item of capital expenditure is sold, the receipt is called a capital receipt. Suppose a motor van is bought for £5,000, and sold five years later for £750. The £5,000 was treated as capital expenditure. The £750 received is treated as a capital receipt.

Revenue receipts are sales or other revenue items, such as rent receivable or commissions receivable.

New terms

Capital expenditure (p 170): When a firm spends money to buy or add value to a fixed asset.
Revenue expenditure (p 170): Expenses needed for the day-to-day running of the business.

Exercises

18.1   For the business of K Thorne, wholesale chemist, classify the following between 'capital' and 'revenue' expenditure:

(a)   Purchase of an extra motor van.
(b)   Cost of rebuilding a warehouse wall which had fallen down.
(c)   Building extension to the warehouse.
(d)   Painting extension to warehouse when it is first built.
(e)   Repainting extension to warehouse three years later than that done in (d).
(f)   Carriage costs on bricks for new warehouse extension.
(g)   Carriage costs on purchases.
(h)   Carriage costs on sales.
(i)   Legal costs of collecting debts.
(j)   Legal charges on acquiring new premises for office.
(k)   Fire insurance premium.
(l)   Costs of erecting new machine.

18.2X   For the business of H Ward, a foodstore, classify the following between 'capital' and 'revenue' expenditure:

(a)   Repairs to meat slicer.
(b)   New tyre for van.
(c)   Additional shop counter.
(d)   Renewing signwriting on store.
(e)   Fitting partitions in store.
(f)   Roof repairs.
(g)   Installing thief detection equipment.
(h)   Wages of store assistant.
(i)   Carriage on returns outwards.
(j)   New cash register.
(k)   Repairs to office safe.
(l)   Installing extra toilet.

18.3   Explain clearly the difference between capital expenditure and revenue expenditure. State which of the following you would classify as capital expenditure, giving your reasons:

(a)   Cost of building extension to factory.
(b)   Purchases of filing cabinets for sales office.
(c)   Cost of repairs to accounting machine.
(d)   Cost of installing reconditioned engine in delivery van.
(e)   Legal fees paid in connection with factory extension.

18.4 The following data was extracted from books of account of H E Worth, a building contractor, on 31 March 1999, his financial year end:

		£
(a)	Wages (including wages of two of Worth's employees who worked on improvements to Worth's premises, amount involved £1,500)	8,000
(b)	Light and heat (including new wiring £500, part of premises improvement)	2,000
(c)	Purchase of extra cement mixer (includes £200 for repair of old dumper)	2,500
(d)	Rent	400
(e)	Carriage (includes £100 carriage on new cement mixer)	800
(f)	Purchase of new lathe (extra)	4,000

You are required to:
Allocate each of the items listed above to either capital or revenue expenditure.
(RSA)

18.5 Geoff worked for many years as a commercial banker but at the recent reorganisation of the staff he decided to take early retirement. One of his and his wife's ambitions has been to own and run a small hotel in the Lake District catering for walkers and climbers. Geoff and Anne are both keen walkers and have been members of walking clubs for many years.

Holly Dale Hotel is situated near Grasmere in its own grounds of approximately one and a half acres. All its six bedrooms are en-suite and amongst its facilities are a dining-room, lounge and two other rooms which can be used for storing climbing and walking equipment and a drying room.

Structurally the hotel is sound and the previous owners have kept up with the maintenance and some refurbishment.

Geoff and Anne have now moved into the private flat situated at the rear of the hotel. They have decided to proceed cautiously with the upgrading of certain parts of the hotel and have produced a budget for the first year's expenditure.

Required

(a) From the attached list classify the following items as either Capital or Revenue Expenditure prior to the books, papers, etc being forwarded to Geoff and Anne's accountant.

Holly Dale Hotel Grasmere
Items of Expenditure
One double and two single beds
10 feather pillows (purchased as a special offer
  @ £5.00 each including a free pillow case)
Bathroom suites
Labour to plumb in bathroom suites
Curtains
Carpeting
Table linen
Cutlery
Vase and dried flower arrangement
Reception desk
Stationery
Portable typewriter
6 waste-paper bins
Towels
Toilet rolls and tissues
Soap and bubble bath

Road tax on estate car
Garage repair account re: estate car
Estate car (second-hand)
2 boxes pansies and wallflowers
6 rose bushes
2 five-litre tins emulsion paint ⎫ Geoff is going to do
20 rolls of wallpaper and paste ⎭ his own decorating
2 storage heaters for drying room
Coat and shoe racks for drying room
  (local joiner to provide materials and labour for making and fitting)

(b) Although Geoff has years of banking experience he is not too familiar with some of the terms used by the accountancy profession. He drops you a line requesting the following explanation:

> *Could you please explain to me the difference between 'Capital' and 'Revenue Expenditure' and why it is so important to make the distinction before I enter the invoices into the books of account.*

Draft a suitable reply to Geoff.
(NVQ Level 3)

18.6X Allocate the following debits between capital and revenue expenditure, giving reasons.

(a) Purchase of new vehicle
(b) Fuel for vehicles
(c) New tyres for vehicles
(d) Vehicles insurance
(e) Radio equipment fitted to vehicle.

(Pitman Qualifications)

18.7 Compupro is a small computer and data processing bureau. In a certain trading period it enters into the following transactions:

(a) The purchase of supplies of computer print-out paper, all of which is expected to be used within the current trading period.
(b) The renewal of insurance on the computer hardware.
(c) Expenditure on increasing the security to the building in which the bureau's facilities are situated.
(d) The wages of the computer operators.
(e) The adding of extra storage capacity to a mainframe computer used within the bureau.

Required
State in respect of each of the above whether you would treat the item as capital expenditure or revenue expenditure, giving the reason for your choice. Set out your answer in two columns as follows:

                Capital or Revenue Expenditure   **Reason**
(a)
(b)
(c)
(d)
(e)
(LCCI)

18.8X Place the following outgoings under capital or revenue expenditure:

  (a)   purchase of premises.
  (b)   repairs to premises.
  (c)   legal costs connected with purchase of premises.
  (d)   payment of ground rent.
  (e)   purchase of second-hand motor van.
  (f)   payment of petrol.
  (g)   payment for telephone charges.
  (h)   depreciation on machinery.
  (i)   wages paid to staff.
  (j)   purchase of patent rights.

(Pitman Qualifications)

19 The sales day book and the sales ledger

19.1 Introduction

In Chapter 12 we saw that the ledger had been split up into a set of day books, journals and ledgers. This chapter explains about sales day books and sales ledgers.

19.2 Cash sales

When goods are paid for immediately by cash there is no need to enter these sales in the sales day book. In such cases we do not need to know the names and addresses of customers and what has been sold to them, as we don't need to keep a record of money owing to us.

19.3 Credit sales

In many businesses most of the sales will be made on credit rather than for cash. In fact, the sales of some businesses will consist entirely of credit sales.

For each credit sale the selling firm will send a document to the buyer showing full details of the goods sold and the prices of the goods. This document is known as an **invoice**, and to the seller it is known as a **sales invoice**. The seller will keep one or more copies of each sales invoice for their own use. Exhibit 19.1 is an example of an invoice.

Exhibit 19.1

Your Purchase Order 10/A/980	J Blake 7 Over Warehouse Leicester LE1 2AP
Invoice No: 16554 **INVOICE** To: D Poole 45 Charles Street Manchester M1 5ZN	1 September 1998

Quantity and description	Per unit	Total
	£	£
21 cases McBrand Pears	20	420
5 cartons Kay's Flour	4	20
6 cases Joy's Vinegar	20	120
		560
Terms: 1¼% cash discount if paid within one month		

You must not think that all invoices will look exactly like the one chosen as Exhibit 19.1. Each business will have its own design. All invoices will be numbered, and they will contain the names and addresses both of the supplier and of the customer. In this case the supplier is J Blake and the customer is D Poole.

19.4 Copies of sales invoices

As soon as the sales invoices for the goods being sent have been made out, they are sent to the customer. The selling firm will keep copies of all these sales invoices. These copies will have been made at the same time as the original, usually by some kind of carbon paper or special copying paper.

19.5 Entering credit sales into the sales day book

From the copy of the sales invoice the seller enters up his sales day book. This book is merely a list, showing the following:

- Date of sale
- Name of customer to whom the goods have been sold
- Invoice number
- Final amount of invoice.

There is no need to show details of the goods sold in the sales day book. This can be found by looking at copy invoices.

We can now look at Exhibit 19.2 which is a sales day book, starting with the record of the sales invoice already shown in Exhibit 19.1. Let us assume that the entries are on page 26 of the day book.

Exhibit 19.2

Sales Day Book		
	Invoice No.	(page 26)
1998		£
Sept 1 D Poole	16554	560
8 T Cockburn	16555	1,640
28 C Carter	16556	220
30 D Stevens & Co	16557	1,100
		3,520

19.6 Posting credit sales to the sales ledger

Instead of having one ledger for all accounts, we now have a sales ledger which is used for recording credit sale transactions.

1 The credit sales are now posted, one by one, to the debit side of each customer's account in the sales ledger.

2 At the end of each period the total of the credit sales is posted to the credit of the sales account in the general ledger. You may find it easier to use 'IN' and 'OUT', as we did in Chapter 3, to post these transactions, i.e. the goods sold go 'into' each individual customer's account and they come 'out' of the sales account. This is now illustrated in Exhibit 19.3.

Exhibit 19.3 **Posting Credit Sales**

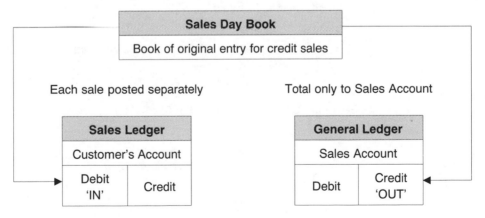

19.7 An example of posting credit sales

The sales day book in Exhibit 19.2 is now shown again. This time posting is made to the sales ledger and the general ledger. Notice the completion of the folio columns with the reference numbers.

Sales Day Book				
		Invoice No.	Folio	(page 26)
1998				£
Sept 1	D Poole	16554	SL 12	560
8	T Cockburn	16555	SL 39	1,640
28	C Carter	16556	SL 125	220
30	D Stevens & Co	16557	SL 249	1,100
	Transferred to Sales Account		GL 44	3,520

Sales Ledger
D Poole Account
Dr   (page 12)
                                                                                                           Cr

1998			£	
Sept 1	Sales	SJ 26	560	

T Cockburn Account
Dr   (page 39)
                                                                                                           Cr

1998			£	
Sept 8	Sales	SJ 26	1,640	

C Carter Account
Dr   (page 125)
                                                                                                           Cr

1998			£	
Sept 28	Sales	SJ 26	220	

D Stevens & Co Account
Dr   (page 249)
                                                                                                           Cr

1998			£	
Sept 30	Sales	SJ 26	1,100	

General Ledger
Sales Account
Dr   (page 44)
                                                                                                           Cr

		1998		£
		Sept 30	Credit Sales for the month	SJ 26 3,520

Alternative names for the sales day book are sales book and sales journal. Before you continue you should attempt exercise 19.1.

19.8 Trade discounts

Suppose you are the proprietor of a business. You are selling to three different kinds of customers:

1 Traders who buy a lot of goods from you.
2 Traders who buy only a few items from you.
3 Direct to the general public.

The traders themselves have to sell the goods to the general public in their own areas. They have to make a profit, so they will want to pay you less than retail price.

The traders who buy in large quantities will not want to pay as much as traders who buy in small quantities. You want to attract large customers, and so you are happy to sell to them at a lower price.

This means that your selling prices are at three levels: **1** to traders buying large quantities, **2** to traders buying small quantities, and **3** to the general public.

So that your staff do not need three different price lists, all goods are shown on your price lists at the same price. However, a reduction (discount), called a **trade discount** is given to traders **1** and **2**. An example illustrating this is shown in Exhibit 19.4.

Exhibit 19.4

You are selling a make of food mixing machine. The retail price is £200. Traders **1** are given 25 per cent trade discount, traders **2**, 20 per cent and the general public pay the full retail price. The prices paid by each type of customer would be:

		Trader 1 £		Trader 2 £	General Public 3 £
Retail price		200		200	200
Less Trade discount	(25%)	50	(20%)	40	nil
Price to be paid by customer		150		160	200

Exhibit 19.5 is an invoice for goods sold to D Poole. It is for the same items as were shown in Exhibit 19.1, but this time the seller is R Grant and he uses trade discounts to get the price down to that paid by his customers.

Exhibit 19.5

Your Purchase Order 11/A/G80		R Grant
		Higher Side
		Preston PR1 2NL
Invoice No: 30756	**INVOICE**	2 September 1998
To: D Poole & Co		Tel (01703) 33122
45 Charles Street		Fax (01703) 22331
Manchester M1 5ZN		

Quantity and description	Per unit	Total
	£	£
21 cases McBrand Pears	25	525
5 cartons Kay's Flour	5	25
6 cases Joy's Vinegar	25	150
		700
Less 20% Trade discount		140
		560

By comparing Exhibits 19.1 and 19.5 you can see that the prices paid by D Poole were the same. It is simply the method of calculating the price that is different.

19.9 No double entry for trade discounts

As trade discount is simply a way of calculating sales prices, no entry for trade discount should be made in the double entry records nor in the sales day book. The recording of Exhibit 19.5 in R Grant's Sales Day Book and D Poole's personal account will appear:

Sales Day Book				
		Invoice No	Folio	(page 87)
1998				
Sept 2	D Poole	30756	SL 32	560

Sales Ledger *(page 32)*
D Poole Account

Dr						Cr
1998				£		
Sept 2	Sales	SJ 87	560			

To compare with cash discounts:
Trade discounts: not shown in double entry accounts.
Cash discounts: are shown in double entry accounts.

19.10 Other documentation

Each firm will have its own system of making out documents. All but the very smallest organisations will have their documents prepared via the computer.

The sales invoice is the document from which the book-keeping records are prepared. There will usually be several other documents prepared at the same time, so that the firm may properly organise the sending of the goods and ensuring that they are safely received.

These extra documents may be as follows:

1 **Advice notes.** These will be sent to the customer before the goods are dispatched. This means that the customer will know that the goods are on the way and when they should arrive. If the goods do not arrive within a reasonable time then the customer will notify the seller, so that enquiries may be made with the carrier to establish what has happened to the goods.

The document will look something like that shown in Exhibit 19.6. Compare it with the invoice sent out as Exhibit 19.5

Exhibit 19.6

ADVICE NOTE	**R GRANT**	No 178554
	Higher Side	
30 August 1998	**Preston**	Tel (01703) 33122
	PR1 2NL	Fax (01703) 22331
J Jones, Head Buyer		
D Poole & Co		
45 Charles Street		
Manchester M1 5ZN		

Your order No 11/A/G80
Despatch details: 27 cases and 5 cartons

Quantity	Cat No	Description	Price
21 cases	M566	McBrand Pears	£25 each
5 cartons	K776	Kay's Flour	£5 each
6 cases	J865	Joy's Vinegar	£25 each
			All less 20%

Delivery to:
   D Poole & Co, Warehouse 2,
   Longmills Trading Estate, Manchester M14 2TT

2 **Delivery note**. When the goods are sent out they usually have a delivery note to accompany them. This means that the customer can check immediately, and easily, what goods are being received. Very often a copy will be retained by the carrier, with the customer having to sign to say that they have received the goods as stated on the note.

In connection with the goods shown on the advice note in Exhibit 19.6 a delivery note may appear as in Exhibit 19.7.

Exhibit 19.7

DELIVERY NOTE	No 194431

R GRANT   Tel (01703) 33122
Higher Side   Fax (01703) 22331
Preston
PR1 2NL

1 September 1998

J Jones, Head Buyer
D Poole & Co
45 Charles Street
Manchester M1 5ZN

Order No 11/A/G80
Despatch details: 27 cases, 5 cartons by road

Quantity	*Cat No*	*Details*
21 cases	M566	McBrand Pears
5 cartons	K776	Kay's Flour
6 cases	J865	Joy's Vinegar

Delivery to: Warehouse 2, Longmills Trading Estate, Manchester M14 2TT

Received 27 cases and 5 cartons

Signed   ....

On behalf of   ....

3 **Other documents**. Each firm may vary in the type and number of documents used. Some of the other documents may be:

- *Despatch notes.* These will resemble the delivery notes, and are used by the despatch department.
- *Acknowledgement letters.* These may be sent to customers to show that their orders have been received, and whether delivery may be made as per the order.

19.11 Manufacturer's recommended retail price

Looking at an item displayed in a shop window, you will frequently see something like the following:

Automatic Washer:	Manufacturer's Recommended Retail Price	£500
	Less discount of 20 per cent	£100
	You pay only	£400

Very often the manufacturer's recommended retail price is a figure above what the manufacturer would expect the public to pay for its product. Probably, in the case shown the manufacturer would have expected the public to pay around £400 for its product.

The inflated figure used for the 'manufacturer's recommended retail price' is simply a sales gimmick. Most people like to feel they are getting a bargain. The salesmen know that someone usually would prefer to get '20 per cent discount' and pay £400, rather than the price simply be shown as £400 with no mention of a discount.

19.12 Credit control

Any organisation which sells goods on credit should keep a close check to ensure that debtors pay their accounts on time. If this is not done properly, the amount of debtors can grow to an amount that will cripple the business.

The following procedures should be carried out:

1 For each debtor a limit should be set and the debtor should not be allowed to owe more than this limit. The amount of the limit will depend on the circumstances. Such things as the size of the customer's firm and the amount of business done with it, as well as its past record of payments, will help in choosing the limit figure.
2 As soon as the payment date has been reached check to see whether payment has been made or not. Failure to pay on time may mean you refusing to supply any more goods unless payment is made quickly.
3 Where payment is not forthcoming, after investigation it may be necessary to take legal action to sue the customer for the debt. This will depend on the circumstances.
4 It is important that the customer is aware of what will happen if they do not pay their account by the due date.

New terms

Advice note (p 183): A note sent to a customer by the supplier prior to goods being despatched, advising them of the goods to be despatched and the estimated date of delivery.

Delivery note (p 183): A note which accompanies goods being despatched, enabling the customer to check what goods have been received. The carrier often retains a copy and asks the customer to sign this to verify that the customer has received the goods.

Sales invoice (p 177): A document showing details of goods sold and the prices of those goods.

Trade discount (p 181): A reduction given to a customer when calculating the selling prices of goods.

Exercises

19.1 You are to enter up the sales day book from the following details. Post the items to the relevant accounts in the sales ledger and then show the transfer to the sales account in the general ledger.

1999

Mar	1	Credit sales to J Gordon	£187
Mar	3	Credit sales to G Abrahams	£166
Mar	6	Credit sales to V White	£12
Mar	10	Credit sales to J Gordon	£55
Mar	17	Credit sales to F Williams	£289
Mar	19	Credit sales to U Richards	£66
Mar	27	Credit sales to V Wood	£28
Mar	31	Credit sales to L Simes	£78

19.2X Enter up the sales day book from the following, then post the items to the relevant accounts in the sales ledger. Then show the transfer to the sales account in the general ledger.

1998

May	1	Credit sales to J Johnson	£305
May	3	Credit sales to T Royes	£164
May	5	Credit sales to B Howe	£45
May	7	Credit sales to M Lee	£100
May	16	Credit sales to J Jakes	£308
May	23	Credit sales to A Vinden	£212
May	30	Credit sales to J Samuels	£1,296

19.3 F Benjamin of 10 Lower Street, Plymouth, is selling the following items, the recommended retail prices as shown: white tape £10 per roll, green baize at £4 per metre, blue cotton at £6 per sheet, black silk at £20 per dress length. He makes the following sales:

1999

May 1   To F Gray, 3 Keswick Road, Portsmouth: 3 rolls white tape, 5 sheets blue cotton, 1 dress length black silk. Less 25 per cent trade discount.

May 4   To A Gray, 1 Shilton Road, Preston: 6 rolls white tape, 30 metres green baize. Less 33⅓ per cent trade discount.

May 8   To E Hines, 1 High Road, Malton: 1 dress length black silk. No trade discount.

May 20   To M Allen, 1 Knott Road, Southport: 10 rolls white tape, 6 sheets blue cotton, 3 dress lengths black silk, 11 metres green baize. Less 25 per cent trade discount.

May 31   To B Cooper, 1 Tops Lane, St Andrews: 12 rolls white tape, 14 sheets blue cotton, 9 metres green baize. Less 33⅓ per cent trade discount.

You are to (a) draw up a sales invoice for each of the above sales, (b) enter them up in the sales day book, post to the personal accounts, (c) transfer the total to the sales account in the general ledger.

19.4X J Fisher, White House, Bolton, is selling the following items, the retail prices as shown: plastic tubing at £1 per metre, polythene sheeting at £2 per length, vinyl padding at £5 per box, foam rubber at £3 per sheet. He makes the following sales:

1998

June 1   To A Portsmouth, 5 Rockley Road, Worthing: 22 metres plastic tubing, 6 sheets foam rubber, 4 boxes vinyl padding. Less 25 per cent trade discount.

" 5   To B Butler, 1 Wembley Road, Colwyn Bay: 50 lengths polythene sheeting, 8 boxes vinyl padding, 20 sheets foam rubber. Less 20 per cent trade discount.

" 11   To A Gate, 1 Bristol Road, Hastings: 4 metres plastic tubing, 33 lengths of polythene sheeting, 30 sheets foam rubber. Less 25 per cent trade discount.

" 21   To L Mackeson, 5 Maine Road, Bath: 29 metres plastic tubing. No trade discount is given.

" 30   To M Alison, Daley Road, Box Hill: 32 metres plastic tubing, 24 lengths polythene sheeting, 20 boxes vinyl padding. Less 33⅓ per cent trade discount.

Required

(a) Draw up a sales invoice for each of the above sales, (b) then enter up in the sales day book and post to the personal accounts, (c) transfer the total to the sales account in the general ledger.

19.5 James Grafton supplies heating and plumbing materials both to the trade (on credit) and to members of the public on a cash sales basis. Invoices are prepared for both cash and credit sales. Customers are grouped as follows:

	Price Paid
Cash Customers	List
Credit Customers:	
Group A	List less 25% trade discount
B	List less 10% trade discount
C	List less 5% trade discount

At the end of each week, he summarises his sales (cash and credit) and posts the *total* to the sales account in the ledger.

In the week ended 31 January 1999 Grafton made the following sales:

Invoice No	List Price	Customer Category
	£	
1040	80	Cash
1041	420	Credit (A)
1042	30	Cash
1043	860	Credit (A)
1044	110	Credit (B)
1045	1040	Credit (A)
1046	15	Cash
1047	32	Cash
1048	320	Credit (C)
1049	100	Credit (B)

Credit customers are offered 1 per cent of the net invoice value as a cash discount for the settlement of accounts within 30 days of the invoice date.

Required

(a)   In your answer book:

(i)   Enter the above invoices in the sales day book (sales journal) for the week, as follows:

Invoice	List (£)	Trade Discount (£)	Net (£)
1040	80	–	80

(ii)   Show the posting to the sales account in the nominal ledger.

(b)   Invoices 1043 and 1045 were for sales to PH Ltd, Invoice 1043 was settled by cheque within 30 days of the invoice date. Show the Personal Account for Customer PH Ltd.

(LCCI)

19.6   Morridge Products Ltd is a small manufacturing company which makes parts for tractors, farm equipment and general machine parts. In addition to manufacturing, the company also carries out repairs.

As accounts assistant, one of your tasks is to prepare sales invoices and enter the details into the books of account. This involves entering them initially in the sales day book then posting each individual item to the respective debtors accounts in the sales ledger; finally, at the end of the month, post the totals in the day book to the respective accounts in the general ledger.

Required

(a)   From the following details prepare invoices, use the blank forms provided (Fig 19.1) and date them 3 December 1999. VAT is to be calculated at 17½ per cent. The next Invoice No is 0932.

Invoice Details

	Name/Address	Details of Order	Price £	Order No
1	Price, Barlow & Co Hulme End Derbyshire	1 Fork for Fordson tractor	240.00	PB 323
2	Rowley Farmers Dove End Farm Bakewell Derbyshire	Repairs to muckspreader Parts Labour	 73.50 38.00	Via telephone

3	Stoke Engineering Co Ltd
	Blythe End Works
	Stoke-on-Trent
		Machine parts
		    to your specification
		    as per quotation
			
			347.30
				
				64394

4	Peak Manufacturing Co Town End Buxton Derbyshire	6 Tractor Back Boxes as per your drawing Price as quoted (each)	 234.70	K 2314

5	Robinson (Plant Hire)
	Leek
	Staffs
		Repair to JCB arm
		    Parts
		    Labour
			
			125.70
			210.00
				
				R 945

6	Bennetts Farm Machinery
	c/o Holly Bank Farm
	Monyash
	Derbyshire
		Baler modified
		    as per our telephone
		    conversation
		As agreed
			
			220.00
			(inclusive)
				Per
				telephone

Note: All invoices subject to VAT except item 6 which includes VAT.

(b) Enter the sales invoices in the day book and post to the various customer accounts in the sales ledger and finally post the day book totals to the accounts in the general ledger.

(NVQ Level 2)

Fig 19.1 Invoice forms

MORRIDGE PRODUCTS LTD Moor Top Lane Leek		Invoice No:	
	INVOICE	Account No:	
Telephone: 0538 703101 Fax: 0538 703203 VAT Reg No 761 9849 16		Date/Tax point:	

Product code	Description	Quantity	Unit price £ p	Total amount £ p

Comments:		Net total	
		VAT @ 17.5%	
		Total	

Registered office: 16 Brook Lane, Manchester   Registered No: 384 1758

Fig 19.1 *(continued)*

MORRIDGE PRODUCTS LTD		Invoice No:
Moor Top Lane		
Leek	**INVOICE**	Account No:

Telephone: 0538 703101
Fax: 0538 703203
VAT Reg No   761 9849 16

Date/Tax point:

Product code	Description	Quantity	Unit price £ p	Total amount £ p
Comments:		Net total		
		VAT @ 17.5%		
		Total		

Registered office: 16 Brook Lane, Manchester   Registered No: 384 1758

Fig 19.1 *(continued)*

MORRIDGE PRODUCTS LTD	Invoice No:
Moor Top Lane	
Leek **INVOICE**	**Account No:**
Telephone: 0538 703101	
Fax: 0538 703203	
VAT Reg No 761 9849 16	Date/Tax point:

Product code	Description	Quantity	Unit price £ p	Total amount £ p
Comments:		Net total		
		VAT @ 17.5%		
		Total		

Registered office: 16 Brook Lane, Manchester   Registered No: 384 1758

Fig 19.1 *(continued)*

				Invoice No:	
MORRIDGE PRODUCTS LTD					

MORRIDGE PRODUCTS LTD
Moor Top Lane
Leek

INVOICE

Telephone: 0538 703101
Fax: 0538 703203
VAT Reg No   761 9849 16

Invoice No:

Account No:

Date/Tax point:

Product code	Description	Quantity	Unit price £ p	Total amount £ p

Comments:	Net total	
	VAT @ 17.5%	
	Total	

Registered office: 16 Brook Lane, Manchester   Registered No: 384 1758

Fig 19.1 *(continued)*

MORRIDGE PRODUCTS LTD **Moor Top Lane** **Leek** Telephone: 0538 703101 Fax: 0538 703203 VAT Reg No 761 9849 16	**INVOICE**	**Invoice No:** **Account No:** Date/Tax point:		

Product code	Description	Quantity	Unit price £ p	Total amount £ p

Comments:	Net total	
	VAT @ 17.5%	
	Total	

Registered office: 16 Brook Lane, Manchester   Registered No: 384 1758

Fig 19.1 *(continued)*

MORRIDGE PRODUCTS LTD **Moor Top Lane** **Leek** Telephone: 0538 703101 Fax: 0538 703203 VAT Reg No 761 9849 16	**INVOICE**	**Invoice No:** **Account No:** Date/Tax point:		

Product code	*Description*	*Quantity*	*Unit price* £ *p*	*Total amount* £ *p*
Comments:		Net total		
		VAT @ 17.5%		
		Total		

Registered office: 16 Brook Lane, Manchester   Registered No: 384 1758

20 The purchases day book and the purchases ledger

20.1 Purchases invoices

An invoice is a **purchases invoice** when it is entered in the books of the firm purchasing the goods. The same invoice, in the books of the seller, would be a sales invoice. For example, look at Exhibit 19.1:

1 In the books of D Poole: it is a purchases invoice.
2 In the books of J Blake: it is a sales invoice.

20.2 Entering into the purchases day book

From the purchases invoices for goods bought on credit, the purchaser enters the details in his purchases day book. This book is merely a list, showing the following:

- date of purchase
- name of supplier from whom the goods were purchased
- the reference number of the invoice
- final amount of invoice

There is no need to show details of the goods bought in the purchases day book. This can be found by looking at the invoices themselves. Exhibit 20.1 is an example of a purchases day book.

Exhibit 20.1

Purchases Day Book				
		Invoice No	Folio	(page 49)
1998				£
Sept 2	R Simpson	9/101		670
8	B Hamilton	9/102		1,380
19	C Brown	9/103		120
30	K Gabriel	9/104		510
				2,680

20.3 Posting credit purchases to the purchases ledger

We now have a separate purchases ledger. The double entry is as follows:

1   The credit purchases are posted one by one, to the credit of each supplier's account in the purchases ledger.
2   At the end of each period the total of the credit purchases is posted to the debit of the purchases account in the general ledger. Again, you may find it easier to use 'IN' and 'OUT' as discussed in Chapters 3 and 19, i.e. the goods purchased come from each supplier, therefore, their accounts are entered on the 'OUT' side. The total purchases for the period are then entered on the 'IN' side of the purchases account since the goods are coming 'IN' to us. This is now illustrated in Exhibit 20.2.

Exhibit 20.2   **Posting Credit Purchases**

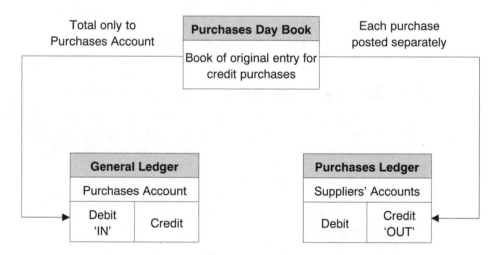

20.4 An example of posting credit purchases

The purchases day book in Exhibit 20.1 is now shown again. This time posting is made to the purchases ledger and the general ledger. Notice the completion of the folio columns.

Purchases Day Book				
		Invoice No	Folio	(page 49)
1998				£
Sept 2	R Simpson	9/101	PL16	670
8	B Hamilton	9/102	PL29	1,380
19	C Brown	9/103	PL55	120
30	K Gabriel	9/104	PL89	510
Transferred to purchases account			GL63	2,680

Purchases Ledger

R Simpson Account *(page 16)*

Dr | | | | | Cr

| | | 1998 | | | £ |
| | | Sept 2 | Purchases | PJ 49 | 670 |

B Hamilton Account *(page 29)*

Dr | | | | | Cr

| | | 1998 | | | £ |
| | | Sept 8 | Purchases | PJ 49 | 1,380 |

C Brown Account *(page 55)*

Dr | | | | | Cr

| | | 1998 | | | £ |
| | | Sept 19 | Purchases | PJ 49 | 120 |

K Gabriel Account *(page 89)*

Dr | | | | | Cr

| | | 1998 | | | £ |
| | | Sept 30 | Purchases | PJ 49 | 510 |

General Ledger

Purchases Account *(page 63)*

Dr | | | | | Cr

1998		£			
Sept 30	Credit purchases				
	for the month				
	PJ 49	2,680			

The purchases day book is often known also as the purchases book or the purchases journal.

New term

> **Purchases invoice** (p 195) A document received by purchaser showing details of goods bought and their prices.

Exercises

20.1   B Mann has the following purchases for the month of May 2000:

2000

May	1	From K King: 4 radios at £30 each, 3 music centres at £160 each. Less 25 per cent trade discount.
May	3	From A Bell: 2 washing machines at £200 each, 5 vacuum cleaners at £60 each, 2 dish dryers at £150 each. Less 20 per cent trade discount.
May	15	From J Kelly: 1 music centre at £300 each, 2 washing machines at £250 each. Less 25 per cent trade discount.
May	20	From B Powell: 6 radios at £70 each, less 33⅓ per cent trade discount.
May	30	From B Lewis: 4 dish dryers at £200 each, less 20 per cent trade discount.

Required

(a)   Enter up the purchases day book for the month.

(b)   Post the transactions to the suppliers' accounts.

(c)   Transfer the total to the purchases account.

20.2X   A Rowland has the following purchases for the month of June 1999:

1999

June	2	From C Lee: 2 sets golf clubs at £250 each, 5 footballs at £20 each. Less 25 per cent trade discount.
June	11	From M Elliott: 6 cricket bats at £20 each, 6 ice skates at £30 each, 4 rugby balls at £25 each. Less 25 per cent trade discount.
June	18	From B Wood: 6 sets golf trophies at £100 each, 4 sets golf clubs at £300 each. Less 33⅓ per cent trade discount.
June	25	From B Parkinson: 5 cricket bats at £40 each. Less 25 per cent trade discount.
June	30	From N Francis: 8 goal posts at £70 each. Less 25 per cent trade discount.

Required

(a)   Enter up the purchases day book for the month.

(b)   Post the items to the suppliers' accounts.

(c)   Transfer the total to the purchases account.

20.3   C Phillips, a sole trader, has the following purchases and sales for March 1998.

1998

Mar	1	Bought from Smith Stores: silk £40, cotton £80, all less 25 per cent trade discount.
Mar	8	Sold to A Grantley: linen goods £28, woollen items £44. No trade discount.
Mar	15	Sold to A Henry: silk £36, linen £144, cotton goods £120. All less 20 per cent trade discount.
Mar	23	Bought from C Kelly: cotton £88, linen £52. All less 25 per cent trade discount.
Mar	24	Sold to D Sangster: linen goods £42, cotton £48. Less 10 per cent trade discount.
Mar	31	Bought from J Hamilton: linen goods £270 less 33⅓ per cent trade discount.

Required

(a)   Prepare the purchases and sales day books of C Phillips from the above.

(b)   Post the items to the personal accounts.

(c)   Post the totals of the day books to the sales and purchases accounts.

20.4 G Bath, a retailer, purchased two items for resale in his shop, one of Product A and one of Product B. The following figures relate to these two items.

	Product A	Product B
Manufacturers' recommended retail price	£1,500	£4,000
Trade discount allowed to retailers	20%	25%

It is G Bath's intention to sell these two products at the recommended retail price.
You are required to:
(a) calculate the price which G Bath will pay for each product;
(b) calculate how much the gross profit will be on each product, if the products are sold at the recommended retail price;
(c) calculate the gross profit as a percentage of cost price for each product.
(Ignore VAT)
(RSA)

20.5X (a) You work in the purchases department of a manufacturing firm, with responsibility for the approval of invoices, prior to settlement by monthly cheque.
   List **five** steps which you would take in the processing of an invoice for approval.
(b) Your firm has received an invoice which shows the catalogue price of a small machine to be £360, subject to a trade discount of 25 per cent and a further 5 per cent cash discount if the invoice is settled within 14 days.

Your firm has purchased three of these machines and pays within seven days of receipt of the invoice. What is the total amount the firm should pay?
(Ignore VAT)
(RSA)

20.6 J Jarvis is a dealer in fancy goods who maintains day books.

4 August	Bought goods from G Mann with a list price of £400, subject to a trade discount of 25%
5 August	Sold goods to B Allen for £240, subject to a cash discount of 5% if paid within 14 days
11 August	Bought goods from B Jollie with a list price of £250, subject to a trade discount of 20% and a cash discount of 5% if paid within 14 days
12 August	Sold goods to G Parker for £360, subject to a cash discount of 10% if paid within 7 days
15 August	Paid cheque to B Jollie for goods bought on 11 August
18 August	Received cheque from G Parker for goods sold on 12 August
21 August	Sold goods to E Todd for £270, less trade discount of 10% and a cash discount of 5% if paid within 7 days
29 August	Paid G Mann a cheque for goods bought on 4 August
31 August	Received cheque from B Allen for goods sold on 5 August

Required
(a) Enter the above transactions in J Jarvis's purchases day book, sales day book and the cash book.
(b) What is trade discount?
(c) Why do traders allow cash discount?
(LCCI)

21 The returns day books

21.1 Returns inwards and credit notes

Sometimes customers return goods to us and we give them an allowance. This might be for reasons such as the following:

- The goods delivered were of the wrong type.
- They were the wrong colour.
- The goods were faulty.
- The customer had bought more than he needed.

Customers might return the goods or agree to keep the goods if an allowance is made to reduce the price of the goods.

In each of these cases a document known as a **credit note** will be sent to the customer, showing the amount of the allowance given by us for the returns or the faulty goods. It is called a credit note because the customer's account will be credited with the amount of the allowance, to show the reduction in the amount they owe. Exhibit 21.1 shows an example of a credit note.

Exhibit 21.1

		R Grant Higher Side Preston PR1 2NL
To:	D Poole 45 Charles Street, Manchester M1 5ZN	8 September 1998

CREDIT NOTE No 9/37

	Per Unit	Total
	£	£
2 cases McBrand Pears	25	50
Less 20% Trade discount		10
		40

To stop them being mistaken for invoices, credit notes are often printed in red.

21.2 Returns inwards day book

The credit notes are listed in a returns inwards day book. This is then used for posting the items, as follows:

1 Sales ledger. Credit the amount of credit notes, one by one, to the accounts of the customers in the sales ledger.
2 General ledger. At the end of the period the total of the returns inwards day book is posted to the debit of the returns inwards account.

Again, you may find it easier to use 'IN' and 'OUT' as discussed previously, i.e. goods returned to us are entered on the 'IN' side of the returns inwards account since the goods are coming 'IN' to us, and on the 'OUT' side of the individual customers' accounts.

21.3 Example of a returns inwards day book

An example of a returns inwards day book showing the items posted to the sales ledger and the general ledger is now shown:

Returns Inwards Day Book			
	Note No	Folio	(page 10)
1998			£
Sept 2 D Poole	9/37	SL 12	40
17 A Brewster	9/38	SL 58	120
19 C Vickers	9/39	SL 99	290
29 M Nelson	9/40	SL 112	160
Transferred to returns inwards account		GL 114	610

Sales Ledger
D Poole Account (page 12)

Dr				Cr
	1998			£
	Sept 8	Returns inwards	RI 10	40

A Brewster Account (page 58)

Dr				Cr
	1998			£
	Sept 17	Returns inwards	RI 10	120

C Vickers Account (page 99)

Dr   Cr

	1998 £
	Sept 19 Returns
	inwards RI 10 290

M Nelson Account (page 112)

Dr   Cr

	1998 £
	Sept 29 Returns
	inwards RI 10 160

General Ledger

Returns Inwards Account (page 114)

Dr   Cr

1998 £	
Sept 30 Returns for	
the month RI 10 610	

Alternative names in use for the returns inwards day book are returns inwards journal or sales returns book.

21.4 Returns outwards and debit notes

If the supplier agrees, goods bought previously may be returned. When this happens a **debit note** is sent to the supplier giving details of the goods and the reason for their return.

Also, an allowance might be given by the supplier for any faults in the goods. Here also, a debit note should be sent to the supplier. Exhibit 21.2 shows an example of a debit note.

Exhibit 21.2

	R. Grant Higher Side Preston PR1 2NL
To: B Hamilton 20 Fourth Street Kidderminster KD2 4PP	11 September 1998

DEBIT NOTE No 9/34

	Per Unit	Total
	£	£
4 cases	60	240
Less 25% Trade discount		60
		180

21.5 Returns outwards day book

The debit notes are listed in a returns outwards day book. This is then used for posting the items, as follows:

1   Purchases ledger. Debit the amounts of debit notes, one by one, to the accounts of the suppliers in the purchases ledger.
2   General ledger. At the end of the period, the total of the returns outwards day book is posted to the credit of the returns outwards account.

Using 'IN' and 'OUT' the entries would be as follows: the goods returned by us to the supplier go 'IN' to the suppliers' accounts and come 'OUT' of the returns outwards account.

21.6 Example of a returns outwards day book

An example of a returns outwards day book, showing the items posted to the purchases ledger and the general ledger, is now shown.

Returns Outwards Day Book				
		Note No	Folio	*(page 7)*
1998				£
Sept 11	B Hamilton	9/34	PL 29	180
16	B Rose	9/35	PL 46	100
28	C Blake	9/36	PL 55	30
30	S Saunders	9/37	PL 87	360
Transferred to returns outwards account			GL 116	670

Purchases Ledger

B Hamilton Account   *(page 29)*

Dr   Cr

1998			£	
Sept	11	Returns		
		outwards	RO 7	180

B Rose Account   *(page 46)*

Dr   Cr

1998			£	
Sept	16	Returns		
		outwards	RO 7	100

C Blake Account   *(page 55)*

Dr   Cr

1998			£	
Sept	28	Returns		
		outwards	RO 7	30

S Saunders Account   *(page 87)*

Dr   Cr

1998			£	
Sept	30	Returns		
		outwards	RO 7	360

General Ledger

Returns Outwards Account   *(page 116)*

Dr   Cr

		1998			£
		Sept	30	Returns for	
				the month	RO 7	670

Other names in use for the returns outwards day book are returns outwards journal or purchases returns book.

21.7 Double entry and returns

Exhibit 21.3 shows how double entry is made for both returns inwards and returns outwards.

Exhibit 21.3 Posting returns inwards and returns outwards

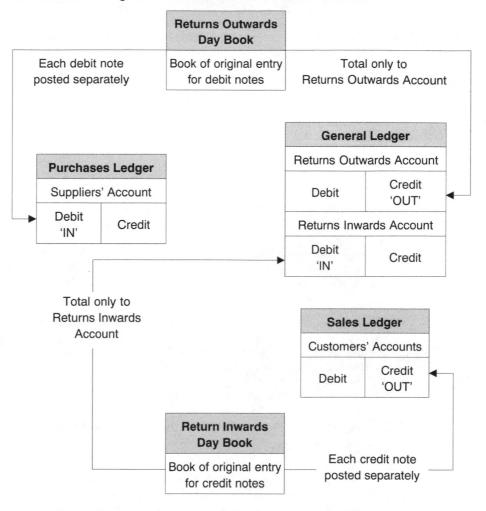

Note: Full coverage of the treatment of returns inwards and returns outwards in the final accounts is shown in Chapter 30: 'Accruals, prepayments and other adjustments'.

New terms

Credit note (p 200): A document sent to a customer showing allowance given by supplier in respect of unsatisfactory goods.
Debit note (p 202): A document sent to a supplier showing allowance given for unsatisfactory goods.

Exercises

21.1 You are to enter up the purchases day book and the returns outwards day book from the following details, then to post the items to the relevant accounts in the purchases ledger and to show the transfers to the general ledger at the end of the month.

1999
May   1   Credit purchase from H Lloyd £119
May   4   Credit purchases from the following: D Scott £98; A Simpson £114;
            A Williams £25; S Wood £56
May   7   Goods returned by us to the following: H Lloyd £16; D Scott £14
May   10   Credit purchase from A Simpson £59
May   18   Credit purchases from the following: M White £89; J Wong £67;
            H Miller £196; H Lewis £119
May   25   Goods returned by us to the following: J Wong £5; A Simpson £11
May   31   Credit purchases from: A Williams £56; C Cooper £98.

21.2X Enter up the sales day book and the returns inwards day book from the following details. Then post to the customer's accounts and show the transfers to the general ledger.

1999
June   1   Credit sales to: A Simes £188; P Tulloch £60; J Flynn £77; B Lopez £88
June   6   Credit sales to: M Howells £114; S Thompson £118; J Flynn £66
June   10   Goods returned to us by: A Simes £12; B Lopez £17
June   20   Credit sales to M Barrow £970
June   24   Goods returned to us by S Thompson £5
June   30   Credit sales to M Parkin £91.

21.3 You are to enter the following items in the books, post to personal accounts, and show transfers to the general ledger:

1999
July   1   Credit purchases from: K Hill £380; M Norman £500; N Senior £106
July   3   Credit sales to: E Rigby £510; E Phillips £246; F Thompson £356
July   5   Credit purchases from: R Morton £200; J Cook £180; D Edwards £410;
            C Davies £66
July   8   Credit sales to: A Green £307; H George £250; J Ferguson £185
July   12   Returns outwards to: M Norman £30; N Senior £16
July   14   Returns inwards from: E Phillips £18; F Thompson £22
July   20   Credit sales to: E Phillips £188; F Powell £310; E Lee £420
July   24   Credit purchases from: C Ferguson £550; K Ennevor £900
July   31   Returns inwards from E Phillips £27; E Rigby £30
July   31   Returns outwards to: J Cook £13; C Davies £11.

21.4X A Whitehead is a manufacturer of handbags. He keeps both a purchases ledger and a sales ledger. On 1 May he owed:

		£
Swade & Co		347
Fittings Ltd		264

Among his credit purchases during the month of May were:

4 May	Fittings Ltd	132
6 May	Swade & Co	202
14 May	Swade & Co	356
20 May	Fittings Ltd	118
26 May	Swade & Co	297
30 May	Swade & Co	145

Goods returned during the month were:

28 May	Swade & Co	28

Payments made during the month were:

10 May	Swade & Co	347
22 May	Fittings Ltd	257
	allowed discount	7

Among his credit sales during the month was:

21 May	Swade & Co	165

On 31 May, the balance of Swade & Co's account in the sales ledger was transferred to Swade & Co's account in the purchases ledger.

Required

Write up the accounts of Swade & Co and Fittings Ltd in Whitehead's ledgers, indicating clearly in which ledger you are entering the account.

Note: The accounts should be set out in three columns:

     Dr   Cr   Balance

(LCCI)

21.5 On 30 September 2000 the trial balance of Maurice Norman was as follows:

	Dr	Cr
	£	£
Capital		9,151
A Birch	4,251	
H Jameson	1,260	
Cash at bank	7,200	
S Franklin		1,780
P Greenbank		670
E Oliver		1,110
	12,711	12,711

The following transactions, as shown in the books of original entry, took place during the month of October 2000.

Sales Day Book				*Purchases Day Book*		
Oct		£		Oct		£
9	A Birch	1,095		8	E Oliver	348
15	H Jameson	740		12	S Franklin	206
19	H Jameson	205		23	E Oliver	1,050

Returns Outwards Day Book				*Returns Inwards Day Book*		
Oct		£		Oct		£
19	S Franklin	80		24	H Jameson	140

Payments Made by Cheque

Oct	To	Discounts received £	Cheque value £
2	P Greenbank	67	603
18	S Franklin	120	1,080
29	E Oliver		1,110

Payments Received by Cheque

Oct	From	Discounts allowed £	Cheque value £
7	A Birch	151	4,100
23	H Jameson		900

You are required to:

(a) open the accounts in the appropriate ledgers for all the above items shown in the trial balance (including Bank) and enter the balances shown as at 30 September 2000;

(b) post the transactions indicated in the books of original entry direct to the appropriate ledger accounts, indicating the sub-divisions of the ledger involved;

(c) balance the personal accounts and bank accounts as at the end of the month.

(RSA)

22 Further considerations regarding sales and purchases

22.1 Statements

At the end of each month a **statement** (or statement of account) should be sent to each debtor who owes money on the last day of each month. It is really a copy of their account in our books. It should show:

1 the amount owing at start of month;
2 the amount of each sales invoice sent to them during the month;
3 the amount of any credit notes sent to them during the month;
4 all cash and cheques received from them during the month;
5 the amount due from them at the end of the month;
6 the date by which payment of the amount owed is due.

The debtor will use this to see if the account in their accounting records agrees with their account in our records. If in our books they are shown as owing £798 then, depending on items in transit between us, their books should show us as a creditor for £798. The statement also acts as a reminder to the debtor that they owe us money.

An example of a statement might be as follows:

STATEMENT OF ACCOUNT

R GRANT
Higher Side
Preston PR1 2NL
Tel (01703) 33122
Fax (01703) 22331

Accounts Dept
D Poole & Co
45 Charles Street
Manchester M1 5ZN

Date	Details	Debit	Credit	Balance
1998		£	£	£
Sept 1	Balance b/f			880
Sept 2	Invoice 30756	560		1,440
Sept 8	Returns 9/37		40	1,400
Sept 25	Bank		880	520
Sept 30	Balance owing c/f			520
All accounts due and payable within 1 month				

22.2 Sales and purchases via credit cards

Various banks, building societies and other financial organisations issue credit cards to their customers. Examples are Visa, Access and American Express. The holder of the credit card purchases items or services without giving cash or cheques, but simply signs a special voucher used by the store or selling organisation. Later on, usually several weeks later, the credit card holder pays the organisation for which they hold the card, e.g. Visa, for all/or part of their previous month's outgoings.

The sellers of the goods or services then present the vouchers to the credit card company and the total of the vouchers less commission is paid to them by that credit card company.

In effect the sales are 'cash sales' for as far as the purchasers are concerned they have seen goods (or obtained services) and have received them, and in their eyes they have paid for them by using their credit card. Such sales are very rarely sales to anyone other than the general public, as compared with sales to professionals in a specific trade.

Once the customer has received the goods or services from the seller, they do not need to be entered in the sales ledger as a debtor. All the selling company is then interested in, from a recording point of view, is collecting the money from the credit card company.

The double entry needed is:

Sale of items via credit cards:	Dr: Credit card company
	Cr: Cash sales
Receipt of money from credit card company:	Dr: Bank
	Cr: Credit card company
Commission charged by credit card company:	Dr: Selling expenses
	Cr: Credit card company

22.3 Internal check

When sales invoices are being made out they should be scrutinised very carefully. A system is usually set up so that each stage of the preparation of the invoice is checked by someone other than the person whose job it is to send out the invoice. If this was not done then it would be possible for someone inside a firm to send out an invoice, as an instance, at a price less than the true price. Any difference could then be split between that person and someone outside the firm. If an invoice should have been sent to Ivor Twister & Co for £2,000, but the invoice clerk made it out deliberately for £200, then, if there was no cross-check, the difference of £1,800 could be split between the invoice clerk and Ivor Twister & Co.

Similarly outside firms could send invoices for goods which were never received by the firm. This might be in collaboration with an employee within the firm, but there are firms sending false invoices which rely on the firms receiving them being inefficient and paying for items never received. There have been firms sending invoices for such items as advertisements which have never been published. The cashier of the firm receiving the invoice, if the firm is an inefficient one, might possibly think that someone in the firm had authorised the advertisements and would pay the bill.

Besides these there are, of course, genuine errors, and these should also be detected. A system is, therefore, set up whereby the invoices have to be subject to scrutiny, at each stage, by someone other than the person who sends out the invoices or is responsible for paying them (refer to section 22.6).

Naturally in a small firm, simply because the office staff might be quite small, this cross-check may be in the hands of only one person other than the person who will pay it. A similar sort of check will be made in respect of sales invoices being sent out.

22.4 Factoring

One of the problems that face many businesses is the time taken by debtors to pay their accounts. Few businesses have so much cash available to them that they do not mind how long the debtor takes to pay. It is a fact that a lot of businesses which become bankrupt do so, not because the business is not making profits, but because the business has run out of cash funds. Once that happens, the confidence factor in business evaporates, and the business then finds that very few people will supply it with goods, and it also cannot pay its employees. Closure of the firm then happens fairly quickly in many cases.

In the case of debtors, the cash problem may be alleviated by using the services of a financial intermediary called a factor.

Factoring is a financial service designed to improve the cash flow of healthy, growing companies, enabling them to make better use of management time and the money tied up in trade credit to customers.

In essence, factors provide their clients with three closely integrated services covering sales accounting and collection, credit management which can include protection against bad debts, and the availability of finance against sales invoices.

22.5 E & OE

On some invoices and other documents you will see the initials 'E & OE' printed at the bottom of the invoice. This abbreviation stands for 'Errors and Omissions Excepted'. Basically, this is a warning that there may possibly be errors or omissions which could mean that the figures shown could be incorrect, and that the recipient should check the figures carefully before taking any action concerning them.

22.6 Authorisation and coding of invoices

1 **Authorisation of purchase invoices**. When purchase invoices are received from various suppliers of goods or services it is important to

check the invoice for accuracy in the calculations and to ensure that the goods invoiced have been received and agree with the purchase order and specifications.

On receipt the purchase invoice should be numbered, recorded and stamped with an appropriate rubber stamp (*see* Exhibit 22.1), to enable the invoice to be checked and coded.

Exhibit 22.1

Invoice no	
Purchase order no	
Goods received	
Extensions	
Passed for payment	
Code	

2 **Coding of invoices**. After stamping, the invoice is sent to the department responsible for ordering the goods, the invoice is checked and if everything is satisfactory it is coded, passed for payment by a department head and returned to the accounts department for entry into the books and payment.

Organisations using computer accounting systems need to give unique numbers to all their various accounts which the computer can easily recognise.

Exhibit 22.2

Purchases Ledger

Suppliers are given account numbers, i.e.:

	Account Number
Blackshaws	0207
Harvey Construction Ltd	0243
Morridge Products	0275
Travis and Humphreys	0284

Sales Ledger

Customers' account numbers may be:

	Account Number
Heath Manufacturing Ltd	1084
Office Supplies Ltd	1095
Seddon & Sons	1098
Yeoman's Supplies	1099

General Ledger

Examples of account codes are as follows:

	Account Number
Capital account	4003
Motor expenses account	4022
Printing and stationery account	4074
Sales account	4098

A register of code numbers allocated to specific accounts must be maintained and updated as necessary. This register may be a manual one or held on the computer system.

New term

Statement (p 209): A copy of a customer's personal account taken from the supplier's books.

Exercise

22.1

STATEMENT

In account with

J Hunt
24 Coventry Road
Nuneaton C4

Mr R J Cook
14 Thorn Street
Derby DE3

			£	£	£	31 March 1999
February	1	Balance			130.42	
"	6	Invoice 512	140.64		271.06	
"	8	Cheque		127.16		
		Discount		3.26	140.64	
"	12	Returns		16.30	124.34	
"	26	Invoice 540	184.42		308.76	
"	28	Undercharge	3.60		312.36	

Study the statement above.

(a) Name the person who is supplying goods.

(b) Explain in simple terms the meaning of each item in the statement from February 1–26 and state the document used for the item on February 28 and the names of the sender and the receiver.

(c) Give the names of the debtor and the creditor and the amount owed on 28 February 1999.

(RSA)

23 Value Added Tax

23.1 Introduction

Value Added Tax (VAT) is a tax on turnover, and not on profits. It is described as an indirect tax, and ultimately the tax is paid by the final consumer of the goods or services. VAT is administered by HM Customs and Excise.

23.2 The scope of VAT

VAT is charged on the supply of most goods or services, by a VAT registered trader. A VAT registered trader may be a sole proprietor, partnership or limited company.

Not all goods and services are subject to VAT. Some goods and services are **zero rated**. This means that VAT is charged at the rate of 0%. Examples of zero-rated supplies are:

Human and animal food
Water and sewerage charges
Books and periodicals
Clothing and footwear for young children

Some goods and services are **exempt** from VAT. This means such supplies are outside the scope of VAT, and VAT cannot be charged. Examples of exempt supplies are:

Financial services
Postal services provided by the post office
Education

It is very important to differentiate between zero-rated and exempt supplies, as we will see later.

23.3 The rate of VAT

The rate of VAT is decided by Parliament in the Finance Acts, passed each year after the budget(s). The rates at the publication of this book were:

All zero rated goods and services	0%
Fuel and Power for domestic or charity use only	5%
All other standard rated supplies	17.5%

The VAT charged *by* a business on its supplies (**outputs**), is called **output VAT**, and is payable by the business to HM Customs and Excise.

The VAT charged *to* a business on its purchases and expenses (**inputs**), is called **input VAT**, and is reclaimable by the business from HM Customs and Excise.

23.4 Example: how the VAT system works

A toymaker manufactures toys from scraps of material and sells them to a wholesaler for £200 plus VAT. The wholesaler sells these toys to a chain of retailers for £300 plus VAT, who in turn retail the toys in their shops for £400 plus VAT.

1   The toymaker accounts for VAT as follows:

	Net (£)	VAT (£) @ 17.5%
Sale of toys	200.00	35.00
Cost	–	–
VAT payable to HMC&E		35.00

2   The wholesaler accounts for VAT as follows:

	Net (£)	VAT (£) @ 17.5%
Sale of toys	300.00	52.50
Cost of toys	200.00	35.00
VAT payable to HMC&E		17.50

3   The retailer accounts for VAT as follows:

	Net (£)	VAT (£) @ 17.5%
Sale of toys	400.00	70.00
Cost of toys	300.00	52.50
VAT payable to HMC&E		17.50

It will be seen that the total output VAT paid to HM Customs and Excise is £70.00, as charged by the retailer to its customers. The VAT, however, has been paid to HM Customs and Excise at various stages in the distribution of the toys as follows:

	£
Toymaker	35.00
Wholesaler	17.50
Retailer	17.50
	70.00

23.5 Zero-rated supplies

In 23.2 we introduced the concept of zero-rated supplies. The important matter to note is that items are charged to VAT at 0 per cent which is a rate of VAT. In some EU countries, supplies which are zero rated in the UK, are charged to VAT at that country's VAT rate.

As the supplies are sold at a rate of VAT, (albeit 0 per cent), any input VAT incurred, relating to the business, can all be reclaimed.

Example 1

A book dealer sells £100,000 worth of books in a year, and during that year, purchases book shelving for £10,000 plus VAT.

The VAT reclaimable is therefore:

	Net (£)	VAT (£) @ 17.5%
Sales	100,000	Nil
Purchases	10,000	1,750
VAT reclaimable		1,750

23.6 Exempt supplies

In 23.2 we introduced the concept of exempt supplies. There are two types of exempt supplies:

1 Supplies of specifically exempted items, examples of which are stated in section 23.2
2 All supplies of goods and services by non-VAT registered businesses, for example:

   (a) Exempt businesses like bank and insurance companies.
   (b) Businesses who do not need to register, as their turnover is below the VAT registration limit.

The important matter to note is that input VAT directly attributable to exempt supplies, or non-VAT registered businesses, cannot be reclaimed from HM Customs and Excise.

Example 2

An insurance company sells £100,000 worth of insurance, and purchases furniture for its office for £10,000 plus VAT.

This business cannot reclaim the £1,750 input VAT on the furniture as it does not have any vatable supplies. The total amount paid for the furniture of £11,750 will be the cost to the business.

Note: Contrast this with the zero-rated supplier in Example 1 above who was able to reclaim £1,750.

23.7 Partly exempt traders

Some VAT registered traders will sell some goods which are exempt from VAT, and some which are either standard rated or zero rated. These businesses may reclaim part of the input VAT paid by them, but not all of it. The rules are complicated, but in essence, the input VAT reclaimable will be proportionate to the standard and zero rated percentage of the business's total turnover.

23.8 Firms which can recover VAT paid

1 Taxable firms

Value Added Tax and sales invoices

A taxable firm will have to add VAT to the value of the sales invoices. It must be pointed out that this is based on the amount of the invoice *after* any trade discount has been deducted. Exhibit 23.1 is an invoice drawn up from the following details:

On 2 March 1998, W Frank & Co, Hayburn Road, Stockport, sold the following goods to R Bainbridge Ltd, 267 Star Road, Colchester: Bainbridge's Order No was A/4/559, for the following items:

220 Rolls T56 Black Tape at £6 per 10 rolls
600 Sheets R64 Polythene at £10 per 100 sheets
7000 Blank Perspex B49 Markers at £20 per 1000

All of these goods are subject to VAT at the rate of 17.5 per cent.
A trade discount of 25 per cent is given by Frank & Co. The sales invoice is numbered 8851.

Exhibit 23.1

	£
W Frank & Co	
Hayburn Road	
Stockport SK2 5DB	
INVOICE No 8851 Date: 2 March 1998	
To: R Bainbridge Your order no A/4/559	
267 Star Road	
Colchester CO1 1BT	
200 Rolls T56 Black Tape @ £6 per 10 rolls	120
600 Sheets R64 Polythene @ £10 per 100 sheets	60
7000 Blank Perspex B49 Markers @ £20 per 1000	140
	320
Less Trade Discount 25%	80
	240
Add VAT 17$\frac{1}{2}$%	42
	282

Where a cash discount is offered for speedy payment, VAT is calculated on an amount represented by the value of the invoice less such a discount. Even if the cash discount is lost because of late payments, the VAT will not change.

The sales day book will normally have an extra column for the VAT contents of the sales invoice (*see* chapter 24). This is needed to make it easier to account for VAT. The entry of several sales invoices in the sales book and in the ledger accounts can now be examined:

W Frank & Co sold the following goods during the month of March 1998:

			Total of invoice, after trade discount deducted but before VAT added	VAT 17.5%
1998			£	£
March	2	R Bainbridge Ltd (*see* Exhibit 23.1)	240	42
March	10	S Lange & Son	200	35
March	17	K Bishop	160	28
March	31	R Andrews & Associates	80	14

Sales Day Book						Page 58
		Invoice No	Folio	Total	Net	VAT
1998				£	£	£
March 2	R Bainbridge Ltd	8851	SL 77	282	240	42
March 10	S Lange & Son	8852	SL 119	235	200	35
March 17	K Bishop	8853	SL 185	188	160	28
March 31	R Andrews & Associates	8854	SL 221	94	80	14
Transferred to General Ledger				799	680	119
					GL 76	GL 90

Now that the sales day book has been written up, the next task is to enter the amounts of the invoices in the individual customer's accounts in the Sales Ledger. These are simply charged with the full amounts of the invoices including VAT.

As an instance of this K Bishop will be shown as owing £188. When he pays his account he will pay £188. It will then be the responsibility of W Frank & Co to ensure that the figure of £28 VAT in respect of this item is included in the total cheque payable to HM Customs and Excise.

Sales Ledger
R Bainbridge Ltd Account

Dr					Cr
				Page 77	
1998			£		
March	2	Sales SB 58	282		

		S Lange & Son Account		Page 119
Dr				*Cr*
1998		£		
March 10	Sales SB 58	235		

		K Bishop Account		Page 185
Dr				*Cr*
1998		£		
March 17	Sales SB 58	188		

		R Andrews & Associates Account		Page 221
Dr				*Cr*
1998		£		
March 31	Sales SB 58	94		

In total, therefore, the personal accounts have been debited with £799, this being the total of the amounts which the customers will have to pay. The actual sales of the firm are not £799, the amount which is actually sales is £680, the other £119 being simply the VAT that W Frank & Co are collecting on behalf of the Government.

The double entry is made in the general ledger:

1   Credit the Sales Account with the sales content only, i.e. £680.
2   Credit the Value Added Tax Account with the VAT content only, i.e. £119.

These are shown as:

General Ledger
Sales Account — Page 76

Dr					*Cr*
		1998			£
		March 31	Credit Sales		
			for the month	SB 58	680

Value Added Tax Account — Page 90

Dr					*Cr*
		1998			£
		March 31	Sales Book:		
			VAT content	SB58	119

Value Added Tax and purchases

In the case of a taxable firm, the firm will have to add VAT to its sales invoices, but it will *also* be able to get a refund of the VAT which it pays on its purchases.

Instead of paying VAT to HM Customs and Excise and then claiming a refund of the VAT on purchases, the firm can set off the amount paid as VAT on purchases against the amount payable as VAT on sales. This means that only the difference has to be paid to HM Customs and Excise. It is shown as:

		£
(a)	Output VAT collected on sales invoices	xxx
(b)	Less Input VAT already paid on purchases	xxx
(c)	Net amount to be paid to HM Customs and Excise	xxx

In certain fairly rare circumstances (a) may be less than (b). If that was the case then it would be HM Customs and Excise that would refund the difference (c) to the firm. Such a settlement between the firm and HM Customs and Excise will take place at least every three months.

The recording of purchases in the purchases day book and purchases ledger follows a similar method to that of sales, but with the personal accounts being debited instead of credited. We can now look at the records of purchases for the same firm whose sales have been dealt with, W Frank & Co. The firm made the following purchases for March 1998.

			Total invoice, after trade discount deducted but before VAT added	VAT 17.5%
1998			£	£
March	1	E Lyal Ltd (*see* Exhibit 23.2)	200	35
March	11	P Portsmouth & Co	280	49
March	24	J Davidson	40	7
March	29	B Cofie & Son Ltd	80	14

Before looking at the recording of these in the Purchases Records, compare the first entry for E Lyal Ltd with Exhibit 23.2 to ensure that the correct amounts have been shown.

Exhibit 23.2

E Lyal Ltd
College Avenue
St Albans
Hertfordshire ST2 4JA

INVOICE No K 453/A

Date: 1/3/1998
Your order no BB/667

To: W Frank & Co   Terms: Strictly net 30 days
     Hayburn Road
     Stockport

	£
50 metres of BYC plastic 1 metre wide × £3.60 per metre	180
1200 metal tags 500mm x 10p each	120
	300
Less Trade Discount at 33$\frac{1}{3}$%	100
	200
Add VAT 17$\frac{1}{2}$%	35
	235

The purchases day book can now be entered up.

Purchases Day Book				Page 38
	Folio	Total	Net	VAT
1998	£	£	£	£
March 1 E Lyal Ltd	PL 15	235	200	35
March 11 P Portsmouth & Co	PL 70	329	280	49
March 24 J Davidson	PL 114	47	40	7
March 29 B Cofie & Son Ltd	PL 166	94	80	14
Transferred to General Ledger		705	GL54 600	GL90 105

These are entered in the purchases ledger. Once again there is no need for the VAT to be shown as separate amounts in the accounts of the suppliers.

Purchases Ledger
E Lyal Ltd Account   *Page 15*

Dr   Cr

	1998			£
	March 1 Purchases	PB 38	235

P Portsmouth & Co Account   Page 70
Dr   Cr

	1998		£
	March 11 Purchases PB 38		329

J Davidson Account   Page 114
Dr   Cr

	1998		£
	March 24 Purchases PB 38		47

B Cofie & Son Ltd Account   Page 166
Dr   Cr

	1998		£
	March 29 Purchases PB 38		94

The personal accounts have been credited with a total of £705, this being the total of the amounts which W Frank & Co will have to pay to them.

The actual cost of purchases is not however, £705. You can see that the correct amount is £600. The other £105 is the VAT which the various firms are collecting for HM Customs and Excise. This amount is also the figure for VAT which is reclaimable from HM Customs and Excise by W Frank & Co. The debit entry in the Purchases account is, therefore, £600, as this is the actual cost of the goods to the firm. The other £105 is entered on the debit side of the VAT account.

Notice that there is already a credit of £119 in the VAT account in respect of the VAT added to sales.

General Ledger
Purchases Account   Page 54
Dr   Cr

1998		£	
March 31	Credit Purchases for the month	600	

Value Added Tax Account   Page 90
Dr   Cr

		£			£
1998			1998		
March 31	Purchases Day Book: VAT content PB 38	105	March 31	Sales Day Book: VAT content SB 58	119
March 31	Balance c/d	14			
		119			119
			April 1	Balance b/d	14

In the final accounts of W Frank & Co, the following entries would be made:

Trading Account for the month ended 31 March 1998:
  Debited with £600 as a transfer from the Purchases Account
  Credited with £680 as a transfer from the Sales Account

Balance Sheet as at 31 March 1998:
  Balance of £14 (credit) on the VAT account would be shown as a current liability, as it represents the amount owing to HM Customs and Excise for VAT.

2 Zero-rated firms

These firms:

(a) Do not have to add VAT on to their sales invoices, as their rate of VAT is zero or nil.
(b) They can, however, reclaim from HM Customs and Excise any VAT paid on goods or services bought.

Accordingly, because of (a) no VAT is entered in the Sales Day Book. VAT on sales does not exist. Because of (b) the Purchases Day Book and Purchases Ledger will appear exactly in the same manner as for taxable firms, as already shown in the case of W Frank & Co.

The VAT account will only have debits in it, being the VAT on Purchases. Any balance on this account will be shown in the Balance Sheet as a debtor.

23.9 Firms which cannot get refunds of VAT paid

As these firms do not add VAT on to the value of their sales invoices, there is obviously no entry for VAT in the Sales Day Book or the Sales Ledger. They do not get a refund of VAT on purchases. This means that there will not be a VAT account. All that will happen is that VAT paid is included as part of the cost of the goods bought.

In the Purchases Day Book, goods bought for £80 + VAT £14 will simply appear as Purchases £94. The double entry will show a credit of £94 in the supplier's account.

Both the Sales and Purchases records will, therefore, not show anything separately for VAT. For comparison let us look at the accounting records of two firms for an item which costs £120 + VAT £21, the item being bought from D Oswald Ltd. The records for the month of May 1998 would appear as follows:

1 Firm which cannot recover VAT:

Purchases Day Book

1998		£
May 16 D Oswald Ltd		141

Purchases Ledger
D Oswald Ltd Account

Dr		Cr
	1998	£
	May 16 D Oswald Ltd	141

General Ledger
Purchases Account

Dr			Cr
1998	£	1998	£
May 31 Credit Purchases for the month	141	May 31 Transfer to Trading Account	141

Trading Account for the month ended 31 May 1998 (extract)

	£	
Purchases	141	

2   Firm which can recover VAT (e.g. zero-rated firm):

Purchases Day Book

	Net	VAT
1998	£	£
May 16 D Oswald Ltd	120	21

Purchases Ledger
D Oswald Ltd Account

Dr		Cr
	1998	£
	May 16 Purchases	141

General Ledger
Purchases Account

Dr			Cr
1998	£	1998	£
May 31 Credit Purchases for the month	120	May 31 Transfer to Trading Account	120

Value Added Tax Account

Dr			Cr
1998	£		
May 31 Purchases Book	21		

Trading Account for the month ended 31 May 1998 (extract)

	£
Purchases	120

Balance Sheet as at 31 May 1998 (extract)

	£
Debtor	21

23.10 VAT included in gross amount

You will often know only the gross amount of an item, this figure will be made up of the net amount plus VAT. To find the amount of VAT which has been added to the net amount, a formula capable of being used with any rate of VAT is:

$$\frac{\% \text{ rate of VAT}}{100 + \% \text{ Rate of VAT}} \times \text{Gross Amount} = \text{VAT in £}$$

Suppose that the gross amount of sales was £940 and the rate of VAT was 17.5 per cent. Find the amount of VAT and the net amount before VAT was added. Using the formula:

$$\frac{17.5}{100 + 17.5} \times £940 = \frac{17.5}{117.5} \times £940 = £140.$$

Therefore, the net amount was £800, which with VAT £140 added, becomes £940 gross.

23.11 VAT on items other than sales and purchases

VAT is not just paid on purchases. It is also payable on many items of expense and on the purchase of fixed assets.

Firms which *can* get refunds of VAT paid will not include VAT as part of the cost of the expense or fixed asset. Firms which *cannot* get refunds of VAT paid will include the VAT cost as part of the expense or fixed asset. For example, two firms buying similar items would treat the following items as shown:

	Firm which can reclaim VAT		Firm which cannot reclaim VAT	
Buys Machinery £200 + VAT £35	Debit Machinery	£200	Debit Machinery	£235
	Debit VAT Account	£35		
Buys Stationery £160 + VAT £28	Debit Stationery	£160	Debit Stationery	£188
	Debit VAT Account	£28		

23.12 VAT owing

VAT owing by or to the firm can be included with debtors or creditors, as the case may be. There is no need to show the amount(s) owing as separate items.

New terms

Exempted firms (p 216): Firms which do not have to add VAT to the price of goods and services supplied by them and which cannot obtain a refund of VAT paid on goods and services purchased by them.

Inputs (p 215): The value of goods and services purchased by a business.

Input tax (p 215): The VAT charged to a business on its purchases and expenses (inputs).

Outputs (p 215): The value of goods and services sold to a business.

Output tax (p 215): The VAT charged *by* a business on its supplies (outputs).

Value Added Tax (VAT) (p 215): A tax charged on the supply of most goods and services. The tax is borne by the final consumer of the goods or services, not by the business selling them to the consumer. VAT is administered by HM Customs and Excise.

Zero-rated firm (p 223): Firms which do not have to add VAT to goods and services supplied by them, to others, and which receive a refund of VAT paid on goods and services purchased by them.

Exercises

23.1 On 1 May 1998, D Wilson Ltd, 1 Hawk Green Road, Stockport, sold the following goods on credit to G Christie & Son, The Golf Shop, Hole-in-One Lane, Marple, Cheshire:

Order No. A/496
3 sets of 'Boy Michael' golf clubs at £240 per set.
150 Watson golf balls at £8 per 10 balls.
4 Faldo golf bags at £30 per bag.
Trade discount is given at the rate of $33\frac{1}{3}\%$.
All goods are subject to VAT at 17.5%.

(a) Prepare the Sales Invoice to be sent to G Christie & Son. The invoice number will be 10586.

(b) Show the entries in the Personal Ledgers of D Wilson Ltd and G Christie & Son.

23.2 The following sales have been made by S Thompson Ltd during the month of June 1997. All the figures are shown net after deducting trade discount, but before adding VAT at the rate of 17.5 per cent.

1997
August	1	to M Sinclair & Co	£160
"	8	to M Brown & Associates	£240
"	19	to A Axton Ltd	£80
"	31	to T Christie	£40

You are required to enter up the sales day book, sales ledger and general ledger in respect of the above items for the month.

23.3 The following sales and purchases were made by R Colman Ltd during the month of May 1998.

				Net	VAT added
1998				£	£
May	1	Sold goods on credit to B Davies & Co		160	28
"	4	Sold goods on credit to C Grant Ltd		200	35
"	10	Bought goods on credit from:			
		G Cooper & Son		400	70
		J Wayne Ltd		240	42
"	14	Bought goods on credit from B Lugosi		40	7
"	16	Sold goods on credit to C Grant Ltd		120	21
"	23	Bought goods on credit from S Hayward		40	7
"	31	Sold goods on credit to B Karloff		80	14

Enter up the sales and purchases day books, sales and purchases ledgers and the general ledger for the month of May 1998. Carry the balance down on the VAT account.

23.4X On 1 March 1998 C Black, Curzon Road, Stockport, sold the following goods on credit to J Booth, 89 Andrew Lane, Stockport. Order No 1697.

20,000 Coils Sealing Tape @ £4.70 per 1,000 coils
40,000 Sheets Bank A5 @ £4.50 per 1,000 sheets
30,000 Sheets Bank A4 @ £4.20 per 1,000 sheets
All goods are subject to VAT at 17.5%.

(a) Prepare the sales invoice to be sent to J Booth.
(b) Show the entries in the personal ledgers of J Booth and C Black.

23.5 C Emberson, a sole trader, buys and sells goods on credit. A bank account is kept through which all amounts received and paid are entered. On 30 November 1998 the following balances remain in the books:

	£	£
C Hills		154
L Lowe		275
K Harris	330	
Bank	740	
Capital		641
	1,070	1,070

You are required to:
(a) open appropriate ledger accounts for the above and enter the balances as at 1 December 1998;
(b) post the transactions indicated in the day books direct to the ledger and open any other accounts which may be required;
(c) balance the accounts where necessary and extract a trial balance on 31 December 1998.

Purchases Day Book				Sales Day Book				
December		NET	VAT	TOTAL	December	NET	VAT	TOTAL
13	C Hills	80	14	94	11 K Harris	240	42	282
20	C Hills	160	28	188	15 K Harris	80	14	94
21	L Lowe	40	7	47				
		280	49	329		320	56	376

Payments Received			Payments Made		
December		£	December		£
16	K Harris	612	8	C Hills	154
			15	Printing	20

(RSA)

23.6X At 1 February 1998 K Murphy's debtors included D Hanson £103.30 and P Newbury £48.60. His creditors included E Goodman £178.20. The balance on Murphy's Value Added Tax account was £237.14 credit. During February his credit transactions with those named above were as follows:

		Sales					Purchases	
Feb	4	P Newbury	£217.10		Feb	6	E Goodman	£83.00
Feb	20	D Hanson	£133.50					

All of these transactions were subject to Value Added Tax at 17.5 per cent. In the bank account in Murphy's books were recorded the following:

		Debit					Credit	
Feb	8	P Newbury	£48.60		Feb	10	E Goodman	£178.20

You are required to write up in the books of Murphy the accounts of Hanson, Newbury and Goodman, and the VAT account, all for the month of February 1998
(RSA)

23.7 The following is a summary of purchases and sales and the relevant figures for VAT for the three months ended 31 March 1998.

Purchases			VAT
		£	£
1998	January	20,000	3,500
	February	21,000	3,675
	March	22,000	3,850
Sales			
	January	21,000	3,675
	February	20,000	3,500
	March	15,000	2,625

Required
(a) Write up and balance the VAT account for the three months to 31 March 1998.
(b) Explain briefly the significance of the balance and how it will be cleared.
(RSA)

24 Columnar sales and purchases day books

24.1 Introduction

In Chapters 19 and 20 the sales and purchases day books were shown using only one total column for the value of the goods sold or purchased. Sometimes goods are subject to VAT, as discussed in Chapter 23. Here you will have noticed that additional columns were used to take account of the VAT, as shown in the Sales Day Book Exhibit 23.1 and the Purchases Day Book in Exhibit 23.2.

In addition to accounting for VAT many businesses find it useful to analyse their sales and purchases between different types of goods bought and sold or perhaps between different departments. For example a coffee shop may sell refreshments and gifts and wish to ascertain the profit on the two different sales areas. In this example it would be advantageous to analyse both sales and purchases to reflect the goods/services bought or sold in each area. The purchases day book could be ruled as follows:

Purchases Day Book						
Date	Details	Folio	Total	Gifts	Food	VAT
			£	£	£	£

24.2 Entering sales invoices into a columnar sales day book

When a business requires additional information from its records then the books can easily be adapted to meet the particular needs.

Let us consider a retail computer shop which sells hardware and software to the public, local businesses and schools.

The proprietor, Mr Harlow, wishes to monitor the sales of each of these lines separately.

Exhibit 24.1 shows an example of Mr Harlow's **columnar sales day book**.

Exhibit 24.1

	Sales Day Book					
Date	*Details*	*Folio*	*Total*	*Software*	*Hardware*	*VAT*
			£	£	£	£
April 1	Mount Hey School	SL1	705		600	105
3	Ashby Marketing	SL2	564	480		84
15	Davenport Manufacturing	SL3	4,700		4,000	700
20	St James College	SL4	23,500		20,000	3,500
			29,469	480	24,600	4,389
				GL1	GL2	GL3

24.3 Posting credit sales

Each sale now has to be posted to the individual debtors accounts in the sales ledger as follows:

1   The total of each sales invoice (i.e. the net price of the goods plus VAT) is posted to each individual debtors account on the debit side, since the goods are going 'into' their account.
2   At the end of the period the sales day book is added up and the totals posted on the credit side, or 'OUT' side of the following accounts:

- Sales of software account
- Sales of hardware account
- VAT account.

Exhibit 24.2   **Posting credit sales**

Sales Ledger
Mount Hey School Account   SL 1

Dr				Cr
		£		
April	1 Sales	705		

Ashby Marketing Co Account   SL 2

Dr				Cr
		£		
April	3 Sales	564		

Exhibit 24.2 *(continued)*

	Davenport Manufacturing Co Account	SL 3
Dr		Cr

	£
April 15 Sales	4,700

	St James College Account	SL 4
Dr		Cr

	£
April 22 Sales	23,500

General Ledger

	Sale of Software Account	GL 1
Dr		Cr

		£
	April 30 Credit sales for April	480

	Sale of Hardware Account	GL 2
Dr		Cr

		£
	April 30 Credit sales for April	24,600

	VAT Account	GL 3
Dr		Cr

		£
	April 30 VAT on credit sales for April	4,389

24.4 Entering purchase invoices into a columnar purchases day book

Another business might wish to monitor its purchases which may include the purchase of goods for resale and business expenses such as electricity, motor expenses etc.

The following example illustrates how a business would analyse its purchase invoices.

Exhibit 24.3

Purchases Day Book							
Date	Details	Folio	Total	Goods	Motor Exp	Stationery	VAT
			£	£	£	£	£
Nov 1	Bould & Co	PL1	4,230	3,600			630
10	Sigley's (Stat)	PL2	47			40	7
17	T Adams Ltd	PL3	940	800			140
30	Robinson's Garage	PL4	188		160		28
			5,405	4,400	160	40	805
				GL 1	GL 2	GL 3	GL 3

24.5 Posting credit purchases

Each purchase now has to be posted to the individual creditors accounts in the purchase ledger as follows:

1 The *total* of each purchase invoice (i.e. the net price of the goods plus VAT) is posted to each individual creditor's account on the *Credit* side, since the goods are coming 'OUT' of their accounts.
2 At the end of the period the purchases day book is added up and the totals posted on the *Debit* side, or 'IN' side of the following accounts:

- Purchases account
- Motor expenses account
- Stationery account
- VAT account.

Exhibit 24.4 **Posting credit purchases/expenses**

Purchases Ledger

Bould & Co Account   *PL 1*

Dr				Cr
				£
	Nov	1	Purchases	4,230

Sigley's Stationers Account   *PL 2*

Dr				Cr
				£
	Nov	10	Purchases	47

Exhibit 24.4 (continued)

<table>
<tr><td>Dr</td><td colspan="2" style="text-align:center">*T Adams Ltd Account*</td><td style="text-align:right">PL 3
Cr</td></tr>
<tr><td></td><td></td><td></td><td style="text-align:right">£</td></tr>
<tr><td></td><td>Nov   17</td><td>Purchases</td><td style="text-align:right">940</td></tr>
</table>

<table>
<tr><td>Dr</td><td colspan="2" style="text-align:center">*Robinson's Garage Account*</td><td style="text-align:right">PL 4
Cr</td></tr>
<tr><td></td><td></td><td></td><td style="text-align:right">£</td></tr>
<tr><td></td><td>Nov   30</td><td>Purchases</td><td style="text-align:right">188</td></tr>
</table>

General Ledger

<table>
<tr><td>Dr</td><td colspan="2" style="text-align:center">*Purchases Account*</td><td style="text-align:right">GL 1
Cr</td></tr>
<tr><td></td><td></td><td style="text-align:right">£</td><td></td></tr>
<tr><td>Nov   30</td><td>Credit purchases
for November</td><td style="text-align:right">4,400</td><td></td></tr>
</table>

<table>
<tr><td>Dr</td><td colspan="2" style="text-align:center">*Motor Expenses Account*</td><td style="text-align:right">GL 2
Cr</td></tr>
<tr><td></td><td></td><td style="text-align:right">£</td><td></td></tr>
<tr><td>Nov   30</td><td>Purchases
day book</td><td style="text-align:right">160</td><td></td></tr>
</table>

<table>
<tr><td>Dr</td><td colspan="2" style="text-align:center">*Stationery Account*</td><td style="text-align:right">GL 3
Cr</td></tr>
<tr><td></td><td></td><td style="text-align:right">£</td><td></td></tr>
<tr><td>Nov   30</td><td>Purchases
day book</td><td style="text-align:right">40</td><td></td></tr>
</table>

<table>
<tr><td>Dr</td><td colspan="2" style="text-align:center">*VAT Account*</td><td style="text-align:right">GL 4
Cr</td></tr>
<tr><td></td><td></td><td style="text-align:right">£</td><td></td></tr>
<tr><td>Nov   30</td><td>Purchases
day book</td><td style="text-align:right">805</td><td></td></tr>
</table>

New term

Columnar day books (p 229): Book of original entry in which invoices are entered. The book has various analysis columns which are totalled at the end of the month and posted to the general ledger and control accounts.

Exercises

24.1 The Curtain Design Company sells both ready-made and custom-made curtains to local hotels, nursing homes and the public.

It operates a columnar sales day book where it analyses the sales into sales of ready-made curtains and custom-made curtains.

The following invoices were sent during November 1998:

Date	Customer	Ready-made £	Custom-made £
Nov 1	Jarvis Arms Hotel		2,300
Nov 8	Springs Nursing Home	1,000	
Nov 15	J P Morten	220	
Nov 17	Queen's Hotel		1,500
Nov 30	W Blackshaw	90	

All goods are subject to VAT at 17.5%.

You are required to:
(a) Record the above transactions in a columnar sales day book;
(b) Post the invoices to the personal accounts in the sales ledger;
(c) Post the totals to the appropriate accounts in the general ledger.

24.2 The Hall Engineering Company manufactures small engineering components for the motor car industry. It operates a columnar purchases day book in which the purchases invoices are recorded.

During May 1998 the following invoices were received:

			£
May 1	Black's Engineering Co	Engineering goods	520
May 3	Ace Printing Co	Printing catalogues	145
May 24	Morgan's Garage	Petrol Account	120
May 26	Martin's Foundry	Engineering parts	700
May 28	Office Supplies	Stationery	126
May 29	Black's Engineering Co	Engineering parts	220

All goods are subject to VAT at 17.5 per cent.

You are required to:
(a) Enter the purchase invoices in a columnar purchases day book using the following analysis columns:

- Engineering parts
- Printing and stationery
- Motor expenses
- VAT

(b) Post the transactions to the personal accounts in the purchases ledger;
(c) Post the totals to the appropriate accounts in the general ledger.

24.3 Harkers Electrical Wholesalers Ltd, Brighton, employs you as accounts assistant responsible for the purchases ledger.

The following details relate to the purchase invoices and credit notes received for April. The company uses an analytical day book with the following column headings and references for spreadsheet purposes.

	Account Reference
Total	E
Electrical goods	F
Motor expenses	G
Office expenses	H
Telephone	I
Sundries	J
VAT	K

Suppliers' Account Nos are as follows:

Supplier	*Account No*
British Telecom	007
Leigh Electrics	030
Office Cleaning Co	043
Peak Electrical Installations Ltd	051
PCD Electrical	060
Smith Stationers	079
Star Manufacturing Co	080
Thomas Motors	090

Purchase Invoices and Credit Notes for April

Invoices

Our Inv No	Date 1999	*Supplier*	*Details*
2306	April 6	Leigh Electrics	Electrical goods £723.52 including VAT £107.75
2307	April 8	PCD Electrical	Cable, etc. £299.13 plus VAT £52.35
2308	April 10	Star Manufacturing Co	Plugs, sockets, etc. £32.17 including VAT £4.79
2309	April 12	British Telecom	Telephone A/c £112.70 including VAT £16.78
2310	April 14	Peak Electrical Installations Ltd	Electrical goods £425.00 plus VAT @ 17½%
2311	April 16	Office Cleaning Co	Cleaning offices (as per contract) £105.00 plus VAT @ 17½%
2312	April 17	Leigh Electrics	Electrical goods £663.68 including VAT
2313	April 19	Thomas Motors	Petrol for March £84.10 including VAT £14.72
2314	April 21	Star Manufacturing Co	Cable, sockets, etc. £160.38 including VAT
2315	April 25	Thomas Motors	Repairs to Renault £131.93 plus VAT £23.09 MOT £24.00 (zero-rated)

| 2316 | April 28 | Smith Stationers | Office stationery £68.95 including VAT £10.27 |

Credit Notes

| 27CN | April 16 | Leigh Electrics | Credit re: faulty goods £57.00 including VAT |
| 28CN | April 30 | Star Manufacturing Co | Credit re: overcharge £2.25 including VAT 34p |

Required

As accounts assistant, you are required to record the purchases invoices and credit notes, but these need to be done in a specific sequence.

(a) Using the headings shown below, draw up an account postings schedule for both the invoices and credit notes, making sure that you check the VAT calculations given in the list of invoices and credit notes.

ACCOUNT POSTINGS – INVOICES   Date..................................

Date	Supplier	Supplier A/c No	A/c Ref	Total	Goods	VAT

ACCOUNT POSTINGS – CREDIT NOTES   Date..................................

Date	Supplier	Supplier A/c No	A/c Ref	Total	Goods	VAT

(b) Rule up a columnar purchases day book and returns outward day book and enter the purchase invoices and credit notes for April 1999. Ensure that all the totals and cross-totals agree.

(c) Post the invoices and credit notes to the suppliers' accounts in the purchases ledger.

(d) Post the totals to the respective accounts in the general ledger.

(NVQ Level 2)

25 Control accounts

25.1 Need for control accounts

When all accounts were kept in one ledger a trial balance could be drawn up as a test of the arithmetical accuracy of the accounts. It must be remembered that certain errors were not revealed by such a trial balance. If the trial balance totals disagreed, for a small business the books could easily and quickly be checked so as to find the errors.

However, when the firm has grown and the accounting work has been so divided up that there are several or many ledgers, any errors could be very difficult to find. We could have to check every item in every ledger. What is required is a type of trial balance for each ledger, and this requirement is met by the **control account**. Thus it is only the ledgers whose control accounts do not balance that need detailed checking to find errors.

25.2 Principle of control accounts

The principle on which the control account is based is simple, and is as follows. If the opening balance of an account is known, together with information of the additions and deductions entered in the account, the closing balance can be calculated.

Applying this to a complete ledger, the total of opening balances together with the additions and deductions during the period should give the total of closing balances. This can be illustrated by reference to a sales ledger for entries for a month.

	£
Total of opening balances at 1 January 1998	3,000
Add Total of entries which have increased the balances	9,500
	12,500
less Total of entries which have reduced the balances	8,000
Total of closing balances at 31 January 1998 should be	4,500

It must be emphasised that control accounts are *not* necessarily a part of the double entry system (see 25.7). They are merely arithmetical proofs performing the same function as a trial balance to a particular ledger.

25.3 Form of control accounts

Sales ledger control account

It is usual to find them in the same form as an account, with the totals of the debit entries in the ledger on the left-hand side of the control account, and the totals of the various credit entries in the ledger on the right-hand side of the control account.

Exhibit 25.1 shows an example of a sales ledger control account for a sales ledger in which all the entries are arithmetically correct.

Exhibit 25.1

Sales ledger	£
Debit balances on 1 January 1998	1,894
Total credit sales for the month	10,290
Cheques received from customers in the month	7,284
Cash received from customers in the month	1,236
Returns inwards from customers during the month	296
Debit balances on 31 January 1998 as extracted from the sales ledger	3,368

Sales Ledger Control Account

Dr			£	Cr			£
1998				1998			
Jan	1	Balances b/d	1,894	Jan	31	Bank	7,284
Jan	31	Sales	10,290			Cash	1,236
						Returns inwards	296
						Balances c/d	3,368
			12,184				12,184

We have proved the ledger to be arithmetically correct, because the totals of the control account equal each other. If the totals are not equal, then this proves there is an error somewhere.

Purchases ledger control account

Exhibit 25.2 shows an example where an error is found to exist in a purchases ledger. The ledger will have to be checked in detail, the error found, and the control account then corrected.

Exhibit 25.2

Purchases ledger	£
Credit balances on 1 January 1998	3,890
Cheques paid to suppliers during the month	3,620
Returns outwards to suppliers in the month	95
Bought from suppliers in the month	4,936
Credit balances on 31 January as extracted from the purchases ledger	5,151

Purchases Ledger Control Account

Dr   Cr

1998			£	1998			£
Jan	31	Bank	3,620	Jan	1	Balances b/d	3,890
Jan	31	Returns outwards	95	Jan	31	Purchases	4,936
Jan	31	Balances c/d	5,151				
			8,866*				8,826*

*There is a £40 error in the purchases ledger. We will have to check that ledger in detail to find the error.

25.4 Information for control accounts

The following tables show where information is obtained from to draw up control accounts.

Sales Ledger Control	Source
1 Opening debtors	List of debtors drawn up at end of previous period
2 Credit sales	Total from sales day book
3 Returns inwards	Total of returns inwards day book
4 Cheques received	Cash book: bank column on received side. List extracted
5 Cash received	Cash book: cash column on received side. List extracted
6 Closing debtors	List of debtors drawn up at end of the period

Purchases Ledger Control	Source
1 Opening creditors	List of creditors drawn up at end of previous period
2 Credit purchases	Total from purchases day book
3 Returns outwards	Total of returns outwards day book
4 Cheques paid	Cash book: bank column on payments side. List extracted
5 Cash paid	Cash book: cash column on payments side. List extracted
6 Closing creditors	List of creditors drawn up at end of the period

25.5 Other transfers

Transfers to bad debt accounts will have to be recorded in the sales ledger control account as they involve entries in the sales ledgers.

Similarly, a contra account whereby the same firm is both a supplier and a customer, and inter-indebtedness is set off, will also need entering in the control accounts. An example of this follows:

1   The firm has sold A Hughes £600 goods.
2   Hughes has supplied the firm with £880 goods.
3   The £600 owing by Hughes is set off against £880 owing to him.
4   This leaves £280 owing to Hughes.

Sales Ledger

Dr			A Hughes Account		Cr
			£		
Sales	1	600			

Purchases Ledger

Dr		A Hughes Account			Cr
					£
			Purchases	2	880

The set-off now takes place.

Sales Ledger

Dr			A Hughes Account			Cr
		£				£
Sales	1	600	Set-off Purchases			
			ledger	3	600	

Purchases Ledger

Dr			A Hughes Account			Cr
		£				£
Set-off: Sales ledger	3	600	Purchases		2	880
Balance c/d	4	280				
		880				880
			Balance b/d		4	280

The transfer of the £600 will therefore appear on the credit side of the sales ledger control account and on the debit side of the purchases ledger control account.

25.6   A more complicated example

Exhibit 25.3 shows a worked example of a more complicated control account.

You will see that there are sometimes credit balances in the sales ledger as well as debit balances. Suppose for instance we sold £500 goods to W Young, he then paid in full for them, and then afterwards he returned £40 goods to us. This would leave a credit balance of £40 on the account, whereas usually the balances in the sales ledger are debit balances.

There may also be reason to write off a debt as bad where a business finds it impossible to collect the debt. If this happens the double entry would be as follows:

Debit Bad debts account
Credit Individual debtors' accounts

Ultimately, the bad debts account would be credited and the profit and loss account would be debited (see Chapter 27). If the business uses control accounts, then the sales ledger control account would also be credited as shown in Exhibit 25.3.

Exhibit 25.3

1998		£
Aug 1	Sales ledger – debit balances	3,816
Aug 1	Sales ledger – credit balances	22
Aug 31	Transactions for the month:	
	Cash received	104
	Cheques received	6,239
	Sales	7,090
	Bad debts written off	306
	Discounts allowed	298
	Returns inwards	664
	Cash refunded to a customer who had overpaid his account	37
	Dishonoured cheques	29
	Interest charged by us on overdue debt	50
	At the end of the month:	
	Sales ledger – debit balances	3,429
	Sales ledger – credit balances	40

Sales Ledger Control Account

Dr			£	Cr			£
1998				1998			
Aug 1	Balances b/d		3,816	Aug 1	Balances b/d		22
Aug 31	Sales		7,090	Aug 31	Cash		104
	Cash refunded		37		Bank		6,239
	Bank: dishonoured				Bad debts		306
	cheques		29		Discounts allowed		298
	Interest on debt		50		Returns inwards		664
	Balances c/d		40		Balances c/d		3,429
			11,062				11,062

25.7 Control accounts and double entry

When a business operates control accounts it has to decide where the 'control accounts' should be kept within the book-keeping system. There are two options:

1 In order to maintain the control account within the general ledger the control account becomes part of the double entry system and the individual debtors and creditors accounts become memorandum accounts, *see* Exhibit 25.4.

Exhibit 25.4 **Control Account as Part of a Double Entry System**

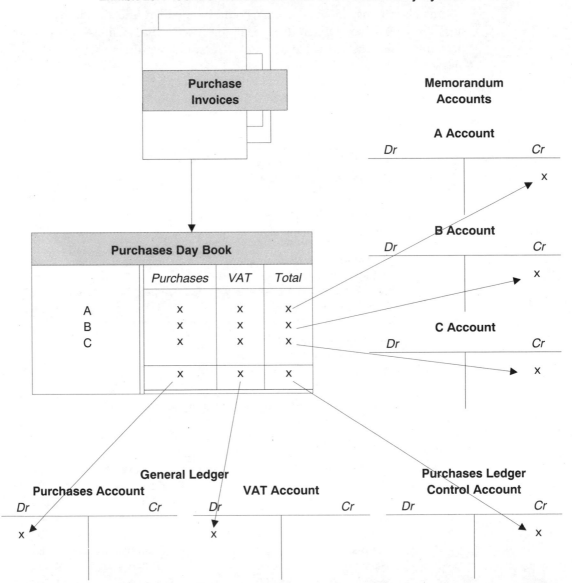

In the above exhibit the balance of outstanding debtors and creditors is taken from the control accounts and included in the trial balance at the end of the month or year end, as required. In this case the personal accounts of the debtors and creditors i.e. A Account, B Account, C Account etc. are not part of the double entry and are referred to as memorandum accounts. It is, however, important to balance the memorandum accounts periodically with the sales and purchases ledger control accounts so that errors can be located and corrected.

2   In order to maintain the control accounts in the sales and purchases ledgers the control accounts become memorandum accounts. Using this method, the debtors and creditors personal accounts are included in the double entry system via the sales and purchases ledgers whilst the control account becomes the memorandum account (*see* Exhibit 25.5).

Exhibit 25.5 **Control Account as a Memorandum Account**

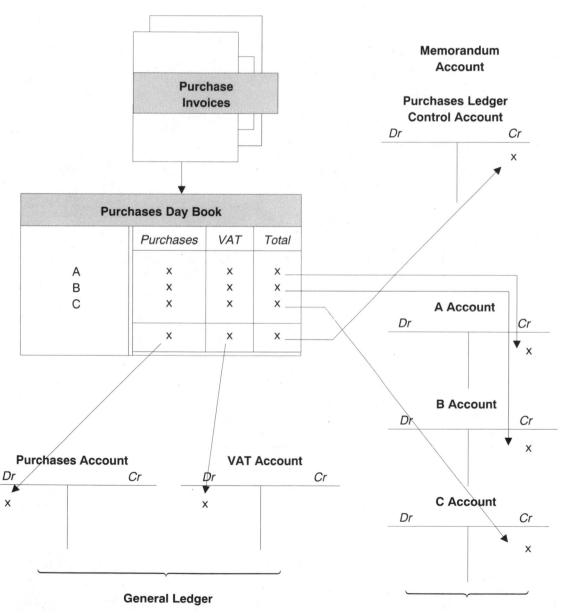

Note: Many students become confused when making postings to control accounts and might find it useful to remember that when posting entries to control accounts the entry goes on the same side as it would in the personal account. Another useful hint can also be applied when entering 'Contra' or 'Set-off' items; here think of the contra or set-off as *cash* and enter the item where you would normally enter cash on the respective control account.

New term

Control account (p 237): An account which checks the arithmetical accuracy of a ledger.

Exercises

25.1 You are required to prepare a sales ledger control account from the following:

1998		£
May 1	Sales ledger balances	4,560
	Total of entries for May:	
	Sales day book	10,870
	Returns inwards day book	460
	Cheques and cash received from customers	9,615
	Discounts allowed	305
May 31	Sales ledger balances	5,050

25.2 You are to prepare a sales ledger control account from the following. Deduce the closing figure of sales ledger balances as at 31 March 1998.

1998		£
Mar 1	Sales ledger balances	6,708
	Totals for March:	
	Discounts allowed	300
	Cash and cheques received from debtors	8,970
	Sales day book	11,500
	Bad debts written off	115
	Returns inwards day book	210
Mar 31	Sales ledger balances	?

25.3X Draw up a purchases ledger control account from the following:

1998		£
June 1	Purchases ledger balances	3,890
	Totals for June:	
	Purchases day book	5,640
	Returns outwards day book	315
	Cash and cheques paid to creditors	5,230
	Discounts received	110
June 30	Purchases ledger balances	?

25.4X You are to prepare a purchases ledger control account from the following. As the final figure of purchases ledger balances at 30 November 1998 is missing, you will have to deduce that figure.

1998		£
Nov 1	Purchases ledger balances	7,560
	Totals for November:	
	Discounts received	240
	Returns outwards day book	355
	Cash and cheques paid to creditors	9,850
	Purchases day book	11,100
Nov 30	Purchases ledger balances	?

25.5 The following balances have been extracted from the books of R Stevenson at 31 December 1998:

1 January 1998	£
Sales ledger balances	6,840
Further Balances:	
Sales	46,801
Discounts allowed	420
Bad debts written off	494
Receipts from customers	43,780
Returns inwards	296

Required

(a) Prepare the sales ledger control account for R Stevenson, showing clearly the balance carried forward at 31 December 1998.

(b) An explanation of the meaning and use of the final balance.

(RSA)

25.6X The following balances are included in the purchases ledger of Ambrose Artichoke as at 1 January 1998:

J Carrot	£86.14
F Parsnip	£20.28
B Sprout	£14.10
C Beetroot	£3.90

During January the following transactions took place:

3 January	Purchased stock on credit from F Parsnip £19.72 and from M Mushroom £55.90
10 January	Purchases on credit from C Beetroot £11.91, B Sprout £25.90 and M Mushroom £28.32
15 January	Returned goods to J Carrot £6.00 and B Sprout £7.40
25 January	Paid by cash J Carrot £20.00 on account
30 January	Paid F Parsnip by cheque the balance owing on her account after deducting a 5% cash discount.

You are required to:

(a) write up and balance off the personal accounts in the purchases ledger;

(b) prepare a purchase ledger control account as at 31 January 1998;

(c) make up a simple reconciliation of the control account balance with the actual creditors as at 31 January 1998.

(RSA)

26 The journal

26.1 Main books of original entry

We have seen in earlier chapters that most transactions are entered in one of the following books of original entry:

- Cash book
- Sales day book
- Purchases day book
- Returns inwards day book
- Returns outwards day book

These books have grouped together similar things, e.g. all credit sales are in the sales day book. To trace any of them would be relatively easy, as we know exactly which book would contain the item.

26.2 The journal: the other book of original entry

The other items which do not pass through the above books are much less common, and sometimes much more complicated. It would be easy for a book-keeper to forget the details of these transactions.

If the book-keeper left the firm it could be impossible to understand such book-keeping entries.

What is needed is a form of diary to record such transactions, before the entries are made in the double entry accounts. This book is called *the journal*. It will contain, for each transaction:

- The date
- The name of account(s) to be debited and the amount(s)
- The name of the account(s) to be credited and the amount(s)
- A description of the transaction (this is called a 'narrative')
- A reference number should be given for the documents giving proof of the transaction

The use of the journal makes errors or fraud by book-keepers more difficult. It also reduces the risk of entering the item once only instead of having double entry. Despite these advantages there are many firms which do not have such a book.

26.3 Typical uses of the journal

Some of the main uses of the journal are listed below. It must not be thought that this list is a fully detailed one.

- The purchase and sale of fixed assets on credit
- The correction of errors
- Writing off bad debts
- Opening entries. These are the entries needed to open a new set of books
- Other items

The layout of the journal can be shown:

The Journal

Date	Folio	Dr	Cr

The name of the account to be debited.
    The name of the account to be credited.
The narrative.

You can see that we put on the first line the account to be debited. The second line gives the account to be credited. We do not write the name of the account to be credited directly under the name of the account to be debited. This makes it easier to see which is the debit and which is the credit.

We should remember that the journal is not a double entry account. It is a form of diary, and entering an item in the journal is not the same as recording an item in an account. Once the journal entry is made the entry in the double entry accounts can then be made. Examples of the uses of the journal are now given.

Purchase and sale on credit of fixed assets

1   A machine is bought on credit from Toolmakers for £550 on 1 July 1997.

		Dr	Cr
1997		£	£
July 1	Machinery	550	
	Toolmakers		550
	Purchase of milling machine on credit, Capital		
	Purchases invoice no 7/159		

2   Sale of a motor vehicle for £300 on credit to K Lamb on 2 July 1997.

		Dr	Cr
1997		£	£
July 2	K Lamb	300	
	Motor vehicles disposal		300
	Sales of motor vehicles per Capital		
	Sales invoice no 7/43		

Correction of errors

These are explained in detail in Chapters 31 and 32.

Bad debts

A debt of £78 owing to us from H Mander is written off as a bad debt on 31 August 1998.

			Dr	Cr
			£	£
1998				
Aug	31	Bad debts	78	
		H Mander		78
		Debt written off as bad. See letter in file 7/8906		

Opening entries

J Brew, after being in business for some years without keeping proper records, now decides to keep a double entry set of books. On 1 July 1998 he establishes that his assets and liabilities are as follows:

Assets:　　Motor van £840, Fixtures £700, Stock £390,
　　　　　Debtors – B Young £95, D Blake £45,
　　　　　Bank £80, Cash £20.
Liabilities:　Creditors – M Quinn £129, C Walters £41.

The Assets therefore total £840 + £700 + £390 + £95 + £45 + £80 + £20 = £2,170; and the Liabilities total £129 + £41 = £170.

The Capital consists of: Assets – Liabilities, £2,170 – £170 = £2,000

We must start the writing up of the books on 1 July 1998. To do this we:

1　Open asset accounts, one for each asset. Each opening asset is shown as a debit balance.
2　Open liability accounts, one for each liability. Each opening liability is shown as a credit balance.
3　Open an account for the capital. Show it as a credit balance.

The journal records what you are doing, and why.
　Exhibit 26.1 shows:

• The journal
• The opening entries in the double entry accounts

Exhibit 26.1

The Journal

		Fol	Dr	Cr
			Page 5	
1998			£	£
July 1	Motor van	GL 1	840	
	Fixtures	GL 2	700	
	Stock	GL 3	390	
	Debtors – B Young	SL 1	95	
	D Blake	SL 2	45	
	Bank	CB 1	80	
	Cash	CB 1	20	
	Creditors – M Quinn	PL 1		129
	C Walters	PL 2		41
	Capital	GL 4		2,000
	Assets and liabilities at the date entered			
	to open the books		2,170	2,170

General Ledger

Motor Van Account

Dr				£			Cr
1998							Page 1
July	1	Balance	J 5	840			

Fixtures Account

Dr				£			Cr
1998							Page 2
July	1	Balance	J 5	700			

Stock Account

Dr				£			Cr
1998							Page 3
July	1	Balance	J 5	390			

Capital Account

Dr							Cr
				1998			Page 4
							£
				July	1	Balance	J 5	2,000

Sales Ledger

B Young Account

Dr				£			Cr
1998							Page 1
July	1	Balance	J 5	95			

D Blake

Dr					Cr Page 2
1998				£	
July	1	Balance	J 5	45	

Purchases Ledger

M Quinn Account

Dr			Cr Page 1			
			1998			£
			July	1	Balance J 5	129

C Walters Account

Dr			Cr Page 2			
			1998			£
			July	1	Balance J 5	41

Cash Book

Cash Bank

Dr				£	£	Cr Page 1
1998						
July	1	Balances	J 5	20	80	

Other items

These can be of many kinds and it is impossible to write out a complete list. Several examples are now shown:

1 K Young, a debtor, owed £200 on 1 July 1998. He was unable to pay his account in cash, but offers a motor car in full settlement of the debt. The offer is accepted on 5 July 1998.

   The personal account is, therefore, not now owed and needs crediting. On the other hand the firm now has an extra asset, a motor car, therefore the motor car account needs to be debited.

The Journal

			Dr	Cr
1998			£	£
July	5	Motor car	200	
		K Young		200
		Accepted motor car in full settlement of debt per letter dated 5/7/1998		

2 T Jones is a creditor. On 10 July 1998 his business is taken over by A Lee to whom the debt now is to be paid.

   Here one creditor is being exchanged for another one. The action needed is to cancel the amount owing to T Jones by debiting his account, and to show it owing to Lee by opening an account for Lee and crediting it.

The Journal

			Dr	Cr
1998			£	£
July	10	T Jones	150	
		A Lee		150
		Transfer of indebtedness as per letter		
		ref G/1335		

3 We had previously bought an office typewriter for £310. It is faulty. On 12 July 1998 we return it to the supplier, RS Ltd. An allowance of £310 is agreed, so that we will not have to pay for it.

The Journal

			Dr	Cr
1998			£	£
July	12	RS Ltd	310	
		Office machinery		310
		Faulty typewriter returned to supplier		
		Full allowance given. See letter 10/7/1998		

26.4 Multiple-choice questions

Now attempt Set No 2 which contains 35 multiple-choice questions (on page 416).

Exercises

26.1 You are to show the journal entries necessary to record the following items:

1998
(a) May 1 Bought a motor vehicle on credit from Kingston Garage for £6,790
(b) May 3 A debt of £34 owing from H Newman was written off as a bad debt
(c) May 8 Office furniture bought by us for £490 was returned to the supplier, Unique Offices, as it was unsuitable. Full allowance will be given to us
(d) May 12 We are owed £150 by W Charles. He is declared bankrupt and we receive £39 in full settlement of the debt
(e) May 14 We take £45 goods out of the business stock without paying for them
(f) May 28 Some time ago we paid an insurance bill thinking that it was all in respect of the business. We now discover that £76 of the amount paid was in fact insurance of our private house
(g) May 29 Bought machinery £980 on credit from Systems Accelerated.

26.2X Show the journal entries for April 1998 necessary to record the following items:

Apr 1 Bought fixtures on credit from J Harper £1,809

Apr 4 We take £500 goods out of the business stock without paying for them

Apr 9 £28 worth of the goods taken by us on 4 April are not returned back into stock by us. We do not take any money for the return of the goods

Apr 12 K Lamb owes us £500. He is unable to pay his debt. We agree to take some office equipment from him at the value and so cancel the debt

Apr 18 Some of the fixtures bought from J Harper, £65 worth, are found to be unsuitable and are returned to him for full allowance

Apr 24 A debt owing to us by J Brown of £68 is written off as a bad debt

Apr 30 Office equipment bought on credit from Super Offices for £2,190

26.3 On 1 May 1998 the financial position of Carol Green was as follows:

	£
Freehold premises	45,000
Fixtures and fittings	12,500
Motor vehicles	9,500
Bank overdraft	2,800
Cash in hand	650
Stock in hand	1,320
F Hardy (a trade debtor)	160
A Darby (a trade creditor)	270

Required

(a) Make a journal entry for the above showing clearly the capital of Carol Green on 1 May 1998.

(b) On examination of her books on 1 May 1998 Sue Baker discovered the following adjustments were necessary:

   (i) When Parker, a debtor for £350, paid his account he was allowed discount of 2 per cent for prompt payment. The actual amount of cash received has been entered in Parker's account and in the cash book, no entry having been made for the discount allowed.

   (ii) The purchase of a motor van for £4,500 had not been entered in the books. The van was purchased from Supervans Ltd paying a deposit of 25 per cent, the balance being due in six months' time.

   (iii) I M Broke, a debtor for £250, has been declared bankrupt. On 1 May 1998 a payment of 20p in the pound was received with notification that it will be the only payment. The remaining balance on the account is therefore to be written off as a bad debt.

Make journal entries giving effect to all of the above transactions including the payment received from Broke and the writing off of the bad debt.

(c) Show I M Broke's account and the bad debts account in the ledger.

Note: Narratives must be given with all journal entries.

(RSA)

26.4X The following transactions relate to the business of Martin Cooper, a sole trader:

(a) A debtor, G Holt, was declared bankrupt, owing Cooper £250. On 1 May 1998, he gave Cooper a cheque for £50, as a first and final payment. Cooper decided to write off the remainder of the debt as bad on the same day.

(b) During the month of June 1998, Cooper had taken goods which had cost the business £180, for use outside the business.

(c) On 1 July 1998, Cooper purchased on credit from Cousins & Co a motor car costing £3,850. He paid a deposit of £1,000 by cheque. He took out comprehensive insurance with Byline Insurance Company for the year from 1 July 1998 for £300. He settled the premium by cheque on that date.

Required

Draw up the journal entries to record the above transactions and adjustments in the books of Martin Cooper.

Note: Cash entries should be journalised.

(LCCI)

26.5 Write the journal entries needed to effect the following:

(a) 1 July   Interest at 6 per cent per annum charged to the account of James Crawford whose debit balance was due to be paid by the previous 31 March when he owed us £120.

(b) 30 Aug   Purchased on credit from 'Mechweights' a new weighing machine worth £1,500, less (i) 10 per cent trade discount, and (ii) less a second-hand weighing machine from us worth £400, in part exchange.

(c) 10 Sept A dividend of £0.35p in the £ received from the bankrupt estate of Thomas Watson whose debt of £150 had previously been written off as irrecoverable. The amount received had been entered in the cash book and posted to Thomas Watson's old account in the ledger, which had been re-opened for the purpose.

(d) 31 Dec   The proprietor of the business, A Walker, had taken stock from the shop for his own use to the value of £39.50.

(Pitman Qualifications)

26.6 You are to open the books of K Mullings, a trader, via the journal to record the assets and liabilities, and are then to record the daily transactions for the month of May. A trial balance is to be extracted as on 31 May 1998.

1998

May 1 *Assets* – Premises £2,000; Motor van £450; Fixtures £600; Stock £1,289. Debtors – N Hardy £40; M Nelson £180. Cash at bank £1,254; Cash in hand £45.
         Liabilities – Creditors: B Blake £60; V Reagan £200.

May 1 Paid rent by cheque £15

May 2 Goods bought on credit from B Blake £20; C Harris £56; H Gordon £38; N Lee £69

May 3 Goods sold on credit to: K O'Connor £56; M Benjamin £78; L Staines £98; N Duffy £48; B Green £118; M Nelson £40

May 4 Paid for motor expenses in cash £13

May 7 Cash drawings by proprietor £20

May 9 Goods sold on credit to: M Benjamin £22; L Pearson £67

May 11 Goods returned to Mullings by: K O'Connor £16; L Staines £18

May 14 Bought another motor van on credit from Better Motors Ltd £300

May 16 The following paid Mullings their accounts by cheque less 5 per cent cash discount: N Hardy; M Nelson; K O'Connor; L Staines

May 19 Goods returned by Mullings to N Lee £9

May 22 Goods bought on credit from: J Johnson £89; T Best £72

May 24 The following accounts were settled by Mullings by cheque less 5 per cent cash discount: B Blake; V Reagan; N Lee

May 27 Salaries paid by cheque £56

May 30 Paid rates by cheque £66

May 31 Paid Better Motors Ltd a cheque for £300.

PART 4

Adjustments required before preparing final accounts

27 Depreciation of fixed assets 1: theory and methods

27.1 Nature of fixed assets

Fixed assets are those assets of significant value which:

- are of long life, and
- are to be used in the business, and
- are not bought with the intention of being resold.

27.2 Depreciation of fixed assets

However, fixed assets such as machinery, motor vans, fixtures and even buildings, do not last for ever. If the amount received (if any) on disposal is deducted from the cost of buying them, the difference is called depreciation.

The only time that depreciation can be calculated accurately is when the fixed asset is disposed of, and the difference between the cost to its owner and the amount received on disposal is then calculated. If a motor van was bought for £10,000 and sold five years later for £2,000 then the amount of depreciation is £10,000 – £2,000 = £8,000.

27.3 Depreciation is an expense

Depreciation is the part of the cost of the fixed asset consumed during its period of use by the firm. It is an expense for services consumed in the same way as expenses for items such as wages, rent or electricity. Because it is an expense, depreciation will have to be charged to the profit and loss account, and will therefore reduce net profit.

You can see that the only real difference between the cost of depreciation for a motor vehicle, and the cost of petrol for the motor vehicle, is that the petrol cost is used up in a day or two, whereas the cost for the motor vehicle is spread over several years. Both costs are costs of the business.

27.4 Causes of depreciation

The principal causes of depreciation are (i) physical deterioration, (ii) economic factors, (iii) the time factor, (iv) depletion. Let us look at these in more detail.

Physical depreciation

1 **Wear and tear**. When a motor vehicle or machinery or fixtures and fittings are used they eventually wear out. Some last many years, others last only a few years. This is true of buildings, although some may last for a long time.

2 **Erosion, rust, rot and decay**. Land may be eroded or wasted away by the action of wind, rain, sun and other elements of nature. Similarly, the metals in motor vehicles or machinery will rust away. Wood will rot eventually. Decay is a process which will also be present due to the elements of nature and the lack of proper attention.

Economic factors

These may be said to be the reasons for an asset being put out of use even though it is in good physical condition. The two main factors are usually **obsolescence** and **inadequacy**.

1 **Obsolescence**. This is the process of becoming obsolete or out of date. For example, propeller-driven aeroplanes, which, although in good physical condition, were made obsolete by the introduction of jet aircraft. The propeller-driven aircraft were put out of use by large airlines when they still had quite a few more years of potential use, because the newer aircraft were suited far better to the needs of the airlines.

2 **Inadequacy**. This is when an asset is no longer used because of the growth and changes in the size of firm. For instance, a small ferryboat that is operated by a firm at a seaside resort is entirely inadequate when the resort becomes more popular. It is found that it would be more efficient and economical to operate a large ferryboat, and so the smaller boat is put out of use by the firm.

Both obsolescence and inadequacy do not necessarily mean that the asset is destroyed. It is merely put out of use by the firm. Another firm will often buy it. For example, many of the aeroplanes no longer used by large airlines are bought by smaller firms.

The time factor

Wear and tear, erosion, obsolescence and inadequacy take time. However, there are fixed assets to which the time factor is connected in a different way. These are assets which have a legal life fixed in terms of years.

For instance, you may agree to rent some buildings for 10 years. This is normally called a lease. When the years are finished the lease is worth nothing to you, as it has finished. Whatever you paid for the lease is now of no value.

A similar asset is where you buy a patent with complete rights so that only you are able to produce something. When the patent's time has finished it then has no value.

Instead of using the term depreciation, the term *amortisation* is often used for these assets.

Depletion

Some assets are of 'wasting' character, perhaps due to the extraction of raw materials from them. These materials are then either used by the firm to make something else, or are sold in their raw state to other firms. Natural resources such as mines, quarries and oil wells come under this heading. **Depletion** is the term used to describe the consumption of an asset of a wasting nature.

27.5 Land and buildings

Prior to SSAP 12, which applied after 1977, freehold and long leasehold properties were very rarely subject to a charge for depreciation. It was contended that, as property values tended to rise instead of fall, it was inappropriate to charge depreciation.

However, SSAP 12 requires that depreciation be written off over the property's useful life, with the exception that freehold land will not normally require a provision for depreciation. This is because land does not normally depreciate. Buildings do, however, eventually fall into disrepair or become obsolete and must be subject to a charge for depreciation each year. When a revaluation of property takes place, the depreciation charge must be on the revalued figure.

An exception to all this is investment properties. These are properties owned not for use but simply for investment. In this case investment properties will be shown in the balance sheet at their open market value.

27.6 Appreciation

At this stage you may begin to ask about the assets that increase (appreciate) in value. The answer to this is that normal accounting procedure would be to ignore any such appreciation, as to bring appreciation into account would be to contravene both the cost concept and the prudence concept as discussed in Chapter 11. Nevertheless, in certain circumstances appreciation is taken into account in partnership and limited company accounts, but this is left until partnerships and limited companies are considered.

27.7 Provision for depreciation as allocation of cost

Depreciation in total over the life of an asset can be calculated quite simply as cost less amount receivable when the asset is put out of use by the firm. If the item is bought and sold within the one accounting period, then the depreciation for that period is charged as a revenue expense in arriving at that period's net profit. The difficulties start when the asset is used for more than one accounting period, and an attempt has to be made to charge each period with the depreciation for that period.

Even though depreciation provisions are now regarded as allocating cost to each accounting period (except for accounting for inflation), it does not follow that there is any 'true' method of performing even this task. All that can be said is that the cost should be allocated over the life of the asset in such a way as to charge it as equitably as possible to the periods in which the asset is used. The difficulties involved are considerable and some of them are now listed.

1   Apart from a few assets, such as a lease, how accurately can a firm assess an asset's useful life? Even a lease may be put out of use if the premises leased have become inadequate.

2   How does one measure use? A car owned by a firm for two years may have been driven one year by a very careful driver and another year by a reckless driver. The standard of driving will affect the motor car and also the amount of cash receivable on its disposal. How should such a firm apportion the car's depreciation costs?

3   There are other expenses besides depreciation, such as repairs and maintenance of the fixed asset. As both of these affect the rate and amount of depreciation should they not also affect the depreciation provision calculations?

4   How can a firm possibly know the amount receivable in x years' time when the asset is put out of use?

These are only some of the difficulties. Therefore, the methods of calculating provisions for depreciation are mainly accounting customs.

27.8 Methods of calculating depreciation charges

The two main methods in use are the **straight line method** and the **reducing balance method**. Most accountants think that, although other methods may be needed in certain cases, the straight line method is the one that is generally most suitable.

Straight line method

We use the straight line method to make an estimate of the number of years of useful life of the asset together with the estimated residual value of the asset.

The cost of the asset less the estimated residual value (the amount which the asset is likely to be sold for) is divided by the number of years of estimated life of the asset to give the **annual depreciation charge**.

For example, if a motor lorry was bought for £22,000 and we thought we would keep it for four years and then sell it for £2,000, the depreciation to be charged would be:

$$\frac{\text{Cost (£22,000)} - \text{Disposal value (£2,000)}}{\text{Number of years of use (4)}} = \frac{\text{£20,000}}{4}$$

$$= \text{£5,000 depreciation each year for four years.}$$

If, after four years, the motor lorry would have had no disposal value, the charge for depreciation would have been:

$$\frac{\text{Cost (£22,000)}}{\text{Number of years use (4)}} = \frac{£22,000}{4}$$

= £5,500 depreciation each year for four years.

Reducing balance method

When using the reducing balance method, the depreciation charge is a fixed percentage each year ex 20 per cent. The first year the fixed percentage is deducted from the cost of the asset but in the second and later years it is deducted from the cost of the asset less depreciation already charged (i.e. the reduced balance).

If a machine is bought for £10,000, and depreciation is to be charged at 20 per cent, the calculations for the first three years would be as follows:

	£
Cost	10,000
First year: depreciation (20%)	2,000
	8,000
Second year: depreciation (20% of £8,000)	1,600
	6,400
Third year: depreciation (20% of £6,400)	1,280
	5,120

Using this method much larger amounts are charged in the earlier years of use as compared with the last years of use. It is often said that repairs and upkeep in the early years will not cost as much as when the asset becomes old.

This mean that:

In the early years		**In the later years**
A higher charge for depreciation	will tend	A lower charge for depreciation
+	to be	+
A lower charge for repairs	fairly	A higher charge for repairs
and upkeep	equal to	and upkeep

Exhibit 27.1 gives a comparison of the calculations using the two methods, if the same cost is given for the two methods.

Exhibit 27.1

A firm has just bought a machine for £8,000. it will be kept in use for four years, then it will be disposed of for an estimated amount of £500. They ask for a comparison of the amounts charged as depreciation using both methods.

For the straight line method a figure of (£8,000 – £500) ÷ 4 = £7,500 ÷ 4 = £1,875 per annum is to be used. For the reducing balance method a percentage figure of 50 per cent will be used.

	Method 1 Straight Line £		Method 2 Reducing Balance £
Cost	8,000		8,000
Depreciation: year 1	1,875	(50% of £8,000)	4,000
	6,125		4,000
Depreciation: year 2	1,875	(50% of £4,000)	2,000
	4,250		2,000
Depreciation: year 3	1,875	(50% of £2,000)	1,000
	2,375		1,000
Depreciation: year 4	1,875	(50% of £1,000)	500
Disposal value	500		500

This illustrates the fact that using the reducing balance method there is a much higher charge for depreciation in the early years, and lower charges in the later years.

27.9 Other methods of calculating depreciation

There are many more methods of calculating depreciation but they are outside the scope of this volume. Special methods are often used in particular industries where there are circumstances which are peculiar to that industry.

New terms

Depletion (p 259): The wasting away of an asset as it is used up.
Depreciation (p 257): The part of the cost of the fixed asset consumed during its period of use by the firm.
Inadequacy (p 258): When an asset is no longer used because of changes within an organisation due to growth, competition or product range changes.
Obsolescence (p 258): Becoming out of date.
Reducing balance method (p 261): Depreciation calculation which is at a lesser amount every following period.
Straight line method (p 260): Depreciation calculation which remains at an equal amount each year.

Exercises

27.1 D Sankey, a manufacturer, purchases a lathe for the sum of £4,000. It has an estimated life of five years and a scrap value of £500.

Sankey is not certain whether he should use the 'straight line' or the 'reducing balance' basis for the purpose of calculating depreciation on the machine.

You are required to calculate the depreciation on the lathe using both methods, showing clearly the balance remaining in the lathe account at the end of each of the five years for each method. (Assume that 40 per cent per annum is to be used for the reducing balance method.)

(Calculations to the nearest £.)

27.2 A machine costs £12,500. It will be kept for four years, and then sold for an estimated figure of £5,120. Show the calculations of the figures for depreciation for each of the four years using *(a)* the straight line method, *(b)* the reducing balance method, for this method using a depreciation rate of 20 per cent.

27.3 A motor vehicle costs £6,400. It will be kept for five years, and then sold for scrap £200. Calculate the depreciation for each year using *(a)* the reducing balance method, using a depreciation rate of 50 per cent, *(b)* the straight line method.

27.4X A machine costs £5,120. It will be kept for five years, and then sold at an estimated figure of £1,215. Show the calculations of the figures for depreciation each year using *(a)* the straight line method, *(b)* the reducing balance method using a depreciation rate of 25 per cent.

27.5X A bulldozer costs £12,150. It will be kept in use for five years. At the end of that time agreement has already been made that it will be sold for £1600. Show your calculation of the amount of depreciation each year if *(a)* the reducing balance method at a rate of 33⅓ per cent was used, *(b)* the straight line method was used.

27.6X A tractor is bought for £6,000. It will be used for three years, and then sold back to the supplier for £3,072. Show the depreciation calculations for each year using *(a)* the reducing balance method with a rate of 20 per cent, *(b)* the straight line method.

27.7 A company, which makes up its accounts annually to 31 December, provides for depreciation of its machinery at the rate of 10 per cent per annum on the reducing balance method.

On 31 December 1998, the machinery consisted of three items purchased as under:

	£
On 1 January 1996 Machine A	Cost 3,000
On 1 April 1997 Machine B	Cost 2,000
On 1 July 1998 Machine C	Cost 1,000

Required

Your calculations showing the depreciation provision for the year 1998.

28 Depreciation of fixed assets 2: double entry records

28.1 Recording depreciation

Fixed assets accounts are always kept for showing the assets at cost price. The depreciation is shown accumulating in a separate 'provision for depreciation' account.

Example

In a business with financial years ending 31 December a machine is bought for £2,000 on 1 January 1997. It is to be depreciated at the rate of 20 per cent using the reducing balance method. The records for the first three years are now shown in Exhibit 28.1.

Notice that no entry is made in the asset account for depreciation. This means that the fixed asset accounts will normally be shown at cost price.

The double entry for depreciation is:

1 Debit the profit and loss account.
2 Credit the provision for depreciation account.

Exhibit 28.1

Machinery Account

Dr					Cr
1997			£		
Jan	1	Cash	2,000		

Provision for Depreciation – Machinery Account

Dr							Cr
1997			£	1997			£
				Dec 31	Profit and		
Dec 31	Balance c/d		400		loss a/c		400
1998				1998			
Dec 31	Balance c/d		720	Jan 1	Balance b/d		400
				Dec 31	Profit and		
					loss a/c		320
			720				720
1999				1999			
Dec 31	Balance c/d		976	Jan 1	Balance b/d		720
				Dec 31	Profit and		
					loss a/c		256
			976				976
				2000			
				Jan 1	Balance b/d		976

Profit and Loss account for the year ended 31 December

Dr				Cr
		£		
1997	Depreciation	400		
1998	Depreciation	320		
1999	Depreciation	256		

Now the balance on the Machinery Account is shown on the balance sheet at the end of each year less the balance on the Provision for Depreciation Account.

Balance Sheets as at 31 December

	Cost	Total depreciation	Net book value
1997	£	£	£
Machinery	2,000	400	1,600
1998			
Machinery	2,000	720	1,280
1999			
Machinery	2,000	976	1,024

Another example can now be given in Exhibit 28.2. This is of a business with financial years ended 30 June. A motor lorry is bought on 1 July 1997 for

£8,000. Another motor lorry is bought on 1 July 1998 for £11,000. Each lorry is expected to be in use for five years, and the disposal value of the first lorry is expected to be £500 and the second lorry is expected to fetch £1,000 disposal value. The method of depreciation to be used is the straight line method. The first two years' accounts are shown.

Exhibit 28.2

Motor Lorries Account

Dr							Cr
1997			£	1997			£
Jul	1	Bank	8,000	Jun 30	Balance c/d		19,000
1998							
Jul	1	Bank	11,000				
			19,000				19,000

Provision for Depreciation – Motor Lorries Account

Dr			£	Cr			£
1998				1998			
				Jun 30	Profit and		
Jun 30	Balance c/d		1,500		loss a/c		1,500
				Jul 1	Balance b/d		1,500
1999				1999			
Jun 30	Balance c/d		5,000	Jun 30	Profit and		
					loss a/c		3,500
			5,000				5,000
				Jul 1	Balance b/d		5,000

Profit and Loss Account for the year ended 30 June (extracts)

		£	
1998	Depreciation	1,500	
1999	Depreciation	3,500	

Balance Sheet as at 30 June 1998

	Cost	Total depreciation	Net book value
	£	£	£
Motor lorry	8,000	1,500	6,500

Balance Sheet as at 30 June 1999

	Cost	Total depreciation	Net book value
	£	£	£
Motor lorries	19,000	5,000	14,000

28.2 The sale of an asset

Reason for accounting entries

Upon the sale of an asset we will want to delete it from our accounts. This means that the cost of that asset needs to be taken out of the asset account. In addition, the depreciation of the sold asset will have to be taken out of the depreciation provision.

Finally, the profit or loss on sale, if any, will have to be calculated.

When we charge depreciation on a fixed asset we are having to make guesses.

We cannot be absolutely certain how long we will keep the asset in use, nor can we be certain at the date of purchase how much the asset will be sold for when we dispose of it. We will not often get our guesses correct. This means that when we dispose of an asset, the cash received for it is usually different from our original guess.

Accounting entries needed

On the sale of a fixed asset the following entries are needed; for instance, let us assume the sale of machinery.

(A)	Transfer the cost price of the asset sold to an assets disposal account (in this case a machinery disposals account).	Debit machinery disposals account. Credit machinery account.
(B)	Transfer the depreciation already charged to the assets disposal account.	Debit provision for depreciation – machinery. Credit machinery disposals account.
(C)	For remittance received on disposal.	Debit cash book. Credit machinery disposals account.
(D)	Transfer balance (difference on machinery disposals account) to the profit and loss account.	
	If the difference is on the debit side of the disposals account, it is a profit on sale.	Debit machinery disposals account. Credit profit and loss account.
	If the difference is on the credit side of the disposal account, it is a loss on sale.	Debit profit and loss account. Credit machinery disposals account.

We can now look at Exhibit 28.3 which shows the entries for an asset sold at a profit. In Exhibit 28.1 the machinery was bought for £2,000 on 1 January 1997 and had been depreciated by £976 by 31 December 1999, and then sold for £1,070 on 2 January 2000. The entries shown in Exhibit 28.4 are those needed if the machinery was instead sold for £950 on 2 January 2000. The letters (A) to (D) shown are references to the table of instructions shown above.

Exhibit 28.3 **Asset sold at a profit**

Machinery Account

Dr						Cr
1997			£	2000		£
				Jan 2 Machinery		
Jan 1	Cash		2,000	disposals	(A)	2,000

Provision for Depreciation: Machinery Account

Dr						Cr
2000			£	2000		£
Jan 2	Machinery					
	disposals	(B)	976	Jan 1 Balance b/d		976

Machinery Disposals Account

Dr						Cr
2000			£	2000		£
Jan 2	Machinery	(A)	2,000	Jan 2 Cash	(C)	1,070
Dec 31	Profit and			2 Provision for		
	loss a/c	(D)	46	depreciation	(B)	976
			2,046			2,046

Profit and Loss Account for the year ended 31 December 2000

			£
	Profit on sale of		
	machinery	(D)	46

Exhibit 28.4 now shows what the entries would be for the same asset if, instead of being sold at a profit, the asset had been sold for £950 only, which would mean that a loss was incurred on sale.

Exhibit 28.4 **Asset sold at a loss**

Machinery Account

Dr						Cr
1997			£	2000		£
				Jan 2 Machinery		
Jan 1	Cash		2,000	disposals	(A)	2,000

Provision for Depreciation: Machinery Account

Dr   Cr

2000			£	2000			£
Jan	2	Machinery disposals (B)	976	Jan	1	Balance b/d	976

Machinery Disposals Account

Dr   Cr

2000				£	2000				£
Jan	2	Machinery	(A)	2,000	Jan	2	Cash	(C)	950
						2	Provision for depreciation	(B)	976
					Dec	31	Profit and loss	(D)	74
				2,000					2,000

Profit and Loss Account for the year ended 31 December 1998

	£	
Loss on sale of machinery (D)	74	

Exercises

28.1 On 1 July 1996 R Burge, a greengrocer, purchased a motor delivery van for £2,000.

You are required to:
(a) Show how the motor delivery van account would appear in the books of R Burge for the four years ending 30 June 2000.
Depreciation is written off at the rate of 20 per cent on a reducing instalment basis.
(b) Explain the difference between the straight line method and the reducing balance method of depreciation.
(RSA)

28.2 David Moore, who is a sole trader, decides to purchase a delivery van for the sum of £1,500. He cannot decide whether to write off depreciation of the new van on the straight line method or the reducing balance method.

Required
In order to assist Moore in reaching a decision, draw up the delivery van account for the first three years – taking a rate of 10 per cent for depreciation – as it would appear:
(a) Under the straight line method.
(b) Under the reducing balance method.
(LCCI)

28.3 Charles Dudley, a sole trader, purchases on 1 November 1997, a new delivery van for £1,200. His business year end is 31 October but he cannot decide which method of depreciation he should use in respect of the new van – the straight line method or the reducing balance method.

Required
In order to assist Charles Dudley in making his decision, draw up the delivery van account for the three years from 1 November 1997 using:
(a)   the straight line method; and
(b)   the reducing balance method.
Each account must indicate which method is being used and each account be balanced at the end of each of the three years.

Notes:
(i)   In both cases the rate of depreciation is to be 10 per cent.
(ii) Calculations should be made to the nearest £.
(LCCI)

28.4X (a)   What is meant by depreciation and why is it important that a businessman should provide for depreciation in his accounts?
(b)   On 1 January 1997 A Swain, a haulage contractor, purchased three tipper lorries for £4,800 each. Mr Swain estimated that his lorries would have an effective working life of five years with a disposal value of £300 each. The straight line method of depreciation is to be used. The financial year ends on 31 December. One of the lorries kept breaking down and was sold on 1 January 1999 for £2,500.
     You are required to show the relevant entries for the years 1997, 1998 and 1999 in the following ledger accounts:
     (i)   Lorries.
     (ii) Lorries disposal.
     (iii) Provision for depreciation on lorries.
All workings are to be shown.
(RSA)

28.5X Reconstruct in good form the following balance sheet after taking into account the transactions for December.

Balance Sheet as at 30 November

Liabilities	£	Assets	£
Capital	3,000	Cash	500
+ Net profit	1,000	Machinery	1,000
	4,000	Vans	2,000
– Drawings	300	Debtors	1,500
	3,700	Stock	1,000
Creditors	2,300		
	6,000		6,000

Dec 1 Received a cheque from debtors £200
Dec 5 Took drawings in cash £150
Dec 10 Sold goods which cost £100 for £300 cash
Dec 15 Purchased goods on credit for £200
Dec 19 Depreciated machinery by £170
Dec 21 Took a loan from the bank to buy machine costing £2,000
Dec 31 Paid £25 cash into bank.
(Pitman Qualifications)

28.6 The financial year of Muldane plc ended on 31 May 1999.

At 1 June 1998 the company owned motor vehicles costing £124,000 which had been depreciated by a total of £88,000.

On 1 August 1998 Muldane plc sold motor vehicles which had cost £54,000 and which had been depreciated by £49,000 for £3,900 and purchased new motor vehicles costing £71,000.

It is the policy of Muldane plc to depreciate its motor vehicles at 35 per cent per annum using the diminishing balance method. A full year's depreciation is charged on all motor vehicles in use at the end of each year. No depreciation is charged for the year on assets disposed of during that year.

Required
(a) Identify the four factors which can cause fixed assets to depreciate.
(b) Which of the four factors from (a) is the most important for each of the following fixed assets?
   (i) A 90-year lease on a building.
   (ii) Land.
   (iii) A forest of mature trees to be felled for timber.
   (iv) A stamping press after the launch of an improved press capable of increased output of higher quality at lower cost.
(c) Show the following accounts as they would appear in the ledger of Muldane plc for the year ended 31 May 1999 only:
   (i) The motor vehicles account.
   (ii) The provision for depreciation – motor vehicles account.
   (iii) The assets disposals account.
(Association of Accounting Technicians)

29 Bad debts and provisions for bad debts

29.1 Bad debts

If a firm finds that it is impossible to collect a debt then that debt should be written off as a **bad debt**. This would happen if the debtor could not pay the debt.

An example of debts being written off as bad is shown in Exhibit 29.1.

Exhibit 29.1

We sold £50 goods to K Lee on 5 January 1998, but he became bankrupt. On 16 February 1998 we sold £240 goods to T Young. He managed to pay £200 on 17 May 1998, but it became obvious that he would never be able to pay the final £40.

When drawing up our final accounts to 31 December 1998 we decided to write these off as bad debts. The accounts would appear as follows:

K Lee Account

Dr				Cr
1998		£	1998	£
Jan 5 Sales		50	Dec 31 Bad debts	50

T Young Account

Dr				Cr
1998		£	1998	£
Feb 16 Sales		240	May 17 Cash	200
			Dec 31 Bad debts	40
		240		240

Bad Debts Account

Dr				Cr
1998		£	1998	£
Dec 31 K Lee		50	Dec 31 Profit and	
T Young		40	loss a/c	90
		90		90

Profit and Loss Account for the year ended 31 December 1998

	£
Bad debts	90

29.2 Provision for bad debts

Why provisions are needed

The total of the trade debtors appears in the balance sheet as an asset. If they all paid their accounts then this would mean that the trade debtors figure was correct. If some of the trade debtors do not pay, the figure of trade debtors will have been overstated in the balance sheet. To try to get as accurate a figure as possible for trade debtors, a firm will make the best estimate it can of the number of trade debtors who will never pay their accounts. This estimate can be made:

1   By looking at each debt, and estimating which ones will be bad debts.
2   By estimating, on the basis of experience, what percentage of the debts will prove to be bad debts.

It is logical to assume that the longer a debt is outstanding the more likely it is that it will become a bad debt. Some firms draw up an ageing schedule, showing how long debts have been owing. Older trade debtors need higher percentage estimates of bad debts than newer debts. Exhibit 29.2 gives an example of such an ageing schedule.

Exhibit 29.2

Ageing Schedule for Doubtful Debts			
Period debt owing	*Amount*	*Estimated percentage doubtful*	*Provision for bad debts*
	£		£
Less than one month	5,000	1	50
1 month to 2 months	3,000	3	90
2 months to 3 months	800	4	32
3 months to 1 year	200	5	10
Over 1 year	160	20	32
	9,160		214

Accounting entries for provisions for bad debts

When the decision has been taken as to the amount of the provision to be made, then the accounting entries are needed for the year in which the provision is first made.

1 Debit profit and loss account with amount of provision.
2 Credit provision for bad debts account.

Exhibit 29.3 shows the entries needed for a provision for bad debts.

Exhibit 29.3

At 31 December 1998 the trade debtors figure amounted to £10,000. It is estimated that two per cent of debts (i.e. £200) will prove to be bad debts, and it is decided to make a provision for these. The accounts would appear as follows:

Profit and Loss Account for the year ended 31 December 1998

Dr			Cr
	£		
Provision for bad debts	200		

Provision for Bad Debts Account

Dr		Cr
	1998	£
	Dec 31 Profit and loss a/c	200

In the balance sheet the balance on the provision for bad debts will be deducted from the total of trade debtors:

Balance Sheet (extracts) as on 31 December 1998

Current Assets	£	£
Debtors	10,000	
Less Provision for bad debts	200	
		9,800

29.3 Increasing the provision

Let us suppose that for the same firm as in Exhibit 29.3, at the end of the following year 31 December 1999, the bad debts provision needed to be increased. This was because the provision was kept at 2 per cent, but the trade debtors had risen to £12,000. A provision of £200 had been brought forward from the *previous* year, but we now want a total provision of £240 (i.e. 2 per cent of £12,000). All that is needed is a provision for an extra £40.

The double entry will be:

1 Debit profit and loss account.
2 Credit provision for bad debts account.

Profit and Loss Account for the year ended 31 December 1999

	£	
Provision for bad debts	40	

Provision for Bad Debts Account

Dr			Cr	
1999		£	1999		£
Dec 31	Balance c/d	240	Jan 1	Balance b/d	200
			Dec 31	Profit and loss a/c	40
		240			240
			2000		
			Jan 1	Balance b/d	240

The balance sheet as at 31 December 1999 will appear as:

Balance Sheet (extract) as on 31 December 1999

Current Assets	£	£
Debtors	12,000	
Less Provision for bad debts	240	
		11,760

29.4 Reducing the provision

The provision is shown as a credit balance. Therefore to reduce it we would need a debit entry in the provision account. The credit would be in the profit and loss account. Let us assume that at 31 December 2000, in the firm already examined, the debtors figure had fallen to £10,500 but the provision remained at 2 per cent, i.e. £210 (2 per cent of £10,500). Thus the provision needs a reduction of £30. The double entry is:

1 Debit provision for bad debts account.
2 Credit profit and loss account.

Profit and Loss Account for the year ended 31 December 2000

Dr	Cr	
		£
	Provision for bad debts: Reduction	30

Provision for Bad Debts Account

Dr						Cr
2000			£	2000		£
Dec 31	Profit and loss a/c		30	Jan 1 Balance b/d		240
Dec 31	Balance c/d		210			
			240			240
				2001		
				Jan 1 Balance b/d		210

The balance sheet will appear:

Balance Sheet (extracts) as on 31 December 2000

Current Assets	£	£
Debtors	10,500	
Less Provision for bad debts	210	
		10,290

Let us now look at a comprehensive example, Exhibit 29.4.

Exhibit 29.4

A business starts on 1 January 1997 and its financial year end is 31 December annually. A table of the trade debtors, the bad debts written off and the estimated bad debts at the rate of two per cent of trade debtors at the end of each year is given below. The double entry accounts, and the extracts from the final accounts follow.

Year to 31 December	Debtors at end of year (after bad debts written off)	Bad debts written off during year	Debts thought at end of year to be impossible to collect: 2% of debtors
	£	£	£
1997	6,000	423	120 (2% of £6,000)
1998	7,000	510	140 (2% of £7,000)
1999	7,750	604	155 (2% of £7,750)
2000	6,500	610	130 (2% of £6,500)

Profit and Loss accounts for the year ended 31 December (extracts)

		£			£
1997	Bad debts	423			
	Provision for bad debts	120			
1998	Bad debts	510			
	Increase in provision for bad debts	20			
1999	Bad debts	604			
	Increase in provision for bad debts	15			
			2000	Reduction in provision for bad debts	25
2000	Bad debts	610			

Provision for Bad Debts Account

Dr			£				Cr £
				1997			
				Dec 31	Profit and loss a/c		120
1998				1998			
Dec 31	Balance c/d		140	Dec 31	Profit and loss a/c		20
			140				140
1999				1999			
Dec 31	Balance c/d		155	Jan 1	Balance b/d		140
				Dec 31	Profit and loss a/c		15
			155				155
2000				2000			
Dec 31	Profit and loss a/c		25	Jan 1	Balance b/d		155
	Balance c/d		130				
			155				155
				2001			
				Jan 1	Balance b/d		130

Bad Debts Account

Dr			£				Cr £
1997				1997			
Dec 31	Various debtors		423	Dec 31	Profit and loss a/c		423
1998				1998			
Dec 31	Various debtors		510	Dec 31	Profit and loss a/c		510
1999				1999			
Dec 31	Various debtors		604	Dec 31	Profit and loss a/c		604
2000				2000			
Dec 31	Various debtors		610	Dec 31	Profit and loss a/c		610

Balance Sheets as at 31 December (extracts)

		£	£
1997	Debtors	6,000	
	Less Provision for bad debts	120	5,880
1998	Debtors	7,000	
	Less Provision for bad debts	140	6,860
1999	Debtors	7,750	
	Less Provision for bad debts	155	7,595
2000	Debtors	6,500	
	Less Provision for bad debts	130	6,370

29.5 Diagram of entries

It can be difficult to understand why there should be entries in the profit and loss account for bad debts and also a provision for bad debts. The following example should show why both of the items are needed:

T Kime starts a business. Let us look at some of the figures from his first year's trading:

1   He has sold £50,000 goods on credit.
2   Trade debtors have paid him £39,600.
3   Two trade debtors owing him a total of £400 have been made bankrupt. No money will ever be received from them.
4   There was still another £10,000 owing to him at the year end not including the £400 in (3).
5   Some of the £10,000 in (4) will probably never be paid. Kime did not know exactly how much it would be. He estimates it to be one per cent of trade debtors, i.e. £10,000 × 1% = £100. He decides to make a provision for bad debts account and extracts from the final accounts are now shown.

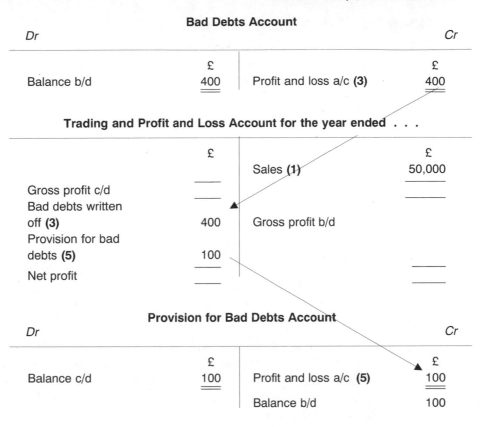

Bad Debts Account

Dr			Cr
	£		£
Balance b/d	400	Profit and loss a/c (3)	400

Trading and Profit and Loss Account for the year ended . . .

	£		£
		Sales (1)	50,000
Gross profit c/d	____		____
Bad debts written off (3)	400	Gross profit b/d	
Provision for bad debts (5)	100		
Net profit	____		____

Provision for Bad Debts Account

Dr			Cr
	£		£
Balance c/d	100	Profit and loss a/c (5)	100
		Balance b/d	100

For the balance sheet, the balances for the trade debtors in (4) and the provision for bad debts in (5) have to be shown. There is no balance on the bad debts account, and therefore this will not appear.

Balance Sheet as at . . .

	£	£
Current Assets		
Debtors (4)	10,000	
Less Provision for bad debts (5)	100	9,900

To summarise:
1 Of the £50,000 sales, there are definite bad debts of £400 which have been written off in the year to the bad debts account.
2 Of the £10,000 trade debtors outstanding at the year end, 1 per cent, £100, is estimated to be the amount that will not be paid in the future, and is transferred to the provision for bad debts account.
3 The trade debtors are thus, £10,000 less £100, which equals £9,900.
4 The profit and loss account is debited with both the £400 actual bad debts, and £100 provision for bad debts, thus reducing the profit by £500 in total, which is the expected amount not to be received for the year.

29.6 Bad debts recovered

It is not uncommon for a debt written off in previous years to be recovered in later years. When this occurs, the book-keeping procedures are as follows:

First, reinstate the debt by making the following entries:

Dr Debtors account
Cr Bad debts recovered account.

The reason for reinstating the debt in the ledger account of the debtor is to have a detailed history of their account as a guide for granting credit in future. By the time a debt is written off as bad, it will be recorded in the debtor's ledger account. Therefore, when such debt is recovered, it also must be shown in the debtor's ledger account.

When payment is later received from the debtor in settlement of the account or part thereof,

Dr Cash/Bank
Cr Debtor's account

with the amount received.

At the end of the financial year, the credit balance in the bad debts recovered account will be transferred to either bad debts account or direct to the credit side of the profit and loss account. The effect is the same since the bad debts account will in itself be transferred to the profit and loss account at the end of the financial year.

New terms

Bad debt (p 272): A debt which will not be collected.
Provision for bad debt (p 273): A provision for a debt, or estimate of debts, that may not be recovered.

Exercises

29.1 On 1 January 1997 the balances below appeared in the sales ledger of S Sowerby:

	£
D Plim	200
C Mike	120

During the year the following events took place:
Feb   1 After negotiation Sowerby agreed to accept £150 cash from D Plim and regarded the outstanding balance as irrecoverable.
Mar 10 C Mike was declared bankrupt. A payment of 30 pence in the £ was received in full settlement.
Show how these matters would be dealt with in Sowerby's ledger assuming that the financial year ends on 30 June 1997.
(RSA)

29.2 On 30 September 1997 B Fox's trade debtors totalled £12,000. He decided to write off the following as bad debts:

£

G Green   60
H Wilson 80

He further decided to make a provision for bad debts of 10 per cent on the remaining debtors.

Debtors on 30 September 1998 totalled £10,000 when Fox decided to maintain the provision at 10 per cent.

You are required to show for each of the years ended 30 September 1997 and 1998:

(a) provision for bad debts account;
(b) the appropriate entries in the profit and loss account; and
(c) the necessary balance sheet entries on each of the above dates.
(RSA)

29.3

Date: 31 Dec	Total debtors	Profit and loss	Dr/Cr	Final figure for balance Sheet
	£	£		£
1997	7,000			
1998	8,000			
1999	6,000			
2000	7,000			

The above table shows the figure for debtors appearing in a trader's books on 31 December of each year from 1997 to 2000. The provision for bad debts is to be 1 per cent of debtors from 31 December 1997. Complete the above table indicating the amount to be debited or credited to the profit and loss account for the year ended on each 31 December, and the amount for the final figure of debtors to appear in the balance sheet on each date.
(RSA)

29.4X A business started on 1 January 1997 and its financial year end is 31 December annually. A table of the debtors, the bad debts written off and the estimated bad debts at the end of the year is now given.

Year to 31 December	Debtors at end of year (after bad debts written off)	Bad debts written off during the year	Debts thought at end of year to be impossible to collect
	£	£	£
1997	12,000	298	100
1998	15,000	386	130
1999	14,000	344	115
2000	18,000	477	150

You are required to show the above in the double entry accounts, as well as the extracts from the profit and loss account for each year and the balance sheet extracts.

29.5X   T Pitt owes you £59.00 on 1 January. He pays you £29.00 on 31 January but ignores all further requests for payment. On 6 May you hear that he has been made a bankrupt, and his trustee in bankruptcy announces that a dividend of 25 per cent in the £ will paid on 30 September. This payment was received in due course.

      Show Pitt's ledger account and the bad debts account at 31 December, the end of your financial year.

(Pitman Qualifications)

29.6X   The following data is available in relation to Thermogen Suppliers:

		£
(1)	Balance of debtors at 31 December Year 6 – *before* writing off bad debts	81,600
(2)	Bad debts written off in Year 6	1,200
(3)	A provision of 2% of debtors for bad debts was set up at 31 December Year 6	
(4)	Bad debts written off in Year 7	1,800
(5)	Balance of debtors at 31 December Year 7 – *before* writing off bad debts	122,700
(6)	The provision for bad debts is increased to 4% at 31 December Year 7	
(7)	Bad debts written off in Year 8	2,100
(8)	Balance of debtors at 31 December Year 8 – *after* writing off bad debts	103,500
(9)	The provision for bad debts is reduced to 3% at 31 December Year 8	

Required

(a) Prepare the following accounts for Years 6, 7 and 8, showing the transfer to profit and loss account at the end of each year:

     (i)   Bad debts account

     (ii)   Provision for bad debts account

(b) Show balance sheet extracts in respect of debtors at the following dates:

     31 December Year 6

     31 December Year 7

     31 December Year 8

(c) If one of the debts, written off early in Year 8, was to be recovered later in Year 8, what accounting entries would you expect to be made?

(LCCI)

30 Accruals, prepayments and other adjustments

30.1 Final accounts so far

The trading and profit and loss accounts studied so far have taken the sales for a period and deducted all the expenses for that period, the result being a net profit (or a net loss).

It has always been assumed that the expenses belonged exactly to the period of the trading and profit and loss account. If the trading and profit and loss account for the year ended 31 December 1997 was being drawn up, then for instance, the rent paid as shown in the trial balance was exactly for 1997. There was no rent owing at the beginning of 1997 nor any owing at the end of 1997, nor had any rent been paid in advance.

30.2 Adjustments needed

Let us look at two firms who pay rent for buildings. The rent for each building is £1,200 a year.

1   Firm A pays £1,000 in the year. At the year end it owes £200 for rent.
    Rent expense used up   = £1,200
    Rent paid for   = £1,000
2   Firm B pays £1,300 in the year. This figure includes £100 in advance for the following year.
    Rent expense used up   = £1,200
    Rent paid for   = £1,300

A profit and loss account for 12 months needs 12 months' rent as an expense = £1,200.

This means that in both (1) and (2) the double entry accounts will have to be adjusted.

30.3 Accrued expenses

Assume that rent of £1,000 per year is payable at the end of every three months. The rent was not always paid on time. Details were:

Amount	Rent due	Rent paid
£250	31 March 1997	31 March 1997
£250	30 June 1997	2 July 1997
£250	30 September 1997	4 October 1997
£250	31 December 1997	5 January 1998

The rent account appeared as:

Rent Account

Dr				Cr

1997			£
Mar	31	Cash	250
Jul	2	"	250
Oct	4	"	250

The rent paid 5 January 1998 will appear in the books of the year 1998 as part of the double entry.

The expenses for 1997 are £1,000, as that is the year's rent, and this is the amount needed to be transferred to the profit and loss account. But if £1,000 was put on the credit side of the rent account (the debit being in the profit and loss account) the account would not balance. We would have £1,000 on the credit side of the account and only £750 on the debit side.

To make the account balance the £250 rent owing for 1997, but paid in 1998, must be carried down to 1998 as a credit balance because it is a liability at 31 December 1997. Instead of rent owing it could be called rent accrued or just simply an accrual. The completed account can now be shown.

Rent Account

Dr							Cr

1997			£	1997			£
Mar	31	Cash	250	Dec	31	Profit and loss	1,000
Jul	2	"	250				
Oct	4	"	250				
Dec	31	Accrued c/d	250				
			1,000				1,000
				1998			
				Jan	1	Accrued b/d	250

The balance c/d has been described as accrued c/d, rather than as a balance. This is to explain what the balance is for; it is for an **accrued expense**.

30.4 Prepaid expenses

A firm has insurance at the rate of £840 a year, starting from 1 January 1998. The firm has agreed to pay this at the rate of £210 every three months. However, payments were not made at the correct times. Details were:

Amount	Insurance due	Insurance paid
£210	31 March 1998	£210 28 February 1998
£210	30 June 1998	
£210	30 September 1998	£420 31 August 1998
£210	31 December 1998	£420 18 November 1998

The insurance account will be shown in the books:

Insurance Account

Dr   Cr

1998		£
Feb 28	Cash	210
Aug 31	"	420
Nov 18	"	420

The last payment of £420 is not just for 1998; it will need to be split, as £210 is for the three months to 31 December 1998 and £210 is for the three months ended 31 March 1999. For a period of 12 months the cost of insurance is £840 and this is the figure that needs to be transferred to the profit and loss account.

The amount needed to balance the account will therefore be £210 and at 31 December 1998 this is a benefit paid for but not used up; it is an asset and needs carrying forward as such to 1999 as a debit balance. It is a **prepaid expense**.

The account can now be completed.

Insurance Account

Dr   Cr

1998		£	1998		£
Feb 28	Cash	210	Dec 31	Profit and	
Aug 31	"	420		loss	840
Nov 18	"	420	" 31	Prepaid c/d	210
		1,050			1,050
1999					
Jan 1	Prepaid b/d	210			

Prepayment will also happen when items other than purchases are bought for use in the business, and they are not fully used up in the period.

For instance, packing materials are normally not entirely used up over the period in which they are bought, there being a stock of packing materials in hand at the end of the period. This stock is, therefore, a form of prepayment and needs carrying down to the following period in which it will be used.

This can be seen in the following example:

Year ended 31 December 1998.
Packing materials bought in the year £2,200.
Stock of packing materials in hand as at 31 December 1998 £400.

Looking at the example, it can be seen that in 1998 the packing materials used up will have been £2,200 – £400 = £1,800. We will still have a stock of £400 packing materials at 31 December 1998 to be carried forward to 1999. The £400 stock of packing materials will be carried forward as an asset balance (debit balance) to 1999.

Packing Materials Account

Dr		£			£
1998			1998		
Dec 31	Cash	2,200	Dec 31	Profit and loss	1,800
				Stock c/d	400
		2,200			2,200
1999					
Jan 1	Stock b/d	400			

The stock of packing materials is not added to the stock of unsold goods in hand in the balance sheet, but is added to the other prepayments of expenses.

30.5 Revenue owing at the end of period

The **revenue** owing for sales is already shown in the books. These are the debit balances on our customers' accounts, i.e. trade debtors. There may be other kinds of revenue, e.g. rent receivable. An example now follows:

30.6 Worked example

Our warehouse is larger than we need. We rent part of it to another firm for £800 per annum. Details for the year ended 31 December 1998 were as follows:

Amount	Rent due	Rent received
£200	31 March 1998	4 April 1998
£200	30 June 1998	6 July 1998
£200	30 September 1998	9 October 1998
£200	31 December 1998	7 January 1999

The account for 1998 appeared:

Rent Receivable Account

Dr					Cr
	1998				£
	Apr	4	Bank		200
	Jul	6	Bank		200
	Oct	9	Bank		200

The rent received of £200 on 7 January 1999 will be entered in the books in 1999.

Any rent paid by the firm would be charged as a debit to the profit and loss account. Any rent received, being the opposite, is transferred to the credit of the profit and loss account.

The amount to be transferred for 1998 is that earned for the twelve months, i.e. £800. The rent received account is completed by carrying down the balance owing as a debit balance to 1999. The £200 owing is an asset on 31 December 1998.

The rent receivable account can now be completed:

Rent Receivable Account

Dr			£	1998				Cr	£
1998				1998					
Dec 31	Profit and			Apr	4	Bank			200
	loss a/c		800	Jul	6	Bank			200
				Oct	9	Bank			200
				Dec	31	Accrued c/d			200
			800						800
1999									
Jan 1	Accrued b/d		200						

30.7 Expenses and revenue account balances and the balance sheet

In all the cases listed dealing with adjustments in the final accounts, there will still be a balance on each account after the preparation of the trading and profit and loss accounts. All such balances remaining should appear in the balance sheet. The only question left is where and how they shall be shown.

The amounts owing for expenses are usually added together and shown as one figure. These could be called expense creditors, expenses owing, or accrued expenses. The item would appear under current liabilities as they are expenses which have to be discharged in the near future.

The items prepaid are also added together and called prepayments, prepaid expenses, or payments in advance. Often they are added to the debtors in the balance sheet, otherwise they are shown next under the debtors. Amounts owing for rents receivable or other revenue owing are usually added to debtors.

The balance sheet in respect of the accounts so far seen in this chapter would appear:

Balance Sheet as at 31 December 1998 (extract)

	£	£
Current assets		
Stock	–	
Debtors	200	
Prepayments (£400 + £210)	610	
Cash at bank	–	
Cash in hand	–	
		810
Current liabilities		
Trade creditors	–	
Accrued expenses	250	
		250
Net current assets		560

30.8 Expenses and revenue accounts covering more than one period

We will now look at how we draw up an expense or revenue account for a full year, when there are amounts owing or prepaid at both the beginning and end of the year.

Example A

The following details are available:

1 On 31 December 1997 three months rent of £3,000 was owing.
2 The rent chargeable per year was £12,000.
3 The following payments were made in the year 1998:
   6 January £3,000; 4 April £3,000; 7 July £3,000; 18 October £3,000.
4 The final three months rent for 1998 is still owing.

Now we can look at the completed rent account. The numbers (**1**) to (**4**) give reference to the details above.

Rent Account

Dr   Cr

1998			£	1998				£
Jan	6	Bank	(3) 3,000	Jan	1	Owing b/f	(1)	3,000
Apr	4	Bank	(3) 3,000	Dec	31	Profit and		
Jul	7	Bank	(3) 3,000			loss a/c	(2)	12,000
Oct	18	Bank	(3) 3,000					
Dec	31	Owing c/d	(4) 3,000					
			15,000					15,000
				Jan	1	Owing b/d		3,000

Example B

The following details are available:

1 On 31 December 1997 packing materials in hand amounted to £1,850.
2 During the year to 31 December 1998 £27,480 was paid for packing materials.
3 There were no stocks of packing materials on 31 December 1998.
4 On 31 December 1998 we still owed £2,750 for packing materials already received and used.

The packing materials account will appear as:

Packing Materials Account

Dr   Cr

1998				£	1998			£
Jan	1	Stocks b/f	(1)	1,850	Dec	31	Profit and	
Dec	31	Bank	(2)	27,480			loss a/c	32,080
Dec	31	Owing c/d	(4)	2,750				
				32,080				32,080
					1999			
					Jan	1	Owing b/d	2,750

The figure of £32,080 is the difference on the account, and is transferred to the profit and loss account.

We can prove it is correct:

	£	£
Stock at start of year		1,850
Add bought and used:		
Paid for	27,480	
Still owed for	2,750	30,230
Cost of packing materials used in the year		32,080

Example C

Where different expenses are put together in one account, it can get even more confusing. Let us look at where rent and rates are joined together.

Here are the details for the year ended 31 December 1998.

1 Rent is payable of £6,000 per annum.
2 Rates of £4,000 per annum are payable by instalments.
3 At 1 January 1998 rent of £1,000 had been prepaid in 1997.
4 On 1 January 1998 rates were owed of £400.
5 During 1998 rent was paid of £4,500.
6 During 1998 rates were paid of £5,000.
7 On 31 December 1998 rent of £500 was owing.
8 On 31 December 1998 rates of £600 had been prepaid.

A combined rent and rates account is to be drawn up for the year 1998 showing the transfer to the profit and loss account, and balances are to be carried down to 1999.

Rent and Rates Account

Dr					Cr	
1998			£	1998		£
Jan 1	Rent prepaid b/f	(3)	1,000	Jan 1	Rates owing b/f (4)	400
Dec 31	Bank: Rent	(5)	4,500	Dec 31	Profit and loss a/c (1 + 2)	10,000
Dec 31	Rates	(6)	5,000	Dec 31	Rates prepaid c/d (8)	600
Dec 31	Rent owing c/d	(7)	500			
			11,000			11,000
1999				1999		
Jan 1	Rates prepaid b/d	(8)	600	Jan 1	Rent owing b/d (7)	500

30.9 Goodwill

When starting in business we could start from nothing. At that time we would have no customers at all. Over the years we might work hard, and then have a lot of customers who would buy or trade with us year after year.

Instead of this we might buy an existing business. We look at it and put a value on the items in the business.

These are:

	£
Premises	50,000
Equipment	20,000
Stock	12,000
	82,000

But the owner wants £100,000 for the business, an extra £18,000. He says it is worth £18,000 extra because he has made the business into a very good one, with a lot of customers. Many of the customers trade continually with him.

We agreed to pay the extra £18,000. This extra amount is known as **goodwill**. We will do this, because we will get a lot of customers immediately. It might take us many years to do this if we start from nothing.

In the balance sheet we will show goodwill as an intangible fixed asset, that is, an asset that cannot be seen or touched.

30.10 Goods for own use

A trader will often take items out of his business stocks for his own use, without paying for them. There is nothing wrong about this, but an entry should be made to record the event. This is done by:

1 Credit purchases account.
2 Debit drawings account.

Adjustments may also be needed for other private items. For instance, if a trader's private insurance had been incorrectly charged to the insurance account, then the correction would be:

1 Credit insurance account.
2 Debit drawings account.

30.11 Treatment of returns inwards and returns outwards in final accounts

You will recall, from Chapter 21, that firms return goods to their supplier (returns outwards) when the goods are either faulty, or, maybe unsuitable, also firms will have goods returned to them (returns inwards) for the same reasons. In Chapter 21 we looked at recording returns in the books of account, now we will consider the treatment in the final accounts.

When calculating the *gross profit* of a business the returns will have to be taken into consideration. Let us assume that the following accounts appear in the books of D Marston as at 31 December 1999.

Exhibit 30.1

**Extracts from the Trial Balance of D Marston
as at 31 December 1999**

	Dr	Cr
	£	£
Opening stock	5,000	
Sales		80,000
Purchases	52,400	
Returns inwards	3,000	
Returns outwards		4,400

The closing stock at 31 December 1999 was valued at £6,500.

The trading and profit and loss account would appear as follows:

**Trading and Profit and Loss Account of D Marston
for the year ended 31 December 1999**

	£	£
Sales		80,000
Less Returns inwards		3,000
		77,000
Less Cost of goods sold		
Opening stock	5,000	
Add Purchases	52,400	
	57,400	
Less Returns outwards	4,400	
	53,000	
Less Closing stock	6,500	
		46,500
Gross profit		30,500

Note: Sales less returns inwards is often called 'turnover'. In Exhibit 30.1 above the turnover is £77,000.

30.12 Treatment of discounts allowed and discounts received in final accounts

In Chapter 16 we dealt with recording cash discounts in the cash book and ledgers and you will recall that such a discount could be either 'discounts allowed', which represents a reduction given to our customers for prompt payment of their account or 'discounts received' when the reduction is given by a supplier to us when we pay their account within a specified period.

Using the previous example of D Marston (Exhibit 30.1) let us assume that the discount allowed amounted to £310 and the discount received totalled £510. These items would appear in the trading and profit and loss account as follows:

Exhibit 30.2

**Trading and Profit and Loss Account of D Marston
for the year ended 31 December 1999**

	£	£
Gross profit		30,500
Less Expenses		
Discounts allowed	310	
Other expenses	10,000	10,310
		20,190
Add Income		
Discounts received		510
Net profit		20,700

30.13 Preparation of final accounts

Students may find it useful to refer to the following exhibits when preparing the final accounts of a business.

Step-by-step guide to preparation of final accounts

Final accounts are often prepared from a trial balance, and the following guidelines should help to ensure speed and accuracy in their preparation, and ensure that confidence and competence is achieved.

1   Before starting the exercise, rule lines connecting each item. This avoids picking up a wrong figure – easily done under the stress of an examination.
2   Decide where each item is going *before* you start to prepare the final accounts.
3   An almost 100 per cent rule!
    - Each item displayed in the trial balance must only be entered *once* in the final accounts.
    - Any item noted below a trial balance exercise should be dealt with *twice*, (i.e. when an item is prepaid at the date of the final accounts).
    - *Exception to the 100 per cent rule!*
      In the case of limited companies showing information on their authorised and issued capital:

      Enter issued capital once in the balance sheet.
      Enter the authorised capital once at the foot of the balance sheet.

Step-by-step guide to deal with adjustments in final accounts

1   Returns inwards and returns outwards:
    (a) Returns inwards – deduct from sales in the trading account.
    (b) Returns outwards – deduct from purchases in the trading account.

2   Carriage inwards and carriage outwards:
    (a) Carriage inwards – add to purchases in the trading account.
    (b) Carriage outwards – charge as an expense in profit and loss account.

3   Prepayments (amounts paid in advance):
    (a) Deduct the amount from expenses in the trial balance.
    (b) Add the amount to debtors in the trial balance.

4   Accruals (amounts owing):
    (a) Add the amount to expenses in the trial balance.
    (b) Add the amount to creditors in the trial balance.

5 Depreciation:
Straight line or on cost
(a) Find cost price of asset (say)   £24,000
(b) Using percentage given (say)   20%
    calculate 20% of £24,000   =   £4,800

then

(c) Charge £4,800 as an expense in the profit and loss account.
(d) In the balance sheet deduct *total* depreciation (i.e. £4,800 from this year plus any depreciation deducted in previous years, see figure on credit side in trial balance) from cost price of asset (£24,000) to arrive at NBV (net book value).

Reducing balance or written down value
(a) Find cost price of asset (say)   £10,000
(b) Find total amount of depreciation
    deducted to date (see credit side
    of trial balance) say   £4,000
(c) Find the difference   £6,000
(d) Using percentage given (say)   10%
    calculate 10 per cent of £6,000 =   £600

then

(a) Charge £600 as an expense in the profit and loss account.
(b) In the balance sheet deduct *total* depreciation (i.e. £600 from this year plus any depreciation deducted in previous years, £4,000, see figure on credit side in the trial balance) from cost price.

6 Bad Debts Provision:
Creation
(a) Decide on the amount of provision to be created (say 1 per cent of debtors of £5,000 = £50).

then

(b) Charge the provision £50 to the profit and loss account as an expense.
(c) In the balance sheet deduct provision £50 from debtors.

Increase in provision
(a) Calculate the new provision (i.e. this year's).
(b) Find out the old provision (i.e. last year's – look in the trial balance – credit side).
(c) Find the difference.

then

(d) Charge the difference only to the profit and loss account.
(e) Deduct the new provision from debtors in the balance sheet.

Reduction in provision
(a) Calculate the new provision (i.e. this year's).

(b) Find out the old provision (i.e. last year's – look in the trial balance – credit side).

(c) Find the difference.

then

(d) Add back the difference as income in the profit and loss account.

(e) Deduct the new provision from debtors in the balance sheet.

7   Bad Debts:
Simply write off as an expense in the profit and loss account.

Exhibit 30.3 **Model layout of final accounts for sole trader**

Trading and Profit and Loss Account of . . . for the year ended . . .		
	£	£
Sales		xxx
Less Returns inwards		xx
		xxx
Less Cost of goods sold		
Opening stock	x	
Add Purchases	x	
Add Carriage inwards	x	
	xx	
Less Returns outwards	x	
	xx	
Less Closing stock	x	xxx
Gross profit		xxx
Less Expenses		
Bad debts (written off)	x	
Wages and salaries	x	
Rates	x	
Insurance	x	
Rent	x	
General expenses	x	
Postages	x	
Stationery	x	
Carriage outwards	x	
Discounts allowed	x	
Heating	x	
Electricity	x	
Depreciation	x	
Increase in provision for bad debts	x	xxx
		xxx
Add income		
Discounts + interest received	x	
Reductions in provision for bad debts	x	xx
Net profit		£xxx

Balance Sheet of . . . as at . . .			
	Cost	Total depreciation	Net book value
Fixed assets	£	£	£
Premises	X	X	X
Motor vehicle	X	X	X
Office furniture	X	X	X
Office equipment	X	X	X
Machinery	X	X	X
	XX	XX	X
Current assets			
Stock (closing)	X		
Debtors (*Less* Provision for bad debts)	X		
Prepayment	X		
Cash at bank	X		
Cash in hand	X	XX	
Less Current liabilities			
Creditors	X		
Expenses owing	X		
Bank overdraft	X	XX	
Net current assets			XX
			XXX
Less Long-term liabilities			
Long-term loan			X
			£XXX
Financed by			
Capital			XXX
Add Profit			X
			XXX
Less Drawings			X
			£XXX

30.14 Final accounts for non-traders

If the final accounts are for someone who is not trading in goods, but providing a service such as accountants, insurance brokers, solicitors etc., there will be no need for a trading account.

All of the revenue and expense items will be shown in a profit and loss account, disclosing a net profit (or net loss). Balance sheets will be the same as for traders.

30.15 Definition of accounting

In Chapter 1 we gave a definition of book-keeping as being concerned with the work of entering information into accounting records and afterwards maintaining such records properly.

However, accounting was not fully defined in Chapter 1 as it would not have meant much to you at that stage. The following is the most widely used definition – *The process of identifying, measuring, and communicating economic information to permit informed judgements and decisions by users of the information.*

New terms

Accrued expenses (p 283): An expense which the firm has used, but which has not yet been paid for, i.e. an amount owing.

Goodwill (p 290): The extra amount paid for an existing firm above the value of its other assets.

Prepaid expenses (p 285): An expense to be used up in a following period, but which has been paid for in advance.

Revenue (p 286): Money earned by the firm.

Exercises

30.1 The financial year of H Saunders ended on 31 December 1998. Show the ledger accounts for the following items including the balance transferred to the necessary part of the final accounts, also the balances carried down to 1999:

(a) Motor expenses: Paid in 1998 £744; Owing at 31 December 1998 £28.

(b) Insurance: Paid in 1998 £420; Prepaid as at 31 December 1998 £35.

(c) Stationery: Paid during 1998: £1,800; Owing as at 31 December 1997 £250; Owing as at 31 December 1998 £490.

(d) Rent: Paid during 1998 £950; Prepaid as at 31 December 1997 £220; Prepaid as at 31 December 1998 £290.

(e) Saunders sub-lets part of the premises. Receives £550 during the year ended 31 December 1998. The tenant owed Saunders £180 on 31 December 1997 and £210 on 31 December 1998.

30.2X J Owen's year ended on 30 June 1998. Write up the ledger accounts, showing the transfers to the final accounts and the balances carried down to the next year for the following:

(a) Stationery: Paid for the year to 30 June 1998 £855; Stocks of stationery at 30 June 1997 £290; at 30 June 1998 £345.

(b) General expenses: Paid for the year to 30 June 1998 £590; Owing at 30 June 1997 £64; Owing at 30 June 1998 £90.

(c) Rent and rates (combined account): Paid in the year to 30 June 1998 £3,890; Rent owing at 30 June 1997 £160; Rent paid in advance at 30 June 1998 £250; Rates owing 30 June 1997 £205; Rates owing 30 June 1998 £360.

(d) Motor expenses: paid in the year to 30 June 1998 £4,750; Owing as at 30 June 1997 £180; Owing as at 30 June 1998 £375.

    (e)   Owen earns commission from the sales of one item. Received for the year to 30 June 1998 £850; Owing at 30 June 1997 £80; Owing at 30 June 1998 £145.

30.3   A Bush is a sole trader who occupies rented premises. The annual rental is £2,400 which he pays quarterly. His lease and financial year commenced on 1 August Year 1.

During his first financial year, A Bush made the following payments in respect of rent:

		£
Year 1	1 August	600
	4 November	600
Year 2	31 March	600
	8 August	600

He paid rates on the premises as follows:

Year 1	31 August	£75 for period 1 August to 30 September Year 1
	22 October	£220 for period 1 October to 31 March Year 2
Year 2	17 April	£270 for period 1 April to 30 September Year 2

He paid electricity bills as follows:

Year 1	17 October	£310
Year 2	21 January	£390
Year 2	10 April	£360

An electricity bill of £420 accrued due had not been paid.

Required

(a)   Open the following accounts and, for the year ended 31 July Year 2, enter the payments and make the necessary year-end adjustments for prepayments or accruals. Enter the transfers to the profit and loss account and bring down balances at 1 August Year 2:
    (i)   Rent payable
    (ii) Rates
    (iii) Electricity

(b)   Show the relevant extracts covering the above items from the balance sheet of A Bush as at 31 July Year 2.

(LCCI)

30.4 The following is the trial balance of J Smailes as at 31 March 1997. Draw up a set of final accounts for the year ended 31 March 1997 in vertical format.

	Dr	Cr
	£	£
Stock 1 April 1996	18,160	
Sales		92,340
Purchases	69,185	
Carriage inwards	420	
Carriage outwards	1,570	
Returns outwards		640
Wages and salaries	10,240	
Rent and rates	3,015	
Communication expenses	624	
Commissions payable	216	
Insurance	405	
Sundry expenses	318	
Buildings	20,000	
Debtors	14,320	
Creditors		8,160
Fixtures	2,850	
Cash at bank	2,970	
Cash in hand	115	
Loan from K Ball		10,000
Drawings	7,620	
Capital		40,888
	152,028	152,028

Stock at 31 March 1997 was £22,390.

30.5 L Stokes drew up the following trial balance as at 30 September 1998. You are to draft trading and profit and loss accounts for the year to 30 September 1998 and a balance sheet as at that date in vertical format.

	Dr	Cr
	£	£
Loan from P Owens		5,000
Capital		25,955
Drawings	8,420	
Cash at bank	3,115	
Cash in hand	295	
Debtors	12,300	
Creditors		9,370
Stock 30 September 1997	23,910	
Motor van	4,100	
Office equipment	6,250	
Sales		130,900
Purchases	92,100	
Returns inwards	550	
Carriage inwards	215	
Returns outwards		307
Carriage outwards	309	
Motor expenses	1,630	
Rent	2,970	
Telephone charges	405	
Wages and salaries	12,810	
Insurance	492	
Office expenses	1,377	
Sundry expenses	284	
	171,532	171,532

Stock at 30 September 1998 was £27,475.

30.6X The following are *some* of the balances existing in the ledger of P Danton at 31 March Year 7:

	£	
Rent	1,265	(Debit balance)
Insurances	480	(Debit balance)
Loan from J Finniston	1,000	(Credit balance)
Motor vehicle at cost	6,200	(Debit balance)
Provision for bad debts	820	(Credit balance)

The following additional information is ascertained:
1 One month's rent, amounting to £115, is due but unpaid.
2 Insurances consist of:
   Property insurance £120 for the year ended 31 March Year 7
   Motor insurance   £360 for the year ended 30 June Year 7
3 Finniston's loan carries interest at 9% per annum. The first half year's interest has been paid and debited to the loan interest account but the second half year's interest is to be provided for.
4 The motor vehicle was purchased on 1 July Year 6. However, a full year's depreciation is to be provided for at 25% per annum on cost.
5 The bad debts provision is to be adjusted to £865.

Required

Prepare ledger accounts for:

(a) Rent

(b) Insurances

(c) Loan interest

(d) Provision for depreciation of motor vehicle

(e) Provision for bad debts

Note: Show clearly in each case the transfer to profit and loss account for the year ended 31 March Year 7.

(LCCI)

30.7 The trial balance of Bilton Potteries prepared after calculation of the gross profit is shown below.

Bilton Potteries

Trial Balance as at 31 January 1998

Details	Debit £	Credit £
Capital		7,000
Premises	5,000	
Bank	3,218	
Debtors	434	
Stock (31 January 1998)	1,000	
Creditors		870
Drawings	3,800	
Insurance	450	
Rent receivable		225
Rates	500	
Wages	5,200	
Gross profit for year ended 31 January 1998		11,507
	£19,602	£19,602

A detailed review by the accountant revealed that the following adjustments were outstanding:

1 Rates amounting to £100 had been paid in advance.

2 Rent receivable of £75 was still outstanding at 31 January 1998.

3 The insurance total included the payment of £50 for private house contents insurance.

4 Wages owing amounted to £300.

Required

(a) Open up the appropriate ledger accounts and post the above adjustments. Balance off these ledger accounts.

(b) Prepare a profit and loss account for the year ended 31 January 1998 and a balance sheet as at that date, after the above adjustments have been posted.

(RSA)

30.8 George Holt, a sole trader, extracted from his books the following trial balance as at the close of business on 31 October 1998.

	Dr £	Cr £
Stock 1 November 1997	1,970	
Debtors and creditors	2,350	1,680
Wages and salaries	1,520	
Rent, rates and insurance	280	
Bad debts	110	
Discounts	130	90
Fixtures and fittings	400	
Purchases and sales	5,930	9,620
Bank overdraft		260
Cash in hand	30	
Capital account 1 November 1997		2,700
Drawings	1,440	
General office expenses	190	
	14,350	14,350

Notes:
(a) Rent prepaid at 31 October 1998 £40.
(b) Stock 31 October 1998 £1,780.
(c) Depreciation £100 for fixtures and fittings.

Required
Prepare the trading and profit and loss accounts for the year ending 31 October 1998 together with a balance sheet as at that date.
(LCCI)

30.9 From the following trial balance of John Brown, a grocery shop owner, prepare a trading account and profit and loss account, taking into consideration the adjustments shown below:

Trial Balance as at 31 December 1997

	Dr £	Cr £
Sales		40,000
Purchases	35,000	
Sales returns	500	
Purchases returns		620
Opening stock at 1 January 1997	10,000	
Provision for bad debt		80
Wages and salaries	3,000	
Rates	600	
Telephone	100	
Shop fittings at cost	4,000	
Van at cost	3,000	
Debtors and creditors	980	700
Bad debts	20	
Capital		17,900
Bank balance	300	
Drawings	1,800	
	59,300	59,300

Adjustments:
(a)   Closing stock at 31 December 1997 £12,000.
(b)   Accrued wages £500.
(c)   Rates prepaid £50.
(d)   The provision for bad debts to be increased to 10 per cent of debtors.
(e)   Telephone account outstanding £22.
(f)   Depreciate shop fittings at 10 per cent per annum, and van at 20 per cent per annum, on cost.
A balance sheet is not required.
(RSA adapted)

30.10X   The following trial balance was extracted from the books of Adam Jenkins at the close of business on 28 February 1998.

	Dr £	Cr £
Purchases and sales	3,760	6,580
Cash at bank	380	
Cash in hand	70	
Capital account 1 March 1997		3,300
Drawings	950	
Office furniture	480	
Rent and rates	340	
Wages and salaries	860	
Discounts	230	120
Debtors and creditors	1,640	830
Stock 1 March 1997	990	
Provision for bad debts 1 March 1997		90
Delivery van	800	
Van running costs	150	
Bad debts written off	270	
	10,920	10,920

Notes:
(a)   Stock 28 February 1998 £1,170.
(b)   Wages and salaries accrued at 28 February 1998 £30.
(c)   Increase the provision for bad debts by £20.
(d)   Provide for depreciation as follows: Office furniture £60; Delivery van £160.

Required
Draw up the trading and profit and loss accounts for the year ending 28 February 1998 together with a balance sheet as on 28 February 1998.
(LCCI)

30.11   Jane Jones is in business as a hairdresser. From the figures below prepare her profit and loss account for the year ended 31 December 1997 and a balance sheet on that date.

	Dr £	Cr £
Capital 1 January 1997		9,740
Drawings	4,500	
Motor car (cost £1,800)	1,320	
Petty cash	40	
Cost of new hair dryer	120	
Equipment (cost £1,000)	600	
Freehold premises	6,000	
Advertising	230	
Cash at bank	5,400	
Motor car expenses	480	
Rates	140	
Telephone	110	
Revenue from hairdressing		10,400
Sundry expenses	1,200	
	20,140	20,140

The following should be taken into consideration.
(a) Rates prepaid 31 December 1997 £30.
(b) One-third of motor car expenses including depreciation for the year is to be regarded as private use.
(c) Provide for cleaning costs £50.
(d) Depreciate all equipment on hand at 31 December 1997 by 10 per cent of cost.
(e) Motor car is to be depreciated by 20 per cent on reduced balance method.
(RSA)

30.12X   Sandra Black operates a secretarial service to farmers and the following trial balance was extracted from her books on 31 May 1998.

	Dr £	Cr £
Income from clients		32,500
Commissions from other sources		800
Discounts received		150
Stationery	2,100	
Wages	7,600	
Equipment	4,500	
Vehicles	6,500	
Rent and rates	2,350	
Vehicle expenses	2,000	
Light and heat	800	
Insurance	850	
Telephone	280	
Sundry expenses	175	
Drawings	11,200	
Debtors	760	
Creditors		670
Bank overdraft		250
Cash in hand	175	
Capital		4,920
	39,290	39,290

Notes:
(a) At 31 May 1998 there is an unpaid telephone bill of £52 and an unpaid electricity bill of £45.
(b) Rates prepaid at 31 May 1998 are £120.
(c) On 31 May 1998 there is an unused stock of stationery valued at £150.

Required
Prepare a profit and loss account for Sandra Black for the year ended 31 May 1998 and a balance sheet as at that date, showing clearly therein the value of her capital, fixed assets, current assets and current liabilities.
(RSA)

30.13 Thomas Williams, a sole trader, extracted the following trial balance from his books at the close of business on 31 March 1998:

	Dr £	Cr £
Purchases and sales	7,620	13,990
Stock 1 April 1997	1,720	
Capital 1 April 1997		2,400
Bank overdraft		1,450
Cash	30	
Discounts	480	310
Returns inwards	270	
Returns outwards		190
Carriage outwards	720	
Rent, rates and insurance	580	
Provision for bad debts		220
Fixtures and fittings	400	
Delivery van	700	
Debtors and creditors	3,970	2,020
Drawings	960	
Wages and salaries	2,980	
General office expenses	150	
	20,580	20,580

Notes:
(a) Stock 31 March 1998 £1,430.
(b) Wages and salaries accrued at 31 March 1998 £70.
(c) Rates prepaid 31 March 1998 £60.
(d) Increase the provision for bad debts by £50 to £270.
(e) Provide for depreciation as follows: Fixtures and fittings £40; Delivery van £100.

Required
Prepare the trading and profit and loss accounts for the year ended 31 March 1998 together with a balance sheet as at that date.
(LCCI)

30.14X Angus Brown is a retail trader. From the following information prepare a trading and profit and loss account for the year ended 31 December 1997 and a balance sheet on that date.

Trial Balance – 31 December 1997

	Dr £	Cr £
Capital 1 January 1997		6,400
Land and buildings	5,000	
Motor vehicles (cost £1,200)	600	
Drawings	1,400	
Stock	910	
Bank overdraft		96
Sales		14,260
Purchases	11,100	
Motor expenses	310	
Sundry expenses	106	
Wages	1,560	
Debtors	820	
Creditors		1,210
Rates and insurance	160	
	21,966	21,966

The following items should be taken into consideration:
(a) Stock at 31 December 1997 £1,820.
(b) A provision for bad debts of 5 per cent on the debtors at 31 December 1997 is to be created.
(c) Depreciation is to be provided on motor vehicles at 20 per cent on cost.
(d) Rates prepaid at 31 December 1997 £12.
(e) Motor expenses bill for December £26 is owing at 31 December 1997.
(f) Sundry expenses includes £15 for a private telephone bill of Angus Brown.
(g) A cheque for £250 was paid to a creditor on 31 December 1997 but had not been entered in the books at the time of extracting the trial balance.
(RSA)

30.15 The following balances remained in the books of G Williams, a sole trader, at 31 October 1998:

	£
Trade creditors	2,065
Stock, 31 October 1998	3,073
Wages owing	225
Premises	27,400
Cash	500
Trade debtors	5,127
Furniture and fittings	3,075
Vehicles	6,100
Plant and machinery	13,840
Bank overdraft	1,875
Insurance paid in advance	50
Five-year loan from Loamshire Finance Co	7,500
Drawings	10,800
Net profit for year ended 31 October 1998	12,970
Capital	?

Required

(a) Answer the following:

    (i)   What is the meaning of the words 'as at' on a balance sheet heading?

    (ii) Why is the stock shown above as being at 31 October 1998 rather than at 1 November 1997?

(b) Prepare the balance sheet for G Williams, using the balances listed above, and thus calculate his capital at the balance sheet date. Pay particular attention to layout and presentation.

(c) Prepare Williams' capital account, as it would appear in his ledger for his financial year to 31 October 1998.

(RSA)

31 Trial balance: correction of errors not affecting trial balance agreement; correction of errors affecting trial balance agreement

31.1 Trial balance agreement and errors

There are two main classifications of errors:

1 Errors not affecting trial balance agreement.
   and
2 Errors affecting trial balance agreement.

31.2 Correction of errors not affecting trial balance agreement

In Chapter 7 we drew up a trial balance from the list of balances in the books of account at the end of an accounting period. Each side of the trial balance was then added up and provided no error had occurred, the two sides should equal each other i.e.:

> **Total debit balances = Total credit balances**

Whilst both sides of the trial balance may agree, complete accuracy cannot be guaranteed. Certain errors can still be made which do not affect the balancing of a trial balance, i.e. the trial balance would still appear to be in 'balance'.

Examples of the different types of errors which come under this heading are as follows:

1 Errors of commission
2 Errors of principle
3 Errors of original entry
4 Errors of omission
5 Compensating error
6 Complete reversal of entries

We will now take each of the above in turn, discuss the error and show how to make the necessary correction.

Errors of commission

An error of commission arises when the correct amounts are entered, but in the wrong person's account.

Example:

D Long paid us by cheque £50 on 18 May 1998. It is correctly entered in the cash book, but it is entered by mistake in the account for D Lee.

This means that there had been both a debit of £50 and a credit of £50. It has appeared in the personal account as:

D Lee Account

Dr			Cr
		1998	£
		May 18 Cash	50

The error was found on 31 May 1998. This will now have to be corrected and needs two entries:

1 A debit of £50 in the account of D Lee to cancel out the error on the credit side in that account.
2 A credit of £50 in the account of D Long. This is where it should have been entered.

The accounts will now appear:

D Lee Account

Dr			Cr	
1998	£	1998		£
May 31 D Long:				
Error corrected (1)	50	May 18 Cash		50

D Long Account

Dr			Cr	
1998	£	1998		£
		May 31 Cash entered in error in D Lee's		
May 1 Balance b/d	50	account (2)		50

The journal

The ways by which errors have been corrected should all be entered in the journal. The correction has already been shown above in double entry.

The journal entry will be:

The Journal

1998		Dr	Cr
		£	£
May 31	D Lee	50	
	D Long		50
	Cash received ... entered in wrong		
	personal account, now corrected.		

Errors of principle

This is where a transaction is entered in the wrong class of account.

For instance the purchase of a fixed asset should be debited to a fixed asset account. If in error it is debited to an expense account, then it has been entered in the wrong class of account.

Example:

The purchase of a motor lorry £5,500 by cheque on 14 May 1998 has been debited in error to a motor expenses account. In the cash book it is shown correctly. This means that there has been both a debit of £5,500 and a credit of £5,500.

It will have appeared in the expense account as:

Motor Expenses Account

Dr				Cr
1998		£		
May 14	Bank	5,500		

The error is found on 31 May 1998. We will now correct it. Two entries are needed:

1   A debit in the motor lorry account of £5,500 to put it where it should have been entered.
2   A credit of £5,500 in the motor expenses account to *cancel* the error. The accounts will now appear as:

Motor Expenses Account

Dr					Cr
1998		£	1998		£
May 14	Bank	5,500	May 31	Motor lorry	
				error corrected **(2)**	5,500

Motor Lorry Account

Dr				Cr
1998		£		
May 31	Bank: entered			
	originally in			
	Motor expenses **(1)**	5,500		

The journal

The journal entries to correct the error will be shown as:

The Journal

		Dr	Cr
1998		£	£
May 31	Motor lorry	5,500	
	Motor expenses		5,500
	Correction of error whereby purchase of motor lorry was debited to motor expenses account.		

Errors of original entry

This occurs when an incorrect figure is posted to the correct sides of the correct accounts. For example, if sales of £150 to T Higgins on 13 May 1998 had been entered as both a debit and a credit as £130, the accounts would appear:

T Higgins Account

Dr				Cr
1998		£		
May 13	Sales	130		

Sales Account

Dr		1998		Cr
		May 31	Sales journal (part of total)	£ 130

The error is found on 31 May 1998. The entries to correct it are now shown:

T Higgins Account

Dr				Cr
1998		£		
May 13	Sales	130		
May 31	Sales: error	20		

Sales Account

Dr		1998		Cr
		May 31	Sales journal	£ 130
		May 31	T Higgins: error corrected	20

The journal

To correct the error the journal entries will be:

The Journal

			Dr	Cr
1998			£	£
May	31	T Higgins	20	
		Sales account		20
		Correction of error. Sales of £150		
		had been incorrectly entered as £130.		

Errors of omission

This type of error occurs when the book-keeper 'omits' to record a transaction.

For example, if we purchased goods from T Hope for £250 but did not enter it in the accounts there would be nil debits and nil credits. We find the error on 31 May 1998. The entries to record it will be:

Purchases Account

Dr				Cr
1998			£	
May	13	T Hope:		
		error corrected	250	

T Hope Account

Dr				Cr
		1998		£
		May 31	Purchases:	
			error corrected	250

The journal

The journal entries to correct the error will be:

The Journal

			Dr	Cr
1998			£	£
May	31	Purchases	250	
		T Hope		250
		Correction of error. Purchases omitted		
		from books.		

Compensating errors

These are where errors cancel each other out. They are known as compensating errors.

Let us take a case where the sales day book is added up to be £100 too much. In the same period the purchases day book is also added up to be £100 too much.

If these were the only errors in our books the trial balance totals would equal each other. Both totals would be wrong, they would both be £100 too much, but they would be equal totals.

If in fact the *incorrect* totals had purchases £7,900 and sales £9,900, the accounts would have appeared as:

Purchases Account

Dr					Cr
1998		£			
May 13	Purchases	7,900			

Sales Account

Dr					Cr
			1998		£
			May 31	Sales	9,900

When corrected, the accounts will appear as:

Purchases Account

Dr					Cr
1998		£	1998		£
May 13	Purchases	7,900	May 31	The Journal: error corrected	100

Sales Account

Dr					Cr
1998		£	1998		£
May 31	The Journal: error corrected	100	May 31	Sales	9,900

The journal

Journal entries to correct these two errors will be:

The Journal

		Dr	Cr
1998		£	£
May 31	Sales account	100	
	Purchases account		100
	Correction of compensating errors. Totals of both purchases and sales day books incorrectly added up £100 too much.		

Complete reversal of entries

Where the correct amounts are entered in the correct accounts, but each item is shown on the wrong side of each account. There has therefore been both a debit and a credit of £200.

For instance we pay a cheque for £200 on 28 May 1998 to D Charles. We enter it as follows in accounts with the letter (A).

Cash Book (A)

Dr								Cr
		Cash £	Bank £				Cash £	Bank £
1998								
May 28 D Charles			200					

D Charles (A)

Dr		Cr
	1998	£
	May 28 Bank	200

This is incorrect. It should have been debit D Charles £200: credit Bank £200. Both items have been entered in the correct accounts, but each is on the wrong side of its account.

The way to correct this is more difficult to understand than with other errors. Let us look at how the items would have appeared if we had done it correctly in the first place. We will show the letter (B) behind the account names.

Cash Book (B)

Dr							Cash £	Bank £
		Cash £	Bank £	1998				
				May 28 D Charles				200

D Charles (B)

Dr		Cr
1998	£	
May 28 Bank	200	

We have found the error on May 31. By using double entry we have to make the amounts shown to cancel the error by twice the amount of the error. This is because:

1 First we have to cancel the error. This would mean entering these amounts:

Dr D Charles £200
Cr Bank   £200

2   Then we have to enter up the transaction:
Dr D Charles £200
Cr Bank   £200

Altogether then, the entries to correct the error are twice the amounts first entered.

When corrected the accounts appear as follows, marked (C).

Cash Book (C)

Dr						*Cr*
	Cash £	Bank £			Cash £	Bank £
1998			1998			
May 8 D Charles		200	May 31 D Charles: error corrected			400

D Charles (C)

Dr			*Cr*
1998	£	1998	£
May 28 Bank: error corrected	400	May 28 Bank	200

You can see that accounts (C) give the same final answer as accounts (B).

		£	£
(B)	*Dr* D Charles	200	
	Cr Bank		200
(C)	*Dr* D Charles (£400 − £200)	200	
	Cr Bank (£400 − £200)		200

The journal

Journal entries. These would be shown:

The Journal

		Dr	Cr
1998		£	£
May 31	D Charles	400	
	Bank		400
	Payment of £200 on 28 May 1998 to D Charles incorrectly credited to his account, and debited to bank. Error now corrected.		

31.3 Correction of errors affecting trial balance agreement

In the previous section we looked at errors which still left equal totals in the trial balance. There are, however, many errors that will affect the balancing of the trial balance. This means that the totals of the debit column in the trial balance will not be the same as the total of the credit column.

For example, suppose we have made only one error in our books. We received cash £103 on 1 May 1998 from H Lee. We enter it as:

Cash Book

Dr			Cr
		Cash	Bank	
1998		£	£	
May 1 H Lee		103		

Sales Ledger
H Lee Account

Dr		Cr
	1998	£
	May 1 Cash	13

We have put £103 on the debit side of our books, and £13 on the credit side. When we draw up a trial balance its totals will be different by £90, i.e. £103 − £13 = £90.

This will be true in every case where a debit entry does not equal a credit entry for the item.

The correction of these types of errors is shown in Chapter 32.

31.4 Casting

You will often notice the use of the expression **to cast**, which means to add up. Overcasting means incorrectly adding up a column of figures to give an answer which is *greater* than it should be. Undercasting means incorrectly adding up a column of figures to give an answer which is *less* than it should be.

New term

> **Casting** (p 316): Adding up figures.

Exercises

31.1 Show the journal entries necessary to correct the following errors:

(a) A sale of goods £678 to J Harkness had been entered in J Harker's account.

(b) The purchase of a machine on credit from L Pearson for £4,390 had been completely omitted from our books.

(c)   The purchase of a motor van £3,800 had been entered in error in the motor expenses account.

(d)   A sale of £221 to E Fletcher had been entered in the books, both debit and credit, as £212.

(e)   Commission received £257 had been entered in error in the sales account.

31.2X   Show the journal entries needed to correct the following errors:

(a)   Purchases £699 on credit from K Webb had been entered in H Weld's account.

(b)   A cheque of £189 paid for advertisements had been entered in the cash column of the cash book instead of in the bank column.

(c)   Sale of goods £443 on credit to B Maxim had been entered in error in B Gunn's account.

(d)   Purchase of goods on credit from K Innes £89 entered in two places in error as £99.

(e)   Cash paid to H Mersey £89 entered on the debit side of the cash book and the credit side of H Mersey's account.

31.3X   Redraft the following balance sheet, correcting the errors in it.

A Smith
Balance Sheet for the year ending 31 December 1999

	£		£
Drawings	20,000	Sundry debtors	43,200
Bank overdraft	9,000	Depreciation on furniture	
Provision for bad debts	2,160	and equipment	5,000
Cash in hand	1,000	Net profit	30,000
Stock at 31 December 1999	38,500	Capital at 1 January 1999	310,000
Furniture and equipment	97,400	Goodwill	14,000
Stock at 1 January 1999	22,200	Rates prepaid	1,000
Creditors	39,680		
Premises	182,000		
Wages accrued	1,260		
	413,200		403,200

31.4   When Daniel Martin prepared his final accounts he calculated his net profit at £8,975. However, on more careful inspection of his accounts he found the following errors. Construct an adjustment of profit statement to show his true net profit.

(a)   A bill for rates of £200 had not been recorded.

(b)   Sales of £28 had not been recorded.

(c)   Closing stock had been overvalued by £48.

(d)   Depreciation of £200 had not been provided for.

(e)   Rent receivable of £50 was outstanding.

(f)   Sales returns of £22 had not been entered.

(g)   Rent of £10 recorded in the profit and loss account related to next year.

(h)   A provision for bad debts of £20 should have been created.

(Pitman Qualifications)

31.5X The following trial balance was extracted from the books of J Sanders on 30 October 1999.

	Debit £	Credit £
Premises	84,000	
Office equipment	2,190	
Fixtures and fittings	1,240	
Trade debtors	2,790	
Trade creditors		1,870
Stock 1 November 1998	2,455	
Purchases	41,000	
Sales		87,257
Wages	3,000	
Insurance	235	
Cash in hand	384	
Bank overdraft		583
Capital 1 November 1998		47,584
	137,294	137,294

Further examination of the books revealed the following:

1 A typewriter bought on 5 October 1999 for £85 had been posted to the purchases account.
2 A payment in cash of £25 had been made to a creditor, entries of £52 had been made in the books.
3 J Sanders had taken £200 from the firm's bank account, the amount had been debited to the wages account.
4 A standing order for £5 had been paid by the bank for insurance, no entry had been made in the cash book.

You are required to:
(a) Redraft the trial balance after making the corrections.
(b) Explain and give an example of each of the following:
    (i) Compensating error.
    (ii) Error of omission.
(RSA)

31.6 R James drew up the following balance sheet on 31 December 1999:

Balance Sheet

	£	£		£	£
Fixed assets			Capital 1 January 1999	7,690	
Furniture and fittings	1,540		*Add* Net profit	3,040	
Motor vehicles	2,980			10,730	
		4,520			
Current assets			*Less* Drawings	2,860	
Stock	2,724				7,870
Sundry debtors	1,241		Sundry creditors		1,850
Cash at bank	1,235				
		5,200			
		9,720			9,720

When checking the books, the following errors and omissions were found:

1   A purchase of fittings, £140, has been included in the purchases account.
2   Motor vehicles should have been depreciated by £280.
3   A debt of £41 included in sundry debtors was considered to be bad.
4   Closing stock had been overvalued by £124.

(a)   Show your calculation of the correct net profit.
(b)   Draw up a corrected balance sheet as at 31 December 1999.
(RSA)

31.7X   At the end of April 1999 C Read extracted a trial balance as follows:

	Dr £	Cr £
Purchases	1,320	
Sales		4,675
Rent	50	
Wages	160	
General expenses	75	
Carriage inwards	100	
Carriage outwards	140	
Salaries	230	
Premises	10,000	
Fixtures and fittings	1,500	
Debtors		680
Creditors	1,050	
Bank overdraft		670
Cash	15	
Drawings	200	
Commission received		130
Capital		7,945
	14,840	14,100

An inspection revealed obvious errors. Further investigations revealed the following:

1   £30 for carriage inwards had been posted to the carriage outwards account.
2   Sales for cash had been entered incorrectly into the bank account instead of the cash account £40.
3   A cheque for £10 from T Murphy had been entered into the S Murphy account. Both T Murphy and S Murphy are debtors.
4   No entry had been made in the books to record a cheque paid to P Sills, a creditor, £70.
5   General expenses included a payment of £10 which should have been entered into a motor expenses account.
6   Wages of £40 had been entered into salaries account.

You are required to:
(a)   make journal entries to record items **1–6** above;
(b)   extract a trial balance having taken notice of the obvious errors as well as the items **1–6** above.
(LCCI)

32 Suspense accounts and errors

32.1 Errors and the trial balance

In the last chapter we looked at errors which still left equal totals in the trial balance. However, many errors will mean that trial balance totals will not be equal. Let us now look at some of these:

- Incorrect additions in any account.
- Making an entry on only one side of the accounts, e.g. a debit but no credit; a credit but no debit.
- Entering a different amount on the debit side from the amount on the credit side.

32.2 Suspense account

We should try very hard to find errors immediately when the trial balance totals are not equal. When they cannot be found, the trial balance totals should be made to agree with each other by inserting the amount of the difference between the two sides in a **suspense account**. This occurs in Exhibit 32.1 where there is a £40 difference.

Exhibit 32.1

Trial Balance as on 31 December 1997

	Dr	Cr
	£	£
Totals after all the accounts have been listed	100,000	99,960
Suspense account		40
	100,000	100,000

To make the two totals the same, a figure of £40 for the suspense account has been shown on the credit side. A suspense account is opened and the £40 difference is also shown there on the credit side.

Suspense Account

Dr			Cr
	1997		£
	Dec 31	Difference per trial balance	40

32.3 Suspense account and the balance sheet

If the errors are not found before the final accounts are prepared, the suspense account balance will be included in the balance sheet. Where the balance is a credit balance, it should be included under current liabilities on the balance sheet. When the balance is a debit balance it should be shown under current assets on the balance sheet.

32.4 Correction of errors

When the errors are found they must be corrected, using double entry. Each correction must also have an entry in the journal describing it.

One error only

We will look at two examples:

Example 1

Assume that the error of £40 as shown in Exhibit 32.1 is found in the following year on 31 March 1998. The error was that the sales account was undercast by £40. The action taken to correct this is:

Debit suspense account to close it: £40.
Credit sales account to show item where it should have been: £40.

The accounts now appear as Exhibit 32.2.

Exhibit 32.2

Suspense Account

Dr				Cr
1998		£	1997	£
			Dec 31 Difference per	
Mar 31 Sales		40	trial balance	40

Sales Account

Dr			Cr
		1998	£
		Mar 31 Suspense	40

This can be shown in journal form as:

The Journal

		Dr	Cr
1998		£	£
Mar 31	Suspense	40	
	Sales		40

Correction of undercasting of sales by £40 in last year's accounts.

Example 2

The trial balance on 31 December 1997 had a difference of £168. It was a shortage on the debit side.

A suspense account is opened, the difference of £168 is entered on the debit side.

On 31 May 1998 the error was found. We had made a payment of £168 to K Leek to close his account. It was correctly entered in the cash book, but it was not entered in K Leek's account.

To correct the error, the account of K Leek is debited with £168, as it should have been in 1997 and the suspense account is credited with £168 so that the account can be closed.

K Leek Account

Dr				Cr
1998		£	1998	£
May 31 Bank		168	Jan 1 Balance b/d	168

The account of K Leek is now correct.

Suspense Account

Dr				Cr
1998		£	1998	£
May 31 Difference per trial balance		168	May 31 K Leek	168

The Journal entries are:

The Journal

		Dr	Cr
1998		£	£
May 31	K Leek	168	
	Suspense		168
	Correction of non-entry of payment last year in K Leek's account.		

More than one error

We can now look at Exhibit 32.3 where the suspense account difference was caused by more than one error.

Exhibit 32.3

The trial balance at 31 December 1997 showed a difference of £77, being a shortage on the debit side. A suspense account is opened, and the difference of £77 is entered on the debit side of the account.

On 28 February 1998 all the errors from the previous year were found.

1 A cheque of £150 paid to L Kent had been correctly entered in the cash book, but had not been entered in Kent's account.
2 The purchases account had been undercast by £20.
3 A cheque of £93 received from K Sand had been correctly entered in the cash book, but had not been entered in Sand's account.

These three errors resulted in a net error of £77, shown by a debit of £77 on the debit side of the suspense account.

These are corrected by:

(a) Making correcting entries in the accounts for (1), (2) and (3).
(b) Recording the double entry for these items in the suspense account.

L Kent Account

Dr				Cr
1998		£		
Feb 28	Suspense (1)	150		

Purchases Account

Dr				Cr
1998		£		
Feb 28	Suspense (2)	20		

K Sand Account

Dr		Cr		
		1998		£
		Feb 28	Suspense (3)	93

Suspense Account

Dr				Cr		
1998		£	1998			£
Jan 1	Balance b/d	77	Feb 28	L Kent (1)		150
Feb 28	K Sand (3)	93	Feb 28	Purchases (2)		20
		170				170

The Journal

				Dr	Cr
1998				£	£
Feb	28	L Kent		150	
		Suspense			150
		Cheque paid omitted from Kent's account			
Feb	28	Purchases		20	
		Suspense			20
		Undercasting of purchases by £20 in last year's accounts			
Feb	28	Suspense		93	
		K Sand			93
		Cheque received omitted from Sand's account			

Only those errors which make the trial balance totals different from each other have to be corrected via the suspense account.

32.5 The effect of errors on profits

Some of the errors will have meant that original profits calculated will be wrong. Other errors will have no effect upon profits. We will use Exhibit 32.4 to illustrate the different kinds of errors.

Exhibit 32.4 shows a set of accounts in which errors have been made.

Exhibit 32.4

K Davis
Trading and Profit and Loss Account for the year ended 31 December 1997

	£	£
Sales		8,200
Less Cost of goods sold		
Opening stock	500	
Purchases	6,100	
	6,600	
Less Closing stock	700	
		5,900
Gross profit		2,350
Less Expenses		
Rent	200	
Insurance	120	
Lighting	180	
Depreciation	250	
		750
Net profit		1,600

K Davis
Balance Sheet as at 31 December 1997

	£	£	£
Fixed assets	Cost	Depreciation	
Fixtures and fittings	2,200	800	1,400
Current assets			
Stock	700		
Debtors	600		
Cash at bank	340		
Suspense	60	1,700	
Current liabilities			
Creditors	600	600	
Net current assets			1,100
Net assets			2,500
Financed by			
Capital Account			
Balance as at 1 January 1997			1,800
Add Net profit for the year			1,600
			3,400
Less Drawings			(900)
			2,500

Errors which do not affect profit calculations

If an error affects items only in the balance sheet, then the original calculated profit will not need altering. Exhibit 32.5 shows this:

Exhibit 32.5

Assume that in Exhibit 32.4 the £60 debit balance on the suspense account was because of the following error:

1 November 1997 we paid £60 to a creditor T Monk. It was correctly entered in the cash book. It was not entered anywhere else. The error was found on 1 June 1998.

The journal entries to correct it will be:

The Journal

			Dr	Cr
1998			£	£
Jun	1	T Monk	60	
		Suspense account		60
		Payment to T Monk on 1 November 1997 not entered in his account. Correction now made.		

Both of these accounts appeared in the balance sheet only with T Monk as part of creditors. The net profit of £1,600 does not have to be changed.

Errors which do affect profit calculations

If the error is in one of the figures shown in the trading and profit and loss account, then the original profit will need altering. Exhibit 32.6 shows this:

Exhibit 32.6

Assume that in Exhibit 32.4 the £60 debit balance was because the rent account was added up incorrectly. It should be shown as £260 instead of £200. The error was found on 1 June 1998. The journal entries to correct it are:

The Journal

			Dr	Cr
			£	£
1998				
Jun	1	Rent	60	
		Suspense		60
		Correction of rent undercast last year.		

Rent last year should have been increased by £60. This would have reduced net profit by £60. A statement of corrected profit for the year is now shown.

K Davis
Statement of Corrected Net Profit for the year ended 31 December 1997

	£
Net profit per the accounts	1,600
Less Rent understated	60
	1,540

Where there have been several errors

If in Exhibit 32.4 there had been four errors in the accounts of K Davis, found on 31 March 1998 their correction can now be seen. Assume that the net difference had also been £60.

1	Sales overcast by	£70
2	Insurance undercast by	£40
3	Cash received from a debtor entered in the cash book only	£50
4	A purchase of £59 is entered in the books, debit and credit entries, as	£95

The entries in the suspense account, and the journal entries will be as follows:

Suspense Account

1998			£	1998			£
Jan	1	Balance b/d	60	Mar	31	Sales	70
Mar	31	Debtor	50	Mar	31	Insurance	40
			110				110

The Journal

				Dr	Cr
1998				£	£
(1)	Mar	31	Sales	70	
			Suspense		70
			Sales overcast of £70 in 1997		
(2)	Mar	31	Insurance	40	
			Suspense		40
			Insurance expense undercast by £40 in 1997		
(3)	Mar	31	Suspense	50	
			Debtor's account		50
			Cash received omitted from debtor's account in 1997		
(4)	Mar	31	Creditor's account	36	
			Purchases		36
			Credit purchase of £59 entered both as debit and credit as £95 in 1997		

Note: In (4), the correction of the understatement of purchases does not pass through the suspense account.

Now we can calculate the corrected net profit for the year 1997. Only items (1), (2) and (4) affect figures in the trading and profit and loss account. These are the only adjustments to be made to profit.

K Davis
Statement of corrected Net Profit for the year ended 31 December 1997

	£	£
Net profit per the accounts		1,600
Add Purchases overstated (4)		36
		1,636
Less Sales overcast (1)	70	
Rent undercast (2)	40	110
Corrected net profit for the year		1,526

Error (3), the cash not posted to a debtor's account, did not affect profit calculations.

32.6 Suspense accounts: businesses and examinations

Businesses

Every attempt should be made to find errors. Opening a suspense account should be done only if all other efforts have failed.

Examinations

Unless it is part of a question, do not make your balance sheet totals agree by using a suspense account. The same applies to trial balances. If you do, you will lose marks.

New term

> **Suspense account** (p 320): Account showing balance equal to difference in trial balance.

Exercises

32.1 Thomas Boyd, a sole trader, extracted a trial balance from his books at the close of business on 31 May 1998. The trial balance did not agree and Boyd entered the difference in a suspense account and prepared the trading and profit and loss accounts in the normal manner. The profit and loss account showed a net profit of £1,170.

During June, Boyd discovered the following errors and these accounted for the trial balance difference:

1 The purchases day book was overcast by £60.
2 Wages paid £76 had been debited to wages account but the workmen concerned had been engaged in installing new shelves in Boyd's office.
3 Discount allowed total of £97, as shown in the cash book, had been entered on the wrong side of discount account.
4 Cash £48 received from a debtor of Boyd – Samuel Lewis – had been correctly entered in the cash book but the double entry had not been completed.

Required
(a) Calculate the correct net profit.
Note: Calculations must be shown.
(b) Indicate the manner and extent to which the above errors affected the trial balance. Your answer should be given under the following headings:

Error	Debit side overstated, or credit side understated	Credit side overstated, or debit side understated
(i)		
(ii)		
(iii)		
(iv)		

(LCCI)

32.2 For question 32.1, show the journal entries necessary to correct the errors.

32.3 The following is a trial balance which has been incorrectly drawn up:

Trial Balance – 31 January 1998

	Cr £	Dr £
Capital 1 February 1997	5,500	
Drawings	2,800	
Stock 1 February 1997		2,597
Trade debtors		2,130
Furniture and fittings	1,750	
Cash in hand	1,020	
Trade creditors		2,735
Sales		7,430
Returns inwards		85
Discount received	46	
Business expenses	950	
Purchases	4,380	
	16,446	14,977

As well as the mistakes evident above, the following errors were also discovered:

(a) A payment of £75 made to a creditor had not been posted from the cash book into the purchases ledger.

(b) A cheque for £56 received from a customer had been correctly entered in the cash book but posted to the customer's account as £50.

(c) A purchase of fittings £120 had been included in the purchases account.

(d) The total of discounts allowed column in the cash book of £38 had not been posted into the general ledger.

(e) A page of the sales day book was correctly totalled at £564 but had been carried forward as £456.

Show the trial balance as it would appear after all the errors had been corrected. You are required to show all workings.

(RSA)

32.4X At the close of business on 26 February 1998, Alfred Bishop, a sole trader, extracted a trial balance from his books. The trial balance did not agree, but Bishop entered the difference in a suspense account. He then prepared his trading and profit and loss account for the year ending 26 February 1998 in the normal way. The profit and loss account so prepared showed a net profit amounting to £2,370.

During March 1998, Bishop discovered the following errors in his books and these accounted for the entire difference in the trial balance:

1 Bad debts account had been debited with items of £31 and £27 in respect of bad debts but the personal accounts of the individual debtors had not been credited.

2 The sales day book was overcast by £70.

3 Cash £36 received from Simon Jones had been correctly entered in the cash book but the double entry had been made on the wrong side of Jones' personal account in Alfred Bishop's ledger.

4 The discount allowed total in the cash book – £42 – had not been entered in the discount account.

Required

(a) State how, and to what extent, each of the above errors would have affected the trial balance, e.g. debit overstated £ …

(b) Calculate the correct figure for net profit.

Note: Calculations must be shown.

(LCCI)

32.5X For question 32.4X show the journal entries necessary to correct the errors.

32.6X J Jones extracted the following trial balance from his books on 31 January 1998.

	£	£
Capital		7,450
Drawings	3,000	
Stock 1 February 1997	2,500	
Trade debtors	2,950	
Trade creditors		2,684
Shop fittings	1,530	
Purchases	5,140	
Sales		7,460
General expenses	860	
Discount received		40
Cash at bank	1,660	
Returns outwards		40
	17,640	17,674

The following errors and omissions were subsequently discovered:
(a) A purchase of shop fittings £320 had been debited to purchases account.
(b) A sales invoice of £150 entered in the sales day book had not been posted to the customer's personal account.
(c) A credit note for £30 issued by J Jones to a customer had been completely omitted from the books.
(d) A credit balance of £16 in the purchases ledger had been omitted from the trial balance.
(e) The sales day book was undercast by £100 in December 1997.
Draw up a corrected trial balance. Show all workings.
(RSA)

32.7X For question 32.6X, show the journal entries necessary to correct the errors.

PART 5

Introduction to single entry

33 Single entry and incomplete records

33.1 Why double entry is not used

For every small shopkeeper, market stall or other small business to keep its books using a full double entry system would not be practical. First of all, a large number of the owners of such firms would not know how to write up double entry records, even if they wanted to.

It is more likely that they would enter details of a transaction once only, using a single entry system. Also many of them would fail to record every transaction, resulting in incomplete records.

Somehow, however, the profits will have to be calculated, if only for the purpose of calculating income tax payable. How can profits be calculated if the book-keeping records are inadequate or incomplete?

33.2 Profit as an increase in capital

Probably the way to start is to recall that, unless there has been an introduction of extra cash or resources into the firm, the only way that capital can be increased is by making profits. Therefore, profits can be found by comparing capital at the end of the last period with that at the end of this period.

Let us look at a firm where capital at the end of 1997 was £2,000. During 1998 there have been no drawings, and no extra capital has been brought in by the owner. At the end of 1998 the capital was £3,000.

	This year's capital		Last year's capital		
Net profit =	£3,000	−	£2,000	=	£1,000

If on the other hand the drawings had been £700, the profits must have been £1,700, calculated thus:

Last year's Capital	+	Profits	−	Drawings	=	This year's Capital
£2,000	+	?	−	£700	=	£3,000

We can see that £1,700 profits was the figure needed to complete the formula, filling in the missing figure by normal arithmetical deduction:

$$£2,000 + £1,700 − £700 = £3,000$$

Exhibit 33.1 shows the calculation of profit where insufficient information is available to draft a trading and profit and loss account, only information of assets and liabilities being known.

Exhibit 33.1

H Taylor has not kept proper book-keeping records, but he has kept notes in diary form of the transactions of his business. He is able to give details of his assets and liabilities as at 31 December 1997 and at 31 December 1998 as follows:

At 31 December 1997. *Assets*: Motor van £1,000; Fixtures £700; Stock £850; Debtors £950; Bank £1,100; Cash £100. *Liabilities*: Creditors £200; Loan from J Ogden £600.

At 31 December 1998. *Assets*: Motor van (after depreciation) £800; Fixtures (after depreciation) £630; Stock £990; Debtors £1,240; Bank £1,700; Cash £200. *Liabilities:* Creditors £300; Loan from J Ogden £400; Drawings were £900.

First of all a statement of affairs is drawn up as at 31 December 1997. This is the name given to what would have been called a balance sheet if it had been drawn up from a set of records. The capital is the difference between the assets and liabilities.

H Taylor
Statement of Affairs as at 31 December 1997

	£	£
Fixed Assets		
Motor van		1,000
Fixtures		1,700
		1,700
Current Assets		
Stock	850	
Debtors	950	
Bank	1,100	
Cash	100	
	3,000	
Less Current Liabilities		
Creditors	200	
Working capital		2,800
		4,500
Financed by		
Capital (difference)		3,900
Long-term liability		
Loan from J Ogden		600
		4,500

A statment of affairs is now drafted up as at the end of 1998. The formula of Opening Capital + Profit – Drawings = Closing Capital is then used to deduce the figure of profit.

H Taylor
Statement of Affairs as at 31 December 1998

	£	£
Fixed Assets		
Motor van		800
Fixtures		630
		1,430
Current Assets		
Stock	990	
Debtors	1,240	
Bank	1,700	
Cash	200	
	4,130	
Less Current Liabilities		
Creditors	300	3,830
		5,260
Financed by		
Capital		
Balance at 1.1.1998	3,900	
Add Net profit (C)	?	
(B)	?	
Less Drawings	900 (A)	?
Long-term loan		
Loan from J Ogden		400
		5,260

Deduction of net profit:

Opening Capital + Net Profit – Drawings = Closing Capital. Finding the missing figures (A), (B) and (C) by deduction:

(A) is the figure needed to make the balance sheet totals equal, i.e. £4,860;

(B) is therefore £4,860 + £900 = £5,760;

(C) is therefore £5,760 – £3,900 = £1,860.

To check:

Capital	3,900	
Add Net profit (C)	1,860	
(B)	5,760	
Less Drawings	900 (A)	4,860

Obviously, this method of calculating profit is very unsatisfactory as it is much more informative when a trading and profit and loss account can be drawn up. Therefore, whenever possible, the comparisons of capital method of ascertaining profit should be avoided and a full set of final accounts drawn up from the available records.

It is important to realise that a business would have exactly the same trading and profit and loss account and balance sheet whether they kept their books by single entry or double entry. However, as you will see, whereas the double entry system uses the trial balance in preparing the final accounts, the single entry system will have to arrive at the same answer by different means.

33.3 Drawing up the final accounts

The following example shows the various stages of drawing up final accounts from a single entry set of records.

The accountant discerns the following details of transactions for J Frank's retail store for the year ended 31 December 1997.

(a) The sales are mostly on a credit basis. No record of sales has been made, but £10,000 has been received, £9,500 by cheque and £500 by cash, from persons to whom goods have been sold.

(b) Amount paid by cheque to suppliers during the year = £7,200.

(c) Expenses paid during the year: by cheque, Rent £200, General expenses £180; by cash, Rent £50.

(d) J Frank took £10 cash per week (for 52 weeks) as drawings.

(e) Other information is available:

	At 31.12.1996	At 31.12.1997
	£	£
Debtors	1,100	1,320
Creditors for goods	400	650
Rent owing	–	50
Bank balance	1,130	3,050
Cash balance	80	10
Stock	1,590	1,700

(f) The only fixed asset consists of fixtures which were valued at 31 December 1996 at £800. These are to be depreciated at 10 per cent per annum.

1 Draw up a statement of affairs on the closing day of the last accounting period. This is now shown:

J Frank
Statement of Affairs as at 31 December 1996

	£	£
Fixed Assets		
Fixtures		800
Current Assets		
Stock	1,590	
Debtors	1,100	
Bank	1,130	
Cash	80	
	3,900	
Less Current Liabilities		
Creditors	400	
Working capital		3,500
		4,300
Financed by		
Capital (difference)		4,300
		4,300

All of these opening figures are then taken into account when drawing up the final accounts for 1997.

2   Next a cash and bank summary, showing the totals of each separate item, plus opening and closing balances, is drawn up.

Dr	Cash	Bank		Cash	Bank Cr
	£	£		£	£
Balances 31.12.1996	80	1,130	Suppliers		7,200
Receipts from debtors	500	9,500	Rent	50	200
			General expenses		180
			Drawings	520	
			Balances 31.12.1997	10	3,050
	580	10,630		580	10,630

3   Calculate the figures for purchases and sales to be shown in the trading account. Remember that the figures needed are the same as those which would have been found if double entry records had been kept.

Purchases

In double entry, purchases means the goods that have been bought in the period irrespective of whether they have been paid for or not during the period. The figure of payments to suppliers must therefore be adjusted to find the figure for purchases.

	£
Paid during the year	7,200
Less Payments made, but which were for goods which were purchased in a previous year (creditors 31.12.1996)	400
	6,800
Add Purchases made in this year, but for which payment has not yet been made (creditors 31.12.1997)	650
Goods bought in this year, i.e. purchases	7,450

The same answer could have been obtained if the information had been shown in the form of a total creditors account, the figure for purchases being the amount required to make the account totals agree.

Total Creditors' Account

Dr				Cr
	£			£
Cash paid to suppliers	7,200	Balances b/f		400
Balances c/d	650	Purchases (missing figure)		7,450
	7,850			7,850

Sales

The sales figure will only equal receipts where all the sales are for cash. Therefore, the receipts figures need adjusting to find sales. This can only be done by constructing a total debtors' account, the sales figure being the one needed to make the totals agree.

Total Debtors' Account

Dr				Cr
	£			£
Balances b/f	1,100	Receipts: Cash	500
		Cheque	9,500
Sales (missing figure)	10,220	Balances c/d	1,320
	11,320		11,320

Expenses

4 Where there are no accruals or prepayments either at the beginning or end of the accounting period, then expenses paid will equal expenses used up during the period. These figures will be charged to the trading and profit and loss account.

On the other hand, where such prepayments or accruals exist, then an expense account should be drawn up for that particular item. When all known items are entered, the missing figure will be the expenses to be charged for the accounting period. In this case only the rent account needs to be drawn up.

Rent Account

Dr				Cr
	£			£
Cheques	200	Rent (missing figure)		300
Cash	50			
Accrued c/d	50			
	300			300

5   Now draw up the final accounts.

J Frank
Trading and Profit and Loss Account for the year ended 31 December 1997

	£	£
Sales (stage 3)		10,220
Less Cost of goods sold		
Stock at 1.1.1997	1,590	
Add Purchases (stage 3)	7,450	
	9,040	
Less Stock at 31.12.1997	1,700	7,340
Gross profit		2,880
Less Expenses		
Rent (stage 4)	300	
General expenses	180	
Depreciation: Fixtures	80	560
Net profit		2,320

Balance Sheet as at 31 December 1997

	£	£	£
Fixed Assets			
Fixtures at 1.1.1997		800	
Less Depreciation		80	720
Current Assets			
Stock		1,700	
Debtors		1,320	
Bank		3,050	
Cash		10	
		6,080	
Less Current Liabilities			
Creditors	650		
Rent owing	50	700	
Working capital			5,380
			6,100
Financed by			
Capital			
Balance 1.1.1997 (per Opening statement of affairs)			4,300
Add Net profit			2,320
			6,620
Less Drawings			520
			6,100

33.4 Incomplete records and missing figures

In practice, part of the information relating to cash receipts or payments is often missing. If the missing information is in respect of one type of payment, then it is normal to assume that the missing figure is the amount required to make both totals agree in the cash column of the cash and bank summary. This does not happen with bank items owing to the fact that another copy of the bank statement can always be obtained from the bank. Exhibit 33.2 shows an example when the drawings figure is unknown; exhibit 33.3 is an example where the receipts from debtors had not been recorded.

Exhibit 33.2

The following information on cash and bank receipts and payments is available:

	Cash	Bank
	£	£
Cash paid into the bank during the year	5,500	
Receipts from debtors	7,250	800
Paid to suppliers	320	4,930
Drawings during the year	?	–
Expenses paid	150	900
Balances at 1.1.1997	35	1,200
Balances at 31.12.1997	50	1,670

Dr	Cash	Bank		Cash	Bank Cr
	£	£		£	£
Balances 1.1.1997	35	1,200	Bankings C	5,500	
Received from debtors	7,250	800	Suppliers	320	4,930
Bankings C		5,500	Expenses	150	900
			Drawings	?	
			Balances 31.12.1997	50	1,670
	7,285	7,500		7,285	7,500

The amount needed to make the two sides of the cash columns agree is £1,265. Therefore, this is taken as the figure of drawings.

Exhibit 33.3

Information of cash and bank transactions is available as follows:

	Cash	Bank
	£	£
Receipts from debtors	?	6,080
Cash withdrawn from the bank for business use (this is the amount which is used besides cash receipts from debtors to pay drawings and expenses)		920
Paid to suppliers		5,800
Expenses paid	640	230
Drawings	1,180	315
Balances at 1.1.1997	40	1,560
Balances at 31.12.1997	70	375

Dr	Cash	Bank		Cash	Bank Cr
	£	£		£	£
Balances 1.1.1997	40	1,560	Suppliers		5,800
Received from debtors	?	6,080	Expenses	640	230
Withdrawn from Bank C	920		Withdrawn from Bank C		920
			Drawings	1,180	315
			Balances 31.12.1997	70	375
	1,890	7,640		1,890	7,640

Cash receipts from debtors is, therefore, the amount needed to make each side of the cash column agree, £930.

It must be emphasised that balancing figures are acceptable only when all the other figures have been verified. Should, for instance, a cash expense be omitted when cash received from debtors is being calculated, then this would result in an understatement not only of expenses but also ultimately of sales.

New terms

Incomplete records (p 333): Where only some transactions are recorded in the books of account, the missing information has to be obtained by other means.

Single entry (p 333): Where transactions are only recorded once in the books of account.

Statement of affairs (p 334): A statement from which the capital of the owner is deduced by estimating assets and liabilities. Then: Capital = Assets *less* Liabilities.

Exercises

33.1 On 1 August 1997 S Pea started his business with £1,000 in his bank account. After the end of his first year of trading he realised that because of his lack of book-keeping knowledge he was unable to prepare a balance sheet. S Pea was, however, able to produce the following data for the year ended 31 July 1998.

	£
Furniture (cost £900)	800
Motor vehicles (cost £2,100)	1,600
Stock-in-trade	2,700
Creditors	3,300
Cash in hand	50
Balance at bank (overdrawn)	1,000
Debtors	1,600
Loan from B Smith	200
Drawings	3,000

You are required to:
(a) Ascertain S Pea's profit or loss for the year ended 31 July 1998.
(b) Prepare S Pea's balance sheet as at 31 July 1998, showing clearly all the totals and sub-totals normally found in a balance sheet.
(RSA)

33.2 Arthur Hobson is a sole trader who, although keeping very good records, does not operate a full double entry system. The following figures have been taken from his records:

	31 March 1997	31 March 1998
	£	£
Cash at bank	730	870
Office furniture	300	250
Stock	1,160	1,310
Cash in hand	30	40

Debtors on 31 March 1997 amounted to £1,490 and sales for the year ended 31 March 1998 to £5,760. During the year ended 31 March 1998 cash received from debtors amounted to £5,410.

Creditors on 31 March 1997 amounted to £940 and purchases for the year ended 31 March 1998 to £4,060. During the year ended 31 March 1998 cash paid to creditors amounted to £3,890.

During the year to 31 March 1998 no bad debts were incurred. Also during the same period there was neither discount allowed nor discount received.

Required
(a) Calculate debtors and creditors as at 31 March 1998.
(b) Calculate Hobson's capital as at 31 March 1997 and 31 March 1998.
(c) Calculate Hobson's net profit for the year ended 31 March 1998 allowing for the fact that during that year his drawings amounted to £1,270.
Note: Calculations must be shown.
(LCCI)

33.3 From the following information ascertain the profit made by C Cat during 1997. On 1 January he started business with £4,000 in the bank. His position on the following 31 December was as follows:

	£		£
Sundry creditors	350	Machinery	2,000
Cash at bank	400	Furniture	1,500
Stock	1,000		
Debtors	350		

(Pitman Qualifications)

33.4 Joseph Adams is a sole trader who does not keep complete book-keeping entries on the double entry system. From his records, however, the following figures have been extracted:

	31 May 1997	31 May 1998
	£	£
Stock-in-trade	1,980	2,160
Debtors	7,250	8,080
Creditors	4,140	5,630

During the year ended 31 May 1998 Adams received from his debtors cash amounting to £22,460. The debtors total of £8,080 at 31 May 1998 was arrived at after writing off bad debts amounting to £410 and allowing for discount of £670.

Also during the year ended 31 May 1998 Adams paid to his creditors cash amounting to £17,190. The creditors total of £5,630 at 31 May 1998 was arrived at after allowing for discount received amounting to £470.

Required

For the year ended 31 May 1998:
(a) Calculate the total of sales.
(b) Calculate the total of purchases.
(c) Draw up Adams' trading account.

Note: Calculations must be shown.
(LCCI)

33.5X

G Browning
Balance Sheet as at 31 May 1997

	£		£
Fixtures	5,000	Capital	14,000
Motor vans	4,000	Creditors	1,500
Stock	3,000		
Debtors	1,300		
Bank	2,000		
Cash	200		
	15,500		15,500

The following transactions took place on 1 June 1997:

	£
Purchases on credit	350
Sales on credit (cost £350)	500
Cash sales (cost £100)	150
A motor van, book value £1,000, was sold for £950. A cheque was received in full settlement.	
Payment to creditors by cheque	800
Cheques received from debtors	700
A bad debt written off	100
Cash received from debtors	50
Stock taken by proprietor	150

Reconstruct the balance sheet as it would appear at close of business on 1 June 1997. You should set out neatly all your calculations.
(RSA)

33.6X Malcolm Price is a sole trader who does not keep his books on the double entry system. From his records, however, the following information is available:

	31 March 1997	31 March 1998
	£	£
Fixed assets	3,120	3,400
Current assets	3,990	4,260
Current liabilities	1,960	1,880

During the year ending 31 March 1998 Price used his private banking account to purchase additional office furniture costing £360, and this was brought into his business. Also during the same period Price made drawings of £1,280 in cash and £60 in goods (cost price).

Required
(a) Calculate the amount of Price's capital as at 31 March 1997 and 31 March 1998.
(b) Calculate his net profit for the year ending 31 March 1998.
(c) Draw up his capital account for the year ending 31 March 1998 as it would appear under the double entry system.

Note: Calculations must be shown.
(LCCI)

33.7X On 1 July 1997 D Loss commenced business with £6,000 in his bank account. After trading for a full year, he ascertained that his position on 30 June 1998 was as follows:

	£		£
Plant	3,600	Fixtures	360
Creditors	720	Bank balance	600
Debtors	930	Stock-in-trade	1,350
Cash in hand	135	Drawings	1,600

You are required to:
(a) Calculate D Loss's capital at 30 June 1998.
(b) Prepare D Loss's balance sheet at 30 June 1998 (assuming a profit of £1,855), set out in such a manner as to show clearly the totals normally shown in a balance sheet.
(RSA)

Receipts and payments accounts and income and expenditure accounts

34.1 Non-trading organisations

Clubs, associations and other non-profit making organisations do not have trading and profit and loss accounts drawn up for them, as their main purpose is not trading or profit making. They are run so that their members can do things such as play football or chess. The kind of final accounts prepared by these organisations are either **receipts and payments accounts** or **income and expenditure accounts**.

34.2 Receipts and payments accounts

Receipts and payments accounts are a summary of the cash book for the period.

Exhibit 34.1 is an example.

Exhibit 34.1

The Homers Running Club
Receipts and Payments Account for the year ended 31 December 1998

Receipts	£	Payments	£
Bank balance 1.1.1998	236	Groundsman's wages	728
Subscriptions received		Sports stadium	
for 1998	1,148	expenses	296
Rent received	116	Committee expenses	58
		Printing and stationery	33
		Bank balance	
		31.12.1998	385
	1,500		1,500

34.3 Income and expenditure accounts

When assets are owned, and there are liabilities, the receipts and payments account is not a good way of drawing up final accounts. Other than the cash received and paid out, it shows only the cash balances. The other assets and liabilities are not shown at all.

What is required is:

1   a balance sheet, and
2   an account showing whether the association's capital has increased.

In a profit making firm (**2**) would be a trading and profit and loss account. In a non-profit organisation (**2**) will be an income and expenditure account.

An income and expenditure account follows the same rules as trading and profit and loss accounts. The only differences are the terms used. A comparison now follows:

Terms used

Profit Making Firm	Non-profit Organisation
1 Trading and Profit and Loss Account	1 Income and Expenditure Account
2 Net Profit	2 Surplus of Income over Expenditure
3 Net Loss	3 Excess of Expenditure over Income

34.4 Profit or loss for a special purpose

Sometimes there are reasons why a non-profit making organisation would want a profit and loss account.

This is where something is done to make a profit. The profit is not to be kept, but used to pay for the main purpose of the organisation.

For instance, a football club may have discos or dances which people pay to go to. Any profit from these helps to pay football expenses. For these discos and dances a trading and profit and loss account would be drawn up. Any profit (or loss) would be transferred to the income and expenditure account.

34.5 Accumulated fund

A sole trader or a partnership would have capital accounts. A non-profit making organisation would instead have an **accumulated fund**. It is in effect the same as a capital account, as it is the difference between assets and liabilities.

In a sole trader or partnership:

> **Capital + Liabilities = Assets**

In a non-profit making organisation:

> **Accumulated Fund + Liabilities = Assets**

34.6 Drawing up income and expenditure accounts

We can now look at the preparation of an income and expenditure account and a balance sheet of a club. A separate trading account is to be prepared for a bar, where beer and alcohol is sold to make a profit.

Long Lane Football Club Trial Balance as at 31 December 1998		
	Dr £	Cr £
Sports equipment	8,500	
Club premises	29,600	
Subscriptions received		6,490
Wages of staff	4,750	
Furniture and fittings	5,260	
Rates and insurance	1,910	
General expenses	605	
Accumulated fund 1 January 1998		42,016
Donations received		360
Telephone and postage	448	
Bank	2,040	
Bar purchases	9,572	
Creditors for bar supplies		1,040
Bar sales		14,825
Bar stocks 1 January 1998	2,046	
	64,731	64,731

The following information is also available:

1 Bar stocks at 31 December 1998 £2,362.
2 Provide for depreciation: Sports equipment £1,700; Furniture and fittings £1,315.

Long Lane Football Club Bar
Trading Account for the year ended 31 December 1998

	£	£
Sales		14,825
Less Cost of goods sold		
Opening stock	2,046	
Purchases	9,572	
	11,618	
Closing stock	2,362	
		9,256
Gross profit		5,569

Income and Expenditure Account for the year ended 31 December 1998

	£	£
Income		
Gross profit from bar		5,569
Subscriptions		6,490
Donations received		360
		12,419
Less Expenditure		
Wages to staff	4,750	
Rates and insurance	1,910	
Telephone and postage	448	
General expenses	605	
Depreciation: Furniture	1,315	
Sports equipment	1,700	
		10,728
Surplus of income over expenditure		1,691

Balance Sheet at 31 December 1998

	£	£	£
Fixed assets	Cost	Depreciation	
Club premises	29,600	–	29,600
Furniture and fittings	5,260	1,315	3,945
Sports equipment	8,500	1,700	6,800
	43,360	3,015	40,345
Current assets			
Bar stocks		2,362	
Cash at bank		2,040	
		4,402	
Current liabilities			
Creditors for bar supplies		1,040	
Net current assets			3,362
Net assets			43,707
Accumulated fund			
Balance at 1 January 1998			42,016
Add Surplus of income over expenditure			1,691
			43,707

34.7 Subscriptions

In an examination you may be told how to deal with subscriptions.

Where the examiner does not give instructions, you are to follow normal accounting rules.

Let us take the following as an example:

Hightown Football Club has received the following subscriptions during the year ended 31 December 1998:

Subscriptions for 1997, received late	£55
Subscriptions for 1998	£6,300

Subscriptions for 1998, owing at 31 December 1998 were £80.

The subscriptions to be shown in the income and expenditure account are those which should have been paid for membership for the year 1998. This is £6,300 + £80 = £6,380. The amount owing at 31 December 1998 £80 will be shown (as debtors would be in a business firm) as a current asset in the balance sheet at 31 December 1998. The following illustrates this:

Hightown Football Club
Income and Expenditure Account for the year ended 31 December 1998

Expenditure	£	Income	£
		Subscriptions	6,380

Balance Sheet as at 31 December 1998

Current Assets	£		
Debtors for subscriptions	80		

The £55 subscriptions received late for 1997 will have been shown included in subscriptions for 1997 and also shown as a debtor in the balance sheet as at 31 December 1997.

34.8 Donations

Any donations received are shown as income in the year that they are received.

34.9 Entrance fees

New members often have to pay an entrance fee in the year that they join, in addition to the membership fee for that year. Entrance fees are normally included as income in the year that they are received.

34.10 Life membership

Sometimes members can pay one amount for life membership, and they will never have to pay any more money. This membership will last for their lifetime.

The committee of the club will have to decide how to enter these in the accounts. Such a receipt will probably be posted to a life membership account, and transfers made to the income and expenditure account over a number of years.

You should follow the examiner's instructions.

New terms

> **Accumulated fund** (p 346): A form of capital account for a non-profit organisation.
> **Income and expenditure account** (p 345): An account for a non-profit making organisation to find the surplus or loss made during a period.
> **Receipts and payments account** (p 345): A summary of the cash book of a non-profit making organisation.

Exercises

34.1 The Town Society was formed on 1 July 1997 and at the end of the first year the treasurer submitted the following statement to members:

Receipts and Payments Account for the year ended 30 June 1998

	£		£
Subscriptions	320	Cost of refreshments	20
Sale of dance tickets	80	Printing and stationery	15
Proceeds of sales of		Rent	10
refreshments	30	Furniture	150
		Dance expenses	45
		Sundry expenses	15
		Balance	175
	430		430

You are required to prepare an income and expenditure account for the year ended 30 June 1998, and a balance sheet as at that date.

You are given the following information:
  No subscriptions were paid in advance;
  No depreciation on the furniture;
  Stock of stationery £5;
  Rent owing £10.
(Pitman Qualifications)

34.2X From the following receipts and payments account and notes prepare the income and expenditure account, showing clearly within it the profit or loss on the bar and disco.

Receipts and Payments Account for the year ended 31 December 1998

	£		£
Bar sales	5,000	Furniture	265
Sale of disco tickets	100	Loss on raffle	40
Subscriptions	2,350	Hire of disco equipment	400
		Rent	100
		Rates	625
		Purchases of bar stock	3,000
		Secretary's expenses	20
		Bar staff wages	2,000
		Balance	1,000
	£7,450		£7,450

Subscriptions due amounted to £45
Rent paid in advance was £25
Bar stock remaining was valued at £250
Depreciate furniture by 20%
Rates due amounted to £15.
(Pitman Qualifications)

34.3 The following receipts and payments account for the year ending 31 May 1998 was prepared by the treasurer of the Down Town Sports and Social Club.

Receipts	£	Payments	£
Balance at bank 1 June 1997	286	Purchases of new equipment	166
Subscriptions	135	Bar stocks purchased	397
Net proceeds of jumble sale	91	Hire of rooms	64
Net proceeds of dance	122	Wages of part-time staff	198
Sale of equipment	80	Balance at bank 31 May 1998	352
Bar takings	463		
	1,177		1,177

Notes:
(1) On 1 June 1997 the club's equipment was valued at £340. Included in this total, valued at £92, was the equipment sold during the year for £80.
(2) Bar stocks were valued as follows:
    31 May 1997 £88   31 May 1998 £101

There were no creditors for bar supplies on either of these dates.
(3) Allow £30 for depreciation of equipment during the year ending 31 May 1998. This is additional to the loss on equipment sold during the year.
(4) No subscriptions were outstanding at 31 May 1997, but on 31 May 1998 subscriptions due but unpaid amounted to £14.

Required
(a) Calculate the accumulated fund of the club as at 1 June 1997. (This is the equivalent of the capital account in the case of a sole trader.)
(b) Draw up the income and expenditure account of the club for the year ending 31 May 1998.
Note: Calculations must be shown.

34.4 Shown below is the balance sheet of the Deepdale Church Youth Centre at 31 December 1998.

Balance Sheet for the Deepdale Church Youth Centre at 31 December 1988

	£	£	£
Fixed Assets	Cost	Depreciation	
Furniture and fittings	2,000	500	1,500
Games and equipment	1,000	360	640
Motor van	1,500	500	1,000
	4,500	1,360	3,140
Current assets			
Cash at bank and in hand		460	
Net current assets			460
Net assets			3,600
Accumulated fund			
Balance at 31 December 1988			3,600

The following summarised transactions took place during the period 1 January 1999 to 31 December 1999.

Receipts	£	Payments	£
Subscriptions (160 members		Light and heat	205
at £5 per annum)	800	Expenses of annual fête	310
Donation (treated as a		New games equipment	160
revenue receipt)	80	Cleaner's wages	104
Sale of tickets from annual		Repairs and renewals	83
fête	540	Motor van repairs	126

Note:
An electricity bill of £45 was owing at 31 December 1999 (analysed under Light and heat)

Required
Prepare:
(a) A receipts and payments account showing clearly the balance in hand at 1 January 2000.
(b) An income and expenditure account for the year ended 31 December 1999.
(c) A balance sheet as at 31 December 1999.
(RSA)

34.5X The Drones Sports and Social Club was formed on 1 January 1998. The treasurer kept the accounts by double entry and extracted the following trial balance on 31 December 1998:

	£	£
Cash at bank	320	
Cash in hand	50	
Bar takings		1,571
Lighting and heating	172	
Sundry expenses	63	
Bar supplies purchased	924	
Equipment	260	
Rates	180	
Rent	106	
Cleaning expenses	96	
Caretaker's wages	120	
Members' subscriptions		580
Christmas dance expenses	158	
Sales of Christmas dance tickets		298
	2,449	2,449

The treasurer has asked you to check his accounting records before the presentation of the annual accounts to the members. In doing this you find that account needs to be taken of the following:

1   Rates prepaid £40 at 31 December 1998.
2   £14 was still outstanding for cleaning expenses, at 31 December 1998.
3   Bar stock of refreshments at 31 December 1998 was valued at £36.

Required
(a) An income and expenditure account for the year ended 31 December 1998, showing clearly the profit or loss on the bar and the Christmas dance.
(b) A balance sheet as at 31 December 1998.
(RSA)

PART 6

Other considerations

35 Stock valuation

35.1 Different valuations of stock

Most people would think that there can be only one figure for the valuation of stock. This is not true. We will examine in this chapter how we can calculate different figures for stock.

Assume that a firm has just completed its first financial year and is about to value stock at cost price. It has dealt in only one type of goods. A record of the transactions is now shown in Exhibit 35.1.

Exhibit 35.1

Bought				Sold			
1998			£	1998			£
January	10	at £30 each	300	May	8	for £50 each	400
April	10	at £34 each	340	November	24	for £60 each	1,440
October	20	at £40 each	800				
	40		1,440		32		1,840

Still in stock at 31 December, 8 units.

The total figure of purchases is £1,440 and that of sales is £1,840. The trading account for the first year of trading can now be completed if the closing stock is brought into the calculations.

But what value do we put on each of the 8 units left in stock at the end of the year? If all of the units bought during the year had cost £30 each, then the closing stock would be 8 × £30 = £240. However, we have bought goods at different prices. This means that the valuation depends on which goods are taken for this calculation, the units at £30, or at £34, or at £40.

Many firms do not know exactly whether they have sold all the oldest units before they sell the newer units. For instance, a firm selling spanners may not know if the oldest spanners had been sold before the newest spanners.

The stock valuation will therefore be based on an accounting custom, and not on the facts of exactly which units were still in stock at the year end. The three main methods of doing this are now shown.

35.2 First in, first out method

This is usually known as **FIFO**, the first letters of each word.

This method says that the first goods to be received are the first to be issued. Using the figures in Exhibit 35.1 we can now calculate the closing figure of stock as follows:

	Received	Issued	Stock after each transaction		
1998				£	£
January	10 at £30 each		10 at £30 each		300
April	10 at £34 each		10 at £30 each	300	
			10 at £34 each	340	640
May		8 at £30 each	2 at £30 each	60	
			10 at £34 each	340	400
October	20 at £40 each		2 at £30 each	60	
			10 at £34 each	340	
			20 at £40 each	800	1,200
November		2 at £30 each			
		10 at £34 each			
		12 at £40 each			
		24	8 at £40 each		320

The closing stock at 31 December 1998 is therefore valued at £320.

35.3 Last in, first out method

This is usually known as **LIFO**. As each issue of goods are made they are said to be from the last lot of goods received before that date. Where there is not enough left of the last lot of goods, then the balance of goods needed is said to come from the previous lot still unsold.

From the information shown in Exhibit 35.1 the calculation can now be shown.

	Received	Issued	Stock after each transaction		
1998 January	10 at £30 each		10 at £30 each	£	£ 300
April	10 at £34 each		10 at £30 each 10 at £34 each	300 340	640
May		8 at £34 each	10 at £30 each 2 at £34 each	300 68	368
October	20 at £40 each		10 at £30 each 2 at £34 each 20 at £40 each	300 68 800	1,168
November		20 at £40 each 2 at £34 each 2 at £30 each 24	8 at £30 each		240

The closing stock at 31 December 1998 is, therefore, valued at £240.

35.4 Average cost method (AVCO)

Using the **AVCO** method, with each receipt of goods the average cost for each item of stock is recalculated. Further issues of goods are then at that figure, until another receipt of goods means that another recalculation is needed.

From the information in Exhibit 35.1 the calculation can be shown.

Received		Issued	Average cost per unit of stock held	Number of units in stock	Total value of stock
			£		£
January	10 at £30		30	10	300
April	10 at £34		32*	20	640
May		8 at £32	32	12	384
October	20 at £40		37*	32	1,184
November		24 at £37	37	8	296

The closing stock at 31 December 1998 is therefore valued at £296.

*In April, this is calculated as follows:
stock 10 × £30 = £300 + stock received (10 × £34) £340 = total £640.
20 units in stock, so the average is £640 ÷ 20 = £32.

In October this is calculated as follows:
stock 12 × £32 = £384 + stock received (20 × £40) £800 = £1,184.
32 units in stock, so the average is £1,184 ÷ 32 = £37.

35.5 Stock valuation and the calculation of profits

Using the figures from Exhibit 35.1, with stock valuations shown by the three methods of FIFO, LIFO, and AVCO, the trading accounts would appear:

Trading Account for the year ended 31 December 1998							
	FIFO	*LIFO*	*AVCO*		*FIFO*	*LIFO*	*AVCO*
	£	£	£		£	£	£
Purchases	1,440	1,440	1,440	Sales	1,840	1,840	1,840
Less Closing stock	320	240	296				
Cost of goods sold	1,120	1,200	1,144				
Gross profit	720	640	696				
	1,840	1,840	1,840		1,840	1,840	1,840

As you can see, different methods of stock valuation will mean that different profits are shown.

35.6 Reduction to net realisable value

The **net realisable value** of stock is calculated as follows:

Saleable value – expenses needed before completion of sale = Net realisable value.

If saleable value is £300 and expenses needed would be £20, the net realisable value would be £280. Now if the net realisable value of stock is lower than the valuation at cost, the figure to be taken for the final accounts will be the net realisable value. If stock at cost valuation is £500 and net realisable value is £400, then the figure of £400 will be used in the trading account and the balance sheet.

35.7 Stock groups and valuation

If there is only one sort of goods in stock, calculating the lower of cost or net realisable value is easy. If we have several or many types of goods in stock we can use one of two ways of making the calculation.

From the information given in Exhibit 35.2 we will calculate the stock in two different ways.

Exhibit 35.2

Stock at 31 December 1998			
Article	*Different categories*	*Cost*	*Net realisable value*
		£	£
1	A	100	80
2	A	120	150
3	A	300	400
4	B	180	170
5	B	150	130
6	B	260	210
7	C	410	540
8	C	360	410
9	C	420	310
		2,300	2,400

Articles 1, 2 and 3 are televisions. Articles 4, 5 and 6 are radios. Articles 7, 8 and 9 are videos.

The category method

The same sorts of items are put together in categories. Thus articles 1, 2 and 3 are televisions and shown as category A. Articles 4, 5 and 6 are radios and shown as category B. Articles 7, 8 and 9 are videos and shown as category C.

A calculation showing a comparison of cost valuation and net realisable value for each category is now shown.

Category	Cost	Net Realisable Value
A	£100 + £120 + £300 = £520	£80 + £150 + £400 = £630
B	£180 + £150 + £260 = £590	£170 + £130 + £210 = £510
C	£410 + £360 + £420 = £1,190	£540 + £410 + £310 = £1,260

The lower of cost and net realisable value is, therefore:

			£
Category A: lower of £520 or £630	=		520
Category B: lower of £590 or £510	=		510
Category C: lower of £1,190 or £1,260	=		1,190
Stock is valued for final accounts at			2,220

Article method

By this method, the lower of cost or net realisable value for each article is compared and the lowest figure taken. From Exhibit 35.2 this gives us the following valuation:

Articles	Valuation
	£
1	80
2	120
3	300
4	170
5	130
6	210
7	410
8	360
9	310
	£2,090

35.8 Goods on sale or return

Goods received on sale or return

Sometimes we may receive goods from one of our suppliers on a **sale or return** basis. What this means is that we do not have to pay for the goods until we sell them. If we do not sell them we have to return them to our supplier.

This means that the goods do not belong to us. If we have some goods on sale or return at the stock-taking date they should not be included in our stock valuation.

Goods sent to our customers on sale or return

We may send goods on a sale or return basis to our customers. The stock will belong to us until it is sold. At our stock-taking date any goods held by our customers on sale or return should be included in our stock valuation.

35.9 Stock-taking and the balance sheet date

Students often think that all the counting and valuing of stock is done on the last day of the accounting period. This might be true in a small business, but it is often impossible in larger businesses. There may be too many items of stock to do it so quickly.

This means that stock-taking may take place over a period of days. To get the figure of the stock valuation as on the last day of the accounting period, we will have to make adjustments. Exhibit 35.3 gives an example of such calculations.

Exhibit 35.3

Lee Ltd has a financial year which ends on 31 December 1998. The stock-taking is not in fact done until 8 January 1999. When the items in stock on that date are priced out, it is found that the stock value amounted to £28,850. The following information is available about transactions between 31 December 1998 and 8 January 1999.

1 Purchases since 31 December 1998 amounted to £2,370 at cost.
2 Returns inwards since 31 December 1998 were £350 at selling price.
3 Sales since 31 December 1998 amounted to £3,800 at selling price.
4 The selling price is always cost price + 25 per cent.

Lee Ltd
Computation of stock as on 31 December 1998

			£
Stock (at cost)			28,850
Add Items which were in stock on 31 December 1998 (at cost)			
		£	
Sales		3,800	
Less Profit content (20 per cent of selling price)*		760	3,040
			31,890
Less Items which were not in stock on 31 December 1998 (at cost)			
	£	£	
Returns inwards	350		
Less Profit content (20 per cent of selling price)*	70	280	
Purchases (at cost)		2,370	2,650
Stock in hand as on 31 December 1998			29,240

*Stock is at cost (or net realisable value), and not at selling price. As this calculation has a sales figure in it which includes profit, we must deduct the profit part to get to the cost price. This is true also for returns inwards.

35.10 Stock records: quantities only

Quite often a firm will keep records of quantities only, to keep a check as to whether items are being stolen, broken, wasted or lost.

Exhibit 35.4 shows the stock quantity records for two items of stock, components FG and JK.

Exhibit 35.4

Component FG			Component JK		
Component FG			**Component JK**		
1999		*No of items*			*No of items*
Jan 1	Stock b/fwd	86	Jan 1	Stock b/fwd	28
" 2	Received (invoice 5543)	20	" 2	Received (invoice 5549)	300
" 4	Issue P67	16	" 3	Issue R323	44
" 6	Issue P68	29	" 5	Issue R324	23
" 10	Issue P132	19	" 9	Issue R129	107
" 21	Received (invoice 5874)	70	" 11	Issue R325	79
" 25	Issue P69	33	" 13	Return in RA229	18
" 31	Issue P243	18	" 19	Received (invoice 5799)	200
			" 22	Issue R354	96
			" 29	Issue R130	64
			" 31	Return in RA230	5

From these stock records we should be able to work out exactly how many of component FG and of component JK are in store on 31 January 1999. We also do a physical stockcheck (i.e. we actually look at and count the items in the store) and find that we have 61 of FG and 134 of JK on that date.

We can now draft up a stock record card for each of these components. As each item is issued or received we alter the balance of stock in hand.

Component FG					
Date		*Ref*	*In*	*Out*	*Balance*
1999					
Jan	1	Opening balance			86
"	2	5543	20		106
"	4	P67		16	90
"	6	P68		29	61
"	10	P132		19	42
"	21	5874	70		112
"	25	P69		33	79
"	31	P243		18	61

With component FG the actual stock equals the stock per the stock card, verifying that there has been no stock losses.

With component JK we will see that the stock card records will disclose a stock loss of four items.

Component JK				
Date	Ref	In	Out	Balance
1999				
Jan 1	Opening balance			28
" 2	5549	300		328
" 3	R323		44	284
" 5	R324		23	261
" 9	R129		107	154
" 11	R325		79	75
" 13	RA229	18		93
" 19	5799	200		293
" 22	R354		96	197
" 29	R130		64	133
" 31	RA230	5		138
" 31	Stock loss		4	134

The stock loss for four items of component JK will now have to be investigated. There may be a satisfactory explanation, or it might even be the case of theft with the police being called in to investigate. It is up to the individual firm to decide what course of action is to be taken, but the stock loss should be looked into to establish the reasons for the deficiency.

New terms

AVCO (p 357): A method by which the goods used are priced out at average cost.

FIFO (p 356): A method by which the first goods to be received are said to be the first to be sold.

LIFO (p 356): A method by which the goods sold are said to have come from the last lot of goods to be received.

Net realisable value (p 358): The value of goods calculated as the selling price less expenses before sale.

Sale or return (p 360): Goods that do not belong to the person holding them.

Exercises

35.1 From the following figures you are to calculate the figures for stock valuation, using (a) the category method, and (b) the article method.

Stock at 31 December 1998			
Article	Categories	Cost	Net realisable value
		£	£
1	A	280	330
2	A	440	370
3	A	390	480
4	B	170	250
5	B	210	310
6	C	400	350
7	C	860	600
8	D	570	660
9	D	770	990

35.2X You are given the information as shown. From it you are to calculate the figures of stock valuation. Show the possible figures using (a) the category method, and (b) the article method.

Stock at 31 March 1998			
Article	Categories	Cost	Net realisable value
		£	£
1	A	600	900
2	A	550	730
3	B	990	890
4	B	220	190
5	B	450	510
6	B	380	440
7	C	490	430
8	C	410	410
9	C	330	280

35.3 (a) From the following figures calculate the closing stock-in-trade that would be shown using (i) FIFO, (ii) LIFO, (iii) AVCO methods.

1998	Bought	Sold	
January	24 at £10 each	June	30 at £16 each
April	16 at £12.50 each	November	34 at £18 each
October	30 at £13 each		

(b) Draw up trading accounts for 1998 using each of the three methods for stock valuation.

35.4X   (a)   From the following figures calculate the closing stock-in-trade that would be shown using (i) FIFO, (ii) LIFO, (iii) AVCO methods.

1999	Bought	Sold	
January	30 at £12 each	July	24 at £15.50 each
May	30 at £14 each	November	16 at £18 each

(b)   Draw up trading accounts for 1999 using each of the three methods for stock valuation.

35.5X   Edward Greenwood is a sole trader whose year end is 31 January each year. Owing to pressure of business, he is unable to value his stock-in-trade at the close of business on 31 January 1998 but he does so on 7 February 1998 when the value, *at cost price*, is calculated at £2830.

For the period 1–7 February his purchases were £296, of which goods costing £54 were in transit at the time of stock-taking.

Sales for the period 1–7 February amounted to £460, all of which had left the warehouse at the time of stock-taking. Greenwood's gross profit is 20% of sales.

Also during the period 1–7 February, Greenwood took goods costing £38 for his personal use.

Included in the valuation figure of £2,830 given above were goods which cost £120, but which had a *market price* of £97 only at the date of the year end, i.e. 31 January 1998.

Required
Calculate the figure which should be shown as 'Stock at 31 January 1998' in Greenwood's trading account for the year ended 31 January 1998.
Note: Calculations must be shown.
(RSA)

35.6   Chung Ltd make up their accounts to 31 December each year. The valuation of the stock, at cost, as at 31 December 1998 was not attempted until 11 January 1999 when a physical stock-check revealed a total per stock sheets of £198,444 at cost.
Further investigation revealed that:
(a)   All goods are sold at a uniform profit of 50 per cent on cost.
(b)   Sales for the period 1 January 1999 to 11 January 1999, and for which goods had been despatched, amounted to £6,960.
(c)   One stock sheet was undercast by £50 and another one overcast by £1,000.
(d)   An extension of 660 articles at £0.80 each was shown as £560.
(e)   The stock figure includes goods held on approval £3,000 and for which no invoices had been received, nor were the goods to be kept by Chung Ltd.
(f)   A total at the bottom of one page, £105,680, had been carried forward to the next page as £106,850.
Calculate the figure of stock for the final accounts as at 31 December 1998.

35.7   The accounting year of Ceramics Ltd ended on 30 June each year. Owing to holidays it was impossible to carry out stock-taking until 5 July 1998. When this was done the total stock as per the stock sheets was £15,705 valued at cost. The normal rate of gross profit earned was $33\frac{1}{3}\%$ of selling price.

Adjustments were necessary to the stock sheet valuation to arrive at the stock figure for 30 June 1998. While these adjustments were being made, certain errors came to light and the following matters had to be considered:

(a)   A parcel of goods purchased in January at an enhanced price of £500 to complete a rush selling order was still in stock and the market price was now £390.

(b) An item valued at cost £500 was a standby generator for use if and when the electricity supply failed. It had been included on the stock sheets.

(c) Goods to the value of £900 had been received from suppliers in the period 1 to 4 July 1998. These goods had been invoiced dated 30 June 1998 and the amount included in creditors.

(d) Goods selling price £630 had been sent to Sang Ltd on approval. They had not been included in stock nor had any entries been made in the books.

(e) Sales for the period 1 to 4 July 1998 and invoiced dated July 1998 totalled £993.

(f) Sales credit notes issued before 30 June 1998 totalling £150 had been omitted from the books in error.

(g) In the stock-taking sheets a sub-total of £240 had been wrongly carried forward as £420 and a sheet had been overcast by £100.

(h) Ceramics Ltd had agreed to take back from Wood goods invoiced at £540 but these were still in transit at 30 June 1998 and no credit note had been issued.

(i) Goods valued at £600 cost were obsolete and it would cost £350 to convert them to 'good' stock. There would be no increase in the selling price obtainable.

Required

Prepare a statement item by item to show the amount at which the stock should be shown in the accounts as at 30 June 1998. State which, if any, of the items (a) to (i) above do not affect the stock.

(LCCI)

35.8 The following are four different business situations:

Business 1

R Simpson, a retail shopkeeper, determines his unsold stock at 31 December 1998 to be £15,600, valued at normal selling prices. His normal selling prices are determined by adding 20% to the purchase cost of the goods.

Business 2

R Bendall's manufacturing and trading account for the year ended 31 December 1998 (in summarised form) showed:

	£
Opening stock raw materials	12,200
Raw material purchases	136,000
	148,200
Closing stock raw materials	14,700
	133,500
Direct wages	205,700
	339,200
Production overhead	193,670
	532,870
Opening stock of work in progress	12,100
	544,970
Closing stock of work in progress	17,390
	527,580
Opening stock finished goods	23,262
	550,842
Closing stock finished goods	28,910
Cost of goods sold	521,932
Sales	620,000
Gross profit	98,068

Business 3

J Gilbert took physical stock on 26 December 1998 and this, valued at cost, amounted to £24,280. In the period 26 December to 31 December:

(a) Purchases delivered, at cost, amounted to £870.

(b) Sales, at a normal profit margin of 25% on cost, amounted to £500.

Business 4

Artimus Ltd has a stock of raw material X at 31 December 1998 which had cost £3,730. It has a replacement price of £4,395. However, material X is no longer used by Artimus Ltd and it will have to be sold as scrap for £2,780.

Required

Calculate the stock valuation which should appear on the balance sheet for each of the businesses as at 31 December 1998.

Note: All workings should be shown.

(LCCI)

35.9 Rule up a card suitable for the recording of the quantity of an item in stock.

The card should show receipts, issues, and balance. The name of suppliers should be shown against receipts, and the requisition number against issues.

Item number 24

1 May 1998	Balance in stock		500
Receipts			
2 May 1998	Starlight Co Ltd		300
8 May 1998	Moonbeam & Sons		200
24 May 1998	Starlight Co Ltd		350
Issues			
8 May 1998	Requisition number	740	173
10 May 1998	" "	810	294
14 May 1998	" "	976	104
28 May 1998	" "	981	206

(RSA)

35.10 D Brown owns a petrol filling station. Petrol is sold at cost plus 25 per cent. The petrol pumps automatically record by meter the number of litres sold. Stock of premium unleaded petrol on 1 January was 40,000 litres valued at 60 pence per litre.

During the month of January 1999 Brown took delivery of premium unleaded petrol as follows:

1999

Jan 8 30,000 litres costing 60 pence per litre

" 16 40,000 litres costing 62 pence per litre

" 24 60,000 litres costing 64 pence per litre

Meter readings taken from the premium unleaded petrol pump were:

1999

Jan 1 178,045

" 31 283,045

You are required to calculate:

(a) The number of litres of premium unleaded petrol in stock on 31 January 1999.

(b) The value of that stock of petrol on 31 January 1999.

(c)   The number of litres of premium unleaded petrol sold during January 1999.

(d)   The revenue from sales of premium unleaded petrol during January 1999.

(e)   The gross profit on sales of premium unleaded petrol for January 1999.

Show your workings.

Ignore VAT.

(RSA)

35.11X   Y Uck, a builders' merchant, has no reliable method of recording his stock receipts and issues. At the present time he has no means of obtaining a valuation for his stock-in-trade (without undertaking a lengthy and costly stock-taking).

Y Uck has produced the following data from the month ended 30 September 1998.

Marble chippings stock	1 Sept 1998	2 tonnes
Purchased from J Brown	4 "	8 "
Sold to T Williams	10 "	6 "
Purchased from B Green	14 "	9 "
Sold to W Thomas	20 "	2 "
Sold to B Dunstan	25 "	7 "

All stock and purchases are priced at £50 per tonne. All issues of stock are priced at £65 per tonne.

You are required to show:

Y Uck's trading account for the month ended 30 September 1998.

(RSA)

36 Wages and salaries

36.1 Introduction

To enable the payment of **wages** and **salaries** to be carried out efficiently and accurately, all organisations, whether large or small, need to keep records of their **employees**. The need for this is essential not only for recording the payment of wages and income tax etc. but also for recording basic personal details. Such personal records are usually kept in the personnel department of an organisation.

36.2 Functions of the payroll

The payroll is a list of employees that specifies the wage or salary that each employee receives.

The procedures and calculations that are necessary to produce this list need to be fully understood and applied to ensure that all employees are paid promptly and correctly.

The responsibility for producing the payroll will depend on the size of the organisation. A large organisation will probably have a wages department, whereas a small one will rely on a wages clerk. Irrespective of who carries out the function they must ensure that the payments are:

1 **Accurate**
   - Correct basic payment for work done.
   - Additional entitlements such as **bonus**, overtime, expenses, etc.
   - Deduction of taxes, national insurance contributions due to the government.
   - Deduction of contributions to pension and medical schemes.
   - Wage cost information for the **employer**.

2 **Regular and on time**
   - Enables the employees to meet their own financial commitments and plan their future expenditure.
   - Late or irregular payment would harm the morale of the employees and cause them to doubt the financial stability of the organisation.

3 **Confidential**
   - Staff involved in preparing the payroll must not divulge any of its

contents except to authorised people, i.e. company executives, the Inland Revenue.

- Staff must only discuss with an employee that employee's wage/salary details.

4 Secure

- The handling of cash and cheques must be done in a secure environment to prevent loss, theft or loss of confidentiality.
- Checks must be built into the procedures to guard against the possibility of fraud by wages staff.
- The distribution of wages must be organised so that each employee receives their own wage.
- All employee records must be kept securely. If a manual system is used it should be held in a locked cabinet with access limited to staff from the personnel/wages department. If a computerised system is used, a password should be given to authorised personnel only so that the information may be accessed only by them.

36.3 Payments to employees

Payments to employees may be made by wage or salary. Wages are usually paid weekly, in cash, often to manual workers. Salaries are paid monthly by cheque, credit transfer (i.e. paid direct into the employee's bank account) or direct into a building society account.

Pay may also be referred to as remuneration, which simply means to reward or pay for work carried out. This term 'remuneration' is often attached to pay given to the directors of a company where their pay is recorded in the accounts as directors' remuneration.

36.4 Gross pay and net pay

All employees are subject to Income Tax (PAYE: Pay As You Earn) and National Insurance Contributions (NIC). These and other deductions have to be made by the employer from the gross pay so it is important to distinguish between the gross pay and net pay.

- Gross pay is the amount of wage or salary due to the employee before deductions are made.
- Net pay is the amount of wage or salary received by the employee after all deductions have been made. Many employees talk about 'take home pay'; this is in fact the net pay.

36.5 Methods of calculating pay

The methods of calculating pay vary between employers and also the employees within an organisation. The main methods are as follows:

1 Fixed amount salary or wage

These are an agreed annual or weekly wage.

Example

For an annual salary of £11,604 the monthly salary would be:

$$\frac{£11,604}{12} = £967 \text{ per month}$$

whereas a weekly wage would be a set figure, e.g. £200 per week.

2 Time rates

Here a fixed basic rate per hour is paid multiplied by the number of hours worked.

Example A

A bricklayer receives £5.20 per hour: if he works for 40 hours during a particular week his gross pay =

$$40 \text{ hours} \times £5.20 = £208 \text{ per week}$$

If additional hours are worked it is usual to pay the workers overtime; this payment is normally at a higher rate. Extra hours worked during the week are often paid at 'time and a half' and 'double time' is freqently paid for weekend work.

Example B

Richard Kerr worked the following hours during the week ended 31 March 1999:

	Hours
Monday	9
Tuesday	8
Wednesday	8.5
Thursday	10
Friday	8
Saturday	4

His basic rate of pay is £4.60 per hour and he works a standard week of 40 hours (i.e. 8 hours a day). Overtime is paid at time and a half during the week and double time on Saturday and Sunday.

Richard Kerr's **gross wage** for week ending 31 March 1999 is calculated as follows:

		£
Basic pay 40 hours at £4.60	=	184.00
Overtime:		
Week 3.5 hours at (4.60 × 1.5)		
= £6.90 per hour	=	24.15
Saturday 4 hours at (£4.60 × 2)		
= £9.20 per hour	=	36.80
Gross wage	=	£244.95

3 Basic rate plus bonus

Many organisations offer bonus payments as an incentive to workers to reach and exceed set targets. Sometimes the bonus is referred to as a 'Productivity Bonus' and can be either a set sum of money or as a percentage of the basic wage.

Example

Electronic Supreme Ltd manufacture television sets for both the home and overseas markets. They pay their workers a basic wage of £168 per week plus a productivity bonus of £20 per worker if 1,500 televisions are produced in the factory per week; this increases to £30 per week if production exceeds 2000 televisions.

During the first week of November the company produces 1,600 televisions, therefore, the workers will receive:

	£
Basic wage	168.00
Bonus	20.00
	£188.00

4 Piece rate

Here payment is based on the number of units produced or operations completed. The employee is paid only for work completed although most employers agree a minimum wage regardless of work completed. **Piece rate** payment is an incentive to encourage workers to work faster although it is important to ensure that quality does not suffer as a result of faster production.

Example

Lowe Production Co manufacture parts for the motor car industry. They pay their workers piecework rates as follows:

Part PCD 27 = £2.10 per unit
Part JB 10 = £7.45 per unit

They also have a minimum wage agreement of £175.00 per week.

During the first week of January one of the workers, Jack Murphy, produced 60 Part PCD 27s and 12 Part JB 103s.

His wage for the week would be:

		£
60 × £2.10	=	126.00
12 × £7.45	=	89.40
		£215.40

Another worker, Thomas Hobson, produced 50 Part PCD 27s and 8 Part JB 103s; his wage would be:

		£
50 × £2.10	=	105.00
8 × £7.45	=	59.60
		£164.60

but because there is a minimum wage agreement Thomas Hobson would receive £175.00.

5 Commission

Commission is a percentage based on the amount of sales made by an employee. Commission may be paid in addition to a basic salary or instead of a salary.

Example

Carol Chapman and Dianne Dawson work for a computer software company. Their salaries were £12,000 and £10,800 a year respectively, plus commission of 1 per cent of total sales made each month.

During July, Carol's sales totalled £30,000 and Dianne's £17,000. Their July salaries would be as follows:

Carol	$\dfrac{£12,000}{12}$	= £1,000 per month
	Plus 1% of £30,000	= 300
	Salary	= £1,300
Dianne	$\dfrac{£10,800}{12}$	= £900
	Plus 1% of £17,000	= 170
	Salary	= £1,070

36.6 Clock cards

Some organisations require their workers to 'clock in and out' of work to enable accurate payment to be made in respect of time spent at work.

On arrival at work each employee removes their personal **clock card** from a rack and slots it into a time recorder clock which records the time of arrival. The same procedure is carried out on leaving work.

At the end of the week the card is passed to the wages department to enable them to calculate the actual hours worked by each employee.

A clock card prior to handing to the wages department is shown in Exhibit 36.1 and a clock card after completion by the wages department is shown in Exhibit 36.2.

Exhibit 36.1

A clock card (prior to handing to the wages department).

CLOCK CARD

Name: B. Sullivan   **No:** 98

Week ending: 11 April 1999

Day	In	Out	In	Out	Total hours
Mon	8.00	12.01	1.00	5.03	
Tue	8.10	12.00	1.00	5.00	
Wed	8.01	12.02	12.57	5.01	
Thu	8.03	12.00	12.59	5.30	
Fri	8.00	12.01	1.01	4.00	
Sat	7.30	12.00			
Total					

Ordinary time

Overtime

Bonus

Gross pay

Exhibit 36.2

A clock card, completed by the wages department, showing the hours worked and a calculation of gross pay.

CLOCK CARD						
Name: *B. Sullivan*				**No:** *98*		
Week ending: *11 April 1999*						

Day	In	Out	In	Out	Total hours	
Mon	8.00	12.01	1.00	5.03	*8*	
Tue	8.10	12.00	1.00	5.00	*7 3/4*	
Wed	8.01	12.02	12.57	5.01	*8*	
Thu	8.03	12.00	12.59	5.30	*8 1/2*	
Fri	8.00	12.01	1.01	4.00	*7*	
Sat	7.30	12.00			*4 1/2*	
Total					*43 3/4*	

Ordinary time	*39 hrs x £3.60*	*140.40*
Overtime	*1/2 hr x £5.00 plus 4 1/4 hrs x £7.20*	*33.10*
Bonus		
	Gross pay	*£173.50*

36.7 Time sheets

Time sheets are usually used by employees who work away from the main business premises, i.e. a decorating company, whose workers are employed at various locations according to the requirements of the individual jobs (*see* Exhibits 36.3 and 36.4) showing time sheets completed by an employee called Gary Lester. You will notice that Gary is required to complete details of work carried out, the hours worked on the job, together with the time spent on travelling to the job.

At the end of the week the time sheet will be checked by the supervisor or foreman before being passed to the wages department for completion.

Time sheets can also be used by workers based at the main office but involved in work for various clients or customers. A typical example here would be a firm of solicitors or accountants who carry out specific duties for clients and need to record the time spent on each particular job to enable correct costings to be carried out prior to invoicing the client.

One of the main advantages of using this method of recording time spent on each job is that employees are more conscious of their time and deploy time more effectively. Also clients are charged fairly according to the time spent on a particular job. However, one of the disadvantages is that they could be over-charged if an employee records their time inaccurately or charges time to a particular client's job when that time was spent in other areas of work or inactivity.

Many organisations also require payroll information and data to be fed into the costing system to enable management information to be available for budgeting, costing and profitability analysis.

Exhibit 36.3

A time sheet completed by employee.

	TIME SHEET			
Name: _Gary Lester_		**Week ending:** _20 March 1999_		
Day	Job description	Hours worked	Travel time	Total
Mon	_Decorating Casino_	8	½	
Tue	_"_	8½	½	
Wed	_"_	8	½	
Thu	_External work at Stanton offices_	9	1	
Fri	_"_	8½	1	
Sat	_Decorating office — Black's Estate Agents_	6	1	
Sun	_"_	4	1	
	Totals			

Basic: _____ hrs × _____   **Total**

O/T – Week: _____ hrs × _____

– Weekend: _____ hrs × _____

Travel: _____ hrs × _____

Foreman: _____   **Gross pay**

Exhibit 36.4

A time sheet showing calculations of hours worked and gross pay.

\	\	\	\	\
TIME SHEET				
Name: _Gary Lester_		**Week ending:** _20 March 1999_		
Day	Job description	Hours worked	Travel time	Total
Mon	*Decorating Casino*	8	1/2	8 1/2
Tue	"	8 1/2	1/2	9
Wed	"	8	1/2	8 1/2
Thu	*External work at Stanton offices*	9	1	10
Fri	"	8 1/2	1	9 1/2
Sat	*Decorating office — Black's Estate Agents*	6	1	7
Sun	"	4	1	5
	Totals	52	5 1/2	57 1/2

Basic:	_40_ hrs × _£5.20_	**Total**	208.00
O/T – Week:	_2_ hrs × _£7.80_		15.60
– Weekend:	_10_ hrs × _£10.40_		104.00
Travel:	_5 1/2_ hrs × _£4.00_		22.00
Foreman:	_R Derbyshire_	**Gross pay**	349.60

36.8 Computer cards

Many organisations are adapting **computerised card** systems whereby employees carry computer cards which they insert into a computerised time clock on arrival and departure. In the same way as clock cards the computerised card automatically records their hours of work.

This method of recording hours worked is often used by employers using a **flexitime system** (*see* section 36.9).

36.9 Flexitime system

Flexitime is a system permitting flexibility of working hours at the beginning or end of the day provided an agreed period of time, called the core time, is spent at work.

Staff are usually free to choose their starting and finishing times but must work the normal number of hours per week. However, it is possible to carry forward time worked in excess of the normal time, or owed, to another period and then take time off in lieu, although the time allowed to be carried forward is usually limited, say only one day per fortnight.

Flexitime is widely used in many large organisations and local authorities while not so popular in smaller private companies.

36.10 Deductions from pay

There are two types of deductions which are made from wages and salaries:
1   Statutory
2   Voluntary

Statutory deductions

Deductions which an employer has to make by law (statute) from their employees' gross pay are:
- Income tax
- National Insurance Contributions

Income tax

In the United Kingdom the wages and salaries of all employees are liable to **income tax** deductions. This does not mean, however, that everyone will pay income tax; it depends upon the amount of earnings and the **tax allowances** that can be offset against that **income**. If income tax is found to be payable then the employer will deduct the tax from the employee's wage or salary. This is then paid to the Inland Revenue, the government department responsible for collection of income tax.

National Insurance Contributions (NIC)

National Insurance Contributions (NIC) are also deducted by the employer from the employee in a similar way to income tax deductions but the employer also has to contribute a certain amount of money, again depending upon the amount of gross pay.

All contributions are again sent to the Inland Revenue, which collects them on behalf of the government Department of Social Security.

Voluntary deductions

As the name suggests these are deductions made from pay at the employee's request. They include payments to:

1   Occupational **pension funds** or **superannuation schemes**
2   Charitable organisations
3   Savings schemes
4   Trade unions and/or social clubs

36.11   Income tax (PAYE)

Introduction

PAYE is the system used in the United Kingdom for the calculation and collection of income tax and Class 1 National Insurance Contributions (NIC) from employees' gross wages. As previously mentioned, the income tax and NIC collected are then paid to the Inland Revenue by the employer.

The PAYE system simply means that workers pay tax as they earn their wages or salaries. In other words they pay income tax weekly, if paid weekly wages, and monthly if salaried. This avoids a large tax bill at the end of each year, which is what some self-employed people are faced with.

Note: PAYE applies to all employees of a business including directors, both full-time and part-time staff, casuals and pensioners who are being paid superannuation/pension from an approved company scheme.

Tax year

The income tax year runs from 6 April of one year to 5 April of the following year. The tax year for 1997/98 is as follows:

> 6 April 1997 to 5 April 1998
> and for 1998/99:
> 6 April 1998 to 5 April 1999

For PAYE purposes each tax year is divided into either weeks (for weekly paid staff) or months for salaried staff.

Pay/income (for PAYE purposes)

It is important to be aware of what counts as pay for PAYE tax purposes.
Examples of such pay include:

* Salaries, wages, fees, overtime, bonuses, commission
* Cash payments such as Christmas gifts
* Payment in respect of absence from work

- Statutory sick pay
- Statutory maternity pay
- Holiday pay
- Lump sum payments (i.e. when an employee leaves)
- Tips paid in addition to normal pay

Tax allowances

All of the above items under the heading 'Pay' constitute income which is subject to income tax. However, each individual is given a personal allowance. This is a tax-free allowance (i.e. an amount of money that a person can earn without paying tax). This amount is deducted from the income to arrive at the **taxable income**. The personal allowance is known as a tax allowance and is announced each year by the Chancellor of the Exchequer in the Budget. The Chancellor also announces the rates of income tax each year. These allowances and **rates of tax** can change each year according to the Budget.

For the income tax year 1997/98 tax allowances are as follows:

Personal allowance (basic amount)	£4,045
Personal allowance (aged 65–74)*	£5,220
Personal allowance (age 75 and over)*	£5,400
Married couple's allowance**	£1,830
Married couple's allowance (age 65–74)*	£3,185
Married couple's allowance (age 75 and over)*	£3,225

Notes: *These allowances are reduced if the taxpayer's income exceeds the income limit, which is £15,600 for the tax year 1997/98.

**This is an extra allowance in addition to the personal allowance that a married man or his wife may claim; or they may agree to split the allowance between them.

In addition to the personal allowance individuals may be entitled to other allowances such as relief on mortgage interest, maintenance payments, etc. People may also claim for professional expenses incurred in employment such as fees paid to a professional body like the Chartered Institute of Management Accountants. Allowance may also be given for expenditure on specialist equipment and working clothes such as safety shoes, overalls etc. It is the employee's responsibility to ensure that he or she receives the right amount of allowances.

Rates of tax

When the tax allowance is deducted from the total income the difference is the taxable income; this is the amount of income which is subject to income tax. For the income tax year 1997/98 the rates of tax and bands of taxable income are as follows:

Lower rate at	20%	£0–£4,100
Basic rate at	23%	on the next £22,000
Higher rate at	40%	on income over £26,100

Calculation of income tax by the PAYE system

We will now look at the income tax payable in the following examples:

1 Matthew Roberts earns £3,000 a year as a part-time gardener. His personal allowance is £4,045 for the year; therefore, no tax will be payable as his personal allowance exceeds his income.

2 Adrian Duffy earns £12,400 a year as a joiner, his personal relief totals £5,120. This means Adrian can earn £5,120 tax free. Therefore, Adrian's taxable pay will be as follows:

Gross pay	£12,400
Less Tax allowance	5,120
Taxable pay	£7,280

We can now see that the amount of pay Adrian has to pay tax on is £7,280; if we were to deduct the tax under the PAYE system, Adrian would pay an amount of tax each week as he earns his wages. To enable us to calculate the amount of tax payable we would use the various tax tables, code numbers and the income tax form P11: Deductions Working Sheet.

For the time being we will calculate the total amount of income tax Adrian has to pay for the year as follows:

Tax due =	£
Income tax at 20% on £4,100	820.00
Basic rate at 23% on £3,180	731.40
Tax payable	£1,551.40

3 Let us consider another example by looking at the case of Alice McGuire who, as director of a marketing company, earns considerably more than either of the two previous examples. Her salary amounts to £34,000 a year and she has allowances of £5,165; the tax payable for the year is as follows:

Gross pay	£34,000
Less Tax allowance	5,165
Taxable pay	£28,835
Tax due =	£
Income tax at 20% on £4,100	820.00
Basic rate at 23% on £22,000	5,060.00
Higher rate at 40% on £2,735	1,094.00
Tax due	£6,974.00

Now we have calculated the amount of income tax due for the above employees let us assume that National Insurance Contributions are 5 per cent of gross pay. In addition we will assume that two of the employees, Adrian Duffy and Alice McGuire also contribute to the company pension scheme to which they contribute 10 per cent of their gross salary.

The **net wage/salary** each employee would receive is calculated as follows:

1 Matthew Roberts

	£	£
Gross wage		3,000
Less Income tax	Nil	
Less NIC	Nil	
Less Pension fund	Nil	Nil
Net wage for the year		£3,000

Note: As Matthew earns less than the threshold for NIC, he is not liable for NIC.

2 Adrian Duffy

	£	£
Gross wage/salary		12,400.00
Less Income tax	1,551.40	
Less NIC	620.00	
Less Pension fund	1,240.00	3,411.40
Net wage/salary for the year		£8,988.60

3 Alice McGuire

	£	£
Gross wage/salary		34,000
Less Income tax	6,974	
Less NIC	1,700	
Less Pension fund	3,400	12,074
Net wage/salary for the year		£21,926

Tax code numbers

To enable employers to calculate the correct amount of taxable income and tax payable by their employees they need to know each individual employee's tax allowance. This allowance is communicated to both the employee and employer by the Inland Revenue using Income Tax Form P6 in the form of a tax code.

The tax code will incorporate all the reliefs to which the employee is entitled, i.e. personal allowance, married allowance, plus relief for mortgage interest, etc. The way the tax codes are arrived at is very simple to understand:

- The total of all the allowances is added up, i.e. £3,525, then the last digit is removed, so £3,525 becomes 352.

- The number will also be followed by a letter. The most common ones used are *L* (for Lower); this code letter is used where an individual is entitled to the basic personal allowance, usually single people. *H* (for Higher), is used for a person entitled to both the personal and married allowance.

- So our **tax code number** of 352 becomes *352L*, indicating that it is a single person's allowance.

There are other tax code numbers but at this stage of your studies it is not necessary to consider these.

36.11 Tax Tables

Tax Tables are issued by the Inland Revenue to enable organisations to operate the PAYE system as easily and smoothly as possible, always ensuring that the correct amount of tax is deducted from or refunded to employees.

The tables help employers to work out how much to deduct from, or refund to, each of their employees every time they are paid. Tax Tables are used in conjunction with the employee's tax code, (see previous section, Tax code numbers).

A set of Tax Tables consists of:

> **Table A** – called Pay Adjustment Tables
> **Tables LR and B to D** – called Taxable Pay Tables

36.12 Worked example

The following example shows the preparation of a wages book, cash analysis and finally the cheque for withdrawing the money from the bank.

Example

Spencers (Exhibition Suppliers) Co of Nottingham is a small company specialising in the supply of exhibition display units and materials to industrial and commercial organisations. They employ a small work-force of four people, details of which are as follows:

Employee's name	Gross weekly wage	Income tax due	NIC employee	NIC employer
Julie L Gibbons	£185.00	£25.17	£13.91	£12.98
David R Hall	£265.00	£40.17	£21.91	£27.08
Andrew M Turner	£250.00	£35.92	£20.41	£25.55
Amanda Whitehouse	£220.00	£33.42	£17.41	£22.49

Each of the above employees also contributes £1.00 per week each to the company's social club.

The completed wages book for Spencers (Exhibition Suppliers) Co is now shown in Exhibit 36.5.

Exhibit 36.5

Completed wages book for Spencers (Exhibition Suppliers) Co.

		WAGES BOOK									
Week ending: *6 April 1997*											
		Earnings				**Deductions**					
Number	**Name**	Basic	Over-time	Bonus	Total gross pay	PAYE (Income Tax)	National Insur-ance	Other deduc-tions	Total deduc-tions	Net pay	Employer's NI contri-butions
		£	£	£	£	£	£	£	£	£	£
	J. L. Gibbons	185–			185–	25.17	13.91	1.00	40.08	144.92	12.98
	D. R. Hall	265–			265–	40.17	21.91	1.00	63.08	201.92	27.08
	A. M. Turner	250–			250–	35.92	20.41	1.00	57.33	192.67	25.55
	A. Whitehouse	220–			220–	33.42	17.41	1.00	51.83	168.17	22.49
	Totals	920–			920–	134.68	73.64	4.00	212.32	707.68	88.10

The wages clerk would then prepare a cash analysis to ensure that the notes and coins obtained from the bank will enable the wage packets to be filled with the correct amount of money.

Note: The company pays the first £100 in £20 notes and any amount thereafter in £10 and £5 notes or £1 coins as appropriate.

To carry out the calculation it is necessary to make a list of the note and coin values across the top and list the employees down the side. After working out what is needed for each single employee the quantities required for all the employees is added up; this is now shown in Exhibit 36.6.

Exhibit 36.6

Completed cash analysis – Spencers (Exhibition Suppliers) Co.

CASH ANALYSIS

Week ending: *6 April 1997*

Name	£20	£10	£5	£1	50p	20p	10p	5p	2p	1p	Amount £ p
J. L. Gibbons	5	4		4	1	2			1		144.92
D. R. Hall	5	10		1	1	2			1		201.92
A. M. Turner	5	9		2	1		1	1	1		192.67
A. Whitehouse	5	6	1	3			1	1	1		168.17
Number of notes and coins required	20	29	1	10	3	4	2	2	4		
Totals Cross-check	400	290	5	10	1.50	.80p	.20p	.10p	.8p		707.68

Now we need to check that we have carried out the cash analysis correctly by adding up the notes and coins required as follows:

Notes and coins required

			£
20	×	£20	= 400.00
29	×	£10	= 290.00
1	×	£5	= 5.00
10	×	£1	= 10.00
3	×	50p	= 1.50
4	×	20p	= 0.80
2	×	10p	= 0.20
2	×	5p	= 0.10
4	×	2p	= 0.08
			707.68

The total of the coin analysis agrees with the net pay figure as shown in the wages book (Exhibit 36.5) so we can assume that the analysis has been carried out correctly.

Finally, a cheque is made out to enable the cash to be withdrawn from the bank (*see* Exhibit 36.7).

Exhibit 36.7

Completed cheque for payment of the wages.

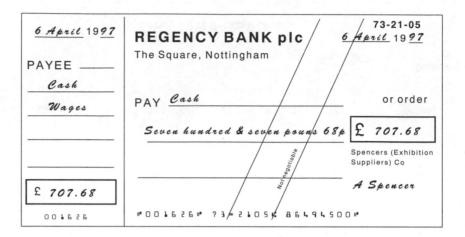

New terms

Bonus (p 372): An additional amount paid to an employee if a set target is achieved.

Clock Card (p 373): Card issued to employees to enable them to 'clock in and out' of work. The card is then used to calculate the employees' wages according to the number of hours spent at work.

Commission (p 373): A percentage, based on the amount of sales made by an employee, may be paid in addition to a basic salary or instead of a salary.

Computer Card (p 377): Card used by staff to record the time spent on the business premises by inserting the card into a computerised time clock on arrival and departure.

Flexitime System (p 378): System of permitting flexibility of working hours at the beginning and end of the day provided an agreed 'core time' is spent on the premises.

Employee (p 369): A person who is hired to work for an organisation in return for payment.

Employer (p 369): A person or organisation that employs workers and pays them wages or salaries in return for services rendered.

Gross Pay (p 370): This is the amount of wages or salary before deductions are made.

Income (p 379): Pay which is subject to income tax.

Income Tax (PAYE) (p 379): System used in the UK for the calculation and collection of Income Tax and Class 1 National Insurance Contributions (NIC) from payments made to employees.

Net Pay (p 370): This is the amount of wages or salary after deductions are made (the net wage is often referred to as 'take home pay').

Pension Fund/Superannuation Scheme (p 379): Schemes set up by employers to provide their employees with a pension.

Personnel department (p 369): An organisation's department that deals with interviewing and appointing staff together with the keeping of accurate employee records.

Piece Rate (p 372): Pay based on the number of units produced or operations completed.

Rates of Tax (p 380): The rates of income tax which are levied by the Government through the Inland Revenue.

Salary (p 370): Fixed payment, usually paid monthly, to an employee for professional or office work.

Statutory Deductions (p 378): Deductions which an employer has to make by law (statute) from their workers' gross pay.

Tax Allowance (p 380): An allowance of tax free income to which an individual is entitled. Also known as the personal allowance.

Tax Code Numbers (p 382): A PAYE code number issued by the Inland Revenue which reflects the tax allowances to which the employee is entitled.

Taxable Income (p 381): The difference between income and the tax allowance is known as taxable income. This amount is subject to income tax and is known as the taxable income.

Time Rate (p 371): A fixed basic rate per hour is paid multiplied by the number of hours worked.

Time Sheet (p 376): Form used by employees, who often work away from the main business premises, to record the time spent on various jobs and the overall weekly attendance.

Voluntary Deductions (p 379): Deductions made from pay at the employee's request.

Wage (p 370): Payment made to a worker in return for services rendered, usually paid weekly.

Exercises

36.1 H Smith is employed by a firm of carpenters at a rate of £5.50 per hour. During the week to 18 May 1998 he worked his basic week of 40 hours. The income tax due on his wages was £36, and he is also liable to pay National Insurance contributions of 6 per cent. Calculate his net wages.

36.2 M Marchand works as an electrician with a basic rate of pay of £4.40 per hour for a 40 hour week, overtime is paid at a rate of 1½ times the basic.

During the week ending 28 April 1999 M Marchand worked 50 hours. He pays National Insurance at 10% of the gross pay, pensions at 8% of the basic pay and income tax at 30% on all earnings after deducting £30 tax free pay. £2 is also paid in union contributions.

You are required to:
(a) Calculate M Marchand's gross pay.
(b) Calculate each of the deductions.
(c) Show the amount M Marchand will take home.
(*Note:* Marks will be awarded if presented in the form of a payslip.)
(RSA)

36.3 The following details relate to the earnings of two employees during the week ended 25 May 1998.

Employee	J Brown	A White
Piecework rate per unit	120p	130p
Units produced	200	140
Hours worked	40	44
Hourly rate of pay	375p	410p

A 40 hour week is in operation and overtime is paid at time and a quarter.

If an employee's piecework earnings fall below his earnings at the hourly rate then the hourly rate earnings are paid.

Both employees have the following deductions:

Company pension scheme	2% of gross earnings
National Insurance	10% of gross earnings
PAYE	25% of all earnings in excess of £75 per week

You are required to calculate:
The gross and net wage of each employee showing clearly the amount of each deduction.
(RSA)

36.4 The wages of the five employees for the first week are: (1) £112.86; (2) £97.19; (3) £128.47; (4) £134.75; (5) £84.77. Bearing in mind that £20 notes are not to be used, and that each employee will have a minimum of five £1 coins in his wage packet, you are required to work out the quantities of the various coins and notes needed when paying out the wages.

36.5 As question 36.4 for the week following. This time the wages are: (1) £99.68; (2) £119.43; (3) £122.55; (4) £94.77; (5) £104.35.

36.6 As question 36.4 for the third week. The wages are: (1) £96.99; (2) £133.46; (3) £128.86; (4) £112.36; (5) £101.26.

36.7X C Ponsford manages a small firm employing four workers. During the week ending 31 December 1999 each worker earned take home pay as follows:

L Jennett	£160.56
J Smith	£90.75
J Grala	£100.20
G Thomas	£136.40

C Ponsford pays wages at the end of each week in cash using notes and coins of £10, £5, £1, 50p, 20p, 10p, 5p, 2p and 1p. C Ponsford insists that each worker receives at least one £1 coin.

You are required to:
(a) rule up and complete a note and coin analysis in table form using the least number of notes and coins permissible;
(b) reconcile the value of the total notes and coins with the total pay bill.
(RSA)

36.8X The wages to be paid to five employees are:

	£
G Billison	74.63
P Farraday	91.17
H Oliver	82.53
R Watt	78.76
T Yeoman	87.80

Calculate the number of each denomination of note and coin required. £10 is the highest denomination of note used and each employee must receive the lowest number of coins or notes possible.
(RSA)

36.9X You are the general clerk in a small manufacturing business which employs four weekly paid assembly line workers.

The net wages for the week ending Saturday, 27 October, which will be paid on Friday, 2 November are as follows:

	£
C Ford	89.25
P Woodbine	76.90
J Swan	65.47
A Gill	101.22

You are required to:
(a) Rule up a note-coin analysis.
(b) Calculate the number and denominations of notes and coins required to pay the four workers.

The owner of the business will not pay with notes greater than £5 and insists that at least one £1 piece should be present in every pay packet. The least number of coins/notes should be used.
(RSA)

36.10X A firm employs John Jones at a standard rate of £1.10 per hour. Time and a half is paid for all hours worked in excess of 40. All employees pay a superannuation contribution of five per cent of all wages earned in a normal working week (40 hours). Time worked in excess of 40 hours is not subject to superannuation. National Insurance contributions are five per cent of gross wages. In the week ending 7 June John Jones has worked 45 hours. He pays income tax at 30 per cent on all he earns over £35 per week after superannuation has been deducted.

You are required to:
(a) Calculate his gross wages.
(b) Show the value of each deduction and calculate his net wages.
(RSA)

36.11X Ace Garden Services employs John Brooke and Philip Daly to lay turves on new housing estates. Each is paid £5 for every 100 turves laid and if any week a worker lays more than 2,000 turves he receives a bonus of 50% for laying the extra turves, in addition to the normal rate for all turves laid.

In the week ended 15 March Brooke laid 2,200 turves and Daly laid 2,600 turves. Income tax of £18 is due from Brooke, and £32 from Daly. Five per cent of the gross earnings of each must be deducted for social security contributions. Each makes a voluntary contribution of £2 weekly to the Lawn Layers Union.

You are required to calculate the net pay of each employee and set out their payslips for the week ended 15 March.
(RSA)

36.12X Calculate the gross wages for each of the following employees using the following information:

Normal working week is 40 hours.

Overtime is paid as follows:

Weekdays	Time and a quarter
Saturdays	Time and a half
Sundays	Double time

Employee	*Hours Worked*			
	Normal	*Weekday*	*Sat*	*Sun*
R Giles	40	4	4	–
R Paskes	40	6	–	4
I Hargreaves	40	–	–	4
S Worrall	40	3	4	4

The basic rate of pay is £4.28 per hour.

36.13 R & R Production Co manufactures exhaust clips for the motor car industry. They pay their workers £3.75 per hour for a 40 hour week plus a weekly bonus of £2.50 for every 500 clips produced. You are required to calculate the gross wages for the week ending 30 November for the following workers:

Employee	*Hours Worked*	*Clips Produced*
S Crawley	40	5,000
D Brookes	44	8,000
J Burns	40	7,000
V Newman	42	4,000

36.14 Calculate the gross pay which each of the following workers would receive from the details below:

Normal hours worked: 40 hours of £5.20 per hour plus incentive bonus scheme of 75 pence for each unit of output.

Employee	*Hours Worked*	*Output*
A Taylor	35	30
S McKenzie	42	40
R Brindley	40	36
W Baseley	44	36
W Warburton	45	52

36.15 Morton's Garages Ltd, who sell new and used cars pay their sales representatives an annual salary of £12,300 plus commission of 1 per cent of sales.

You are required to calculate the gross wages of the area representatives for August 1999.

Area	Representative	Sales for Month
		£
North West	M D Ross	50,000
Midlands	J T Cross	45,000
South East	P Kent	80,000
Wales	B Knott	40,000
Scotland	H McDonald	60,000

37 Manufacturing accounts

37.1 Manufacturing: not retailing

We now have to deal with firms which are manufacturers. For these firms a **manufacturing account** is prepared in addition to the trading and profit and loss accounts.

37.2 Divisions of costs

In a manufacturing firm the costs are divided into different types. These may be summarised in chart form as follows:

Direct materials ⎫
Direct labour   ⎬ Prime cost ⎫
Direct expenses ⎭   ⎬ Production cost ⎫
Plus   ⎬ Total
Factory or Work overhead expenses ⎭   cost
Plus   ⎭
Administrative expenses
Selling and distribution expenses

37.3 Direct and indirect costs

When you see the words **direct costs** you know that the costs of making an item have been able to be traced to the item being manufactured. If it cannot easily be traced to the item being manufactured then it is an indirect expense, and will be included under factory overhead expenses.

For example, the wages of a machine operator making a particular item will be direct labour. The wages of a foreman in charge of many men on different jobs will be indirect labour, and will be part of factory overhead expenses.

Other instances of costs being direct costs:

1 Cost of direct materials will include carriage inwards on raw materials.
2 Hire of special machinery for a job.

37.4　Factory overhead expenses

Factory overhead costs are all those costs which occur in the factory where production is being done, but which cannot easily be traced to the items being manufactured. Examples are:

- Wages of cleaners.
- Wages of crane drivers.
- Rent and rates of the factory.
- Depreciation of plant and machinery.
- Costs of operating fork-lift trucks.
- Factory power.
- Factory lighting.

37.5　Administration expenses

Administration expenses consist of such items as managers' salaries, legal and accountancy charges, the depreciation of office equipment and secretarial salaries.

37.6　Selling and distribution expenses

Selling and distribution expenses are items such as sales staff salaries and commission, carriage outwards, depreciation of delivery vans, advertising and display expenses.

37.7　Format of final accounts

Manufacturing account part

This is debited with the production cost of goods completed during the accounting period.

It contains costs of:

- Direct materials.
- Direct labour.
- Direct expenses.
- Factory overhead expenses.

When completed this account will show the total of production cost. This figure will then be transferred down to the trading account.

Trading account part

This account includes:

- Production cost brought down from the manufacturing account.

- Opening and closing stocks of finished goods.
- Sales.

When completed this account will disclose the gross profit. This will then be carried down to the profit and loss account part.

The Manufacturing Account and the Trading Account can be shown in the form of a diagram:

Manufacturing Account

	£
Production costs for the period:	
Direct materials	xxx
Direct labour	xxx
Direct expenses	xxx
Production cost of goods completed c/d to trading account	xxx

Trading Account

		£	£
Sales			
Less Production cost of goods sold:			
Opening stock of finished goods	(A)	xxx	
Add Production costs of goods completed b/d		xxx	
		xxx	
Less Closing stock of finished goods	(B)	xxx	xxx
Gross profit			xxx

(A) is production costs of goods unsold in previous period
(B) is production costs of goods unsold at end of the period

Profit and loss account part

This account includes:

- Gross profit brought down from the trading account.
- All administration expenses.
- All selling and distribution expenses.

When completed, this account will show the net profit.

37.8 A worked example of a manufacturing account

Exhibit 37.1 shows the necessary details for a manufacturing account. It has been assumed that there were no partly completed units (known as **work in progress**) either at the beginning or end of the period.

Exhibit 37.1

Details of production cost for the year ended 31 December 1998:

	£
1 January 1998, stock of raw materials	500
31 December 1998, stock of raw materials	700
Raw materials purchased	8,000
Manufacturing (direct) wages	21,000
Royalties	150
Indirect wages	9,000
Rent of factory – excluding administration and selling and	
distribution blocks	440
Depreciation of plant and machinery in factory	400
General indirect expenses	310

Manufacturing Account for the year ended 31 December 1998

	£	£
Stock of raw materials 1.1.1998		500
Add Purchases		8,000
		8,500
Less Stock of raw materials 31.12.1998		700
Cost of raw materials consumed		7,800
Manufacturing wages		21,000
Royalties		150
Prime cost		28,950
Factory Overhead Expenses		
Rent	440	
Indirect wages	9,000	
General expenses	310	
Depreciation of plant and machinery	400	10,150
Production cost of goods completed c/d		39,100

Sometimes, if a firm has produced less than the customers have demanded, then the firm may well have bought an outside supply of finished goods. In this case, the trading account will have both a figure for purchases and for production cost of goods completed.

37.9 Work in progress

The production cost to be carried down to the trading account is that of production cost of goods completed during the period. If items have not been completed they cannot be sold. Therefore, they should not appear in the trading account.

For instance, if we have the following information, we can calculate the transfer to the trading account:

	£
Total production costs expended during the year	5,000
Production costs last year on goods not completed last year, but completed in this year (work in progress)	300
Production costs this year on goods which were not completed by the year end (work in progress)	440

The calculation is:	
Total production costs expended this year	5,000
Add Costs from last year, in respect of goods completed in this year (work in progress)	300
	5,300
Less Costs in this year, for goods to be completed next year (work in progress)	440
Production costs expended on goods completed this year	4,860

37.10 Another worked example

Exhibit 37.2

	£
1 January 1998, Stock of raw materials	800
31 December 1998, Stock of raw materials	1,050
1 January 1998, Work in progress	350
31 December 1998, Work in progress	420
Year to 31 December 1998.	
Wages: Direct	3,960
Indirect	2,550
Purchase of raw materials	8,700
Fuel and power	990
Direct expenses	140
Lubricants	300
Carriage inwards on raw materials	200
Rent of factory	720
Depreciation of factory plant and machinery	420
Internal transport expenses	180
Insurance of factory buildings and plant	150
General factory expenses	330

Manufacturing Account for the year ended 31 December 1998

	£	£
Stock of raw materials 1.1.1998		800
Add Purchases		8,700
Carriage inwards		200
		9,700
Less Stock of raw materials 31.12.1998		1,050
Cost of raw materials consumed		8,650
Direct wages		3,960
Direct expenses		140
Prime cost		12,750
Factory Overhead Expenses		
Fuel and power	990	
Indirect wages	2,550	
Lubricants	300	
Rent	720	
Depreciation of plant	420	
Internal transport expenses	180	
Insurance	150	
General factory expenses	330	5,640
		18,390
Add Work in progress 1.1.1998		350
		18,740
Less Work in progress 31.12.1998		420
Production cost of goods completed c/d		18,320

The trading account is concerned with finished goods. If in the foregoing exhibit there had been £3,500 stock of finished goods at 1 January 1998 and £4,400 at 31 December 1998, and the sales of finished goods amounted to £25,000, then the trading account would appear:

Trading Account for the year 31 December 1998

	£	£
Sales		25,000
Less Cost of goods sold		
Stock of finished goods 1.1.1998	3,500	
Add Production cost of goods completed b/d	18,320	
	21,820	
Less Stock of finished goods 31.12.1998	4,400	17,420
Gross profit c/d		7,580

The profit and loss account is then constructed in the normal way.

37.11 Apportionment of expenses

Quite often expenses will have to be split between:

- Factory overhead expenses: to be charged in the manufacturing account section

- Administration expenses:
- Selling and distribution expenses: } to be charged in the profit and loss account section

An instance of this could be the rent expense. If the rent is paid separately for each part of the organisation, then it is easy to charge the rent to each sort of expense. However, only one figure of rent may be paid, without any indication as to how much is for the factory part, how much is for the selling and distribution part and that for the administration buildings.

How the rent expense will be apportioned in the latter case will depend on circumstances, using the most equitable way of doing it. For instance, one of the following methods may be used.

- by floor area
- by property valuations of each part of the buildings and land

37.12 Full set of final accounts

A complete worked example is now given. Note that in the profit and loss account the expenses have been separated so as to show whether they are administration expenses, selling and distribution expenses, or financial charges.

The trial balance in Exhibit 37.3 has been extracted from the books of J Jarvis, Toy Manufacturer, as on 31 December 1998:

Exhibit 37.3

J Jarvis
Trial Balance as on 31 December 1998

	Dr	Cr
	£	£
Stock of raw materials 1.1.1998	2,100	
Stock of finished goods 1.1.1998	3,890	
Work in progress 1.1.1998	1,350	
Wages (direct £18,000); factory indirect £14,500)	32,500	
Royalties	700	
Carriage inwards (on raw materials)	350	
Purchases of raw materials	37,000	
Productive machinery (cost £28,000)	23,000	
Accounting machinery (cost £2,000)	1,200	
General factory expenses	3,100	
Lighting	750	
Factory power	1,370	
Administrative salaries	4,400	
Salesmen's salaries	3,000	
Commission on sales	1,150	
Rent	1,200	
Insurance	420	
General administration expenses	1,340	
Bank charges	230	
Discounts allowed	480	
Carriage outwards	590	
Sales		100,000
Debtors and creditors	14,230	12,500
Bank	5,680	
Cash	150	
Drawings	2,000	
Capital as at 1.1.1998		29,680
	142,180	142,180

Notes at 31.12. 1998:

1 Stock of raw materials £2,400, stock of finished goods £4,000, work in progress £1,500.

2 Lighting, rent and insurance are to be apportioned: factory ⅚ths, administration ⅙th.

3 Depreciation on productive and accounting machinery at 10 per cent per annum on cost.

J Jarvis
Manufacturing, Trading and Profit and Loss Account for the year ended
31 December 1998

	£	£	£
Stock of raw materials 1.1.1998			2,100
Add Purchases			37,000
Carriage inwards			350
			39,450
Less Stock raw materials 31.12.1998			2,400
Cost of raw materials consumed			37,050
Direct labour			18,000
Royalties			700
Prime cost			55,750
Factory Overhead Expenses			
General factory expenses		3,100	
Lighting ⅚ths		625	
Power		1,370	
Rent ⅚ths		1,000	
Insurance ⅚ths		350	
Depreciation of plant		2,800	
Indirect labour		14,500	23,745
			79,495
Add Work in progress 1.1.1998			1,350
			80,845
Less Work in progress 31.12.1998			1,500
Production cost of goods completed c/d			79,345
Sales			100,000
Less Cost of goods sold			
Stock of finished goods 1.1.1998		3,890	
Add Production cost of goods completed		79,345	
		83,235	
Less Stock of finished goods 31.12.1998		4,000	79,235
Gross profit			20,765
Administration Expenses			
Administrative salaries	4,400		
Rent ⅙th	200		
Insurance ⅙th	70		
General expenses	1,340		
Lighting ⅙th	125		
Depreciation of accounting machinery	200	6,335	
Selling and Distribution Expenses			
Sales representatives' salaries	3,000		
Commission on sales	1,150		
Carriage outwards	590	4,740	
Financial Charges			
Bank charges	230		
Discounts allowed	480	710	11,785
Net profit			8,980

J Jarvis
Balance Sheet as at 31 December 1998

Fixed Assets	£	£
Productive machinery at cost	28,000	
Less Depreciation to date	7,800	20,200
Accounting machinery at cost	2,000	
Less Depreciation to date	1,000	1,000
		21,200
Current Assets		
Stock:		
raw materials	2,400	
finished goods	4,000	
Work in progress	1,500	
Debtors	14,230	
Bank	5,680	
Cash	150	
	27,960	
Less Current Liabilities		
Creditors	12,500	
Working capital		15,460
		36,660
Financed by		
Capital		
Balance as at 1.1.1998		29,680
Add Net profit		8,980
		38,660
Less Drawings		2,000
		36,660

New terms

Direct costs (p 392): Costs which can be traced to the item being manufactured.
Factory overhead costs (p 393): Costs in the factory for production, but not traced to the item being manufactured.
Manufacturing account (p 393): An account in which production cost is calculated.
Work in progress (p 395): Items not completed at the end of a period.

Exercises

37.1 From the following information prepare the manufacturing and trading accounts of E Smith for the year ended 31 March 1998.

	£
Stocks at 1 April 1997:	
Finished goods	6,724
Raw materials	2,400
Work in progress	955
Carriage on purchases (raw materials)	321
Sales	69,830
Purchases of raw materials	21,340
Manufacturing wages	13,280
Factory power	6,220
Other manufacturing expenses	1,430
Factory rent and rates	2,300
Stocks at 31 March 1998:	
Raw materials	2,620
Work in progress	870
Finished goods	7,230

37.2X From the following details you are to draw up a manufacturing, trading and profit and loss account of P Lucas for the year ended 30 September 1998.

	30.9.1997	30.9.1998
	£	£
Stocks of raw materials, at cost	8,460	10,970
Work in progress	3,070	2,460
Finished goods stock	12,380	14,570

For the year:	£
Raw materials purchased	38,720
Manufacturing wages	20,970
Factory expenses	12,650
Depreciation:	
Plant and machinery	7,560
Delivery vans	3,040
Office equipment	807
Factory power	6,120
Advertising	5,080
Office and administration expenses	5,910
Sales representatives' salaries and expenses	6,420
Delivery van expenses	5,890
Sales	134,610
Carriage inwards	2,720

37.3 Prepare manufacturing, trading and profit and loss accounts from the following balances of T Shaw for the year ended 31 December 1998.

	£
Stocks at 1 January 1998:	
Raw materials	18,450
Work in progress	23,600
Finished goods	17,470
Purchases: raw materials	64,300
Carriage on raw materials	1,605
Direct labour	65,810
Office salaries	16,920
Rent	2,700
Office lighting and heating	5,760
Depreciation: Works machinery	8,300
Office equipment	1,950
Sales	200,600
Factory fuel and power	5,920

Rent is to be apportioned: Factory ⅔rds; Office ⅓rd. Stocks at 31 December 1998 were: Raw materials £20,210; Work in progress £17,390; Finished goods £21,485.

37.4 The financial year of Excelsior Pressings, a manufacturer of small household equipment, ends on 31 December. The following balances are in the books of the firm as at 31 December 1998:

	£
Stocks as at 1 January 1998:	
Raw materials	28,315
Work in progress (at factory cost)	6,200
Finished goods	33,700
Heating and lighting	3,450
Wages of indirect manufacturing personnel	45,820
Rent and rates	16,400
Purchases of raw materials	172,300
Manufacturing wages	194,500
Factory expenses and maintenance	3,700
Salaries	32,400
Sales of finished goods	652,500
Advertising	60,800
Administration expenses	27,500

The following information is also available:

1 Stocks have been valued as at 31 December 1998 as follows:

	£
Raw materials	30,200
Work in progress (at factory cost)	7,100
Finished goods	37,500

2 In respect of 1998, the following apportionments are to be made:

	Factory	General Office
Heating and lighting	⅘	⅕
Rent and rates	¾	¼
Salaries	⅓	⅔

3   Depreciation is to be allowed as follows:

	£
Plant and machinery	20,000
Office equipment	4,000

Required
Prepare the manufacturing, trading and profit and loss accounts of Excelsior Pressings for the year ended 31 December 1998.
Note: A balance sheet is *not* required.
(LCCI)

37.5X   Gordon Dace, a manufacturer, extracted the following trial balance at the end of his financial year, 30 September 1998.

	Dr £	Cr £
Freehold premises (cost)	120,000	
Plant and machinery (cost)	60,000	
Provision for depreciation: Plant and machinery		18,000
Office fixtures and fittings (cost)	8,000	
Provision for depreciation: Fixtures and fittings		1,600
Stocks at 1 October 1997:		
Raw materials	8,500	
Finished goods	6,320	
Purchases of raw materials	56,000	
Bad debts	170	
Debtors and creditors	4,820	2,780
Office wages and salaries	30,140	
Rates [Factory £610, Office £220]	830	
Insurance [Factory £450, Office £150]	600	
Light/heat and power [Factory £1210, Office £210]	1,420	
Miscellaneous expenses	350	
Repairs and renewals [Factory £1070, Office £230]	1,300	
Telephone [Factory £150, Office £250]	400	
Drawings	15,000	
Balance at bank	12,170	
Cash in hand	100	
Manufacturing wages	62,000	
Sales		186,600
Capital account		179,140
	388,120	388,120

The following additional information is available:

1   Closing stocks at 30 September 1998 are as follows:

Raw materials	£10,500
Finished goods	£7,410

2   Provide for depreciation as follows:

Plant and machinery [Factory]	£6,000
Fixtures and fittings [Office]	£800

Required
Prepare Gordon Dace's manufacturing, trading and profit and loss accounts for the year ended 30 September 1998, using such information as is required from the above trial balance.
Note: A balance sheet is *not* required.
(LCCI)

38 Introduction to accounting ratios

38.1 Mark-up and margin

The purchase and sale of goods may be shown as

> **Cost price + Profit = Selling Price**

The profit when shown as a fraction, or percentage, of the cost price is known as the **mark-up**.

The profit when shown as a fraction, or percentage, of the selling price is known as the **margin**.

We can now calculate these using this example.

$$\text{Cost Price} + \text{Profit} = \text{Selling Price.}$$
$$£4 \quad + \quad £1 \quad = £5.$$

$\text{Mark-up} = \dfrac{\text{Profit}}{\text{Cost Price}}$ as a fraction, or if required as a percentage, multiply by 100:

$$£\tfrac{1}{4} = \tfrac{1}{4}, \text{ or } \tfrac{1}{4} \times 100 = 25 \text{ per cent.}$$

$\text{Margin} = \dfrac{\text{Profit}}{\text{Selling Price}}$ as a fraction, or if required as a percentage, multiply by 100:

$$£\tfrac{1}{5} = \tfrac{1}{5} \text{ or } \tfrac{1}{5} \times 100 = 20 \text{ per cent.}$$

38.2 Calculating missing figures

Now we can use these ratios to complete trading accounts where some of the figures are missing.

All examples in this chapter:

- assume that all the goods in a firm have the same rate of mark-ups, and
- ignore wastages and theft of goods.

Example 1

The following figures are for the year 1999:

	£
Stock 1.1.1999	400
Stock 31.12.1999	600
Purchases	5,200

A uniform rate of mark-up of 20 per cent is applied.
  Find the gross profit and the sales figure:

Trading Account for the year ended 31 December 1999

	£	£
Sales		?
Less Cost of goods sold		
Stock 1.1.1999	400	
Add Purchases	5,200	
	5,600	
Less Stock 31.12.1999	600	5,000
Gross profit		?

Answer:

It is known that:	Cost of goods sold + Profit = Sales
and also that:	Cost of goods sold + Percentage Mark-up = Sales

The following figures are
  also known: £5,000 + 20 per cent = Sales
After doing the arithmetic: £5,000 + £1,000 = £6,000

The trading account can be completed by inserting the gross profit £1,000 and £6,000 for Sales.

Example 2

Another firm has the following figures for 1998:

	£
Stock 1.1.1998	500
Stock 31.12.1998	800
Sales	6,400

A uniform rate of margin of 25 per cent is in use. Find the gross profit and the figure of purchases.

Trading Account for the year ended 31 December 1998

	£	£
Sales		6,400
Less Cost of goods sold		
Stock 1.1.1998	500	
Add Purchases	?	
	?	
Less Stock 31.12.1998	800	?
Gross profit		?

Answer: Cost of goods sold + Gross profit = Sales
Therefore   Sales – Gross profit   = Cost of goods sold
            Sales – 25 per cent margin   = Cost of goods sold
            £6,400 – £1,600   = £4,800

Now the following figures are known:

		£	£
Cost of goods sold			
Stock 1.1.1998		500	
Add Purchases	(1)	?	
	(2)	?	
Less Stock 31.12.1998		800	4,800

The two missing figures are found by normal arithmetical deduction:

No (**2**) less £800   = £4,800
Therefore No (**2**)   = £5,600
So that: £500 opening stock + No (**1**)   = £5,600
Therefore No (**1**)   = £5,100

The completed trading account can now be shown:

Trading Account for the year ended 31 December 1998

	£	£
Sales		6,400
Less Cost of goods sold		
Stock 1.1.1998	500	
Add Purchases	5,100	
	5,600	
Less Stock 31.12. 1998	800	4,800
Gross profit		1,600

This technique is found very useful by retail stores when estimating the amount to be bought if a certain sales target is to be achieved. Alternatively, stock levels or sales figures can be estimated given information as to purchases and opening stock figures.

38.3 Commonly used accounting ratios

There are some ratios that are often used to compare one period's results against those of a previous period. Two ratios in most common use are the ratio of gross profit to sales and the rate of turnover or **stockturn**.

Gross profit as percentage of sales

The basic formula is:

$$\frac{\text{Gross Profit}}{\text{Sales}} \times 100 = \text{Gross profit as percentage of sales.}$$

This is the amount of gross profit for every £100 of sales. If the answer turned out to be 15 per cent, this would mean that for every £100 of sales £15 gross profit was made before any expenses were paid.

This ratio is used as a test of the profitability of the sales. Just because the sales are increased may not mean that the gross profit will increase. The trading accounts in Exhibit 38.1 illustrate this.

Exhibit 38.1

Trading Accounts for the years ended 31 December

	1997		1993	
	£	£	£	£
Sales		7,000		8,000
Less Cost of goods sold				
Opening stock	500		900	
Add Purchases	6,000		7,200	
	6,500		8,100	
Less Closing stock	900	5,600	1,100	7,000
Gross profit		1,400		1,000

In the year 1997 the gross profit as a percentage of sales was:

$$\frac{1,400}{7,000} \times \frac{100}{1} = 20 \text{ per cent.}$$

In the year 1998 it became:

$$\frac{1,000}{8,000} \times \frac{100}{1} = 12\frac{1}{2} \text{ per cent.}$$

Sales had increased, but as the gross profit percentage had fallen by a relatively greater amount the gross profit has fallen. There can be many reasons for such a fall in the gross profit percentage. Some are now listed:

1   Perhaps the goods being sold have cost more, but the selling price of the goods has not risen to the same extent.
2   Perhaps in order to increase sales, reductions have been made in the selling price of goods.
3   There could be a difference in how much has been sold of each sort of goods, called the sales-mix, between this year and last, with different kinds of goods carrying different rates of gross profit per £100 of sales.
4   There may have been a greater wastage or theft of goods.

These are only some of the possible reasons for the decrease. The idea of calculating the ratio is to show that the profitability per £100 of sales has changed. The firm would then try to find out why and how such a change has taken place.

Stockturn or rate of turnover

If we always kept just £100 of stock at cost, which when we sold it would sell for £125, then if we sold this amount eight times in a year we would make 8 × £25 = £200 gross profit. The quicker we sell our stock (we could say the quicker we turn over our stock) the more the profit we will make, if our gross profit percentage stays the same.

To check on how quickly we are turning over our stock we can use the formula:

$$\frac{\text{Cost of goods sold}}{\text{Average stock}} = \text{Number of times stock is turned over within a period}$$

It would be best if the average stock held could be calculated by valuing the stock quite a few times each year, then dividing the totals of the figures obtained by the number of valuations. For instance, monthly stock figures are added up then divided by twelve.

However, it is quite common, especially in examinations or in cases where no other information is available, to calculate the average stock as the opening stock plus the closing stock and the answer divided by two. Using the figures in Exhibit 38.1 we can calculate the **stockturn** for 1997 and 1998:

$$1997 \quad \frac{5600}{(500 + 900) \div 2} = \frac{5600}{700} = 8 \text{ times per annum}$$

$$1998 \quad \frac{7000}{(900 + 1100) \div 2} = \frac{7000}{1000} = 7 \text{ times per annum}$$

Instead of saying that the stockturn is so many times per annum, we could instead say on average how long we keep stock before we sell it. We do this by the formula:

To express it in months: 12 ÷ Stockturn = x months
To express it in days: 365 ÷ Stockturn = x days

From Exhibit 38.1:

	1997		1998	
In months	$\frac{12}{8}$	= 1.5 months	$\frac{12}{7}$	= 1.7 months
In days	$\frac{365}{8}$	= 45.6 days	$\frac{365}{7}$	= 52.1 days

All the above figures are rounded off to the nearest decimal point.

38.4 The relationship between mark-up and margin

As both of these figures refer to the same profit, but are expressed as a fraction or a percentage of different figures, there is a relationship between them. If one is known as a fraction, the other can soon be found.

If the mark-up is known, to find the margin take the same numerator to be the numerator of the margin. Then for the denominator of the margin take the total of the mark-up's denominator plus the numerator. An example can now be shown:

Mark-up	Margin	
$\dfrac{1}{4}$	$\dfrac{1}{4+1}$	$= \dfrac{1}{5}$
$\dfrac{2}{11}$	$\dfrac{2}{11+2}$	$= \dfrac{2}{13}$

If the margin is known, to find the mark-up take the same numerator to be the numerator of the mark-up. Then for the denominator of the mark-up take the figure of the margin's denominator less the numerator:

Margin	Mark-up	
$\dfrac{1}{6}$	$\dfrac{2}{6-1}$	$= \dfrac{1}{5}$
$\dfrac{3}{13}$	$\dfrac{3}{13-3}$	$= \dfrac{3}{10}$

38.5 Multiple-choice questions

Now attempt Set No 3, which contains 27 multiple-choice questions, on pages 421–6.

New terms

Margin (p 405): Profit shown as a percentage or fraction of selling price.
Mark-up (p 405): Profit shown as a percentage or fraction of cost price.
Stockturn (p 409): Number of times we sell our stock in an accounting period.

Exercises

38.1 J Jackson is a trader who marks the selling price of his goods at 25 per cent above cost. His books give the following information at 31 July 1998:

	£
Stock 1 August 1997	4,936
Stock 31 July 1998	6,310
Sales for year	30,000

You are required to:

(a) Find 'cost of goods sold'.

(b) Show the value of purchases during the year.

(c) Ascertain the profit Jackson made.

Note: Your answer should take the form of a trading account.

(RSA)

38.2 P R Match produces from his trial balance at 31 August 1998 the following information.

	£
Stock 1 September 1997	2,000
Purchases	18,000

Match has a mark-up of 50 per cent on cost of sales.

His average stock during the year was £4,000.

You are required to:

(a) Calculate the closing stock for P R Match at 31 August 1998.

(b) Prepare his trading account for the year ended 31 August 1998.

(c) Ascertain the total amount of profit and loss expenditure that Match must not exceed if he is to maintain a net profit on sales of 10 per cent.

(RSA)

38.3X A business has a rate of turnover of seven times. The average stock is £4,200. Trade discount allowed is 33⅓ per cent off all selling prices. Expenses are given as 70 per cent of gross profit. Calculate:

(a) Cost of goods sold.

(b) Gross profit.

(c) Turnover.

(d) Total expenses.

(e) Net profit.

(RSA)

38.4X The following figures relate to the retail business of W Watson for the month of May 1998. Goods which are on sale fall into two categories, A and B.

	Category A	Category B
Sales to the public at manufacturer's recommended list price	£3,000	£7,000
Trade discount allowed to retailers	20%	25%
Total expenses as a percentage of sales	10%	10%
Annual rate of stock turnover	12	20

Calculate for each category:

(a) Cost of goods sold.

(b) Gross profit.

(c) Total expenses.

(d) Net profit.

(e) Average stock at cost, assuming that sales are distributed evenly over the year, and that there are twelve equal months in the year.

(RSA)

Multiple-choice questions

Each multiple-choice question has four suggested answers, either letter (A), (B), (C) or (D). You should read each question and then decide which choice is best, either (A) or (B) or (C) or (D). On a separate piece of paper you should then write down your choice. Unless the textbook you are reading belongs to you, you should not make a mark against your choice in the textbook.

Set No 1: Questions MC1–MC20

Answers are on page 427.

MC1   Which of the following statements is incorrect?
- (A) Assets – Liabilities = Capital
- (B) Capital – Liabilities = Assets
- (C) Assets = Capital + Liabilities
- (D) Assets – Capital = Liabilities.

MC2   Which of the following is not an asset?
- (A) Debtor
- (B) Motor Vehicle
- (C) Creditor
- (D) Stock of Goods.

MC3   Which of the following is a liability?
- (A) Cash balance
- (B) Loan from J Owens
- (C) Debtor
- (D) Buildings.

MC4   Which of the following is incorrect?

	Assets	Liabilities	Capital
	£	£	£
(A)	9,460	2,680	6,780
(B)	7,390	1,140	6,250
(C)	6,120	2,490	4,630
(D)	8,970	3,580	5,390

412

MC5   Which of the following statements is incorrect?

		Effect upon	
		Assets	*Liabilities*
(A)	Paid creditor by cheque	− Bank	+ Creditors
(B)	Bought goods on credit	+ Stock	+ Creditors
(C)	Received cash from debtor	+ Cash	
		− Debtor	
(D)	Sold goods for Cash	+ Cash	
		− Stock	

MC6   Which of the following are correct?

	Accounts	*To record*	*Entry in the account*
(i)	Assets	a decrease	Debit
		an increase	Credit
(ii)	Capital	a decrease	Debit
		an increase	Credit
(iii)	Liabilities	a decrease	Debit
		an increase	Credit

(A) (i) and (ii)
(B) (i) and (iii)
(C) (ii) and (iii)
(D) None of them.

MC7   Which of the following are correct?

		Account to be debited	*Account to be credited*
(i)	Bought motor van by cheque	Motor van	Bank
(ii)	Paid a creditor, T Allen, by cheque	Cash	T Allen
(iii)	Loan repaid to C Kirk by cheque	Loan from Kirk	Bank
(iv)	Sold goods for cash	Sales	Cash

(A) (i) and (ii) only
(B) (ii) and (iii) only
(C) (iii) and (iv) only
(D) (i) and (iii) only.

MC8   Which of the following are incorrect?

		Account to be debited	*Account to be credited*
(i)	Sold goods on credit to P Moore	P Moore	Sales
(ii)	Bought Fixtures on credit from Furnishers Ltd	Fixtures	Furnishers Ltd
(iii)	Introduce more capital in cash	Capital	Cash
(iv)	A debtor, L Sellars, pays by cheque	Cash	L Sellars

(A) (iii) and (iv) only
(B) (ii) and (iii) only
(C) (i) and (iv) only
(D) (i) and (iii) only.

MC9 Which of the following should not be called 'sales'?
(A) Goods sold, to be paid for in one month's time
(B) Goods sold, cash being received immediately
(C) Item previously included in purchases, now sold on credit
(D) Sale of a motor lorry not now required.

MC10 Which of the following should not be called 'purchases'?
(A) Items bought for the prime purpose of resale
(B) Goods bought on credit
(C) Office stationery purchased
(D) Goods bought for cash.

MC11 Which of the following are incorrect?

		Account to be debited	Account to be credited
(i)	B Ash returns goods to us	Returns Inwards	B Ash
(ii)	Goods bought on credit from L Thomas	L Thomas	Purchases
(iii)	Motor van bought on Credit from X L Garages	Purchases	X L Garages
(iv)	Goods sold for cash	Cash	Sales

(A) (i) and (ii) only
(B) (i) and (iii) only
(C) (ii) and (iii) only
(D) (iii) and (iv) only.

MC12 Of the following, which are correct?

		Account to be debited	Account to be credited
(i)	Surplus office furniture sold for cash	Cash	Sales
(ii)	We returned goods to F Ward	F Ward	Returns Inwards
(iii)	Goods bought for cash	Purchases	Cash
(iv)	Goods sold on credit to F Clarke	F Clarke	Sales

(A) (i) and (ii) only
(B) (iii) and (iv) only
(C) (ii) and (iii) only
(D) (ii) only.

MC13 What is the amount of Capital, given the following information? Buildings £30,000, Stock £5,600, Bank £750, Creditors £2,200, Loan from K Noone £7,000:
(A) £29,150
(B) £36,350
(C) £41,150
(D) None of the above.

MC14 Which of these statements is incorrect?
(A) Profit is another word for Capital
(B) A loss decreases Capital
(C) Profit increases Capital
(D) Drawings decreases Capital.

MC15 Which of the following are incorrect?

		Account to be debited	Account to be credited
(i)	Paid insurance by cheque	Insurance	Bank
(ii)	Paid telephone bill by cash	Telephone	Cash
(iii)	Received refund of part of motor expenses by cheque	Cash	Motor Expenses
(iv)	Took cash out of business for personal use	Drawings	Capital

(A) (i) and (iii) only
(B) (ii) and (iv) only
(C) (iii) and (iv) only
(D) (iv) only.

MC16 Of the following, which are correct?

		Account to be debited	Account to be credited
(i)	Paid rent by cheque	Rent	Cash
(ii)	Received commission in cash	Commissions	Cash
(iii)	Introduced extra capital in cash	Cash	Capital
(iv)	Sold surplus stationery for cash	Cash	Stationery

(A) None of them
(B) (i) and (iv) only
(C) (ii) and (iii) only
(D) (iii) and (iv) only.

MC17 What is the balance on the following account on 30 June 1998?

Dr			£		N Garth		Cr	£
1998			£	1998				£
June	18	Bank	400	June	1	Purchases		870
June	22	Returns	44	June	15	Purchases		245
				June	29	Purchases		178

(A) A debit balance of £849
(B) A credit balance of £829
(C) A credit balance of £849
(D) There is a nil balance on the account.

MC18 What was the balance on the account of N Garth, in MC17, on 20 June 1998?
(A) A credit balance of £671
(B) A debit balance of £715
(C) A credit balance of £715
(D) A debit balance of £671.

MC19 Of the following which *best* describes a trial balance?
(A) Is the final account in the books
(B) Shows all the asset balances
(C) Is a list of balances on the books
(D) Discloses the financial position of a business.

MC20 When should the trial balance totals differ?
(A) Only when it is drawn up by the accountant
(B) When drawn up before the profit and loss account is prepared
(C) If drawn up half way through the financial year
(D) Never.

Set No 2: Questions MC21–MC55

Answers are on page 427.

MC21 Gross profit is:
(A) Excess of cost of goods sold over sales
(B) Purchases + Sales
(C) Net profit less expenses
(D) Excess of sales over cost of goods sold.

MC22 Net profit is calculated in the
(A) Trial balance
(B) Trading account
(C) Profit and loss account
(D) Balance sheet.

MC23 The credit entry for net profit is shown in the
(A) Capital account
(B) Profit and loss account
(C) Balance sheet
(D) Trading account.

MC24 The value of closing stock is found by
(A) Adding opening stock to purchases
(B) Deducting purchases from sales
(C) Looking in the stock account
(D) Doing a stock-taking.

MC25 Which of the following are *not* part of the double entry system?
(i) Trading account
(ii) Balance sheet
(iii) Trial balance
(iv) Profit and loss account.

(A) (i) and (ii)
(B) (i) and (iii)
(C) (ii) and (iii)
(D) (ii) and (iv).

MC26   Which is the *best* definition of a balance sheet?
   (A)   A list of balances after calculating net profit
   (B)   A statement of all liabilities
   (C)   A trial balance at a different date
   (D)   A list of balances before calculating net profit.

MC27   The descending order in which current assets should be shown in the balance sheet are:
   (A)   Debtors, Bank, Stock, Cash
   (B)   Stock, Debtors, Bank, Cash
   (C)   Stock, Debtors, Cash, Bank
   (D)   Cash, Bank, Debtors, Stock.

MC28   Carriage inwards is charged to the trading account because:
   (A)   It is not a balance sheet item
   (B)   It is not part of our motor expenses
   (C)   Returns inwards also goes in the trading account
   (D)   It is basically part of the cost of buying goods.

MC29   Given figures showing: Sales £28,500; Opening stock £4,690; Closing stock £7,240; Carriage inwards £570; Purchases £21,360; the cost of goods sold figure is:

   (A)   £19,830
   (B)   £19,380
   (C)   £18,810
   (D)   Another figure.

MC30   If someone owns a grocery store, which of the following are *not* capital expenditure?
   (i)   Rent
   (ii)   Motor van
   (iii)   Fixtures
   (iv)   Fire insurance

   (A)   (ii) and (iii)
   (B)   (i) and (ii)
   (C)   (i) and (iii)
   (D)   (i) and (iv).

MC31   The purchases day book is *best* described as
   (A)   A list of purchases bought on credit
   (B)   Containing suppliers' accounts
   (C)   A list of purchases bought for cash
   (D)   Part of the double entry system.

MC32   Customers' personal accounts are found in
   (A)   The private ledger
   (B)   General ledger
   (C)   Purchases ledger
   (D)   Sales ledger.

MC33   Which of the following are *not* personal accounts
(i)   Debtors
(ii) Drawings
(iii) Rent
(iv) Creditors.

(A) (iii) only
(B) (i) and (ii) only
(C) (i) and (iv) only
(D) (ii) and (iii) only.

MC34   A debit balance of £500 on the cash columns of the cash book would mean
(A) The book-keeper has made a mistake
(B) We have £500 cash in hand
(C) We have spent £500 cash more than we have received
(D) Someone has stolen £500 cash.

MC35   £200 withdrawn from the bank and placed in the cash till is entered:
(A) Debit bank column £200: Credit bank column £200
(B) Debit cash column £200: Credit bank column £200
(C) Debit bank column £200: Credit cash column £200
(D) Debit cash column £400: Credit cash column £400.

MC36   A contra item is where
(A) Cash is banked before it has been paid out
(B) Where double entry is completed within the cash book
(C) Where the proprietor has repaid his capital in cash
(D) Where sales have been paid by cash.

MC37   An invoice shows a total of £3,200 less 2½ per cent cash discount. If this was paid in time, the amount of the cheque paid would be for
(A) £2,960
(B) £3,040
(C) £3,120
(D) £2,800.

MC38   The total of the discounts received column in the cash book is posted to
(A) The credit of the discounts received account
(B) The credit of the discounts allowed account
(C) The debit of the discounts allowed account
(D) The debit of the discounts received account.

MC39   A bank overdraft is *best* described as
(A) A firm wasting its money
(B) Having more receipts than payments
(C) A firm having bought too many goods
(D) A firm having paid more out of its bank account than it has put in it.

MC40　A cash discount is *best* described as a reduction in the sum to be paid
(A)　If goods are bought on credit and not for cash
(B)　If either cheque or cash payment is made within an agreed period
(C)　If cash is paid instead of cheques
(D)　If trade discount is also deducted.

MC41　If a sales invoice shows 12 items of £250 each, less trade discount of 20 per cent and cash discount of 5 per cent, then the amount to be paid, if the payment is made within the credit period, will be for
(A)　£2,440
(B)　£2,360
(C)　£2,280
(D)　£2,500.

MC42　The total of the sales day book is entered on
(A)　The debit side of the sales day book
(B)　The credit side of the sales account in the general ledger
(C)　The debit side of the sales account in the general ledger
(D)　The debit side of the sales day book.

MC43　A trade discount is *best* described as
(A)　A discount given if the invoice is paid
(B)　A discount given for cash payment
(C)　A discount given to suppliers
(D)　A discount given to traders.

MC44　The sales day book does not contain
(A)　Credit sales made without deduction of trade discount
(B)　Credit sales made to overseas customers
(C)　Cash sales
(D)　Credit sales which eventually turn out to be bad debts.

MC45　The purchases day book consists of
(A)　Cash purchases
(B)　Suppliers' ledger accounts
(C)　A list of purchases invoices
(D)　Payments for goods.

MC46　The total of the purchases day book is transferred to the
(A)　Debit side of the purchases account
(B)　Credit side of the purchases day book
(C)　Debit side of the purchases day book
(D)　Debit side of the purchases ledger.

MC47　The balances in the purchases ledger are usually
(A)　Credit balances
(B)　Contras
(C)　Nominal account balances
(D)　Debit balances.

MC48 Debit notes are entered in our
(A) Returns outwards day book
(B) Returns inwards day book
(C) Purchases account
(D) Returns outwards account.

MC49 A statement of account
(A) Is used instead of an invoice
(B) Means that our customers need not keep accounts
(C) Saves us sending out invoices
(D) Acts as a reminder to the purchaser of the amount owed.

MC50 Originally we bought 80 items at £60 each, less trade discount of 25 per cent. We now return 5 items, so we will issue a debit note amounting to
(A) £270
(B) £240
(C) £225
(D) £220.

MC51 A cheque given to you by a customer and banked by you, but for which he has proved not to have enough funds to meet it, is known as
(A) A dishonoured cheque
(B) A debit transfer
(C) A standing order
(D) A bank error.

MC52 Which of the following are not true? A bank reconciliation statement is
(i) Drawn up by the bank monthly
(ii) Not part of the double entry system
(iii) Part of the double entry system
(iv) Drawn up by our cashier.

(A) (i) and (ii)
(B) (i) and (iii)
(C) (ii) and (iv)
(D) (iii) and (iv).

MC53 The journal is
(A) Part of the double entry system
(B) A form of sales day book
(C) A form of diary
(D) A supplement to the balance sheet.

MC54 Given a desired cash float of £700, if £541 is spent in the period, and the opening cash float has been £700, how much will be reimbursed at the end of the period?
(A) £541
(B) £700
(C) £159
(D) None of the above.

MC55 A petty cash book
(A) Is used only in limited companies
(B) Is used when we have a bank overdraft
(C) Is used for small cheque payments
(D) Will keep down the number of entries in the general ledger.

Set No 3: Questions MC56–MC82

Answers are on page 427.

MC56 Straight line method of depreciation consists of
(A) Unequal amounts of depreciation each year
(B) Increasing amounts of depreciation each year
(C) Reducing amounts of depreciation each year
(D) Equal amounts of depreciation each year.

MC57 Depreciation is:
(A) The cost of a current asset wearing away
(B) The cost of a replacement for a fixed asset
(C) The salvage value of a fixed asset plus its original cost
(D) The part of the cost of the fixed asset consumed during its period of use by the firm.

MC58 A firm bought a machine for £50,000. It is expected to be used for 6 years then sold for £5,000. What is the annual amount of depreciation if the straight line method is used?
(A) £7,000
(B) £8,000
(C) £7,500
(D) £6,750.

MC59 When a separate provision for depreciation account is in use then book-keeping entries for the year's depreciation are
(A) Debit profit and loss: Credit the balance sheet
(B) Debit profit and loss: Credit asset account
(C) Debit asset account: Credit provision for depreciation account
(D) Debit profit and loss: Credit provision for depreciation account.

MC60 In the trial balance the balance on the provision for depreciation account is
(A) Shown as a credit item
(B) Not shown, as it is part of depreciation
(C) Shown as a debit item
(D) Sometimes shown as a credit, sometimes as a debit.

MC61 If a provision for depreciation account is not in use then the entries for the year's depreciation would be
(A) Debit asset account, credit profit and loss account
(B) Credit asset account, debit provision for depreciation account
(C) Credit profit and loss account, debit provision for depreciation account
(D) None of the above.

MC62   A provision for bad debts is created
 (A) When debtors become bankrupt
 (B) When debtors cease to be in business
 (C) To provide for possible bad debts
 (D) To write off bad debts.

MC63   When the final accounts are prepared the bad debts account is closed by a transfer to the
 (A) Balance sheet
 (B) Profit and loss account
 (C) Trading account
 (D) Provision for bad debts account.

MC64   These questions relate to the following assets and liabilities:

	£		£
Stock	1,000	Machinery	750
Cash at bank	750	Debtors	750
Cash in hand	50	Fixtures	250
Creditors	500	Motor vehicle	750
Capital	3,800		

 (i) The balance sheet totals are (use the vertical presentation)
 (A) £4,800. (B) £3,800. (C) £4,000. (D) £4,500.
 (ii) Current liabilities are:
 (A) £1,750. (B) £500. (C) £3,800. (D) £2,550.
 (iii) Working capital is:
 (A) £3,050. (B) £2,050. (C) £500. (D) £800.
 (Pitman Qualifications)

MC65   If we take goods for own use we should
 (A) Debit drawings account: Credit purchases account
 (B) Debit purchases account: Credit drawings account
 (C) Debit drawings account: Credit stock account
 (D) Debit sales account: Credit stock account.

MC66   A debit balance brought down on a packing materials account means
 (A) We owe for packing materials
 (B) We have no stock of packing materials
 (C) We have lost money on packing materials
 (D) We have a stock of packing materials unused.

MC67   A credit balance brought down on a rent account means
 (A) We owe that rent at that date
 (B) We have paid that rent in advance at that date
 (C) We have paid too much rent
 (D) We have paid too little in rent.

MC68 Working capital is a term meaning
  (A) The amount of capital invested by the proprietor
  (B) The excess of the current assets over the current liabilities
  (C) The capital less drawings
  (D) The total of fixed assets + current assets.

MC69 In the trading account the returns inwards should be
  (A) Added to cost of goods sold
  (B) Deducted from purchases
  (C) Deducted from sales
  (D) Added to sales.

MC70 If £750 was added to Rent instead of being added to a fixed asset
  (A) Gross profit would not be affected
  (B) Gross profit would be affected
  (C) Both gross and net profits would be affected
  (D) Just the balance sheet items would be affected.

MC71 Of the following, which should *not* be entered in the journal?
  (i)   Cash payments for wages
  (ii)   Bad debts written off
  (iii) Credit purchases of goods
  (iv)   Sale of fixed assets.

  (A) (i) and (ii)
  (B) (i) and (iii)
  (C) (ii) and (iii)
  (D) (iii) and (iv).

MC72 Which of the following do *not* affect trial balance agreement?
  (i)   Purchases £585 from C Owens completely omitted from the books
  (ii)   Sales £99 to R Morgan entered in his account as £90
  (iii) Rent account added up to be £100 too much
  (iv)   Error on sales invoice of £14 being entered in the books.

  (A) (i) and (iv)
  (B) (i) and (ii)
  (C) (i) and (iii)
  (D) (iii) and (iv).

MC73 Which of the following *are* errors of principle?
  (i)   Rent entered in buildings account
  (ii)   Purchases £150 completely omitted from books
  (iii) Sale of machinery £500 entered in sales account
  (iv)   Cheque payment to R Kago entered only in cash book.

  (A) (ii) and (iii)
  (B) (iii) and (iv)
  (C) (i) and (ii)
  (D) (i) and (iii).

MC74 When the trial balance totals do not agree, the difference is entered in
(A) The balance account
(B) A suspense account
(C) An errors account
(D) The profit and loss account.

MC75 Which of these errors would be disclosed by the trial balance?
(A) Error on a purchase invoice
(B) Purchases from T Morgan entered in C Morgan's account
(C) Carriage outwards debited to sales account
(D) Overcast of total on sales account.

MC76 All these questions refer to the following trading and profit and loss account

Trading Account

	£	£		£	£
Opening stock		700	Sales	24,770	
Purchases	18,615		*Less* Returns	270	24,500
Less Returns	280	18,335			
Carriage in		320			
		19,355			
Closing stock		980			
		18,375			
Gross profit carried down		6,125			
		£24,500			£24,500

Profit and Loss Account

		£		£
Wages		1420	Gross profit b/d	6125
Rent Paid	360			
Accrued	90	450		
General expenses		220		
Carriage out		360		
Net profit		???		
		£6,125		£6,125

(i) The missing net profit figure should be:
(A) £1,675. (B) £21,675. (C) £3,675. (D) £4,675.
(ii) Total expenses were:
(A) £210. (B) £2,450. (C) £810. (D) £2,575.
(iii) The cost of goods sold totalled:
(A) £18,375. (B) £19,500. (C) £24,500. (D) £24,770.
(iv) The expense item of Rent totalled:
(A) £360. (B) £270. (C) £90. (D) £450.
(v) The turnover is:
(A) £24,770. (B) £24,500. (C) £19,355. (D) £18,375.
(vi) The net cost of purchases is:
(A) £18,615. (B) £18,335. (C) £18,655. (D) £18,375.
(vii) Purchases returned totalled:
(A) £360. (B) £320. (C) £280. (D) £270.
(viii) Gross profit as a percentage on net sales is:
(A) 20%. (B) 30%. (C) 25%. (D) 33⅓%.

(ix) Net profit as a percentage on net sales is:
 (A) 10%.   (B) 20%.   (C) 25%.   (D) 15%.
(x)   The value of unsold goods was:
 (A) £980.   (B) £24,500.   (C) £6,125.   (D) £19,355.

(PEI)

MC77 Answer the following questions using the following trial balance and the information given below:

Trial Balance as at 31 December

	£	£
Capital		5,600
Furniture and fittings	5,580	
Stock January 1	700	
Drawings	1,200	
Bank overdraft		1,260
Salaries	3,560	
General expenses	190	
Purchases/sales	4,020	9,840
Discount all'd/rec'd	150	130
Rent and rates	820	
Returns in/out	·90	80
Trade debtors/creditors	1,500	1,070
Bad debt provision		130
	£18,110	£18,110

(a) Salaries owing at 31 December – £140
(b) Rent and rates paid in advance – £220
(c) Depreciate furniture and fittings by 10% p.a.
(d) Closing stock valuation – £800
(e) Increase the bad debt provision to bring it up to 10% of debtors' balances.

(i) What will be the yearly depreciation charge?
 (A) £5,292.   (B) £,6468.   (C) £588.   (D) £5,886.
(ii) What will be the salaries figure shown on the profit and loss account?
 (A) £140.   (B) £3,700.   (C) £3,420.   (D) £3,560.
(iii) The rent and rates figure shown on the profit and loss account will be:
 (A) £600.   (B) £820.   (C) £220.   (D) £1,040.
(iv) The new bad debt provision will be:
 (A) £1,650.   (B) £1,450.   (C) £150.   (D) £110.
(v) What will be the gross profit on the trading account?
 (A) £5,910.   (B) £5,830.   (C) £4,630.   (D) £4,430.
(vi) The net profit on the profit and loss account will be:
 (A) £1,420.   (B) £792.   (C) £1,400.   (D) £812.
(vii) The book value of furniture and fittings on the balance sheet will be:
 (A) £5,292.   (B) £6,000.   (C) £6,368.   (D) £5,880.
(viii) What will be the turnover for the year?
 (A) £9,840.   (B) £3,840.   (C) £9,750.   (D) £4,640.
(ix) Using the adjusted sales figure, the stock turnover for the year will be:
 (A) 10.   (B) 11.   (C) 12.   (D) None of these.
(x) What will be the capital figure at end of year?
 (A) £4,100.   (B) £5,600.   (C) £5,192.   (D) £6,392.

(PEI)

MC78   Given last year's capital as £57,500, this year's capital as £64,300, and drawings as £11,800, then profit must have been
(A) £18,600
(B) £18,100
(C) £16,600
(D) £19,600.

MC79   Given last year's capital as £74,500, closing capital as £46,200, and drawings of £13,400, then
(A) Profit for the year was £14,900
(B) Loss for the year was £14,900
(C) Loss for the year was £15,900
(D) Profit for the year was £16,800.

MC80   Given this year's closing capital as £29,360, the year's net profit as £8,460 and drawings as £5,320, what was the capital at the beginning of the year?
(A) £29,360
(B) £26,220
(C) £34,680
(D) None of the above.

MC81   In a commercial firm an 'Accumulated Fund' would be known as
(A) Fixed assets
(B) Total assets
(C) Net current assets
(D) Capital.

MC82   A receipts and payments account does not show
(A) Cheques paid out during the year
(B) The Accumulated Fund
(C) Receipts from sales of assets
(D) Bank balances.

Answers to multiple-choice questions

Set 1

1	B	2	C	3	B	4	C	5	A
6	C	7	D	8	A	9	D	10	C
11	C	12	B	13	D	14	A	15	C
16	D	17	C	18	C	19	C	20	D

Set 2

21	D	22	C	23	A	24	D	25	C
26	A	27	B	28	D	29	B	30	D
31	A	32	D	33	D	34	B	35	B
36	B	37	C	38	A	39	D	40	B
41	C	42	B	43	D	44	C	45	C
46	A	47	A	48	A	49	D	50	C
51	A	52	B	53	C	54	A	55	D

Set 3

56	D	57	D	58	C	59	D	60	A
61	D	62	C	63	B	64 (i) B (ii) B (iii) B		65	A
66	D	67	A	68	B	69	C	70	A
71	B	72	A	73	D	74	B	75	D

76 (i) C (ii) B (iii) A (iv) D (v) B (vi) B (vii) C (viii) C (ix) D (x) A

77 (i) C (ii) B (iii) A (iv) C (v) A (vi) B (vii) A (viii) C (ix) D (x) D

78	A	79	B	80	B	81	D	82	B

Answers to exercises

Chapter 2

2.1

(a) 25,750 (b) 72,820 (c) 34,980 (d) 48,600 (e) 12,500 (f) 30,620

2.3

(i) Asset (ii) Liability (iii) Asset (iv) Asset (v) Liabilities (vi) Asset

2.5

Wrong: Assets: Loan from C Smith; Creditors; Liabilities: Stock of goods; Debtors.

2.7

Assets: Motor 2,000; Premises 5,000; Stock 1,000; Bank 700; Cash 100 = total 8,800; Liabilities: Loan from Bevan 3,000; Creditors 400 = Total 3,400. Capital 8,800 – 3,400 = 5,400.

2.9

Balance Sheet of T Lymer as at 31 December 1997

	£	£	Net book value £
Fixed assets			
Office furniture			8,640
Delivery van			12,000
			20,640
Current assets			
Stock	4,220		
Debtors	10,892		
Cash at Bank	11,722	26,834	
Less Current liabilities			
Creditors	12,651	12,651	
Net current assets			14,183
			£34,823
Financed by			
Capital			34,823
			£34,823

2.11

	Assets	*Liabilities*	*Capital*
(a)	– Cash	– Creditors	
(b)	– Bank		
	+ Fixtures		
(c)	+ Stock	+ Creditors	
(d)	+ Cash		
(e)	+ Cash		+ Loan from J Walker
(f)	+ Bank		
	– Debtors		
(g)	– Stock	– Creditors	
(h)	+ Premises		
	– Bank		

2.13

C Sangster
Balance Sheet as at 7 May 1998

			Net book value £
Fixed assets			
Fixtures			4,500
Motor vehicle			4,200
			8,700
Current assets			
Stock		5,720	
Debtors		3,000	
Bank		5,450	
Cash		400	14,570
Less Current liabilities			
Creditors		2,370	2,370
Net current assets			12,200
			20,900
Less long-term liability			
Loan from T Sharples			2,000
			£18,900
Financed by			
Capital			£18,900

Chapter 3

3.1

	Debited	Credited
(a)	Motor van	Cash
(c)	Cash	Capital
(e)	A Barrett	Cash
(b)	Office machinery	J Grant & Son
(d)	Bank	J Beach

3.2

	Debited	Credited
(a)	Machinery	A Jackson & Son
(c)	Cash	J Brown
(e)	Cash	Office machinery
(b)	A Jackson & Son	Machinery
(d)	Bank	J Smith (Loan)

3.5

Cash

| (1) Capital | 1,000 | (14) Office Mach | 60 |
| | | (31) Speed & Sons | 698 |

Capital

| | | (1) Cash | 1,000 |

Speed & Sons

| (31) Cash | 698 | (3) M lorry | 698 |

Motor Lorry

| (3) Speed & Sons | 698 | | |

Office Machinery

| (14) Cash | 60 | | |

3.6

Bank

(1) Capital	2,500	(2) Office F	150
		(5) Motor van	600
		(15) Planers Ltd	750
		(31) Machinery	280

Capital

| | | (1) Bank | 2,500 |

Office Furniture

| (2) Bank | 150 | (8) J Walker & Sons | 60 |

Machinery

| (3) Planers Ltd | 750 | | |
| (31) Bank | 280 | | |

Cash

| | | (23) J Walker | 60 |

Planers Ltd

| (15) Bank | 750 | (3) Machinery | 750 |

Motor Van

| (5) Bank | 600 | | |

J Walker & Sons

| (8) Office F | 60 | (23) Cash | 60 |

3.8

Bank

(1) Capital	5,000	(2) Motor van	1,200
(25) Cash	800	(12) Cash	100
		(19) Super Motors	800
		(30) Office fixtures	300

Office Fixtures

| (5) Young Ltd | 400 | (15) Cash | 60 |
| (30) Bank | 300 | | |

Capital

| | | (1) Bank | 5,000 |

Cash

(21) Loan: Jarvis	1,000	(12) Bank	100
		(15) Office fixtures	60
		(25) Bank	800

Motor Van

| (2) Bank | 1,200 | (8) Super Motors | 800 |

Young Ltd

| | | (5) Office fixtures | 400 |

Super Motors

| (19) Bank | 800 | (8) Motor van | 800 |

Loan from Jarvis

| | | (21) Cash | 1,000 |

Chapter 4

4.1

(a)	Dr Purchases, Cr Cash
(c)	Dr C Grant, Cr Sales
(e)	Dr Cash, Cr Sales
(b)	Dr Purchases, Cr E Flynn
(d)	Dr Cash, Cr Motor Van

4.3

	Debited	Credited
(a)	Purchases	J Reid
(c)	Motor van	H Thomas
(e)	Cash	Sales
(g)	Cash	Machinery
(i)	Purchases	D Simpson
(b)	B Perkins	Sales
(d)	Bank	Sales
(f)	H Hardy	Returns outwards
(h)	Returns inwards	J Nelson
(j)	H Forbes	Returns outwards

4.5

Cash

(1) Capital	500	(3) Purchases	85
(10) Sales	42	(25) E Morgan	88
(31) A Knight	55		

Purchases

(3) Cash	85		
(7) E Morgan	116		
(18) A Moses	98		

Sales

| | | (10) Cash | 42 |
| | | (24) A Knight | 55 |

Returns Outwards

| | | (14) E Morgan | 28 |
| | | (21) A Moses | 19 |

A Knight

| (24) Sales | 55 | (31) Cash | 55 |

E Morgan

| (14) Returns outwards | 28 | (7) Purchases | 116 |
| (25) Cash | 88 | | |

A Moses

| (21) Returns outwards | 19 | (18) Purchases | 98 |

Capital

| | | (1) Cash | 500 |

4.6

Cash
(1) Capital	1,000	(2) Bank	900
(19) Sales	28	(7) Purchases	55

Bank
(2) Cash	900	(5) Motor van	500
(24) D Watson (Loan)		(29) S Holmes	60
		(31) Kingston Equipment	150

Purchases
(4) S Holmes	78
(7) Cash	55

Sales
(10) D Moore	98
(19) Cash	28

Returns Outwards
(12) S Holmes	18

S Holmes
(12) Returns	18	(4) Purchases	78
(29) Bank	60		

D Moore
(10) Sales	98

Fixtures
(22) Kingston Equipment	150

Motor Van
(5) Bank	500

D Watson (Loan)
(24) Bank	100

Kingston Equipment
(31) Bank	150	(22) Fixtures	150

Capital
(1) Cash	1,000

4.7

Bank
(1) Capital	10,000	(6) Cash	250
(25) F Jones	1,070	(29) Manchester Motors	2,600

Cash
(2) T Cooper (Loan)	200	(6) Bank	250
(4) Sales	180	(20) Purchases	220
(24) Sales		(31) Office furn	100
(28) Capital	500		

Sales
(4) Cash	200
(8) C Moody	180
(10) J Newman	220
(14) H Morgan	190
(14) J Peat	320
(24) Cash	70

Purchases
(3) F Jones	840
(3) S Charles	3,600
(11) F Jones	370
(20) Cash	220

Returns Inwards
(12) C Moody	40
(26) H Morgan	30

Returns Outwards
(15) F Jones	140
(19) S Charles	110

Motor Van
(17) Manchester Motors	2,600

Office Furniture
(18) Faster S	600
(27) Faster S	100

Manchester Motors
(29) Bank	2,600	(17) Motor van	2,600

Faster Supplies Ltd
(27) Office furn	160	(18) Office furn	600

F Jones
(15) Returns	140	(3) Purchases	840
(25) Bank	1,070	(11) Purchases	370

S Charles
(19) Returns	110	(3) Purchases	3,600

Capital
(1) Bank	10,000
(28) Cash	500

J Newman
(10) Sales	220

H Morgan
(14) Sales	190	(26) Returns	30

C Moody
(8) Sales	180	(12) Returns	40

J Peat
(14) Sales	320

T Cooper (Loan)
(2) Cash	400

Chapter 5

5.1

	Account to be debited	Account to be credited
(a)	Rates	Bank
(b)	Wages	Cash
(c)	Bank	Rent received
(d)	Bank	Insurance
(e)	General exps	Cash

5.2

	Account to be debited	Account to be credited
(a)	Rent	Cash
(b)	Purchases	Cash
(c)	Bank	Rates
(d)	General exps	Bank
(e)	Cash	Commissions recd
(f)	T Jones	Returns out
(g)	Cash	Sales
(h)	Office fixtures	Bank
(i)	Wages	Cash
(j)	Drawings	Cash

5.5

Bank
(1) Capital	200	(5) Motor van	250
(2) U Surer (Loan)	1,000	(12) Insurance	22
		(31) Electricity	17

Capital
(1) Bank	200

U Surer (Loan)
(2) Bank	1,000

Motor Van
(5) Bank	250

Insurance
(12) Bank	22

Electricity
(31) Bank	17

Motor Expenses
(7) Cash	15

Cash
(6) Sales	105	(7) Motor exps	15
(15) Commission	15	(8) Wages	18

Purchases
(3) T Parkin	296
(10) C Moore	85

Sales
(6) Cash	105

T Parkin
(3) Purchases	296

C Moore
(10) Purchases	85

Commission
(15) Cash	15

Wages
(8) Cash	18

5.6

Bank
(1) Capital	2,000	(3) Fixtures 150
(21) Rent	5	(24) Motor van 300

Cash
(5) Sales	275	(10) Rent 15
		(12) Stationery 27
		(30) Wages 117
		(31) Drawings 44

Purchases
(2) D Miller 175
(6) S Waites 114

Sales
(5) Cash 275
(23) U Henry 77

Fixtures
(3) Bank 150

Rent
(10) Cash 15

M Mills
(18) Returns out 23 | (2) Purchases 175

S Waites
(6) Purchases 114

U Henry
(23) Sales 77

Rent Received
(21) Bank 5

Stationery
(12) Cash 27

Returns Out
(18) M Mills 23

Motor Van
(24) Bank 300

Wages
(30) Cash 117

Drawings
(31) Cash 44

5.7

Cash
(1) Capital	1,500	(3) Rent 28
(11) Sales	49	(4) Bank 1,000
		(20) B repairs 18
		(28) Purchases 125
		(30) Motor exps 15

Bank
(4) Cash	1,000	(7) Stationery 15
		(27) A Hanson 279
		(29) Motor van 395

Purchases
(2) A Hanson 296
(28) Cash 125

Sales
(5) E Linton 54
(11) Cash 49
(17) S Morgan 29

Stationery
(7) Bank 15

Returns Outwards
(14) A Hanson 17

Fixtures
(31) A Webster 120

Capital
(1) Cash 1,500

Rent
(3) Cash 28

Building Repairs
(20) Cash 18

Motor Expenses
(30) Cash 15

Motor Van
(29) Bank 395

A Hanson
(14) Returns out 17 | (2) Purchases 296
(27) Bank 279

E Linton
(5) Sales 54 | (22) Returns in 14

S Morgan
(17) Sales 29

Returns Inwards
(22) E Linton 14

A Webster
(31) Fixtures 120

Chapter 6

6.1

H Harvey
(1) Sales	690	(10) Returns 40
(4) Sales	66	(24) Cash 300
		(31) Balance c/d 416
	756	756
(1) Balance b/d	416	

L Masters
(4) Sales	418	(31) Balance c/d 621
(31) Sales	203	
	621	621
(1) Balance b/d	621	

N Morgan
153 | (18) Bank 153

J Lindo
420 | (10) Returns 20
 | (20) Bank 400
420 | 420

6.2

J Young
(10) Returns	55	(1) Purchases 458
(28) Cash	250	(15) Purchases 80
(30) Balance c/d	233	
	538	538
		(1) Balance b/d 233

G Norman
(10) Returns	22	(1) Purchases 708
(30) Balance c/d	686	
	708	708
		(1) Balance b/d 686

L Williams
	17	(1) Purchases 120
	180	(3) Purchases 77
	197	
		(1) Balance b/d 180

T Harris
880 | (3) Purchases 880

6.3

H Harvey
1998		Dr	Cr	Balance
May	1 Sales	690		690 Dr
May	4 Sales	66		756 Dr
May	10 Returns		40	716 Dr
May	24 Cash		300	416 Dr

N Morgan
1998		Dr	Cr	Balance
May	1 Sales	153		153 Dr
May	18 Bank		153	0

J Lindo
1998		Dr	Cr	Balance
May	1 Sales	420		420 Dr
May	10 Returns		20	400 Dr
May	20 Bank		400	0

6.5

L Masters

1998		Dr	Cr	Balance
May 4	Sales	418		418 Dr
May 31	Sales	203		621 Dr

D Williams

(1)	Sales	458	(24)	Bank	300
			(28)	Cash	100
			(30)	Balance c/d	58
		458			458
(1)	Balance b/d	58			

A White

		77	(2)	Purchases	77

H Samuels

(17)	Returns	24	(2)	Purchases	231
(30)	Balance c/d	219	(10)	Purchases	12
		243			243
			(1)	Balance b/d	219

J Moore

(1)	Sales	235	(12)	Returns	26
(8)	Sales	444	(20)	Balance c/d	653
		679			679
(1)	Balance b/d	653			

P Owen

(12)	Returns	26	(2)	Purchases	65

G Grant

(1)	Sales	98	(12)	Returns	9
			(30)	Balance c/d	89
		98			98
(1)	Balance b/d	89			

O Oliver

(17)	Returns	12	(2)	Purchases	210
(26)	Cash	210	(10)	Purchases	12
		222			222

F Franklin

(1)	Sales	249	(30)	Bank	249

Chapter 7

7.1

Cash

(1)	Capital	250	(6)	Rent	12
			(15)	Carriage	23
			(31)	Balance c/d	215
		250			250

Bank

(9)	C Bailey	43	(12)	K Gibson	25
(10)	H Spencer	150	(12)	D Ellis	54
			(31)	Rent	18
			(31)	Balance c/d	96
		193			193

Purchases

(2)	D Ellis	54
(2)	C Mendez	87
(2)	K Gibson	25
(2)	D Booth	76
(2)	L Lowe	64
(18)	C Mendez	43
(18)	D Booth	110

Sales

(4)	C Bailey	43
(4)	B Hughes	62
(4)	H Spencer	176
(21)	B Hughes	67

Capital

(1)	Cash	250

Rent

(6)	Cash	12
(31)	Bank	18

Carriage

(15)	Cash	23

D Ellis

(12)	Bank	54	(2)	Purchases	54

C Mendez

			(2)	Purchases	87
			(18)	Purchases	43

K Gibson

(12)	Bank	25	(2)	Purchases	25

D Booth

			(2)	Purchases	76
			(18)	Purchases	110

L Lowe

			(2)	Purchases	64

C Bailey

(4)	Sales	43	(9)	Bank	43

B Hughes

(4)	Sales	62
(21)	Sales	67

H Spencer

(4)	Sales	176	(10)	Bank	150

Trial Balance as at 31 May 1998

	Dr	Cr
Cash	215	
Bank	96	
Capital		250
Rent	30	
Carriage	23	
C Mendez		130
D Booth		186
L Lowe		64
B Hughes	129	
H Spencer	26	
Purchases	459	
Sales		348
	978	978

7.2

Bank

(1)	Capital	800	(17)	M Hyatt	95
(24)	J Carlton	95	(21)	Betta Ltd	50
			(31)	Motor van	400
			(31)	Balance c/d	361
		895			895

Cash

(5)	Sales	87	(6)	Wages	14
(30)	J King (Loan)	60	(9)	Purchases	46
			(12)	Wages	14
			(31)	Balance c/d	73
		147			147

Capital

(1)	Bank	800

Motor Van

(31)	Bank	400

Sales

(5)	Cash	87
(7)	H Elliott	35
(7)	L Lane	42
(7)	J Carlton	72
(13)	L Lane	32
(13)	J Carlton	23

Purchases

(2)	K Henriques	76
(2)	M Hyatt	27
(2)	T Braham	56
(9)	Cash	46
(10)	M Hyatt	57
(10)	T Braham	98

Returns Outwards

(18)	T Braham	20
(27)	K Henriques	24

Trial Balance as on 31 March 1998

	Dr	Cr
Bank	361	
Cash	73	
Capital		800
Motor van	400	
Wages	28	
Shop fixtures	50	
J King (Loan)		60
H Elliott	35	
L Lindo	74	
K Henriques		52
T Braham		134
Sales		291
Purchases	360	
Returns outwards		44
	1381	1381

Wages

| (6) Cash | 14 | | |
| (12) Cash | 14 | | |

Shop Fixtures

| (15) Betta Ltd | 50 | | |

J King (Loan)

| | | (30) Cash | 60 |

H Elliott

| (7) Sales | 35 | | |

L Lane

| (7) Sales | 42 | | |
| (13) Sales | 32 | | |

J Carlton

| (7) Sales | 72 | (24) Bank | 95 |
| (13) Sales | 23 | | |

K Henriques

| (27) Returns | 24 | (2) Purchases | 76 |

M Hyatt

| (17) Bank | 84 | (2) Purchases | 27 |
| | | (10) Purchases | 57 |

T Braham

| (18) Returns | 20 | (2) Purchases | 56 |
| | | (10) Purchases | 98 |

Betta Ltd

| (21) Bank | 50 | (15) S Fixtures | 50 |

7.3

Bank

(1) Capital	600	(5) Motor van	256
(25) P Potter	43	(7) Motor exps	12
		(12) N Moss	62
		(21) O Hughes	46
		(29) Balance	267
	643		643

Cash

(1) Capital	50	(4) Purchases	23
(23) H Henry	66	(15) Motor exps	5
(26) Sales	34	(20) Drawings	10
		(27) Drawings	24
		(29) Postages	4
		Balance	84
	150		150

Motor Van

| (5) Bank | 256 | | |

Motor Expenses

| (7) Bank | 12 | | |
| (15) Cash | 5 | | |

Postages

| (29) Cash | 4 | | |

H Henry

| (3) Sales | 66 | (23) Cash | 66 |

N Neita

| (3) Sales | 25 | (19) Returns in | 11 |
| (30) Sales | 43 | | |

P Potter

| (3) Sales | 43 | (25) Bank | 43 |

B Barnes

| (3) Sales | 24 | | |

K Lyn

| | | (9) Sales | 26 |
| | | (30) Sales | 45 |

M Moore

| | | (9) Sales | 65 |

M Edgar

| | | (9) Sales | 67 |

C Jones

| (13) Returns | 25 | (2) Purchases | 500 |
| (28) Returns | 42 | (11) Purchases | 240 |

N Moss

| (21) Bank | 62 | (11) Purchases | 62 |

O Hughes

| (21) Bank | 46 | (11) Purchases | 46 |

Capital

| | | (1) Bank | 600 |
| | | (25) Cash | 50 |

Drawings

| (20) Cash | 10 | | |
| (27) Cash | 24 | | |

Sales

		(3) H Henry	66
		(3) N Neita	25
		(3) P Potter	43
		(9) B Barnes	24
		(9) K Lyn	26
		(9) M Moore	65
		(26) Cash	34
		(30) N Neita	43
		(30) M Edgar	67
		(30) K Lyn	45

Purchases

(2) C Jones	500		
(4) Cash	23		
(11) C Jones	240		
(11) N Moss	62		
(11) O Hughes	46		

Returns Inwards

| (19) N Neita | 11 | | |

Returns Outwards

| | | (13) C Jones | 25 |
| | | (28) C Jones | 42 |

Trial Balance 30 June 1998

	Dr	Cr
Bank	267	
Cash	84	
Capital		650
Drawings	34	
Sales		438
Purchases	871	
Returns inwards	11	
Returns outwards		67
Motor van	256	
Motor expenses	17	
Postages	4	
N Neita	57	
B Barnes	24	
K Lyn	71	
M Moore	65	
M Edgar	67	
C Jones		673
	1,828	1,828

7.7

Trial Balance of P Brown as at 31 May 1999

	Dr £	Cr £
Capital		20,000
Drawings	7,000	
General expenses	500	
Sales		38,500
Purchases	29,000	
Debtors	6,800	
Creditors		9,000
Bank	15,100	
Cash	200	
Plant and equipment	5,000	
Heating and lighting	1,500	
Rent	2,400	
	67,500	67,500

7.8

Trial Balance of S Higton as at 30 June 1998

	Dr £	Cr £
Capital		19,956
Sales		119,439
Stationery	1,200	
General expenses	2,745	
Motor expenses	4,476	
Cash at bank	1,950	
Stock 1 July 1997	7,668	
Wages and salaries	9,492	
Rent and rates	10,500	
Office equipment	6,000	
Purchases	81,753	
Heating and lighting	2,208	
Rent received		2,139
Debtors	10,353	
Drawings	4,200	
Creditors		10,230
Motor vehicle	7,500	
Interest received		1,725
Insurance	3,444	
	153,489	153,489

7.9

Trial Balance of Ms Anita Hall as at 31 December 1999

	Dr £	Cr £
Plant and machinery	21,450	
Motor vehicles	26,000	
Premises	80,000	
Wages	42,840	
Purchases	119,856	
Sales		179,744
Rent received		3,360
Telephone, printing and stationery	3,600	
Creditors		27,200
Debtors	30,440	
Bank overdraft		2,216
Capital		131,250
Drawings	10,680	
General expenses	3,584	
Lighting and heating	2,960	
Motor expenses	2,360	
	343,770	343,770

Chapter 8

8.1

B Webb

Trading and Profit and Loss Account for the year ended 31 December 1997

Sales			18,462
Less Cost of goods sold			
Purchases		14,629	
Less Closing stock		2,548	12,081
Gross profit			6,381
Less Expenses			
Salaries		2,150	
Motor expenses		520	
Rent and rates		670	
Insurance		111	
General expenses		105	3,556
Net profit			2,825

8.2

C Worth
Trading and Profit and Loss Account for the year ended 30 June 1998

	£	£
Sales		28,794
Less Cost of goods sold		
Purchases	23,803	
Less Closing stock	4,166	
		19,637
Gross profit c/d		9,157
Less Expenses		
Salaries	3,164	
Rent and rates	854	
Lighting expenses	422	
Insurance	105	
Motor running expenses	1,133	
Trade expenses	506	
		6,184
Net profit		2,973

8.3

Mrs P Stewart
Trial Balance as at 31 March 1998

	Dr £	Cr £
Sales		24,765
Purchases	13,545	
Staff wages	2,100	
Drawings	5,500	
Rent and rates	1,580	
Electricity	565	
Motor expenses	845	
Insurance	345	
General expenses	245	
Cash in hand	135	
Cash at bank	2,675	
Creditors		3,285
Vehicle	5,875	
Fixtures and fittings	1,495	
Capital		6,855
	34,905	34,905

Closing stock £2,345

Mrs P Stewart
Trading and Profit and Loss Account for the year ended 31 March 1998

	£	£
Sales		24,765
Less Cost of goods sold		
Purchases	13,545	
Less Closing stock	(2,345)	
		11,200
		13,565
Gross profit		
Less Overheads		
Staff wages	2,100	
Rent and rates	1,580	
Electricity	565	
Motor expenses	845	
Insurance	345	
General expenses	245	
		5,680
Net profit		7,885

Chapter 9

9.1

(Vertical)

B Webb
Balance Sheet as at 31 December 1997

	£	£
Fixed Assets		
Premises		1,500
Motor vehicles		1,200
		2,700
Current Assets		
Stock	2,548	
Debtors	1,950	
Bank	1,654	
Cash	40	
	6,192	
Less Current Liabilities		
Creditors	1,538	
		4,654
		7,354
Capital		
Balance at 1.1.1997		5,424
Add Net profit		2,825
		8,249
Less Drawings		895
		7,354

9.2

C Worth
Balance Sheet as at 30 June 1998

	£	£	£
Fixed Assets			
Buildings		50,000	
Fixtures		1,000	
Motor vans		5,500	56,500
Current Assets			
Stock	4,166		
Debtors	3,166		
Bank	3,847		
	11,179		
Less Current Liabilities			
Creditors	1,206		
Net current assets			9,973
			66,473
Capital			
Balance at 1.7.1997		65,900	
Add Net profit		2,973	
		68,873	
Less Drawings		2,400	
			66,473

9.3

Mrs P Stewart
Balance Sheet as at 31 March 1998

	£	£
Fixed Assets		
Fixtures and fittings		1,495
Motor car		5,875
		7,370
Current Assets		
Stock	2,345	
Debtors	–	
Bank	2,675	
Cash	135	
	5,155	
Less Current Liabilities		
Creditors	3,285	
Net current assets		1,870
Total net assets		9,240
Financed by		
Capital		6,855
Add Net profit		7,885
		14,740
Less Drawings		5,500
		9,240

9.4

Miss V Holland
Balance Sheet as at 30 June 1998

	£	£	£
Fixed Assets			
Equipment			2,885
Van			3,400
			6,285
Current assets			
Stock on hand		1,465	
Trade debtors		2,375	
Cash in hand		150	
		3,990	
Current Liabilities			
Trade creditors		4,565	
Bank overdraft		1,785	
		6,350	
Net current liabilities			(2,360)
			3,925
Long-term Liabilities			
Loan from mother			2,000
Net assets			1,925
Financed by			
Capital account			2,000
Cash introduced			2,525
			4,525
Net profit			2,600
Drawings			1,925

Chapter 10

10.1

Trading Account for the year ended 31 December 1997

	£	£
Sales		38,742
Less cost of goods sold		
Opening stock	6,924	
Add Purchases	26,409	
Add Carriage inwards	670	
	34,003	
Less Closing stock	7,489	
		26,514
Gross profit		12,228

10.2

R Graham
Trading and Profit and Loss Account for the year ended 30 September 1998

	£	£
Sales		18,600
Less Cost of goods sold		
Opening stock	2,368	
Add Purchases	11,874	
Carriage inwards	310	
	14,552	
Less Closing stock	2,946	11,606
Gross profit		6,994
Less Expenses		
Salaries and wages	3,862	
Rent and rates	304	
Carriage out	200	
Insurance	78	
Motor expenses	664	
Office expenses	216	
Lighting and heating	166	
General expenses	314	5,804
Net profit		1,190

Balance Sheet as at 30 September 1998

	£	£
Fixed Assets		
Premises	5,000	
Fixtures	350	
Motor vehicles	1,800	7,150
Current Assets		
Stock	2,946	
Debtors	3,896	
Bank	482	
	7,324	
Less Current Liabilities		
Creditors	1,731	5,593
		12,743
Capital		
Balance at 1.10.1997	12,636	
Add Net profit	1,190	
	13,826	
Less Drawings	1,083	12,743

Chapter 11

11.1

(a) Materiality
(b) Business entity
(c) Prudence
(d) Cost
(e) Money measurement
(f) Accrual
(g) Realisation
(h) Going concern
(i) Consistency
(j) Materiality

Chapter 12

12.1

(a)

Roger Craig
Trading and Profit and Loss Account for the year ended 31 December 1998

	£	£
Sales		36,340
Less Cost of goods sold		18,185
Gross profit		18,155
Less Expenses		
Wages and salaries	8,310	
Rates	1,720	
Insurances	680	
Electricity	1,010	
General expenses	550	12,270
Net profit		£5,885

12.1 (continued)
(b)

Roger Craig
Balance Sheet as at 31 December 1998

Fixed Assets (at Net Book Value)*	£	£	£
			14,500
Current Assets			
Stock	1,836		
Debtors	2,620		
Bank	1,799		
Cash	15		
		6,270	
Less Current Liabilities			
Creditors	1,730		
		1,730	
Net current assets			4,540
			19,040
Financed by			
Capital			17,365
Add Net profit			5,885
			23,250
Less Drawings			4,210
			19,040

* This is *after* depreciation £1,010.

† As Cost of goods sold (9) already calculated, the stock (12) must be the closing stock.

12.2

(a)
(i) Sales day book/sales ledger/personal account
(ii) Cash book/general ledger/nominal ledger
(iii) Purchase day book/purchases ledger/personal account
(iv) Cash book/general ledger/nominal account
(v) Sales day book/sales ledger/personal account
(vi) Returns inwards day book/sales ledger/personal account
(vii) Returns outwards day book/purchases ledger/personal account
(viii) General journal/general ledger/real account

Chapter 13

13.1

Petty Cash Book

				Total	Wages	Stationery	Postage	Ledger
4.67	(1)	Balance b/f						
45.33	(1)	Cash						
	(3)	Wages		8.76	8.76			
	(7)	Postages		2.94			2.94	
	(10)	Wages		9.11	9.11			
	(14)	Envelopes		2.28		2.28		
	(17)	Wages		8.84	8.84			
	(20)	J Smith		4.16				4.16
	(21)	Stationery		2.75		2.75		
	(24)	Wages		8.48	8.48			
				47.32	35.19	5.03	2.94	4.16
	(28)	Balance c/d		2.68				
50.00				50.00				
2.68	(1)	Balance b/d						
47.32	(1)	Cash						

13.3

(a)

Petty Cash Book

Receipts £	Date	Details	Voucher no	Total payment £	Travel-ling £	Post-age £	Station-ery £	Office expenses £	VAT £	Ledger postings £
	1999									
120.00	Mar 1	Cash								
	2	Postage Stamps	1	6.50		6.50				
	3	Rail Fare	2	23.00	23.00					
	7	Parcel	3	4.00		4.00				
	9	Window Cleaning	4	8.00				8.00		
	12	Envelopes	5	3.10			2.64		.46	
	14	Office Tea, etc	6	6.40				6.40		
	16	Petrol	7	10.00	8.51				1.49	
	19	Disks – Computer	8	13.00				11.06	1.94	
	20	Dusters and Polish	9	1.73				1.47	.26	
	23	Postage Stamps	10	2.40		2.40				
	27	Ledger a/c J Cheetham	11	7.30						7.30
	31	Magazine	12	6.40				6.40		
91.83	Mar 31	Cash	CB1	91.83	31.51	12.90	2.64	33.33	4.15	7.30
		Balance	c/d	28.17						
211.83				120.00						
					GL1	GL2	GL3	GL4	GL5	
28.17	Apr 1	Balance	b/d							
91.83	" 1	Cash	CB1							

13.3 (continued)

(b)

General Ledger

Travelling Expenses Account

Dr						GL1	Cr
Date	Details	Fol	£	Date	Details	Fol	£
1999							
Mar 31	Petty Cash	PCB1	31.51				

Postages Account — GL2

Dr							Cr
Date	Details	Fol	£	Date	Details	Fol	£
1999							
Mar 31	Petty Cash	PCB1	12.90				

Stationery Account — GL3

Dr							Cr
Date	Details	Fol	£	Date	Details	Fol	£
1999							
Mar 31	Petty Cash	PCB1	2.64				

Office Expenses Account — GL4

Dr							Cr
Date	Details	Fol	£	Date	Details	Fol	£
1999							
Mar 31	Petty Cash	PCB1	33.33				

VAT Account — GL5

Dr							Cr
Date	Details	Fol	£	Date	Details	Fol	£
1999							
Mar 31	Petty Cash	PCB1	4.15				

Cash Book (Bank Column Only) — CB1

Dr							Cr
Date	Details	Fol	£	Date	Details	Fol	£
				1999			
				Mar 31	Petty Cash	PCB1	91.83

Purchase Ledger

J Cheetham Account

Dr							Cr
Date	Details	Fol	£	Date	Details	Fol	£
1999				1999			
Mar 31	Petty Cash	PCB1	7.30	Feb 1	Purchases	PDB1	7.30

(c)

MEMORANDUM

To	Ms S Dickinson	Ref	
From	Student's Name		
Subject	Petty Cash Imprest System	Date	31 March 1999

Advantages of Imprest System

1. *Control:* The petty cash can be checked easily at any time because cash in hand plus vouchers paid out for the period should always equal the amount of the 'float'.
2. *Responsibility:* It is an ideal opportunity to appoint junior staff and give them some responsibility and test their honesty.
3. It relieves the accountant by dealing with numerous small cash payments and reduces the posting to the general ledger.

Chapter 14

14.1 Refer to text 14.2.

14.2 Drawer – the person filling out a cheque and using it for payment.
Payee – the person to whom the cheque is paid.

14.4 Refer to text section 14.4.

14.5 Refer to text section 14.8.

Chapter 15

15.1

Cash Book

Dr		Cash	Bank			Cash	Bank	Cr
(1)	Capital	100		(2)	Rent	10		
(3)	F Lake (Loan)		500	(4)	B McKenzie		65	
(5)	Sales	98		(9)	B Burton	22		
(7)	N Miller		62	(16)	Bank C	50		
(11)	Sales		53	(19)	F Lake (Loan)		100	
(16)	G Moores	65		(26)	Motor expenses		12	
(22)	Sales		50	(30)	Cash C		100	
(30)	Bank C	100	66	(31)	Wages	97		
				(31)	Balances c/d	184	454	
		363	731			363	731	

15.2

Cash Book

Dr		Cash	Bank			Cash	Bank	Cr
(1)	Balances b/d	56	2,356	(2)	Rates		156	
(5)	Sales	74		(3)	Postages	5		
(7)	Cash C		60	(7)	Bank C	60		
(12)	J Moores	50	100	(8)	T Lee		75	
(20)	P Jones		79	(10)	C Brooks	2		
(22)	Bank C	200		(17)	Drawings	20		
(31)	Sales		105	(22)	Cash C		200	
				(24)	Motor van	195		
				(28)	Rent		40	
				(31)	Balance c/d	98	2,229	
		380	2,700			380	2,700	

15.5

Two Column Cash Book

Date Details	Fol	Cash	Bank	Date Details	Fol	Cash	Bank	
1998				1998				
May 1 Balance	b/d	14.72	432.36	May 1 Balance	b/d		820.54	
3 P Wrench			634.34	2 Stationery		10.00		
" R Whitworth			341.00	6 SW Rail			37.50	
" J Summers				9 Fabulous Fabrics Ltd			450.80	
12 Sales		76.00		11 Mellors Mfg. Co			348.32	
17 Trentham Traders			32.81	14 Inland Revenue			221.30	
24 Sales		350.00		20 Foreign Currency		250.00		
26 Cash C				" Bank Charges			3.20	
31 Summers			1,231.00	26 Bank C		300.00		
" Bradnor Mfg. Co			725.00	27 Salaries			5,720.00	
" Taylors			2,330.50	31 Balance	c/d	130.72		
" Balance	c/d		1,824.65					
		440.72	7,851.66			440.72	7,851.66	
June 1 Balance	b/d	130.72	1,824.65					

15.6

Two Column Cash Book

Dr Date	Details	Fol	Cash	Bank	Date	Details	Fol	Cash	Bank Cr
1999					1999				
Feb 1	Balance	b/d	76.32	2,376.50	Feb 2	Electricity			156.00
6	D Hill			300.00	4	Motor expenses		15.00	
"	A Jackson			275.00	7	Stationery		3.70	
"	H Wardle			93.20	12	Palmer & Sons – Purchases			723.50
10	Sales		57.10		16	Wright Brothers			86.20
14	D Whitman – Loan			500.00	17	Drawings		50.00	
22	J Smith			217.00	"	Post Office re: Telephone a/c Mr S Jepson			140.60
26	Sales			53.00	23	Petrol		21.00	
28	Balance	c/d		590.60	27	Brownsons of M/cr			899.00
					28	Salaries			2,400.00
					"	Balance	c/d	43.72	
			133.42	4,405.30				133.42	4,405.30
			43.72						
Mar 1	Balance	b/d			Mar 1	Balance	b/d	133.42	590.60

Chapter 16

16.1

Cash Book

Dr		Disct	Cash	Bank			Disct	Cash	Bank Cr
(1)	Capital			6,000	(1)	Fixtures			950
(3)	Sales		407		(2)	Purchases			1,240
(5)	N Morgan	10		210	(4)	Rent		200	
(9)	S Cooper	20		380	(7)	S Thompson & Co	4		76
(14)	L Curtis			115	(12)	Rates			410
(20)	P Exeter	2		78	(16)	M Monroe	6	114	
(31)	Sales			88	(31)	Balance c/d		93	4,195
		32	407	6,871			10	407	6,871

In general ledger:
Debit discounts allowed 32: Credit discounts received 10.

16.2

Cash Book

Dr		Disct	Cash	Bank			Cr Disct	Cash	Bank
(1)	Balance b/d		230	4,756	(4)	Rent			120
(2)	R Burton	7		133	(8)	N Black	9		351
(2)	E Taylor	11		209	(8)	P Towers	12		468
(2)	R Harris	15		285	(8)	C Rowse	20		780
(6)	J Cotton: loan			1,000	(10)	Motor expenses		44	
(12)	H Hankins	3		74	(15)	Wages		160	
(18)	C Winston	13		247	(21)	Cash			350
(18)	R Wilson & Son			323	(24)	Drawings		120	
(18)	H Winter	17		437	(25)	T Briers	7	133	
(21)	Bank		350		(29)	Fixtures			650
(31)	Commission	23		88	(31)	Balances c/d		123	4,833
		89	**580**	**7,552**			**48**	**580**	**7,552**

Discounts Received
(31) Total for month 48

Discounts Allowed
(31) Total for month 89

16.3

Cash Book

Dr		Disct	Cash	Bank			Cr Disct	Cash	Bank
(1)	Balances b/f		211	3,984	(2)	T Adams	4		76
(4)	C Potts			98	(2)	C Bibby	13		247
(6)	Sales		49		(2)	D Clarke	22		418
(9)	R Smiley	4		156	(7)	Insurance		65	
(9)	J Turner	16		624	(12)	Motor expenses		100	
(9)	R Pimlott	13		507	(21)	Salaries			120
(18)	Sales		98		(23)	Rent		60	
(28)	R Godfrey (Loan)			500	(31)	Stationery			27
					(31)	Balances c/d		84	5,030
		33	**309**	**5,918**			**39**	**309**	**5,918**

16.6

(a) Depending on the exact nature of the transaction, and whether the provider of goods or services will accept the method of payment.

Any three from:

(i) By handing over an asset at an agreed value, e.g. a motor car to cancel a debt.
(ii) By contra, e.g. an amount owing by him to you may be set off against what he owes.
(iii) By credit card
(iv) By direct debit
(v) By standing order
(vi) By a postal order or money order
(vii) By credit transfer

(b)

Cash Book

Dr		Disct	Cash	Bank			Cr Disct	Cash	Bank
(1)	Balances b/d		419	3,685	(6)	Wages		102	
(2)	A Wood			296	(9)	C Hill	13		211
(12)	Sales		146		(12)	T Jarvis	28		1,023
(17)	Atlas & Co			500	(13)	Wages		104	
(23)	Bank C		200		(19)	Postages		21	
(28)	T Phillips	8		317	(20)	Wages		102	
(31)	Cash			260	(23)	Cash C			200
					(25)	W Moore		105	
					(26)	Wages		260	
					(31)	Bank C			429
					(31)	Balances c/d		71	3,195
		8	**765**	**5,058**			**41**	**765**	**5,058**

Chapter 17

17.1

Bank Reconciliation as on 31 December 1997

Cash at bank as per cash book		678
Add Unpresented cheques	256	
Credit transfers	56	312
		990
Less Bank lodgements		115
Cash at bank as per bank statement		875

17.3

Bank Reconciliation as on 31 March 1999

Balance as per cash book		787
Add Traders' credit	73	
Unpresented cheques	127	
		200
		987
Less Standing order	25	
Bank lodgement	112	
		137
Balance per bank statement		850

17.6

Cash Book

Dr	Details			Cr	Details	
Dec 31	Balance b/d	2,200		Dec 31	Standing order	40
"	Credit transfer	175		"	Bank charges	40
					Balance c/d	2,295
		2,375				2,375
Jan 1	Balance b/d	2,295				

Mitchell: Bank Reconciliation as at 31 December

	£
Balance per bank statement	2,245
Less: Unpresented cheques	250
	1,995
Add: Deposit	300
Balance per cash book	2,295

17.7

(a)

Cash Book (Bank Column Only)

Dr Date	Details	Folio	Bank	Cr Date	Details	Folio	Bank
1999				1999			
July 31	Balance	b/d	1,069.68	July 7	D/D United Insurance		35.00
25	Wheeldons		217.00	9	S/O Uttoxeter CC		76.00
				18	Bank Charges		24.40
				31	Balance	c/d	1,151.28
			1,286.68				1,286.68
Aug 1	Balance	b/d	1,151.28				

(b)

Bank Reconciliation Statement as at 31 July

		£
Balance per bank statement		3,225.63
Add Cash not credited		34.10
		3,259.73
Less Unpresented cheques		
00236	54.00	
00241	450.25	
00242	125.00	
00244	1,427.30	
00245	51.90	
	2,108.45	
Balance per cash book	1,151.28	

(c)

Standing orders are payments made by the bank on the customer's behalf by deducting a regular amount of money from the customer's account to pay for such things as a mortgage payment, insurance premium etc. The customer requests the bank to make the payment on a regular, often monthly, basis until such time as he or she wishes to cancel the order.

Direct debits are also used to enable regular payments to be made by the bank on the customer's behalf. These, however, differ slightly from standing orders in that authority is given to the person/firm receiving the money to make the request for payment to the bank from the payer's account. Often the payment will vary from one payment to another, whereas standing orders remain fixed until altered at the customer's request.

(d) As you are an employee of the firm it is not your duty to divulge confidential information about the business's financial stability to anyone, be they employees or outside personnel. Therefore, to protect both yourself and the firm you should refuse this request.

Chapter 18

18.1

Capital (a) (c) (d) (f) (j) (l)

Revenue (b) (e) (g) (h) (i) (k)

18.3

Capital (a) (b) (e)

Explanation – see text.

18.4

Capital £1,500 of (a); £500 of (b); £2,300 of (c); £100 of (e); £4,000 of (f)

Revenue £6,500 of (a); £1,500 of (b); £200 of (c); £400 of (d); £700 of (e)

18.5

(a)

Items of expenditure

Capital Items
1 double and 2 single beds
Bathroom suites
Labour to plumb-in bathroom suites
Curtains
Carpeting
Reception desk
Portable typewriter
Estate car (second-hand)
2 storage heaters for drying room
Coat and shoe racks for drying room (supplied and fitted)

Revenue Items
10 feather pillows (and pillowcases)
Table linen
Cutlery
Vase and dried flower arrangement
Stationery
6 waste-paper bins
Towels
Toilet rolls and tissues
Soap and bubble bath
Tax on estate car
Garage repair bill
2 boxes pansies and wallflowers
6 rose bushes
2 five-litre tins emulsion
20 rolls wallpaper and paste

(b)

Capital expenditure is money spent on either acquiring a fixed asset or adding value to an existing asset. Examples include the purchase of a motor vehicle, plant and equipment, computer, etc.

Revenue expenditure is money spent on the day-to-day running expenses of the business. Examples include stationery, petrol, rent, rates etc.

Draft reply: It is very important to distinguish between the two types of expenditure as incorrect analysis can affect both the profit figures and the balance sheet figures, i.e. if revenue expenditure is inadvertently charged as a capital item then the profit figure would be overstated. Also the assets in the balance sheet would be overstated.

18.7

	Nature	**Reason**
(a)	Revenue expenditure	Used up in the short term
(b)	Revenue expenditure	Used up in the short term
(c)	Question is not too clear	
	(i) If spent on improving building construction Capital expenditure	Adds to fixed asset value
	(ii) If spent on extra wages for security guards Revenue expediture	
(d)	Revenue expenditure	Used up in the short term
(e)	Capital expenditure	Used up in the short term
		Adds to value of computer

Chapter 19

19.1

Sales Day Book

(1)	J Gordon	187
(3)	G Abrahams	166
(6)	V White	12
(10)	J Gordon	55
(17)	F Williams	289
(19)	U Richards	66
(27)	V Wood	28
(31)	L Simes	78
		881

Sales Ledger

J Gordon
(1)	Sales	187
(10)	Sales	55

G Abrahams
(3)	Sales	166

V White
(6)	Sales	12

F Williams
(17)	Sales	289

U Richards
(19)	Sales	66

V Wood
(27)	Sales	28

L Simes
(31)	Sales	78

General Ledger
Sales Account
(31)	Total for month	881

19.3
Workings of invoices:

(1) F Gray			
3 rolls white tape × 10 =	30		
5 sheets blue cotton × 6 =	30		
1 dress length × 20 =	20	80	
Less trade discount 25%		20	60
(4) A Gray			
6 rolls white tape × 10 =	60		
30 metres green baize × 4 =	120	180	
Less trade discount 33⅓%		60	120
(8) E Hines			
1 dress length black silk × 20 =			20
(20) M Allen			
10 rolls white tape × 10 =	100		
6 sheets blue cotton × 6 =	36		
3 dress lengths black silk × 20 =	60		
11 metres green baize × 4 =	44	240	
Less trade discount 25%		60	180
(31) B Cooper			
12 rolls white tape × 10 =	120		
14 sheets blue cotton × 6 =	84		
9 metres green baize × 4 =	36	240	
Less trade discount 33⅓%		80	160

Sales Day Book

(1)	F Gray	60
(4)	A Gray	120
(8)	E Hines	20
(20)	M Allen	180
(31)	B Cooper	160
		540

Sales Ledger

F Gray
(1) Sales 60

A Gray
(4) Sales 120

E Hines
(8) Sales 20

M Allen
(20) Sales 180

B Cooper
(31) Sales 160

General Ledger
Sales Account
(31) Total for month 540

19.5
(a)(i)

Sales Day Book

Yr 4	Invoice No	Details	List (£)	Trade Discount (£)	Net (£)
Jan	1040	Cash	80	–	80
"	1041	Debtor	420	105	315
"	1042	Cash	30	–	30
"	1043	PH Ltd	860	215	645
"	1044	Debtor	110	11	99
"	1045	PH Ltd	1,040	260	780
"	1046	Cash	15	–	15
"	1047	Cash	32	–	32
"	1048	Debtor	320	16	304
"	1049	Debtor	100	10	90
					2,390

(ii)

Dr | Sales Account | Cr

		Credit Sales	2,233
		Cash Sales	157
		Year 4 Jan 31	2,390

(b)

Dr | PH Ltd | Cr

Year 4				Year 4			
Jan	Sales		645.00	Jan 31	Bank		638.55
"	"		780.00	" 31	Discount		6.45
				"	Balance c/d		780.00
			1,425.00				1,425.00

19.6
(a)

	Name/Address	Invoice No	Total £	Net £	VAT £
1	Price Barlow & Co, Hulme End, Derbyshire	0932	282.00	240.00	42.00
2	Rowley Farmers, Dove End Farm, Bakewell, Derbyshire	0933	131.01	111.50	19.51
3	Stoke Engr Co Ltd, Blythe End Works, Stoke-on-Trent	0934	408.08	347.30	60.78

19.6 (continued)

	Name/Address	Invoice No	Total £	Net £	VAT £
4	Peak Mfr Co, Town End, Buxton, Derbyshire	0935	1,654.64	1,408.20	246.44
5	Robinson (Plant Hire), Leek, Staffs	0936	394.44	335.70	58.74
6	Bennetts Farm Machinery, c/o Holly Bank Farm, Monyash, Derbyshire	0937	220.00	187.23	32.77

(b)

Sales Day Book — Page 9

Date	Name	Invoice No	Folio	Total	Plant and Equipment	Repairs	VAT
Dec 3	Price, Barlow & Co	0932	SL1	282.00	240.00		42.00
"	Rowley Farmers	0933	SL2	131.01		111.50	19.51
"	Stoke Engs Co Ltd	0934	SL3	408.08	347.30		60.78
"	Peak Mfr Co Ltd	0935	SL4	1,654.64	1,408.20		246.44
"	Robinson (Plant Hire)	0936	SL5	394.44	335.70		58.74
"	Bennetts Farm Machinery	0937	SL6	220.00		187.23	32.77
				3,090.17	1,995.50	634.43	460.24
					GL7	GL8	GL22

Sales Ledger

Price, Barlow & Co Account — Page 1

Dr				Cr
Dec 3	Sales	SDB9	282.00	

Rowley Farmers Account

Dr				Cr
Dec 3	Sales	SDB9	131.01	

Stoke Engr Co Ltd Account

Dr				Cr
Dec 3	Sales	SDB9	408.08	

Peak Mfr Co Account

Dr				Cr
Dec 3	Sales	SDB9	1,654.64	

Robinson (Plant Hire) Account

Dr				Cr
Dec 3	Sales	SDB9	394.44	

Bennetts Farm Machinery Account — Page 7

Dr				Cr
Dec 3	Sales	SDB9	220	

General Ledger

Sales of Plant and Equipment Account

Dr				Cr
		Dec 31	Total Sales for Dec	1,995.50

Sales–Repairs Account

Dr				Cr
		Dec 31	Total Sales for Dec	634.43

VAT Account

Dr				Cr
		Dec 31	Total VAT on Sales for Dec	460.24

Chapter 20

20.1

Workings of purchases invoices

(1) K King

4 radios x 30 =	120	
3 music centres x 160 =	480	
	600	
Less trade discount 25%	150	
		450

(3) A Bell

2 washing machines x 200 =	400	
5 vacuum cleaners x 60 =	300	
2 dish dryers x 150 =	300	
	1,000	
Less trade discount 20%	200	
		800

(15) J Kelly

1 music centre x 300 =	300	
2 washing machines x 250 =	500	
	800	
Less trade discount 25%	200	
		600

(20) B Powell

6 radios x 70 =	420	
Less trade discount 33⅓%	140	
		280

(30) B Lewis

4 dish dryers x 200 =	800	
Less trade discount 20%	160	
		640

Purchases Day Book

(1)	K King	450
(3)	A Bell	800
(15)	J Kelly	600
(20)	B Powell	280
(30)	B Lewis	640
		2,770

General Ledger
Purchases Account

(31)	Total for month	2,770

Purchases Ledger

K King

	(1) Purchases	450

A Bell

	(3) Purchases	800

J Kelly

	(15) Purchases	600

B Powell

	(20) Purchases	280

B Lewis

	(30) Purchases	640

20.3

Purchases Day Book

(1)	Smith Stores	90
(23)	C Kelly	105
(31)	J Hamilton	180
		375

Purchases Ledger

Smith Stores
(1)	Purchases	90

C Kelly
(23)	Purchases	105

J Hamilton
(31)	Purchases	180

General Ledger
Purchases Account
(31)	Total for month	375

Sales Day Book

(8)	A Grantley	72
(15)	A Henry	240
(24)	D Sangster	81
		393

Sales Ledger

A Grantley
(8)	Sales	72

A Henry
(15)	Sales	105

D Sangster
(24)	Sales	180

Sales Account
(31)	Purchases	393

20.4

(a)

	Product A	Product B
Manufacturers recommended retail price	1,500	4,000
Less trade discount	(20%) 300	(25%) 1,000
Price paid per product	1,200	3,000

(b) Profit per product (equals trade discount when sold at MRRP) — 300 — 1,000

(c) $\dfrac{300}{1,200} \times \dfrac{100}{1} = 25\%$ $\dfrac{1,000}{3,000} \times \dfrac{100}{1} = 33\frac{1}{3}\%$

20.6

(a)

Purchases Day Book

Aug 4	G Mann	300
" 11	B Jollie	200
		500

Sales Day Book

Aug 5	B Allen	240
" 12	G Parker	360
" 21	E Todd	243
		843

Cash Book

		Discount	Bank			Discount	Bank
Aug 18	G Parker	36	324	Aug 15	B Jollie	10	190
" 31	B Allen	12	228	" 29	G Mann	10	300

(b) Discount allowed to traders as a means of calculating net sales price.

(c) To speed up payments of debtors' accounts.

Chapter 21

21.1

Purchases Day Book

(1)	H Lloyd	119
(4)	D Scott	98
(4)	A Simpson	114
(4)	A Williams	25
(4)	S Wood	56
(10)	A Simpson	59
(18)	M White	89
(18)	J Wong	67
(18)	H Miller	196
(18)	H Lewis	119
(31)	A Williams	56
(31)	C Cooper	98
		1,096

Returns Outwards Day Book

(7)	H Lloyd	16
(7)	D Scott	14
(25)	J Wong	5
(25)	A Simpson	11
		46

General Ledger
Purchases Account
(31)	Total for month	1,096

Returns Outwards Account
	(31)	Total for month 46

Purchases Ledger

H Lloyd
(7)	Returns	16	(1)	Purchases	119

D Scott
(7)	Returns	14	(4)	Purchases	98

A Simpson
(25)	Returns	11	(4)	Purchases	114
			(10)	Purchases	59

A Williams
	(4)	Purchases	25
	(31)	Purchases	56

S Wood
	(4)	Purchases	56

M White
	(18)	Purchases	89

J Wong
(25)	Returns	5	(18)	Purchases	67

H Miller
	(18)	Purchases	196

H Lewis
	(18)	Purchases	119

C Cooper
	(31)	Purchases	98

21.3

Sales Day Book

(3)	E Rigby	510
(3)	E Phillips	246
(3)	F Thompson	356
(8)	A Green	307
(8)	H George	250
(8)	J Ferguson	185
(20)	E Phillips	188
(20)	F Powell	310
(20)	E Lee	420
		2,772

Purchases Day Book

(3)	K Hill	380
(3)	M Norman	500
(3)	N Senior	106
(8)	R Morton	200
(8)	J Cook	180
(8)	D Edwards	410
(20)	C Davies	66
(24)	C Ferguson	550
(24)	K Ennevor	900
		3,292

Returns Inwards Day Book

(14)	E Phillips	18
(14)	F Thompson	22
(31)	E Phillips	27
(31)	E Rigby	30
		97

Returns Outwards Day Book

(12)	M Norman	30
(12)	N Senior	16
(31)	J Cook	13
(31)	C Davies	11
		70

Sales Ledger

E Rigby: (3) Sales 510 | (31) Returns in book 30
E Phillips: (3) Sales 246 / (20) Sales 188 | (14) Returns in 18 / (31) Returns in 27
F Thompson: (3) Sales 356 | (14) Returns in 22
A Green: (8) Sales 307
H George: (8) Sales 250
J Ferguson: (8) Sales 185
F Powell: (20) Sales 310
E Lee: (20) Sales 420

Purchases Ledger

K Hill: (1) Purchases 380
M Norman: (13) Returns out 30 | (1) Purchases 500
N Senior: (12) Returns out 16 | (1) Purchases 106
R Morton: (5) Purchases 200
J Cook: (31) Returns out 13 | (5) Purchases 180
D Edwards: (5) Purchases 410
C Davies: (31) Returns out 11 | (5) Purchases 66
C Ferguson: (24) Purchases 550
K Ennevor: (24) Purchases 900

General Ledger

Sales: (31) Sales book 2,772
Purchases: (31) Purchases book 3,292
Returns Inwards: (31) Returns in book 97
Returns Outwards: (31) Returns out book 70

21.6

(a)

(Sales Ledger)

A Birch

(1)	Balance b/d	4,251	(7)	Bank	4,100	
(9)	Sales	1,095	(7)	Discount	151	
			(31)	Balance c/d	1,095	
		5,346			5,346	

H Jameson

(1)	Balance b/d	1,260	(23)	Bank	900	
(15)	Sales	740	(24)	Returns	140	
(19)	Sales	205	(31)	Balance c/d	1,165	
		2,205			2,205	

(Purchases Ledger)

S Franklin

(18)	Bank	1,080	(1)	Balance b/d	1,780	
(18)	Discount	120	(12)	Purchases	206	
(19)	Returns	80				
(31)	Balance c/d	706				
		1,986			1,986	

P Greenbank

(2)	Bank	603	(1)	Balance b/d	670	
(2)	Discount	67				
		670			670	

E Oliver

(29)	Bank	1,110	(1)	Balance b/d	1,110	
(31)	Balance c/d	1,398	(8)	Purchases	348	
			(23)	Purchases	1,050	
		2,508			2,508	

(b)

(General Ledger)

Capital
(1) Balance b/d 9,151

Sales
(31) Sales book 2,040

Purchases
(31) Purchases book 1,604

Returns Inwards
(31) Returns in book 140

Returns Outwards
(31) Returns out book 80

Discounts Allowed
(31) Cash book 151

Discounts Received
(31) Cash book 187

21.6 (continued)

(c)

Cash Book

Dr	Discount	Bank			Discount	Bank	Cr
(1) Balance b/d		7,200	(2) P Greenbank		67	603	
(7) A Birch	151	4,100	(18) S Franklin		120	1,080	
(23) H Jameson		900	(29) E Oliver			1,110	
			(31) Balance c/d			9,407	
	151	12,200			187	12,200	

Chapter 22

22.1

(a) J Hunt

(b)

Feb 1 Amount owing brought forward from previous month.

Feb 6 Goods bought from Hunt on this date.

Feb 8 Cook paid Hunt a cheque for £127.16. Hunt allowed Cook to deduct this amount from payment because payment was made in good time.

Feb 12 Cook returns goods to Hunt.

Feb 26 Goods brought from Hunt on this date.

Feb 28 Cook was charged extra amount by Hunt because of an undercharge on a past invoice.

Sender: Hunt; Receiver: Cook. An invoice.

(c) Debtor is R J Cook.
Creditor is J Hunt.
Amount owed at 28 February 1999 is £312.36.

Chapter 23

23.1

(a)

Style of invoice will vary.

Calculations:

	£
3 sets of Boy Michael Golf Clubs × £240	720
150 Watson golf balls at £8 per 10 balls	120
4 Faldo golf bags at £30	120
	960
Less trade discount 33⅓%	320
	640
Add VAT 17½%	112
	752

(b)

D Wilson Ltd Ledger
G Christie & Sons

Dr				Cr
				£
1998 May 1	Sales			752

G Christie & Son Ledger
D Wilson Ltd

Dr				Cr
1998 May 1	Purchases			752

23.2

Sales Book

		Net	VAT	£
1997 Aug 1	M Sinclair & Co	160	28	188
" 8	M Brown & Associates	240	42	282
" 19	A Axton Ltd	80	14	94
" 31	T Christie	40	7	47
		520	91	

Sales Ledger

M Sinclair & Co
(1) Sales 188

M Brown & Associates
(8) Sales 282

A Axton Ltd
(19) Sales 94

T Christie
(31) Sales 47

General Ledger

Sales
(31) Credit sales for the month 520

Value Added Tax
(31) Sales book: VAT content 91

23.3

Sales Day Book

		Net	VAT	£
(1)	B Davies & Co	160	28	
(4)	C Grant Ltd	200	35	
(16)	C Grant Ltd	120	21	
(31)	B Karloff	80	14	
		560	98	

23.3 (continued)

Purchases Day Book

		Net	VAT
(10)	G Cooper & Son	400	70
(10)	J Wayne Ltd	240	42
(14)	B Lugosi	40	7
(23)	S Hayward	40	7
		720	126

Sales Ledger

B Davies & Co
(1) Sales 188

C Grant Ltd
(4) Sales 235
(16) Sales 141

B Karloff
(31) Sales 94

Purchases Ledger

G Cooper & Son
(10) Purchases 470

J Wayne Ltd
(10) Purchases 282

B Lugosi
(14) Purchases 47

S Hayward
(23) Purchases 47

General Ledger

Sales
(31) Credit sales for month 560

Purchases
(31) Credit purchases for month 720

Value Added Tax
(31) VAT content in purchase book 126
(31) VAT content in sales book 98
(31) Balance c/d 28
126 | 126

23.5

C Hills

(8) Bank	154	(1) Balance b/d	154
(31) Balance c/d	282	(13) Purchases	94
		(20) Purchases	188
	436		436
		(1) Balance b/d	282

Bank

(1) Balance b/d	740	(8) C Hills	154
(16) K Harris	612	(15) Printing	20
		(31) Balance c/d	1178
	1,352		1,352
(1) Balance b/d	1,178		

H Lowe

(31) Balance c/d	322	(1) Balance b/d	275
		(21) Purchases	47
	322		322
		(1) Balance b/d	322

Capital

		(1) Balance b/d	641

Purchases

(31) Day book	280		

Sales

		(31) Day book	320

K Harris

(1) Balance b/d	330	(16) Bank	612
(11) Sales	282	(31) Balance c/d	94
(15) Sales	94		
	706		706
(1) Balance b/d	94		

Printing

(15) Bank	20		

Value Added Tax

(31) Purchases book	49	(31) Sales book	56
(31) Balance c/d	7		
	56		56
		(1) Balance b/d	7

Trial Balance as at 31.12.1998

	Dr	Cr
C Hills		282
H Lowe		322
K Harris	94	
Printing	20	
Bank	1,178	
Capital		641
Purchases	280	
Sales		320
Value Added Tax		7
	1,572	1,572

23.7

(a)

VAT Account

1998			1998		
Jan 31	Tax on Inputs	3,500	Jan 31	Tax on Outputs	3,675
Jan 31	Balance c/d	175			
		3,675			3,675
Feb 28	Tax on Inputs	3,675	Feb 1	Balance b/d	175
			Feb 28	Tax on Outputs	3,500
		3,675			3,675
Mar 31	Tax on Inputs	3,850	Mar 31	Tax on Outputs	2,625
			Mar 31	Balance c/d	1,225
		3,850			3,850
			Apr 1	Balanced b/d	1,225

(b)

The balance of £1,225 on 31 March 1998 is the amount owing by HM Customs & Excise (VAT) to the firm. This will be cleared by HM Customs & Excise sending a remittance for £1,225.

24.1
(a)

Curtain Design Company
Sales Day Book

Date 1998	Details	Folio	Total £	Ready-made £	Custom-made £	VAT £
Nov 1	Jarvis Arms Hotel	SL1	2,702.50		2,300.00	402.50
8	Springs Nursing Home	SL2	1,175.00	1,000.00		175.00
15	J P Morten	SL3	258.50	220.00		38.50
17	Queen's Hotel	SL4	1,762.50		1,500.00	262.50
30	W Blackshaw	SL5	105.75	90.00		15.75
			6,004.25	1,310.00	3,800.00	894.25
				GL1	GL2	GL3

(b)

Sales Ledger
Jarvis Arms Hotel Account

Dr		SL1		Cr
Nov 1 Sales 2,702.50				

Spring's Nursing Home Account

Dr		SL2		Cr
Nov 8 Sales 1,175.00				

J P Morten Account

Dr		SL3		Cr
Nov 15 Sales 258.50				

Queen's Hotel Account

Dr		SL4		Cr
Nov 17 Sales 1,762.50				

W Blackshaw Account

Dr		SL5		Cr
Nov 30 Sales 105.75				

(c)

General Ledger
Sales – Ready-Made Account

Dr		GL1		Cr
		Nov 30 Day book 1,310.00		

Sales – Custom-Made Account

Dr		GL2		Cr
		Nov 30 Day book 3,800.00		

Value Added Tax Account

Dr		GL3		Cr
		Nov 30 VAT on sales 894.25		

24.2
(a)

Hall Engineering Co
Purchases Day Book

Date 1998	Details	Folio	Total £	Engineering parts £	Printing and stationery £	Motor expenses £	VAT £
May 1	Black's Engineering Co	PL1	611.00	520.00			91.00
" 3	Ace Printing Co	PL2	170.37		145.00		25.37
" 24	Morgan's Garage	PL3	141.00			120.00	21.00
" 26	Martin's Foundry	PL4	822.50	700.00			122.50
" 28	Office Supplies	PL5	148.05		126.00		22.05
" 29	Black's Engineering Co	PL1	258.50	220.00			38.50
			2,151.42	1,440.00	271.00	120.00	320.42
				GL1	GL2	GL3	GL4

(b)

Purchases Ledger
Black's Engineering Account

Dr		PL1		Cr
		May 1 Purchases 611.00		
		" 29 Purchases 258.50		

Ace Printing Co Account

Dr		PL2		Cr
		May 3 Purchases 170.37		

Morgan's Garage Account

Dr		PL3		Cr
		May 24 Purchases 141.00		

Martin's Foundry Account

Dr		PL4		Cr
		May 26 Purchases 822.50		

Office Supplies Account

Dr		PL5		Cr
		May 28 Purchases 148.05		

24.2 (continued)

(c)

General Ledger

Purchases – Engineering Parts Account

Dr			GL1 Cr
May 31	Day book	1,440.00	

Printing and Stationery Account

Dr			GL2 Cr
May 31	Day book	271.00	

Motor Expenses Account

Dr			GL3 Cr
May 31	Day book	120.00	

VAT Account

Dr			GL4 Cr
May 31	VAT on Purchases	320.42	

24.3

(b)

PURCHASES DAY BOOK

Date	Supplier	Invoice No	Account No	Total	Elect-rical	Motor	Office	Tele-phone	Sun-dries	VAT
A	B	C	D	E	F	G	H	I	J	K
1999										
Apr 6	Leigh Electrics	2306	030	723.52	615.77					107.75
8	PCD Electrical	2307	060	351.48	299.13					52.35
10	Star Mfg Co	2308	080	32.17	27.38					4.79
12	British Telecom	2309	007	112.70				95.92		16.78
14	Peak Electrical Installations Ltd	2310	051	499.37	425.00					74.37
16	Office Cleaning Co	2311	043	123.37			105.00			18.37
17	Leigh Electrics	2312	030	663.68	564.83					98.85
19	Thomas Motors	2313	090	84.10		69.38				14.72
21	Star Mfg Co	2314	080	160.38	136.49					23.89
25	Thomas Motors	2315	090	155.02		131.93				23.09
25	"	2315	090	24.00		24.00				
25	Smith Stationers	2316	079	68.95			58.68			10.27
				2,998.74	2,068.60	225.31	163.68	95.92		445.23
				PLC a/c	GL201	GL202	GL203	GL204		GL205

(b)

RETURNS OUTWARDS BOOK

Date	Supplier	Invoice No	Account No	Total	Elect-rical	Motor	Office	Tele-phone	Sun-dries	VAT
A	B	C	D	E	F	G	H	I	J	K
1999										
Apr 16	Leigh Electrics	27CN	030	57.00	48.57					8.43
30	Star Mfrg Co	28CN	080	2.25	1.91					0.34
				59.25	50.48					8.77
				PLC a/c	GL201					GL205

(c)

PURCHASES LEDGER

Leigh Electrics Account

Dr						030	
Date 1999		Fol	£	Date 1999		Fol	Cr £
Apr 16	Returns Outward	27CN	57.00	Apr 6	Purchases	2306	723.52
Apr 30	Balance c/d		1,330.20	Apr 17	Purchases	2312	663.68
			1,387.20				1,387.20

PCD Electrical Account

Dr						060	
Date		Fol	£	Date		Fol	Cr £
				Apr 8	Purchases	2307	351.48

Star Mfg Co Account

Dr						080	
Date		Fol	£	Date		Fol	Cr £
Apr 30	Returns Outward	28CN	2.25	Apr 10	Purchases	2308	32.17
Apr 30	Balance c/d		190.30	Apr 21	"	2314	160.38
			192.55				192.55
				May 1	Balance b/d		190.30

British Telecom Account

Dr						007	
Date		Fol	£	Date		Fol	Cr £
				Apr 12	Purchases	2309	112.70

Peak Electrical Installations Account

Dr						051	
Date		Fol	£	Date		Fol	Cr £
				Apr 14	Purchases	2310	499.37

24.3 (continued)

Office Cleaning Co — 043

Dr			Date		Fol	Cr £
			Apr 16	Purchases	2311	123.37

Thomas Motors Account — 090

Dr	Fol	£	Date		Fol	Cr £
Apr 30 Balance c/d		263.12	Apr 19	Purchases	2313	84.10
			Apr 25	"	2315	155.02
			Apr 25	"	2315	24.00
		263.12				263.12
			May 1	Balance b/d		263.12

Smith Stationers Account

Dr			Date		Fol	Cr £
			Apr 25	Purchases	2316	68.95

GENERAL LEDGER

Electrical Purchases Account — GL201

Dr		£	Date 1999			Cr £
Apr 30 Total Electrical Purchases for April		2,068.60	Apr 30	Returns – April		50.48

Motor Expenses Account — GL202

Dr		£	Date			Cr £
Apr 30 Total Motor expenses for April		225.31				

Office Expenses Account — GL203

Dr		£	Date			Cr £
Apr 30 Total Office expenses for April		163.68				

Telephone Account — GL204

Dr		£	Date		Fol	Cr £
Apr 30 Total Telephone for April		95.92				8.77

VAT Account — GL205

Dr		£	Date		Fol	Cr £
Apr 30 Total VAT on April Purchases		445.23	Apr 30	Returns – April		445.23

Chapter 25

25.1

Sales Ledger Control Account

Dr			Fol	£				Fol	Cr £
(1)	Balance b/f			4,560	(31)	Returns inwards			460
(31)	Sales journal			10,870	(31)	Cheques and cash			9,615
					(31)	Discounts allowed			305
					(31)	Balances c/d			5,050
				15,430					15,430

25.2

Sales Ledger Control Account

Dr			Fol	£				Fol	Cr £
(1)	Balances b/f			6,708	(31)	Discounts			300
(31)	Sales journal			11,500	(31)	Cash and cheques			8,970
					(31)	Bad debts			115
					(31)	Returns inwards			210
					(31)	Balances c/d			8,613
				18,208					18,208

25.5

(a)

Sales Ledger Control Account

Dr			Fol	£				Fol	Cr £
(1)	Balances b/f			6,840	(31)	Discounts			420
(31)	Sales			46,801	(31)	Bad debts			494
					(31)	Receipts			43,780
					(31)	Returns in			296
					(31)	Balances c/f			8,651
				53,641					53,641

(b) See text.

Chapter 26

26.1

			Dr			Cr
(a)	Motor vehicles	Dr	6,790	: Kingston	Cr	6,790
(b)	Bad debts	Dr	34	: H Newman	Cr	34
(c)	Unique Offices	Dr	490	: Office furniture	Cr	490
(d) (i)	Bank	Dr	39	: W Charles	Cr	39
(ii)	Bad debts	Dr	111	: W Charles	Cr	111
(e)	Drawings	Dr	45	: Purchases	Cr	45
(f)	Drawings	Dr	76	: Insurance	Cr	76
(g)	Machinery	Dr	980	: Systems accelerated	Cr	980

26.3

(a) *The Journal (dates omitted)*

	Dr	Cr
Freehold premises	45,000	
Fixtures and fittings	12,500	
Motor vehicles	9,500	
Bank (overdraft)		2,800
Cash	650	
Stock	1,320	
F Hardy	160	
A Derby		270
Capital		66,060
	69,130	69,130

(b)

	Dr	Cr
Discounts Allowed	7	
Parker		7
Being discount allowed to Parker		
Motor Van	4,500	
Supervans Ltd		4,500
Being purchase of van		
Supervans Ltd	1,125	
Bank		1,125
Being payment of deposit on van		
Bank	50	
I M Broke		50
Being final payment by Broke		
Bad debts	200	
I M Broke		200
Being bad debt written off		

(c)

Bad Debts Account

Dr			Cr
I M Broke	200		

I M Broke Account

Dr			Cr
Balance b/d	250	Bank	50
		Bad debts	200
	250		250

26.5

The Journal (narratives omitted)

	Dr	Cr
(a) July 1 James Crawford	1.80	
Interest receivable (6% × 120 × $^3/_{12}$)		1.80
(b) Aug 30 Weighing machines	1,350.00	
Mechweights		1,350.00
Mechweights	400.00	
Weighing machines		400.00
(c) Sept 10 Bank	52.50	
Bad debt recovered		52.50

26.6

The Journal

	Dr	Cr
(1) Premises	2,000	
Motor van	450	
Fixtures	600	
Stock	1,289	
Debtors: N Hardy	40	
M Nelson	180	
Bank	1,254	
Cash	45	
Creditors: B Blake		60
V Reagan		200
Capital		5,598
	5,858	5,858
(14) Motor van	300	
Better Motors		300

Purchases Day Book

(2)	B Blake	20
(2)	C Harris	56
(2)	H Gordon	38
(2)	N Lee	69
(22)	J Johnson	89
(22)	T Best	72
		344

Sales Day Book

(3)	K O'Connor	56
(3)	M Benjamin	78
(3)	L Staines	98
(3)	N Duffy	48
(3)	B Green	118
(3)	M Nelson	40
(9)	M Benjamin	22
(9)	L Pearson	67
		527

Returns Inwards Day Book

(11)	K O'Connor	16
(11)	L Staines	18
		34

Returns Outwards Day Book

(19)	N Lee	9

26.6 (continued)

Cash Book

Dr		Disc	Cash	Bank			Cr		Disc	Cash	Bank
(1)	Balances		45	1,254	(1)	Rent					15
(16)	N Hardy	2		38	(4)	Motor expenses				13	
(16)	M Nelson	11		209	(7)	Drawings				20	
(16)	K O'Connor	2		38	(24)	B Blake			4		76
(16)	L Staines	4		76	(24)	V Reagan			10		190
					(24)	N Lee			3		57
					(27)	Salaries					56
					(30)	Rates					66
					(31)	Better Motors					300
					(31)	Balance c/d				12	855
		19	45	1,615					17	45	1,615

B Blake Account

Dr				Cr	
(24)	Bank	76	(1)	Balance	60
(24)	Discount	4	(2)	Purchases	20
		80			80

V Reagan Account

Dr				Cr	
(24)	Bank and Disct	200	(1)	Balance b/d	200

C Harris Account

Dr			Cr	
			(2) Purchases	56

H Gordon Account

Dr			Cr	
			(2) Purchases	38

N Lee Account

Dr				Cr	
(19)	Returns	9	(2)	Purchases	69
(24)	Bank and Disct	60			
		69			69

M Benjamin Account

Dr			Cr	
(3)	Sales	78		
(9)	Sales	22		

L Staines Account

Dr				Cr	
(3)	Sales	98	(11)	Returns	18
			(16)	Bank & Disct	80
		98			98

N Duffy Account

Dr			Cr	
(3)	Sales	48		

B Green Account

Dr			Cr	
(3)	Sales	118		

L Pearson Account

Dr			Cr	
(9)	Sales	67		

Better Motors Account

Dr				Cr	
(31)	Bank	300	(14)	Motor van	300

General Ledger
Capital Account

Dr			Cr	
			(1) Balance	5,598

Rent Account

Dr			Cr	
(1)	Bank	15		

Motor Expenses Account

Dr			Cr	
(4)	Cash	13		

Drawings Account

Dr			Cr	
(7)	Cash	20		

Salaries Account

Dr			Cr	
(27)	Bank	56		

Rates Account

Dr			Cr	
(30)	Bank	66		

26.6 (continued)

Sales Account

Dr		Cr
	(31) Total for month	527

Purchases Account

Dr		Cr
(31) Total for month	344	

Returns Inwards Account

Dr		Cr
(31) Total for month	34	

Returns Outwards Account

Dr		Cr
	(31) Total for month	9

Premises Account

Dr		Cr
(1) Balance	2,000	

Motor Vans Account

Dr		Cr
(1) Balance	450	
(14) Better Motors	300	

Fixtures Account

Dr		Cr
(1) Balance	600	

Stock Account

Dr		Cr
(1) Balance	1,289	

J Johnson Account

Dr		Cr
	(22) Purchases	89

T Best Account

Dr		Cr
	(22) Purchases	72

N Hardy Account

Dr		Cr
(1) Balance	40	(16) Bank & Disct 40

M Nelson Account

Dr		Cr
(1) Balance	180	(16) Bank & Disct 220
(3) Sales	40	
	220	220

K O'Connor Account

Dr		Cr
(3) Sales	56	(11) Returns 16
		(16) Bank & Disct 40
	56	56

Discounts Allowed Account

Dr		Cr
(31) Total for month	19	

Discounts Received Account

Dr		Cr
	(31) Total for month	17

Trial Balance as at 31 May 1998

	Dr	Cr
C Harris		56
H Gordon		38
J Johnson		89
T Best		72
M Benjamin	100	
N Duffy	48	
B Green	118	
L Pearson	67	
Capital		5,598
Rent	15	
Motor expenses	13	
Drawings	20	
Salaries	56	
Rates	66	
Sales		527
Purchases	344	
Returns inwards	34	
Returns outwards		9
Premises	2,000	
Motor vans	750	

26.6 (continued)

Fixtures		600
Stock		1,289
Discounts allowed		19
Discounts received		17
Bank	855	
Cash	12	
	6,406	6,406

Chapter 27

27.1

Straight Line

Cost		4,000
Yr 1	Depreciation	700
		3,300
Yr 2	Depreciation	700
		2,600
Yr 3	Depreciation	700
		1,900
Yr 4	Depreciation	700
		1,200
Yr 5	Depreciation	700
		500

4,000 – 500 = 3,500 ÷ 5 = 700

Reducing Balance

Cost		4,000
Yr 1	Depn 40% of 4000	1,600
		2,400
Yr 2	Depn 40% of 2400	960
		1,440
Yr 3	Depn 40% of 1440	576
		864
Yr 4	Depn 40% of 864	346
		518
Yr 5	Depn 40% of 518	207
		311

27.2

(a) Straight Line

Cost		12,500
Yr 1	Depreciation	1,845
		10,655
Yr 2	Depreciation	1,845
		8,810
Yr 3	Depreciation	1,845
		6,965
Yr 4	Depreciation	1,845
		5,120

$$\frac{12,500 - 5,120}{4} = 1,845$$

(b) Reducing Balance

Cost		12,500
Yr 1	Depn 20% of 12,500	2,500
		10,000
Yr 2	Depn 20% of 10,000	2,000
		8,000
Yr 3	Depn 20% of 8,000	1,600
		6,400
Yr 4	Depn 20% of 6,400	1,280
		5,120

27.3

(a) Reducing Balance

Cost		6,400
Yr 1	Depn 50% of 6,400	3,200
		3,200
Yr 2	Depn 50% of 3,200	1,600
		1,600
Yr 3	Depn 50% of 1,600	800
		800
Yr 4	Depn 50% of 800	400
		400
Yr 5	Depn 50% of 400	200
		200

(b) Straight Line

Cost		6,400
Yr 1	Depreciation	1,240
		5,160
Yr 2	Depreciation	1,240
		3,920
Yr 3	Depreciation	1,240
		2,680
Yr 4	Depreciation	1,240
		1,440
Yr 5	Depreciation	1,240
		200

$$\frac{6,400 - 200}{5} = 1,240$$

27.7

			Machines		
			A	B	C
Bought 1.1.1996			3,000		
1996	Depreciation	10% for 12 months	300		
			2,700		
Bought 1.4.1997				2,000	
1997	Depreciation	10% × 2,700	270		
	"	10% for 9 months		150	
			2,430	1,850	
Bought 1.7.1998					1,000
1998	Depreciation	10% × 2,430	243		
	"	10% × 1,850		185	
	"	10% for 6 months			50
			2,187	1,665	950

1998 Total Depreciation 243 + 185 + 50 = 478

Chapter 28

28.1

(a)

Motor Delivery Van Account

Dr			Cr
1996 Jul 1 Bank	2,000	1997 Jun 30 Depreciation	400
		Jun 30 Balance c/d	1,600
	2,000		2,000
1997 Jul 1 Balance b/d	1,600	1998 Jun 30 Depreciation	320
		Jun 30 Balance c/d	1,280
	1,600		1,600
1998 Jul 1 Balance b/d	1,280	1999 Jun 30 Depreciation	256
		Jun 30 Balance c/d	1,024
	1,280		1,280
1999 Jul 1 Balance b/d	1,024	2000 Jun 30 Depreciation*	205
		Jun 30 Balance c/d	819
	1,024		1,024

*rounded off to nearest £

(b) per text

28.2

(a)

(Straight line method)
Delivery Van Account

Dr			Cr
Year 1 Bank	1,500	Year 1 Depreciation	150
		Balance c/d	1,350
	1,500		1,500
Year 2 Balance b/d	1,350	Year 2 Depreciation	150
		Balance c/d	1,200
	1,350		1,350
Year 3 Balance b/d	1,200	Year 3 Depreciation	150
		Balance c/d	1,050
	1,200		1,200

(b)

(Reducing balance method)

Dr			Cr
Year 1 Bank	1,500	Year 1 Depreciation	150
		Balance c/d	1,350
	1,500		1,500
Year 2 Balance b/d	1350	Year 2 Depreciation	135
		Balance c/d	1,215
	1,350		1,350
Year 3 Balance b/d	1,215	Year 3 Depreciation	121
		Balance c/d	1,094
	1,215		1,215

28.3

(Showing modern method only)
(a) Straight line method

Delivery Van Account

Dr			Cr
1997 Nov 1 Bank	1,200		

Provision for Depreciation: Delivery Van Account

Dr			Cr
1998		1998	
Oct 31 Balance c/d	120	Oct 31 Profit and loss	120
		1998	
		Nov 1 Balance b/d	120
1999		1999	
Oct 31 Balance c/d	240	Oct 31 Profit and loss	120
	240		240
		1999	
		Nov 1 Balance b/d	240
2000		2000	
Oct 31 Balance c/d	360	Oct 31 Profit and loss	120
	360		360
		2000	
		Nov 1 Balance b/d	360

28.3 (continued)
(b) Reducing balance method

Delivery Van Account

Dr			Cr
1997 Nov 1	Bank	1,200	

Provision for Depreciation: Delivery Van Account

Dr			Cr		
1998 Oct 21	Balance c/d	120	1998 Oct 31	Profit and loss	120
					120
1999 Oct 31	Balance c/d	228	1998 Nov 1	Balance b/d	120
			1999 Oct 31	Profit and loss	108
		228			228
			1999 Nov 1	Balance b/d	228
2000 Oct 31	Balance c/d	325	2000 Oct 31	Profit and loss	97
		325			325
			2000 Nov 1	Balance b/d	325

28.6
(a)
(i) Wear and tear
(ii) Passage of time
(iii) Obsolescence
(iv) Depletion

(b)
(i) A 90-year lease on a building – *passage of time.*
(ii) Land – *none of these, land is not normally subject to depreciation.*
(iii) A forest of mature trees to be felled for timber – *depletion.*
(iv) A stamping press after an improved press capable of increased output of higher quality at lower cost – *obsolescence.*

(c)

Motor Vehicles Account

Dr		£	Cr		£
1998 June 1	Balance b/f	124,000	1998 Aug 1	Assets disposals	54,000
1999 Aug 1	Cash/bank	71,000	1999 May 31	Balance c/f	141,000
		195,000			195,000

Provision for depreciation – Motor Vehicles Account

Dr		£	Cr		£
1998 Aug 1	Assets disposals	49,000	1998 June 1	Balance b/f	88,000
1999 May 31	Balance c/f	74,700	1999 May 31	Profit and loss	35,700
		123,700			123,700

Assets Disposals Account

Dr		£	Cr		£
1998 Aug 1	Motor vehicles	54,000	1998 Aug 1	Provision for depreciation	49,000
			1999 Aug 1	Bank	3,900
			1999 May 31	Profit and loss	1,100
		54,000			54,000

Chapter 29

29.1

D Plim Account

Dr			Cr		
1998 Jan 1	Balance b/f	200	1998 Feb 1	Cash	150
			Feb 1	Bad debts	50
		200			200

C Mike Account

Dr			Cr		
1998 Jan 1	Balance b/f	120	1998 Mar 10	Cash (30p in £)	36
			Mar 10	Bad debts	84
		120			120

Bad Debts Account

Dr			Cr		
1998 Feb 1	D Plim	50	1998 Jun 30	Profit and loss	134
Mar 10	C Mike	84			
		134			134

29.2

(a)

Provision for Bad Debts Account

Dr			Cr
1998		1997	
Sept 30 Profit and loss	186	Sept 30 Profit and loss	1,186
Sept 30 Balance c/d	1,000		
	1,186		1,186

(b)

Profit and Loss Account

1997		1998	
Bad debts	140	Reduction in Provision for bad debts	186
Provision for bad debts	1,186		

(c)

Balance Sheet as at 30 September 1997 & 1998

1997		
Debtors		11,860
Less Provision for bad debts		1,186	10,674
1998		
Debtors		10,000
Less Provision for bad debts		1,000	9,000

29.3

Date 31 Dec	Total Debtors	Profit and Loss	Dr/Cr	Final Figure for Balance Sheet
	£	£		£
1997	7000	70	Dr	6930 (net)
1998	8000	10	Dr	7920 (net)
1999	6000	20	Cr	5940 (net)
2000	7000	10	Dr	6930 (net)

Chapter 30

30.1

Motor Expenses Account

Dr			Cr
1998		1998	
Dec 31 Cash & Bank	744	Dec 31 · Profit and loss	772
Dec 31 Owing c/d	28		
	772		772

Insurance Account

Dr			Cr
1998		1998	
Dec 31 Cash & Bank	420	Dec 31 Prepaid c/d	35
		Dec 31 Profit and loss	385
	420		420

Stationery Account

Dr			Cr
1998		1998	
Dec 31 Cash & Bank	1,800	Jan 1 Owing b/f	250
Dec 31 Owing c/d	490	Dec 31 Profit and loss	2,040
	2,290		2,290

Rent Account

Dr			Cr
1998		1998	
Jan 1 Prepaid b/f	220	Dec 31 Prepaid c/d	290
Dec 31 Cash & Bank	950	Dec 31 Profit and loss	880
	1,170		1,170

Rent Received Account

Dr			Cr
1998		1998	
Jan 1 Owing b/f	180	Dec 31 Cash & Bank	550
Dec 31 Profit & Loss	580	Dec 31 Owing c/d	210
	760		760

30.3
(a)(i)

Rent Payable Account

Dr			Cr
Year 1		Year 2	
Aug 1 Bank	600	Jul 31 Profit and loss	2,400
Nov 4 Bank	600		
Year 2			
Mar 31 Bank	600		
Jul 31 Accrued c/d	600		
	2,400		2,400
		Year 2	
		Aug 1 Accrued b/d	600

Answers to exercises

30.1 (continued)

(ii)

Rates Account

Dr				Cr
Year 1			Year 2	
Aug 31	Bank	75	Jul 31 Profit and loss	475
Oct 22	Bank	220	Jul 31 Prepaid c/d	90
Year 2				
Apr 17	Bank	270		
		565		565

Year 2
Aug 1 Prepaid c/d 90

(iii)

Electricity Account

Dr				Cr
Year 1			Year 2	
Oct 17	Bank	310	Jul 31 Profit and loss	1480
Year 2				
Jan 21	Bank	390		
Apr 10	Bank	360		
Jul 31	Accrued c/d	420		
		1,480		1,480
			Year 2	
			Aug 1 Accrued b/d	420

(b)

Balance Sheet as at 31 July Year 2 (extracts)

Current Assets		Current Liabilities	
Prepayment (b)	90	Accrued Expenses (a) + (c)	1,020

30.4

J Smailes

Trading and Profit and Loss Account for the year ended 31 March 1997

	£	£	£
Sales			92,340
Less Cost of goods sold			
Opening stock		18,160	
Add Purchases	69,185		
Less Returns out	640	68,545	
Carriage inwards		420	
		87,125	
Less Closing stock		22,390	64,735
Gross profit			27,605
Less Expenses			
Wages and salaries		10,240	
Carriage outwards		1,570	
Rent and rates		3,015	
Communication expenses		624	
Commissions payable		216	
Insurance		405	
Sundry expenses		318	16,388
Net profit			11,217

Balance Sheet as at 31 March 1997

	£	£	£
Fixed Assets			
Buildings		20,000	
Fixtures		2,850	22,850
Current Assets			
Stock		22,390	
Debtors		14,320	
Bank		2,970	
Cash		115	
		39,795	
Less Current Liabilities			
Creditors		8,160	
Net current assets			31,635
			54,485
Less Long-term liabilities			
Loan			10,000
			44,485
Capital			
Balance at 1.4.1996			40,888
Add Net profit			11,217
			52,105
Less Drawings			7,620
			44,485

30.5

L Stokes
Trading and Profit and Loss Account for the year ended 30 September 1998

	£	£
Sales		130,900
Less Returns in		550
		130,350
Less Cost of goods sold		
Opening stock		23,910
Add Purchases	92,100	
Less Returns out	307	
		91,793
Carriage inwards		215
		115,918
Less Closing stock		27,475
		88,443
Gross profit		41,907
Less Expenses:		
Wages and salaries	12,810	
Carriage out	309	
Motor expenses	1,630	
Rent and rates	2,970	
Telephone	405	
Insurance	492	
Office expenses	1,377	
Sundry expenses	284	
		20,277
		21,630

Balance Sheet as at 30 September 1998

	£	£
Fixed Assets		
Motor van	4,100	
Office equipment	6,250	
		10,350
Current Assets		
Stock	27,475	
Debtors	12,300	
Bank	3,115	
Cash	295	
	43,185	
Less current liabilities		
Creditors	9,370	
Net current assets		33,815
		44,165
Less Long-term liabilities		
Loan		5,000
		39,165
Capital		
Balance as at 1.10.1997		25,955
Add Net profit		21,630
		47,585
Less Drawings		8,420
		39,165

30.7

(a)

Rates Account

Dr		Cr	
Bank	500	Prepayment c/d	100
		Profit and loss	400
	500		500

Rent Account

Dr		Cr	
Profit and loss	300	Bank	225
		Owing c/d	75
	300		300

Insurance Account

Dr		Cr	
Bank	450	Transfer to Drawings	50
		Profit and loss	400
	450		450

Wages Account

Dr		Cr	
Bank	5,200	Profit and loss	5,500
Owing c/d	300		
	5,500		5,500

(b)

Bilton Potteries
Profit and Loss Account for the year ended 31 January 1998

	£	£
Gross profit b/d		11,507
Rent receivable		300
		11,807
Less Expenses		
Wages	5,500	
Rates	400	
Insurance	400	
		6,300
Net profit		5,507

30.7 (continued)

Balance Sheet as at 31 January 1998

	£	£
Fixed Assets		
Premises		5,000
Current Assets		
Stock	1,000	
Debtors	434	
Prepaid and accrued	175	
Bank	3,218	
	4,827	
Less Current Liabilities		
Creditors	870	
Wages owing	300	
	1,170	
Net current assets		3,657
		8,657
Financed by		
Capital 1.1.97		7,000
Add Net profit		5,507
		12,507
Less Drawings		3,850
		8,657

Balance Sheet as at 31 October 1998

	£	£	£
Fixed Assets			
Fixtures		400	
Less Depreciation		100	
			300
Current Assets			
Stock		1,780	
Debtors		2,350	
Prepayment		40	
Cash		30	
		4,200	
Less Current Liabilities			
Creditors	1,680		
Bank overdraft	260		
		1,940	
Working capital			2,260
			2,560
Financed by			
Capital			
Balance as at 1.11.1997			2,700
Add Net profit			1,300
			4,000
Less Drawings			1,440
			2,560

30.8

George Holt

Trading and Profit and Loss Account for the year ended 31 October 1998

	£	£
Sales		9,620
Less Cost goods sold		
Opening stock	1,970	
Add Purchases	5,930	
	7,900	
Less Closing stock	1,780	
		6,120
Gross profit		3,500
Add Discounts received		90
		3,590
Less Expenses		
Wages	1,520	
Rent	240	
Bad debts	110	
Discounts allowed	130	
General expenses	190	
Depreciation	100	
		2,290
Net profit		1,300

30.9

John Brown

Trading and Profit and Loss Account for the year ended 31 December 1997

	£	£	£
Sales			40,000
Less Returns inwards			500
			39,500
Less Cost of goods sold			
Opening stock		10,000	
Add Purchases	35,000		
Less Returns outwards	620		
		34,380	
		44,380	
Less Closing stock		12,000	
			32,380
Gross profit			7,120
Less Expenses			
Wages		3,500	
Rates		550	
Telephone		122	
Bad debts		20	
Provision for bad debts		18	
Depreciation: Fittings	400		
Van	600		
		1,000	
			5,210
Net profit			1,910

30.9 (continued)

Balance Sheet as at 31 December 1997

	£	£
Fixed Assets		
Fittings	4,000	
Less Depreciation	400	
		3,600
Motor van	3,000	
Less Depreciation	600	
		2,400
		6,000
Current Assets		
Stock		12,000
Debtors	980	
Less Provision for bad debts	98	
		882
Prepayment		50
Bank		300
		13,232
Less Current Liabilities		
Creditors	700	
Expenses owing	522	
		1,222
		18,010
Financed by		
Capital		
Balance at 1.1.1997		17,900
Add Net profit		1,910
		19,810
Less Drawings		1,800
		18,010

30.11

Jane Jones

Profit and Loss Account for the year ended 31 December 1997

	£	£
Revenue		10,400
Less Expenses		
Rates (140 – 30)	110	
Telephone	110	
Advertising	230	
Cleaning	50	
Motor car expenses (480 – 160)	320	
Sundry expenses	1,200	
Depreciation: Equipment	112	
Motor (*see* workings)	176	
	288	
		2,308
Net profit		8,092

Balance Sheet as at 31 December 1997

	£	£
Fixed Assets		
Freehold premises		6,000
Equipment at cost	1,120	
Less Depreciation	512	
		608
Motor car at cost	1,800	
Less Depreciation*	744	
		1,056
		7,664
Current Assets		
Prepaid expenses	30	
Bank	5,400	
Petty Cash	40	
	5,470	
Less Current Liabilities		
Expenses owing	50	
Working capital		5,420
		13,084
Financed by		
Capital		
Balance at 1.1.1997		9,740
Add Net profit		8,092
		17,832
Less Drawings*		4,748
		13,084

Workings:

	£
Depreciation Motor car 1,320 × 20% =	264
Of this charge to Profit and Loss ⅔rds	176
charge to Drawings ⅓rd	88
	264

	£
Drawings: per Trial balance	4,500
⅓ Depreciation of Motor car	88
⅓ Motor car expenses	160
	4,748

	£
Depreciation: Motor car	
To start of year (Cost 1,800 – 1,320)	480
For the year (including private part)	264
	744

30.13

Thomas Williams
Trading and Profit and Loss Account for the year ended 31 March 1998

	£	£
Sales		13,990
Less Returns inwards		270
		13,720
Less Cost of goods sold		
Opening stock		1,720
Purchases	7,620	
Less Returns outwards	190	7,430
		9,150
Less Closing stock		1,430
		7,720
Gross profit		6,000
Add Discounts received		310
		6,310
Less Expenses		
Wages and salaries		3,050
Rent, rates and insurance		520
Discounts allowed		480
Carriage outwards		720
General office expenses		150
Provision for bad debts		50
Depreciation:		
Fixtures and fittings	40	
Delivery van	100	140
		5,110
Net profit		1,200

Balance Sheet as at 31 March 1998

	£	£	£
Fixed Assets			
Fixtures and fittings		400	
Less depreciation		40	360
Delivery van		700	
Less Depreciation		100	600
			960
Current Assets			
Stock		1,430	
Debtors	3,970		
Less Provision	270	3,700	
Prepayments		60	
Cash		30	
		5,220	
Less Current Liabilities			
Creditors		2,020	
Expenses accrued		70	
Bank overdraft		1,450	
		3,540	
Working capital			1,680
			2,640
Financed by			
Capital			
Balance as at 1.4.1997			2,400
Add Net profit			1,200
			3,600
Less Drawings			960
			2,640

30.15

(a)

(i) 'as at' means that the capital, assets and liabilities are shown at their book values at the close of the balance sheet date.

(ii) Because the trading and profit and loss account for the year ended 31 October 1998 has already been drawn up. This is why the net profit of £12,970 is shown. The only balance, therefore, remaining on the stock account is for the stock at 31 October 1998, as the opening stock on 1 November 1997 was transferred to the debit of the Trading Account.

(b)

G Williams
Balance Sheet as at 31 October 1998

	£	£	£
Fixed Assets			
Premises			27,400
Furniture and fittings			3,075
Plant and machinery			13,840
Vehicles			6,100
			50,415
Current Assets			
Stock		3,073	
Debtors		5,127	
Prepayment		50	
Cash		500	
		8,750	
Less Current Liabilities			
Creditors		2,065	
Bank overdraft		1,875	
Expenses owing		225	
		4,165	
			4,585
			55,000

30.15 (continued)

Less Long-term Liability		
5 year loan – Loamshire Finance		7,500
		47,500

Financed by		
Capital 1.11.1997	(C)	45,330
Add Net profit	(B)	12,970
		58,300
Less Drawings	(A)	10,800
		47,500

(A) is figure needed to balance
(B) is 47,500 + 10,800 = 58,300
(C) is 58,300 less 12,970 = 45,330

(c)

Capital Account

Dr					Cr
1998			1997		
Oct 31	Drawings	10,800	Nov 1	Balance b/d	45,330
Oct 31	Balance c/d	47,500	1998		
			Oct 31	Net profit	12,970
		58,300			58,300

Chapter 31

To economise on space, all narratives for journal entries are omitted.

31.1

(a)	J Harkness	Dr	678	:	J Harker	Cr	678
(b)	Machinery	Dr	4,390	:	L Pearson	Cr	4,390
(c)	Motor van	Dr	3,800	:	Motor expenses	Cr	3,800
(d)	E Fletcher	Dr	9	:	Sales	Cr	9
(e)	Sales	Dr	257	:	Commissions received	Cr	257

31.4

D Martin: Corrected net profit calculation

Profit originally calculated			8,975
Add	(B) Sales not recorded	28	
	(E) Rent receivable	50	
	(G) Rent for next year	10	88
			9,063
Less	(A) Rates not recorded	200	
	(C) Closing stock overvalued	48	
	(D) Depreciation	200	
	(F) Sales returns	22	
	(H) Provision for bad debts	20	490
Corrected figure of net profit			8,573

31.6

(a)

R James
Computation of Correct Net Profit
for the year ended 31 December 1999

Net profit per accounts			3,040
Add	(i) Purchases overstated		140
			3,180
Less	(ii) Depreciation omitted	280	
	(iii) Bad debts written off	41	
	(iv) Closing stock overvalued	124	445
Corrected Net profit			2,735

(b)

R James
Balance Sheet as at 31 December 1999

	£	£
Fixed Assets		
Furniture and fittings		1,680
Motor Vehicles	2,980	
Less Depreciation	280	2,700
		4,380
Current Assets		
Stock	2,600	
Debtors	1,200	
Bank	1,235	
	5,035	
Less Current Liabilities		
Creditors	1,850	
Working capital		3,185
		7,565
Financed by		
Capital		
Balance as at 1.1.1999		7,690
Add Net profit		2,735
		10,425
Less Drawings		2,860
		7,565

Chapter 32

32.1

(a)

T Boyd: Computation of correct net profit

	£	£
Net profit originally calculated		1,170
Add (b) Shelves – capital expenditure	76	
(a) Purchases overstated	60	136
		1,306
Less (c) Discount allowed incorrectly entered: to eliminate double the error		194
Corrected net profit figure		1,112
(d) has no effect on profit calculation		

(b)

(i) Excess debit 60 (ii) No effect (iii) Debit side understated 97, Credit side overstated 97
(iv) Credit side understated 48.

32.2

The Journal

	Dr	Cr
(i) Suspense	60	
Purchases		60
(ii) Fittings	76	
Wages		76
(iii) Discount allowed	194	
Suspense		194
(iv) Suspense	48	
S Lewis		48

32.3

Trial Balance as on 31 January 1998

	Dr	Cr
Capital 1.2.1997		5,500
Drawings	2,800	
Stock 1.2.1997	2,597	
Trade debtors (2130 – 6) (ii)	2,124	
Furniture and fittings (1750 + 120) (iii)	1,870	
Cash	1,020	
Trade creditors (2,735 – 75) (i)		2,660
Sales (7,430 + 108*)*564 – 456 (v)		7,538
Returns inwards	85	
Discounts received		46
Discounts allowed (iv)	38	
Business expenses	950	
Purchases (4,380 – 120) (iii)	4,260	
	15,744	15,744

Chapter 33

33.1

S Pea
Balance Sheet as at 31 July 1998

	£	£	£
Fixed Assets			
Furniture		900	
Less Depreciation		100	800
Motor vehicles		2,100	
Less Depreciation		500	1,600
			2,400
Current Assets			
Stock	2,700		
Debtors	1,600		
Cash	50	4,350	
Less Current Liabilities			
Creditors	3,300		
Bank overdraft	1,000	4,300	
Net current assets			50
			2,450
Less Long-term Liability			
Loan to B. Smith			200
			*2,250

	£	
Financed by		
Capital	1,000	(C)
Add Net profit	5,250	(B)
Less Drawings	3,000	
	2,250	(A)

Workings:
(A) (B) & (C) found in that order by filling in figures needed to balance the balance sheet figures.
(A) Equals the total of the balance sheet see *
(B) is 2,250 + 3,000 = 5,250
(C) is 5,250 – 1,000 = 4,250 = net profit

33.2

(a)

Sales Ledger Control Account

Dr	£		Cr	£
Balances b/f	1,490	Cash		5,410
Sales	5,760	Balances (Difference) c/d		1840
	7,250			7,250

Purchases Ledger Control Account

Dr	£		Cr	£
Cash	3,890	Balances b/f		940
Balances c/d	1,110	Purchases		4,060
	5,000			5,000

(b)

Statement of Affairs as at 31 March 1997

	£	£
Fixed Assets		
Office furniture		300
Current Assets		
Stock	1,160	
Debtors	1,490	
Bank	730	
Cash	30	3,410
Less Current Liabilities		
Creditors	940	940
Net current assets		2,470
		2,770
Financed by		
Capital (Difference)		2,770

(c)

Statement of Affairs as at 31 March 1998

	£	£	£
Fixed Assets			
Office furniture			250
Current Assets			
Stock		1,310	
Debtors		1,840	
Bank		870	
Cash		40	4,060
Less Current Liabilities			
Creditors		1,110	1,110
Net current assets			2,950
			3,200
Financed by			
Capital – Balance 31.3.1997	(C)		2,770
Add Net profit	(B)		1,700
			4,470
Less Drawings	(A)		1,270
			3,200

(A) (B) & (C) found in that order by filling in missing figures to make balance sheet totals agree.

33.3

C Cat: Statement of Affairs as at 31.12.97

	£	£
Fixed Assets		
Machinery		2,000
Furniture		1,500
		3,500
Current Assets		
Stock	1,000	
Debtors	350	
Bank	400	1,750
Less Current Liabilities		
Creditors	350	350
Net current assets		1,400
		4,900
Financed by		
Capital Introduced		4,000
Add Net profit (Balancing figure)		900
		4,900

33.4
(a)

Sales Ledger Control Account

Dr			Cr
Balances b/fwd	7,250	Cash	22,460
Sales (Difference)	24,370	Discounts	670
		Bad debts	410
		Balance c/d	8,080
	31,620		31,620

(b)

Purchases Ledger Control Account

Dr			Cr
Cash	17,190	Balances b/fwd	4,140
Discounts	470	Purchases (Difference)	19,150
Balances c/d	5,630		
	23,290		23,290

(c)

J Adams: Trading Account for the year ended 31 May 1998

	£	£
Sales		24,370
Less Cost of sales		
Opening stock	1,980	
Add Purchases	19,150	
	21,130	
Less Closing stock	2,160	18,970
Gross profit		5,400

Chapter 34

34.1

Town Society
Income and Expenditure Account for the year ended 30 June 1998

Income			
Subscriptions			320
Sale of refreshments		30	
Less Cost		20	10
Sale of dance tickets		80	
Less expenses		45	35
			365
Expenditure			
Rent (10 + 10)		20	
Printing and stationery (15 – 5)		10	
Sundry expenses		15	45
Surplus of income over expenditure			320

34.3
(a)

Accumulated fund 1.6.1997:

Bar stocks		88
Equipment		340
Bank		286
		714

(b)

Down Town Sports and Social Club
Income and Expenditure Account for the year ended 31 May 1998

	£	£	£
Income			
Subscriptions			149
Net proceeds of jumble sale			91
Net proceeds of dance			122
Contribution from Bar:			
Bar takings		463	
Less Cost of supplies:			
Opening Stock	88		
Add Purchases	397		
	485		
Less Closing stock	101	384	
			79
			441
Less Expenditure			
Wages		198	
Hire of rooms		64	
Loss on equipment		12	
Depreciation		30	
			304
Surplus of income over expenditure			137

34.4
(a)

Depdale Church Youth Centre
Receipts and Payments Account for the year ended 31 December 1999

Balance 1.1.1999	460	Light and heat	205
Subscriptions	800	Expenses of fête	310
Donation	80	New games equipment	160
Sale of fête tickets	540	Cleaner's wages	104
		Repairs and renewals	83
		Motor van repairs	126
		Balance 31.12.1999	892
	1,880		1,880

34.4 (continued)

(b)

Income and Expenditure Account for the year ended 31 December 1999

	£	£
Income		
Subscriptions		800
Donation		80
Profit on fête: Sale of tickets	540	
Less Expenses	310	230
		1,110
Less Expenditure		
Light and heat (205 + 45)	250	
Cleaner's wages	104	
Repairs and renewals	83	
Motor van repairs	126	563
Surplus of income over expenditure		547

(c)

Balance Sheet as at 31 December 1999

	£	£
Fixed Assets		
Furniture and fittings		1,500
Games and equipment		800
Motor van		1,000
		3,300
Current Assets		
Cash and bank	892	
Less Current Liabilities		
Electricity owing	45	
Working capital		847
		4,147
Financed by		
Accumulated Fund: Balance at 31.12.1998		3,600
Add Surplus		547
		4,147

Chapter 35

35.1

(a)

Category method.

A	Lowest of (280 + 440 + 390) 1,110 or (330 + 370 + 480) 1,180	=	1,110
B	Lowest of (170 + 210) 380 or (250 + 310) 560	=	380
C	Lowest of (400 + 860) 1,260 or (350 + 600) 950	=	950
D	Lowest of (570 + 770) 1,340 or (660 + 990) 1,650	=	1,340
			3,780

(b) Article method: 280 + 370 + 390 + 170 + 210 + 350 + 600 + 570 + 770 = 3,710

35.3

(a)

(i) FIFO 6 × £13 = £78 (you should show full workings)

(ii)

	Issued	Stock after each transaction	
LIFO Received			
Jan 24 × £10		24 × £10 =	240
Apr 16 × £12.50		24 × £10 =	240
		16 × £12.50 =	200	440
Jun	14 × £10		
	16 × £12.50	10 × £10	100
	30		
Oct 30 × £13		10 × £10 =	100
		30 × £13 =	390	490
Nov	4 × £10		
	30 × £13	6 × £10	60
	34		

(iii)

AVCO	Received	Issued	Average cost per unit of stock	No. of units in stock	Total value of stock
Jan	24 × £10		£10	24	£240
Apr	16 × £12.50		£11	40	£440
Jun		30	£11	10	£110
Oct	30 × £13		£12.50	40	£500
Nov		34	£12.50	6	£75

(b)

Trading Accounts for the year ended 31 December 1998

	FIFO	LIFO	AVCO	
				(All methods)
Purchases	830	830	830	
Less Closing stock	78	60	75	
	752	770	755	
				Sales 30 × £16	480
				34 × £18	612	1,092
Gross profit	340	322	337	
	1,092	1,092	1,092	1,092

35.6

Chung Ltd

Computation of Stock as at 31 December 1998

Total per stock sheets			198,444
Add (b)	Sales to 11.1.1999	6,960	
	Less profit 33⅓%	2,320	4,640
(c)	Undercast		50
			203,134
Less (c)	Overcast		1,000
(d)	Incorrect extension 560 − 528		32
(e)	Goods on approval		3,000
(f)	Incorrect total carried forward		
	106,850 − 105,680		1,170
			5,202
			197,932

469

35.7

Ceramics Ltd
Computation actual Stock at 30 June 1998

Stock: 5 July 1998		15,705
Add Cost of goods sent on approval: 66⅔% of 630	420	
Cost of sales for the period 1 to 4 July 1998: 66⅔% of 993	662	
Cost of goods returned and still in transit: 66⅔% of 540	360	1,442
		17,147
Less Stock overvalued: 500 – 390	110	
Fixed asset (generator) wrongly included in stock	500	
Error in carry forward: 420 – 240	180	
Error in casting	100	
Stock overvalued	350	1,240
Stock at 30 June 1998		15,907

Note: Items (c) and (f) do not affect stock.

35.8

Business 1 15,600 – margin ⅙th = 15,600 – 2,600 =		13,000
Business 2 Closing Stocks:		
Raw materials	14,700	
Finished goods	28,910	
Work in progress	17,390	61,000
Business 3 Stock at 26 Dec 1998	24,280	
Add Purchases	870	25,150
Less Sales at cost 500 – 20% margin =		400
Stock at cost 31 Dec 1998		24,750
Business 4 Reduce to net realisable value		2,780

35.9

Item no 24

Date	Ref	In	Out	Balance
1998				
May 1	Opening balance			500
May 2	Starlight Co Ltd	300		800
May 8	740		173	627
May 8	Moonbeam & Sons	200		827
May 10	810		294	533
May 14	976		104	429
May 24	Starlight Co Ltd	350		779
May 28	981		206	573

35.10

1999 Jan 1	Stock		8,000
	Received deliveries		
	Jan 8	6,000	
	Jan 16	8,000	
	Jan 24	12,000	26,000
	Total litres available for sale		34,000
	Less sold	56,609	
		35,609	
	Litres in stock 31.1.1999		

(a)	13,000 litres		13,000
(b)	12,000 litres at Jan 24 price × 64p	7,680	
	1,000 litres at Jan 16 price × 62p	620	8,300
(c)	No of litres sold 56,609 – 35,609 =		21,000
(d)	Sales 8,000 (of opening stock) × 60p + 25% =		6,000
	6,000 (of Jan 8 delivery) × 60p + 25% =		4,500
	7,000 (of Jan 16 delivery) × 62p + 25% =		5,425
			15,925

(e)

Trading Account for January 1999

Sales		15,925
Opening stock 8,000 × 60p =		4,800
Add Purchases 6,000 × 60p =	3,600	
8,000 × 62p =	4,960	
12,000 × 64p =	7,680	16,240
		21,040
Less Closing stock		8,300
		12,740
Gross profit		3,185

Chapter 36

36.1

H Smith: Wages calculations

40 hours × £5.50 : Gross pay		220.00
Less Income tax	36.00	
National Insurance 5% × 60.00	13.20	49.20
Net pay		170.80

36.2

M Marchand
Payslip week ended 28 April 1999

(a)	Gross pay 40 × 4.40 (basic)	176.00	
	10 × 6.60 (overtime)	66.00	242.00
(b)	Less National Insurance 10% × 242.00	24.20	
	" Pension 8% × 176.00	14.08	
	" Income tax 30% × (242.00 – 30.00) 212	63.60	
	" Union contributions	2.00	103.88
(c)	Net take-home pay		138.12

36.3

J Brown: Payslip week ended 25 May 1998

Gross earnings 200 units × 120p		240.00
Less Pension scheme	4.80	
National Insurance	24.00	
PAYE 25% × (240 – 75) 165	41.25	70.05
		169.95

A White: Payslip week ended 25 May 1998

Gross Earnings: 40 hours × 410p		164.00
4 hours × 410p × 1¼		20.50
		184.50
Less Pension scheme	3.69	
National Insurance	18.45	
PAYE 25% × (184.50 – 75) 109.50	27.37	49.51
		134.99

Note: for J Brown the pay is on piecework, as piecework £240.00 exceeds hourly earnings of (40 × 375p) £150.00. For A White pay is on hours worked. Piecework earnings would have been less at 140 × 130p = £182.00

36.4

	Wages	£10	£5	£1	50p	20p	10p	5p	2p	1p
1	112.86	10	1	7		1	1	1		1
2	97.19	9		7	1		1	1	2	
3	128.47	12		8		2			1	1
4	134.75	12	1	9	1	1	1	1		
5	84.77	7	1	9	1	1		1	1	1
	558.04	50	3	40	3	5	3	4	4	1

36.5

	Wages	£10	£5	£1	50p	20p	10p	5p	2p	1p
1	99.68	9		9	1		1	1	1	1
2	119.43	11		9		2		1	1	1
3	122.55	11	1	7	1	1		1	1	
4	94.77	8	1	9	1	1	1	1		1
5	104.35	9	1	9			1	1		
	540.78	48	3	43	3	4	2	5	3	2

36.6

	Wages	£10	£5	£1	50p	20p	10p	5p	2p	1p
1	96.99	9		6	1	2		1		1
2	133.46	12	1	8	1	2	1	1	2	1
3	128.86	12		8		1	1	1		1
4	112.36	10	1	7		1		1		1
5	101.26	9	1	6		1		1		
	572.93	52	3	35	2	7	2	5	2	4

36.13

R&R Production Co

Employee	Basic pay £	Bonus £	Total £
S Crawley	(40 hrs × £3.75) = 150.00	25.00	175.00
D Brookes	(44 hrs × £3.75) = 165.00	40.00	205.00
J Burns	(40 hrs × £3.75) = 150.00	35.00	185.00
V Newman	(42 hrs × £3.75) = 157.50	20.00	177.50
	£622.50	£120.00	£742.50

36.14

Employee		Gross Pay £
		£
A Taylor	35 hrs × £5.20 = 182.00	
	30 hrs × £0.75 = 22.50	204.50
S McKenzie	42 hrs × £5.20 = 218.40	
	40 hrs × £0.75 = 30.00	248.40
R Brindley	40 hrs × £5.20 = 208.00	
	36 hrs × £0.75 = 27.00	235.00
W Baseley	44 hrs × £5.20 = 228.80	
	36 hrs × £0.75 = 27.00	255.80
W Warburton	45 hrs × £5.20 = 234.00	
	52 hrs × £0.75 = 39.00	273.00
		£1,216.70

36.15

Morton's Garages Ltd

Salary = £12,300 per year = £1,025 per month
Commission = 1% of sales

Area Representative	Basic Salary £	Bonus £	Total Gross Salary £
M D Ross	1,025	500	1,525
J T Cross	1,025	450	1,475
P Kent	1,025	800	1,825
B Kent	1,025	400	1,425
H McDonald	1,025	600	1,625
Totals	5,125	2,750	7,875

Chapter 37

37.1

E Smith
Manufacturing and Trading Accounts for the year ended 31 March 1998

	£	£
Stock of raw material 1.4.1997		2,400
Add Purchases		21,340
Carriage inwards		321
		24,061
Less Stock of raw mats 31.3.1998		2,620
Cost of raw materials consumed		21,441
Manufacturing wages		13,280
Prime cost		34,721
Factory overhead expenses:		
Rent and rates	2,300	
Power	6,220	
Other expenses	1,430	9,950
		44,671
Add Work in progress 1.4.1996		955
		45,626
Less Work in progress 31.3.1997		870
Production cost of goods completed c/d		44,756

Sales			69,830
Less Cost of goods sold			
Stock finished goods 1.4.1997		6,724	
Add Production cost of goods completed b/d		44,756	
		51,480	
Less Stock finished goods 31.3.98		7,230	44,250
Gross profit			25,580

37.3

T Shaw
Manufacturing, Trading and Profit and Loss Accounts for the year ended 31 December 1998

Stock raw materials 1.1.1998		18,450
Add Purchases		64,300
Add Carriage inwards		1,605
		84,355
Less Stock raw materials 31.12.1998		20,210
Cost of raw materials consumed		64,145
Direct labour		65,810
Prime cost		129,955
Factory overhead expenses		
Rent ⅔	1,800	
Fuel and power	5,920	
Depreciation: Machinery	8,300	16,020
		145,975
Add Work in progress 1.1.1998		23,600
		169,575
Less Work in progress 31.12.1998		17,390
Production cost goods completed c/d		152,185

Sales		200,600
Less Cost of goods sold		
Stock finished goods 1.1.1998	17,470	
Add Production cost goods completed b/d	152,185	
	169,655	
Less Stock finished goods 31.12.1998	21,485	148,170
Gross profit		52,430
Less Expenses		
Office salaries	16,920	
Rent ⅓	900	
Lighting and heating	5,760	
Depreciation: Office equipment	1,950	25,530
Net profit		26,900

37.4

Excelsior Pressings

Manufacturing, Trading and Profit and Loss Account for year ended 31 December 1998

Cost of raw materials consumed

Stock 1 Jan 1998		28,315
Add Purchases		172,300
		200,615
Less Stock 31 Dec 1998		30,200
		170,415
Direct wages		194,500
Prime cost		364,915

Factory Overhead Expenses

Indirect wages	45,820	
Factory expenses	3,700	
Heating and lighting	2,760	
Rent and rates	12,300	
Salaries	10,800	
Depreciation	20,000	95,380
		460,295

Add Opening		
Work in progress		6,200
		466,495
Less Closing		
Work in progress		7,100
Production cost of goods completed c/d		459,395

Sales		652,500
Less Cost of goods sold		
Opening stock of finished goods	33,700	
Production cost of goods completed b/d	459,395	
	493,095	
Less Closing stock of finished goods	37,500	455,595
Gross Profit		196,905

Less Expenses

Rent and rates	4,100	
Heating and lighting	690	
Salaries	21,600	
Advertising	60,800	
Administration	27,500	
Depreciation: Office equipment	4,000	118,690
Net profit		78,215

Chapter 38

38.1

J Jackson: Trading Account for the year ended 31 July 1998

Sales				30,000
Less Cost of goods sold				
Stock 1.8.1997		4,936		
Add Purchases	(D)	25,374		
		30,310		
Less Stock 31.7.1998	(C)	6,310	(A)	24,000 (B)
Gross profit				6,000

(A) Mark-up is 25%, therefore margin is 20%. Gross Profit is therefore 20% × 30,000 = 6000
(B) Is missing figure, i.e. 30,000 − (A) 6000 = 24,000
(C) and (D) also found by missing figure deduction in that order.

38.2

P R Match – Trading Account for the year ended 31 August 1998

Sales			(D)	21,000
Less Cost of goods sold				
Stock 1.9.1997		2,000		
Add Purchases		18,000		
		20,000		
Less Closing stock	(A)	6,000	(B)	14,000
Gross profit			(C)	7,000

(A) To find, we know average stock is 4,000. Therefore (Opening Stock 2,000 + Closing Stock?) ÷ 2. Therefore Closing Stock must be 6,000, i.e. (2,000 + 6,000) ÷ 2 = 4,000
(B) can then be found, i.e. simply 20,000 − 6,000 = 14,000
(C) As mark-up is 50%, this figure is therefore 14,000 × 50% = 7,000
(D) is then missing figure, i.e. (B) + (C)

Index